ENVIRONMENTAL LAW
PRACTICE

ENVIRONMENTAL LAW PRACTICE

Problems and Exercises for Skills Development

THIRD EDITION

Jerry L. Anderson
DRAKE UNIVERSITY LAW SCHOOL

Dennis D. Hirsch
CAPITAL UNIVERSITY LAW SCHOOL

CAROLINA ACADEMIC PRESS
Durham, North Carolina

Library of Congress Cataloging-in-Publication Data

Anderson, Jerry L. (Jerry Linn), 1959-
  Environmental law practice : problems and exercises for skills development /
Jerry L. Anderson, Dennis D. Hirsch. -- 3rd ed.
      p. cm.
  Includes index.
  ISBN 978-1-59460-813-1 (alk. paper)
  1. Environmental law--United States--Problems, exercises, etc. I. Hirsch,
Dennis D. (Dennis Daniel), 1962- II. Title.

  KF3775.Z9A53 2010
  344.73'046076--dc22

                                        2010002269

CAROLINA ACADEMIC PRESS
700 Kent Street
Durham, North Carolina 27701
Telephone (919) 489-7486
Fax (919) 493-5668
www.cap-press.com

Printed in the United States of America

To my marvelous wife, Susan, and my wonderful parents.
JLA

To my wife Suzanne, who encourages me to pursue my dreams;
and to my parents, who introduced me to writing and the law.
DDH

Contents

LIST OF FIGURES

List of Exercises

List of Problems

FOREWORD

BY ANGUS MACBETH

I began to practice environmental law as a staff attorney with the Natural Resources Defense Council in 1970, shortly after the passage of the National Environmental Policy Act. In those days the landscape had a few large visible monuments—the common law of nuisance; the Second Circuit's decision in the first Scenic Hudson case—but generally the eye and the imagination could peer far and wide with little to impede the view. In the succeeding twenty-five years, during the course of which I have served as a Deputy Assistant Attorney General in the Land and Natural Resources Division at the Department of Justice and as the head of Sidley, Austin, Brown and Wood's environmental law practice group, I have seen a massive growth of statute laws: the Clean Air Act, Clean Water Act, Resource Conservation and Recovery Act, Superfund, and all their state law analogues. Beneath this forest canopy there has been a sturdy growth of both regulations and case law. EPA's regulations at 40 CFR now extend to more than twenty-five volumes. A few years ago I looked through a leading case book on administrative law and found that more than twenty percent of the cases were drawn from environmental law. Hidden in the underbrush we find a thriving culture of guidance documents, regulations which are never made final but are followed nevertheless, and interpretive letters hidden where only the insatiable collector is likely to find them.

In short, environmental law has become a jungle. Or, if you prefer a different metaphor, an excruciating maze. Or a paper palace rivaling the tax code and regulations in complexity and counter-intuitive esoterica.

That history is the first justification for this book and it is a very powerful one. The student has to be taught the path through the jungle and how to use a machete with speed and accuracy if he is ever to be able to give advice to his client with speed and accuracy—and most importantly, with sound judgment.

This problem is there for the government lawyer, the public interest bar, and the private attorney.

I do not think it will go away. The number of Superfund cases with a hundred parties will shrink as we continue and complete the clean up of commercial hazardous waste sites; but the pervading complexity of environmental law will continue. First, the natural world is enormously complex and the regulation of human impact on the natural world will reflect that complexity. Second, the environmental laws of the last twenty-five years have been a tremendous success in reducing pollution. As a consequence, the targets for environmental regulation get smaller over time and the competing interests that must be weighed in deciding how to regulate have become more complex with the result that the law becomes more complex. Third, simplicity and accuracy are in constant tension in this field and so far simplicity has rarely prevailed (unfortunately, it does not follow that accuracy has prevailed). Finally, it is a sad fact that on the jungle floor the lush diversity of semi-legal forms of authority has rooted and spread to the point where they cannot be eradicated. Coherent compilations of basic laws such as State Implementation Plans under the Clean Air Act cannot be found. The meaning of RCRA regulations are hidden in footnotes to Federal Register preambles. It isn't the way things should be, but it certainly is the way they have been for a long time.

In short, the need for this book will persist for a long time to come.

The second real value of this volume lies in its decision to introduce students to the roles of the public interest, government *and* private attorney, instead of focusing on just one of these. In the course of my career, during which I have represented all three of these constituencies, I have come to appreciate the importance of being able to see environmental issues from more than one perspective.

This ability is valuable, first, in that it gives one insight into how the "other side" thinks. For example, a private lawyer entering a negotiation with the EPA would be well advised to have thought through how his opponent is likely to approach the issue—what the EPA attorney's goals, incentives and marching orders are likely to be. The same might be said for the EPA lawyer, who should be able to place himself in the private attorney's shoes. The exercises ask the students to play the roles of private, EPA and public interest attorney in the context of negotiating an EPCRA penalty, settling a Superfund suit and litigating a citizens suit. This should help them see how lawyers from different sides think about an issue, thereby equipping them to deal more effectively with opposing counsel when they enter the world of practice.

Students should also draw another valuable lesson from the experience of representing different sides in environmental disputes. The layperson and the untutored lawyer often assume that environmental laws, like the lights in a crosswalk, give clear signals to the business people seeking to make their way. But the environmental lawyer soon finds out that this is not the case.

Rather, environmental statutes, regulations and policies, with their great complexity and many ambiguities, leave much room for interpretation and judgment. The earlier a lawyer recognizes this, the earlier he can start developing this judgment. By asking students to play a number of roles, and thereby to see environmental law questions from a variety of different perspectives, the book begins to develop this essential skill.

In sum, this volume provides practical training for environmental lawyers of the most useful sort. It not only leads the student through the jungle of the law, it gives him the tools to develop his judgment so that he can wrestle effectively with the tough practical problems and, in time, give his client advice that is mature and wise as well as solidly grounded in the law.

ACKNOWLEDGMENTS

Several people have made important contributions to this third edition. In addition to our spouses, to whom this book is dedicated and who provided much support during the latest revision of the book, we want to acknowledge the contributions of, and to thank, Drake law student Katie Kowalczyk, Stetson law student Samantha Hagio, and Capital law student Daniel Lenert, who provided highly capable, insightful and thorough research assistance. We would also like to thank the Capital University Law School and the Drake University Law School Endowment Trust which provided summer research grants to support the writing of this third edition.

Acknowledgments for the First and Second Editions:

Many people assisted us in bringing this project to fruition. We want to thank the following:

Drake law students Michael Angell, Shraddha Upadhyaya, Letticia Rodriquez, Paul Johnson, Patricia Ashton, Liz Williams, Hayley Hanson, Ronald Bailey, Angela Doss, and Erin Sass, and Capital law students Sonja Rawn and Summer Koladin provided able research assistance. The Rocky Mountain Mineral Law Foundation generously provided a grant to support the research for the book. Aimee Bentlage, Administrative Assistant to the Dean at Drake Law School, did a wonderful job proofing and editing the text. Drake Law Librarian Sandy Placzek went beyond the call of duty solving computer glitches and finding sources. Capital Law School librarians Jacqueline Orlando and Jane Underwood and Boston College Law School librarian Joan Shear provided insights on legal research. Britney Brigner of LexisNexis and Anthony Buscemi of Westlaw gave useful advice on how best to conduct on-line research. Susan Anderson provided her excellent editing acumen as well as her moral support.

We were also assisted by many of our colleagues in practice. From EPA's Region VII, Martha Steincamp, Regional Counsel, and Becky Dolph, Deputy Regional Counsel, provided valuable "real world" input and problem examples. Scott Fulton, Justina Fugh, Michael Goo, Geoffrey Wilcox, and Padmini Singh of the EPA's Office of General Counsel (OGC), and Suzanne Childress, Christina McCulloch, Carol Holmes and Joe Theis of the EPA's Office of Enforcement and Compliance Assurance (OECA) talked with us about the skills that are required for legal practice at the EPA. Angus Macbeth, David Buente, Sam Gutter, Jim Cahan, Larry Gutterridge, Tom Echikson, Margaret Spring and Alan Au of Sidley, Austin, Brown & Wood's environmental group provided input about the skills that are needed for environmental law practice at a private firm and provided us with useful source materials. The authors also thank Bill Beck, Terry Satterlee, and Alok Ahuja at Lathrop and Gage for environmental law practice advice.

Finally, we would like to thank several of our academic colleagues. Professors Jonathan Wiener at Duke, Richard Lazarus at Georgetown and Sandra Zellmer at Toledo provided valuable feedback on the concept for this book. Professors Zyg Plater at Boston College, Clifford Rechtschaffen at Golden Gate and Eileen Gauna at Southwestern provided valuable comments on the book, as did Michael Gerrard of the Arnold & Porter law firm.

In addition, we acknowledge the generosity of Capital University Law School and the Drake University Law School Endowment Trust which provided summer research grants to support the writing of the first and second editions of this book.

INTRODUCTION

The Goals of This Book

The authors of this book remember well our first days as practicing environmental lawyers. Fresh out of law school and clerkships, we set out for the library with sharpened pencils to complete our initial research assignments. We began where most law students are taught to begin, with the law reporters. But the fine interpretations of regulatory law that we needed were not to be found there. We moved on to American Jurisprudence Second, the ALRs, and the law reviews. Still nothing. Stumped, and more than a little embarrassed, we were forced to seek out more senior lawyers for guidance. Thus began our introduction to the new realm of legal materials that includes such sources as the Code of Federal Regulations, the Federal Register, the Environment Reporter, and agency guidance—the materials that environmental lawyers use most.

We also learned early on that environmental lawyers do much more than legal research (this is one of the reasons that the practice of environmental law is so much fun). They counsel clients on regulatory compliance. They bring or defend against enforcement actions. They litigate complex statutory issues. They initiate citizen suits. They participate in rulemaking proceedings where they argue the legal and policy merits of environmental regulations. Our practices required us to undertake many of these activities. Once again, we suffered the rude awakening that law school had hardly touched upon, much less prepared us for, these tasks.

As environmental law professors, we were determined that our students would be better prepared for environmental law practice than we had been. We looked for a book that would introduce students to the resources that environmental lawyers use and the activities in which they routinely engage. We found that such a book did not exist.

The principal objective of *Environmental Law Practice: Problems and Exercises for Skills Development* is to fill this gap. The materials in this book will introduce you to the main sources of environmental law. Some of these are contained in the book itself. In other instances, we teach you how to find them on your own. Those who work though this book should be able to head to the library or computer terminal on their first environmental law research assignment with strategies and skills for finding the information they need.

The book also uses exercises and role plays to introduce you to the day-to-day tasks of environmental law practice. It covers four of the principal areas of environmental law practice: compliance counseling, administrative enforcement, environmental litigation (including citizen suits), and environmental policy. It is comprehensive in its approach to these areas, providing lessons for the aspiring private lawyer, government lawyer, and public interest attorney. The book will teach you how to bring a federal enforcement action against a polluter; negotiate a Superfund settlement; prepare documents and strategy for a citizen's suit; counsel a corporation on environmental compliance; and comment on an EPA proposed rule, as well as develop many other relevant skills.

The problems and exercises are also good opportunities for increasing your knowledge of substantive environmental law. Environmental law consists largely of complex statutory and regulatory schemes, many of which are featured in this book. Often, the best way to learn these doctrines is to use them. More than once, we have seen it all "come together" for a student while working through an exercise in class. The book should help you to master the complexities of environmental law.

This book can serve as a stand-alone text for an upper-level course on environmental practice or as a supplement to an introductory environmental law text. Whichever way you encounter it, we hope that it provides you with a useful introduction to the practice of environmental law.

Environmental Law Practice

CHAPTER I

ENVIRONMENTAL COMPLIANCE

A. Introduction: The Lawyer's Role in Environmental Compliance

Many assume that the primary task of the private sector environmental lawyer is to defend clients against enforcement actions. While this image describes an important aspect of private environmental practice (and one that we will address in Chapter II), it does not tell the whole story. In fact, many private sector environmental lawyers spend a good deal of their time trying to *prevent* their clients from violating environmental requirements.

Consider the following scenario. Company X wants to construct a new manufacturing plant. It knows that, once constructed, the facility will emit air and water pollutants and will generate some solid wastes. But it does not know what the law requires it to do to control this pollution. If the company is to comply—and the environment is to be protected—someone will have to identify what the environmental requirements are and how they apply to the proposed facility. Will the facility be subject to air and water emission standards or permit requirements? Will the plant's wastes qualify as "hazardous" and, if so, how should the company go about handling and disposing of them? Businesses must consider environmental law implications such as these before embarking on almost any significant action.

Businesses rely on their environmental lawyers to provide them with guidance. In this type of work—generally known as "compliance counseling"—the attorney helps her client identify the governing environmental requirements and develop a plan for meeting them.

To perform this work effectively, an attorney must become adept at finding the applicable environmental requirements and at applying them to the facts at hand. This is by no means a simple task. While other litigators can generally limit their legal research to reported cases, environmental lawyers must be able to draw on a host of statutory and administrative materials, some of which are available only in obscure publications or are not formally reported at all. Section I.B will introduce you to specialized techniques for finding and applying environmental law. It will then ask you to counsel a hypothetical client on a Clean Air Act compliance issue.

What if, after extensive research, you find that the law is ambiguous? How should you counsel a client under these conditions? Should you provide the interpretation that is most favorable to the client's interests? Should you err on the side of human health and the environment? Should you refrain from giving any advice at all? Section I.C will give you some tools for approaching these issues. It will then ask you to counsel a hypothetical client on a question where the law is not clear.

B. Ensuring Compliance

Successful compliance counseling requires that you unlearn some of what you have been taught about the relative significance to legal problem solving of Congressional, judicial and administrative agency decisions. By the end of the first year, most law students have come to believe that courts are the principal source of law. It is, after all, *judicial* decisions that one reads during the first year. Congress figures importantly in a few instances. Administrative agencies appear to be of minimal importance, if they enter the picture at all.

In environmental law (as in all other areas of regulatory law), the situation is different. Judicial decisions are still important, but they do not hold a paramount position. Congress initiates the lawmaking process by passing a statute (*e.g.*, the Resource Conservation and Recovery Act (RCRA)) which establishes the broad contours of the regulatory program. The administrative agency (usually EPA) then fills in the details of the program by regulation.[1] For example, RCRA requires facilities that treat, store or dispose of hazardous waste to meet certain performance standards. Since Congress does not possess expertise in the handling of hazardous waste, the statute delegates to EPA the

---

1. While the material that follows focuses largely on EPA regulations and policies, students should note that environmental law practitioners often interact with other agencies such as the Department of the Interior or U.S. Army Corps of Engineers, and deal with issues, such as endangered species or land use, that go beyond pollution control.

task of defining what those performance standards will be.[2] If your client was in the business of disposing of RCRA "hazardous waste" and wanted to know the lawful methods for doing so, you would have to locate the relevant EPA regulations. The statute alone would not provide the answer. Virtually all of federal environmental law is set up this way. Congress, painting in broad strokes, establishes a legal framework. The relevant agency then develops implementing regulations that speak with much greater specificity.

Agencies are not infallible and, on occasion, may promulgate regulations that conflict with the legislation they are supposed to implement. This is one way in which the courts enter the picture.[3] When a party (usually a regulated entity) believes that agency regulations are at odds with a statute it can bring a legal action challenging the regulations on this ground.[4] A court then construes the statute and assesses the validity of the agency's implementing regulations.

The two most important sources of agency-made law are the *Federal Register* and the *Code of Federal Regulations* (CFR).[5] The Administrative Procedure Act (APA) requires that when an agency develops a regulation it must publish two documents in the *Federal Register*.[6] First, it must publish a *proposed rule*. This document generally contains two parts: a *preamble*, which explains in narrative form what the regulation will do; and the *regulation* itself which will, in a later stage, become binding law. The public is then given a period of time (usually 60 days) in which to provide written comments on the proposed rule. The comments become part of the *administrative record*. After the agency has received and considered the comments, it publishes a *final rule* in the Federal Register. As with the proposed rule, this document contains both a preamble and regulatory language. The preamble explains the regulation and responds to each of the significant points raised by those who commented on the proposed rule. The regulatory language, now in its final form,

---

2. *See* 42 U.S.C. §6924(a) ("the Administrator shall promulgate regulations establishing ... performance standards, applicable to owners and operators of facilities for the treatment, storage, or disposal of hazardous waste").

3. Courts also play an important role in common law areas—such as nuisance law—that involve the environment. This book will not focus on this aspect of environmental law.

4. Parties can challenge agency regulations on other grounds as well. For example, a party might claim that a regulation is "arbitrary or capricious" and thus violates the Administrative Procedure Act, 5 U.S.C. §706(2)(A) (2006).

5. Administrative adjudications represent another important set of administrative materials. However, they are more relevant to the enforcement aspect of environmental law than to compliance work. We will therefore address administrative adjudications in the chapter on enforcement. This chapter will focus on administrative rulemaking materials.

6. Administrative Procedure Act, 5 U.S.C. §553 (2006).

becomes law. It is published in the CFR, an annual publication that contains all final regulations issued by federal administrative agencies, including all EPA regulations.[7]

The *Federal Register* and the *CFR* are indispensable tools for environmental law research. Attorneys must look to the regulations contained in the *CFR* to see how the agency has "fleshed out" the statutory framework. If the final regulations themselves do not provide a clear answer (and often they do not), the lawyer must turn to the *Federal Register* and examine the preamble explanations of the proposed and final rules. Another technique that often proves fruitful is to compare the proposed and final versions of the regulation. For example, if a proposed RCRA regulation says that pouring hazardous liquids down the drain is an appropriate "disposal" practice, but the final regulation deletes this language, this would provide strong evidence that EPA has considered, and rejected, this method of disposal.

What if you come across a question that the statute, regulation, and regulatory preambles do not answer? In these situations there are a variety of other resource materials that you will want to consult. The most important of these is known as "agency guidance" and consists of memoranda, drafted by agency officials, that explain and interpret agency regulations. These documents may be critical to your ability to counsel your client. In the discussion (below) of agency guidance, you will learn some tips on how to locate these important documents.

In the following pages, we will guide you through the process of answering an environmental law question regarding the Clean Air Act's Prevention of Significant Deterioration program. Our research will begin with the statute and then lead us through legislative history, regulations, regulatory preambles, and agency guidance. By the time we reach the end, you should have the tools to conduct such research on your own. In the problems and exercises that conclude this section, you will be asked to do just that.

---

7. The Code of Federal Regulations may not contain the most up-to-date version of regulations since it is published annually and cannot include additions or amendments made during the course of each year. When researching an administrative law question for a client it is therefore important that you check not only the CFR but also the Federal Register which is published daily and will contain any amendments or additions that have not yet been incorporated into the CFR.

1. Complying with the Clean Air Act's Prevention of Significant Deterioration Program

Suppose that Carol Client, the general counsel for the Fab Furniture Company, comes to you and presents the following scenario:

Fab Furniture is a large manufacturer of wooden office furniture with facilities located throughout the Midwest. The company is looking to expand its operations and is considering building a new, very large operation in La Porte County, Indiana, for the purpose of manufacturing painted wooden desks. La Porte, Indiana is classified as an "attainment area" for ozone under the Clean Air Act (CAA). For business reasons, the company wants to divide the manufacturing process into two steps, each of which will be housed in its own building. In Building #1, the company will construct the desks and will apply a finish to them. In Building #2, located two miles away, it will paint the desks. The painted desks will be shipped to customers from the loading dock at Building #2. The local railroad has agreed to extend a nearby rail line so that it passes both buildings. The rail line will be used to deliver raw lumber to Building #1, to transport the unpainted desks from Building #1 to Building #2, and to ship the finished desks to customers.

Carol is not very well-versed in environmental law. However, she recently attended a meeting of the Wood Furniture Manufacturers' Trade Association at which she heard that, under the CAA New Source Review program for attainment areas, known as the Prevention of Significant Deterioration (PSD) program, newly constructed facilities that will emit or will have the potential to emit[8] more than a certain amount of volatile organic compounds (VOC)[9]

---

8. As EPA defines it, "[p]otential to emit means the maximum capacity of a stationary source to emit a pollutant under its physical and operational design. Any physical or operational limitation on the capacity of the source to emit a pollutant, including air pollution control equipment and restrictions on hours of operation or on the type or amount of material combusted, stored, or processed, shall be treated as part of its design if the limitation or the effect it would have on emissions is federally enforceable." 40 C.F.R. §51.21(b)(4) (2009). While this definition, and the regulatory interpretations of it, can be quite complex, the central idea is that a facility's potential to emit is based on the maximum amount of pollutants that it could possibly emit if it operated at full capacity 24 hours per day, 365 days per year, taking into account binding restrictions. Most facilities do not operate on a 24-hour per day schedule. It follows that their *actual* emissions (based on their actual operating schedule) are likely to be smaller than their *potential* emissions (based on the 24-hour per day operating scenario).

9. Volatile organic compounds combine with oxides of nitrogen (NOx) and sunlight to produce ground-level ozone, and are regulated under the Clean Air Act.

must obtain a permit prior to beginning construction.[10] Carol knows that the initial finish that Fab applies to its office furniture emits VOC as it dries, and that this VOC will be vented to the atmosphere through a single "smokestack" that will rise from the center of Building #1. Building #1 will have the potential to emit 150 tpy of VOC. In addition, Carol understands that the painting of the desks will also result in substantial VOC emissions which will be emitted through a "smokestack" at the top of Building #2. Engineers at Fab Furniture have estimated that Building #2 will have the potential to emit 225 tons per year (tpy) of VOC. Emissions of other air pollutants from the two buildings will be negligible.

Carol wants to know whether the VOC emissions from the new manufacturing operation will exceed the amount allowed under the PSD program and whether Fab Furniture, as a consequence, will have to obtain a PSD permit prior to commencing construction. She understands that it may take six months to a year to obtain a PSD permit if one is required. The company is poised to begin construction and is just awaiting the "OK" from the general counsel's office, so Carol needs your answer quickly.

As an environmental lawyer, you have some basic familiarity with the New Source Review program's PSD provisions.[11] For example, you know that the PSD provisions apply in "attainment" areas (and in "unclassifiable"

---

10. *See* 40 CFR §52.21(a)(2)(iii).

11. During the past decade the Clean Air Act New Source Review program has been one of the most dynamic areas in environmental law. The EPA has changed (or attempted to change) a number of NSR regulations. In addition the United States, state governments and citizens groups have initiated a host of NSR enforcement actions that have generated an array of court decisions, including one by the U.S. Supreme Court. *See, e.g., Environmental Defense, et al., v. Duke Energy Corp.* 549 U.S. 561 (2007). Some students may be aware of these developments and may wonder whether, in order to handle the NSR and New Source Performance Standard (NSPS) exercises and problems in this chapter, they will need to master this large body of recent regulatory and case law. The answer is "no." All of the major recent legal changes concern the way that the *New Source Review program* applies to facility *modifications*. By contrast, the first set of problems in this chapter concern how the NSR program applies to *newly constructed* sources, not to modifications of existing sources. The law in this area, i.e. how NSR applies to newly constructed sources, has not changed meaningfully in recent years. The recent developments also do not affect the second set of problems and exercises. These materials focus on the New Source Performance Standard (NSPS) program, not the NSR program. Since the recent changes relate only to the NSR program, they do not affect the second set of problems and exercises. Thus, any research required to answer the problems and exercises in this chapter should involve only settled Clean Air Act rules and case law, and should not require students to master the daunting array of new regulations and cases.

areas), whereas the Nonattainment New Source Review program applies in "nonattainment" areas. Carol has informed you that La Porte County, Indiana is an "attainment" area for ozone, so PSD is the correct program to look at. You also know that the PSD program requires pre-construction permits for those new facilities that will emit or will have the potential to emit more than a "threshold" amount of an air pollutant such as VOC.[12] The PSD program calls these large emitters "major sources." Only "major sources" of VOC (or other PSD-regulated pollutants) must obtain a permit prior to construction. The central question is whether the proposed wood furniture manufacturing operation will emit or will have the potential to emit more than a threshold amount of VOC and will qualify as a major source. Carol has told you that Building #1 will have the potential to emit 150 tpy of VOC, and that Building #2 will have the potential to emit 225 tpy. You need to figure out whether either of these emissions amounts exceeds the PSD "threshold" for VOC. In addition, you need to know whether you should combine the emissions from Buildings #1 and #2, or whether you should count them separately, when determining whether the emissions cross the threshold.

a. Statutes: The United States Code Annotated

The logical place to begin your inquiry is with the Clean Air Act itself. To find the Clean Air Act permitting requirements for newly constructed major sources you will need to refer to the General Index of the *United States Code Annotated*. The Index is updated and re-issued each year.

Practice Tip: Researching Statutory Law

You may find the United States Code Annotated (U.S.C.A.) to be preferable to the other published forms of the statute (i.e., slip laws, session laws, and unannotated codifications) because, in addition to providing you with the current statutory language as amended, it contains helpful citations to pertinent legislative history and case law.

The cover page and a relevant page of the U.S.C.A. General Index are reproduced in figures 1.1a and 1.1b.

---

12. *See* 40 CFR 52.21(a)(2)(iii), (b)(1)(i).

Figure 1.1 U.S.C.A. Index.

Problem 1.1: Finding Statutes

Based on your review of the above page from the U.S.C.A. General Index, answer the following questions: (A) Where in the Clean Air Act would you expect to find the requirements applicable to the construction of major emitting facilities? Note that the U.S.C.A. is arranged in fifty subjects, each known as a "title." Each title is divided into chapters, each of which is further subdivided into sections. Individual provisions are usually referred to by their title and section number. What is the title and section number for the relevant CAA provision? (B) What is the title and section number for the related definitions section that defines "major emitting facility" for the purposes of the PSD program?

Practice Tip: Use the Definitions Section

Too often, attorneys fail to consult the definitions sections of statutes and regulations and thereby miss critical information. Environmental statutes and regulations frequently embed substantive consequences in the definitions. When researching an environmental law issue, always be sure to check for a definitions section in the regulation or statute that you are working with. It may contain the crucial piece of information that allows you to answer your client's question.

The relevant portions of the Clean Air Act are reproduced below.

§7475. Preconstruction requirements

(a) Major emitting facilities on which construction is commenced

No major emitting facility on which construction is commenced after August 7, 1977, may be constructed in any area to which this part applies unless—

(1) a permit has been issued for such proposed facility in accordance with this part setting forth emission limitations for such facility which conform to the requirements of this part;

(2) the proposed permit has been subject to a review in accordance with this section, the required analysis has been conducted in accordance with regulations promulgated by the Administrator, and a public hearing has been held with opportunity for interested persons including representatives of the Administrator to appear and submit written or oral presentations on the air quality impact of such source, alternative thereto, control technology requirements, and other appropriate considerations;

(3) the owner or operator of such facility demonstrates, as required pursuant to section 7410(j) of this title, that emissions from construction or operation of such facility will not cause, or contribute to, air pollution in excess of any (A) maximum allowable increase or maximum allowable concentration for any pollutant in any area to which this part applies more than one time per year, (B) national ambient air quality standard in any air quality control region, or (C) any other applicable emission standard or standard of performance under this chapter;

(4) the proposed facility is subject to the best available control technology for each pollutant subject to regulation under this chapter emitted from, or which results from, such facility;

(5) the provisions of subsection (d) of this section with respect to protection of class I areas have been complied with for such facility;

(6) there has been an analysis of any air quality impacts projected for the area as a result of growth associated with such facility;

(7) the person who owns or operates, or proposes to own or operate, a major emitting facility for which a permit is required under this part agrees to conduct such monitoring as may be necessary to determine the effect which emissions from any such facility may have, or is having, on air quality in any area which may be affected by emissions from such source; and

(8) in the case of a source which proposes to construct in a class III area, emissions from which would cause or contribute to exceeding the maximum allowable increments applicable in a class II area and where no standard under section 7411 of this title has been promulgated subsequent to August 7, 1977, for such source category, the Administrator has approved the determination of best available technology as set forth in the permit.

Figure 1.2 42 U.S.C.A. §7475(a).

§ 7479. Definitions

For purpose of this part—

(1) The term "major emitting facility" means any of the following stationary sources of air pollutants which emit, or have the potential to emit, one hundred tons per year or more of any air pollutant from the following types of stationary sources: fossil-fuel fired steam electric plants of more than two hundred and fifty million British thermal units per hour heat input, coal cleaning plants (thermal dryers), kraft pulp mills, Portland Cement plants, primary zinc smelters, iron and steel mill plants, primary aluminum ore reduction plants, primary copper smelters, municipal incinerators capable of charging more than fifty tons of refuse per day, hydrofluoric, sulfuric, and nitric acid plants, petroleum refineries, lime plants, phosphate rock processing plants, coke oven batteries, sulfur recovery plants, carbon black plants (furnace process), primary lead smelters, fuel conversion plants, sintering plants, secondary metal production facilities, chemical process plants, fossil-fuel boilers of more than two hundred and fifty million British thermal units per hour heat input, petroleum storage and transfer facilities with a capacity exceeding three hundred thousand barrels, taconite ore processing facilities, glass fiber processing plants, charcoal production facilities. Such term also includes any other source with the potential to emit two hundred and fifty tons per year or more of any air pollutant. This term shall not include new or modified facilities which are non-profit health or education institutions which have been exempted by the State.

Figure 1.3 42 U.S.C.A. § 7479(1).

Problem 1.2: Applying Statutory Language

Based on these statutory provisions, answer the following questions: (A) What types of facilities must obtain permits under the PSD program? (B) What is the definition of a "major emitting facility"? (C) What is the amount of VOC, in tons per year, that the Fab Furniture plant must have the potential to emit in order for a PSD permit to be required prior to construction of the plant? (D) For the purposes of determining whether a PSD permit will be required, does it matter whether Building #1 and Building #2 are considered as the same facility as opposed to being treated as separate facilities? Explain.

b. Legislative History: The U.S. Code Congressional and Administrative News

As you have probably figured out from the above statutory provisions, the key question is whether the two Fab Furniture buildings should be treated as a single "stationary source," or as two separate "stationary sources" (if you have not arrived at this conclusion, go back and work through Problem 1.2 again). You should also have become aware that the statute alone will not answer this question for you. Where statutory language is ambiguous, courts look to the legislative history for guidance as to the statute's meaning.[13] You can locate the relevant legislative history quite easily. At the end of each statutory section, the U.S.C.A. provides "Historical and Statutory Notes" that cite the most significant legislative materials related to that section. The Historical and Statutory Notes for CAA §7475 are reproduced in Figure 1.4.

Ch. 85 AIR POLLUTION PREVENTION   **42 §7475**

HISTORICAL AND STATUTORY NOTES

Revision Notes and Legislative Reports
  1977 Acts. House Report No. 95–294 and House Conference Report No. 95–564, see 1977 U.S. Code Cong. and Adm. News, p. 1077.

  House Report No. 95–338, see 1977 U.S. Code Cong. and Adm. News, p. 3648.

Amendments
  1977 Amendments. Subsec. (a)(1). Pub.L. 95–190, § 14(a)(44), substituted "part;" for "part:".

  Subsec. (a)(3). Pub.L. 95–190, § 14(a)(45), added provision making applicable requirement of section 7410(j) of this title.

  Subsec. (b). Pub.L. 95–190, § 14(a)(46), struck out "actual" preceding "allowable emissions" and added "cause or" preceding "contribute".

  Subsec. (d)(2)(C). Pub.L. 95–190, § 14(a)(47) to (49), in cl. (ii), substituted "contribute" for "contrbute", in cl. (iii)

substituted "quality-related" for "quality related" and "concentrations which" for "concentrations, which", and in cl. (iv) substituted "such facility" for "such sources" and "will not cause or contribute to concentrations of such pollutant which exceed" for "together with all other sources, will not exceed".

  Subsec. (d)(2)(D). Pub.L. 95–190, § 14(a)(50), (51), in cl. (iii) substituted provisions relating to determinations of amounts of emissions of sulfur oxides from facilities, for provisions relating to determinations of amounts of emissions of sulfur oxides from sources operating under permits issued pursuant to this subparagraph, together with all other sources, and added cl. (iv).

Effective and Applicability Provisions
  1977 Acts. Section effective Aug. 7, 1977, except as otherwise expressly provided, see section 406(d) of Pub.L. 95–95, set out as a note under section 7401 of this title.

Figure 1.4 42 U.S.C.A. §7475 historical note.

As you can see, the Notes identify two House Reports and a House Conference Report and provide citations to them in the U.S. Code Congressional and Administrative News (U.S.C.C.A.N.), an annual publication that contains legislation passed during the year in its original, pre-codified form, as well as the most important legislative history for these statutes. When a bill is introduced into either the House or Senate, it is assigned to one or more committees with jurisdiction over the subject matter of the bill. The committee's duty is to examine the bill and then issue a recommendation as to whether the full chamber should pass it. When the committee recommends passage, it does so in a written report (the bill is said to have been "reported out of committee").

---

13. Norman J. Singer, Sutherland Stat. Const. §48.01 (5th ed. 1992).

Such reports often contain a section-by-section analysis in which the committee conveys its understanding of what the statutory language means. The committee report accompanies the legislation when it is returned to the chamber as a whole for debate and vote, and it can be presumed that each voting member has read it. This makes committee reports some of the strongest pieces of evidence of Congressional intent.[14]

Practice Tip: Use Congressional Committee Reports

When trying to construe a statute, it is often worthwhile to track down the relevant committee reports and see if they address the issue.

The Notes for CAA § 7475 refer to two reports drafted by the House Interstate and Foreign Commerce Committee. The first accompanied the initial legislation; the second is a brief document drafted by the Committee when it reported out a series of technical amendments at the end of the legislative process (e.g., amendments that corrected punctuation errors in the initial bill). More than 70 pages of the first report are devoted to the PSD provisions of the legislation,[15] including a section devoted to "preconstruction review permits."[16] In these pages, the Committee expresses various views about the term "major stationary source."[17] However, it fails to address whether related production divided between two buildings should be treated as a single "stationary source." This is not surprising since, at the time of passing a statute, Congress can hardly be expected to anticipate and address every issue that will arise under the statute.

---

14. See, generally, J. Myron Jacobstein, Rom M. Mersky, Donald J. Dunn, Fundamentals of Legal Research 194 (6th ed. 1994). Another important source of legislative history are the debates over bills that take place on the House and Senate floor. These are published in the Congressional Record.

15. See 1977 U.S.C.C.A.N. at 1181–1257. The 1977 amendments to the Clean Air Act contained more than just the PSD provisions. That is why only a section of the committee report is dedicated to PSD.

16. Id. at 1223.

17. For example, the Report states that the term "major stationary source" applies only to "direct pollution sources" (e.g., smokestacks), and not to "indirect" sources (e.g., dirt roads that create dust) or "mobile" sources (e.g., cars, trains). Id.

c. Regulations: The Code of Federal Regulations

The role of filling in the details falls to the agency. You can find EPA regulations that implement the Clean Air Act's PSD provisions in the Code of Federal Regulations (CFR). The CFR is divided by subject into 50 titles, each of which is further subdivided into chapters, parts and sections. All EPA regulations are located in Title 40, Chapter I.[18] Thus, the key to finding a specific EPA rule is to identify its part and section number.

To do so, consult the last volume of the CFR set, entitled "CFR Index and Finding Aids." This volume contains a comprehensive index that lists subject matter areas and identifies the appropriate Title and Part number for each. Once you have located the correct Title and Part, it is then necessary to scan the table of contents for that Part in order to locate the precise Section you seek.

A portion of the CFR Index listings under the subject heading "air pollution control" is reproduced on the following pages.

---

18. This is not to suggest that EPA is the only federal agency to have developed regulations relevant to environmental law practice. Other agencies have also developed regulations that are important to the field. *See, e.g.,* 43 CFR §11.10 *et seq.* (Department of Interior regulations on CERCLA natural resource damage assessments); 33 CFR §323.1 *et seq.*(Army Corps of Engineers regulations on Clean Water Act permits); 50 CFR §424.01 *et seq.*(Fish and Wildlife Agency, Dept. of the Interior, National Marine Fisheries Service, National Oceanic and Atmospheric Admin. and Depart. of Commerce joint regulations on endangered species).

Code of Federal Regulations

**CFR Index
and Finding Aids**

Revised as of January 1, 2009

Published by
Office of the Federal Register
National Archives and Records
Administration

as a Special Edition of the
Federal Register

Figure 1.5 Code of Federal Regulations Index.

CFR Index **Air pollution control**

Notice that the index identifies Title 40, Part 52 as the location for regulations on "Air quality implementation plans; Approval and promulgation." As you may know, the Clean Air Act follows a cooperative federalism approach. The federal government (*i.e.* EPA) establishes national standards for "clean" air quality, known as National Ambient Air Quality Standards (NAAQS). Each state then figures out exactly how it will go about meeting these federal air quality standards, codifies its strategy in a set of state air regulations known as the state implementation plan (SIP), and submits the SIP to the U.S. EPA for approval. In Part 52, U.S. EPA identifies the SIP provisions that it has approved for each state. Sometimes, U.S. EPA does not approve a state submission. Part 52 accordingly includes default provisions that become applicable in those instances where EPA disapproves a state SIP submission. The default regulations for the Prevention of Significant Deterioration (PSD) program appear in Section 52.21. As it turns out, many states look to these default provisions when writing their state implementation plans, with the result that most state SIPs closely track the default regulations. It follows that Section 52.21, the default PSD regulations, can serve as a good guide to PSD requirements as implemented in most states.[19] When you look at the table of contents for 40 CFR Part 52 (reproduced below), you will see that Section 52.21 is entitled "prevention of significant deterioration of air quality."

In addition to the table of contents, we reproduce a portion of the "definitions" section from the PSD regulations, 40 CFR § 52.21(b).

---

19. When a state has promulgated a SIP and EPA has approved it, a private party's responsibility is to comply with the state regulations in the SIP. Thus, were you conducting compliance counseling for a real client, you would want to check not only EPA regulations but also the state regulations in the SIP that define the term "stationary source." For the present purposes, we will examine only the federal regulations. We do this both to prevent this example from becoming too complex and in recognition of the fact that, in most instances, the state PSD regulations track the federal template that EPA has laid out in the CFR.

Code of Federal Regulations

40

Part 52 (§§ 52.01 to 52.1018)
Revised as of July 1, 2009

Protection of Environment

Containing a codification of documents
of general applicability and future effect

As of July 1, 2009

With Ancillaries

Published by
Office of the Federal Register
National Archives and Records
Administration
Administration

A Special Edition of the Federal Register

Figure 1.6 Code of Federal Regulations Part 52.

SUBCHAPTER C—AIR PROGRAMS (CONTINUED)

PART 52—APPROVAL AND PROMULGATION OF IMPLEMENTATION PLANS

§ 52.18 Abbreviations.

Abbreviations used in this part shall be those set forth in part 60 of this chapter.

[38 FR 12698, May 14, 1973]

§ 52.20 Attainment dates for national standards.

Each subpart contains a section which specifies the latest dates by which national standards are to be attained in each region in the State. An attainment date which only refers to a month and a year (such as July 1975) shall be construed to mean the last day of the month in question. However, the specification of attainment dates for national standards does not relieve any State from the provisions of subpart N of this chapter which require all sources and categories of sources to comply with applicable requirements of the plan—

(a) As expeditiously as practicable where the requirement is part of a control strategy designed to attain a primary standard, and

(b) Within a reasonable time where the requirement is part of a control strategy designed to attain a secondary standard.

[37 FR 19808, Sept. 22, 1972, as amended at 39 FR 34535, Sept. 26, 1974; 51 FR 40676, Nov. 7, 1986]

§ 52.21 Prevention of significant deterioration of air quality.

(a)(1) *Plan disapproval.* The provisions of this section are applicable to any State implementation plan which has been disapproved with respect to prevention of significant deterioration of air quality in any portion of any State where the existing air quality is better than the national ambient air quality standards. Specific disapprovals are listed where applicable, in subparts B through DDD of this part. The provisions of this section have been incorporated by reference into the applicable implementation plans for various States, as provided in subparts B through DDD of this part. Where this section is so incorporated, the provisions shall also be applicable to all lands owned by the Federal Government and Indian Reservations located in such State. No disapproval with respect to a State's failure to prevent significant deterioration of air quality shall invalidate or otherwise affect the obligations of States, emission sources, or other persons with respect to all portions of plans approved or promulgated under this part.

(2) *Applicability procedures.* (i) The requirements of this section apply to the construction of any new major stationary source (as defined in paragraph (b)(1) of this section) or any project at an existing major stationary source in an area designated as attainment or unclassifiable under sections 107(d)(1)(A)(ii) or (iii) of the Act.

(ii) The requirements of paragraphs (j) through (r) of this section apply to the construction of any new major stationary source or the major modification of any existing major stationary source, except as this section otherwise provides.

(iii) No new major stationary source or major modification to which the requirements of paragraphs (j) through (r)(5) of this section apply shall begin actual construction without a permit that states that the major stationary source or major modification will meet those requirements. The Administrator has authority to issue any such permit.

(iv) The requirements of the program will be applied in accordance with the principles set out in paragraphs (a)(2)(iv)(a) through (f) of this section.

(a) Except as otherwise provided in paragraphs (a)(2)(v) and (vi) of this section, and consistent with the definition of major modification contained in paragraph (b)(2) of this section, a project is a major modification for a regulated NSR pollutant if it causes two types of emissions increases—a significant emissions increase (as defined in paragraph (b)(40) of this section), and a significant net emissions increase (as defined in paragraphs (b)(3) and (b)(23) of this section). The project is not a major modification if it does not cause a significant emissions increase. If the project causes a significant emissions increase, then the project is a major modification only if it also results in a significant net emissions increase.

(b) The procedure for calculating (before beginning actual construction)

14

Figure 1.7 40 Code of Federal Regulations §§ 52.18–21

whether a significant emissions increase (i.e., the first step of the process) will occur depends upon the type of emissions units being modified, according to paragraphs (a)(2)(iv)(c) through (f) of this section. For these calculations, fugitive emissions (to the extent quantifiable) are included only if the emissions unit is part of one of the source categories listed in paragraph (b)(1)(iii) of this section or if the emission unit is located at a major stationary source that belongs to one of the listed source categories. Fugitive emissions are not included for those emissions units located at a facility whose primary activity is not represented by one of the source categories listed in paragraph (b)(1)(iii) of this section and that are not, by themselves, part of a listed source category. The procedure for calculating (before beginning actual construction) whether a significant net emissions increase will occur at the major stationary source (i.e., the second step of the process) is contained in the definition in paragraph (b)(3) of this section. Regardless of any such preconstruction projections, a major modification results if the project causes a significant emissions increase and a significant net emissions increase.

(c) *Actual-to-projected-actual applicability test for projects that only involve existing emissions units.* A significant emissions increase of a regulated NSR pollutant is projected to occur if the sum of the difference between the projected actual emissions (as defined in paragraph (b)(41) of this section) and the baseline actual emissions (as defined in paragraphs (b)(48)(i) and (ii) of this section), for each existing emissions unit, equals or exceeds the significant amount for that pollutant (as defined in paragraph (b)(23) of this section).

(d) *Actual-to-potential test for projects that only involve construction of a new emissions unit(s).* A significant emissions increase of a regulated NSR pollutant is projected to occur if the sum of the difference between the potential to emit (as defined in paragraph (b)(4) of this section) from each new emissions unit following completion of the project and the baseline actual emissions (as defined in paragraph

(b)(48)(iii) of this section) of these units before the project equals or exceeds the significant amount for that pollutant (as defined in paragraph (b)(23) of this section).

(e) [Reserved]

(f) *Hybrid test for projects that involve multiple types of emissions units.* A significant emissions increase of a regulated NSR pollutant is projected to occur if the sum of the emissions increases for each emissions unit, using the method specified in paragraphs (a)(2)(iv)(c) through (d) of this section as applicable with respect to each emissions unit, for each type of emissions unit equals or exceeds the significant amount for that pollutant (as defined in paragraph (b)(23) of this section).

(v) For any major stationary source for a PAL for a regulated NSR pollutant, the major stationary source shall comply with the requirements under paragraph (aa) of this section.

(b) *Definitions.* For the purposes of this section:

(1)(i) *Major stationary source means:*

(a) Any of the following stationary sources of air pollutants which emits, or has the potential to emit, 100 tons per year or more of any regulated NSR pollutant: Fossil fuel-fired steam electric plants of more than 250 million British thermal units per hour heat input, coal cleaning plants (with thermal dryers), kraft pulp mills, portland cement plants, primary zinc smelters, iron and steel mill plants, primary aluminum ore reduction plants (with thermal dryers), primary copper smelters, municipal incinerators capable of charging more than 250 tons of refuse per day, hydrofluoric, sulfuric, and nitric acid plants, petroleum refineries, lime plants, phosphate rock processing plants, coke oven batteries, sulfur recovery plants, carbon black plants (furnace process), primary lead smelters, fuel conversion plants, sintering plants, secondary metal production plants, chemical process plants (which does not include ethanol production facilities that produce ethanol by natural fermentation included in NAICS codes 325193 or 312140), fossil-fuel boilers (or combinations thereof) totaling more than 250 million British thermal units per hour heat input, petroleum storage and transfer units with a total storage capacity exceeding 300,000 barrels, taconite ore processing plants, glass fiber processing plants, and charcoal production plants;

(b) Notwithstanding the stationary source size specified in paragraph (b)(1)(i) of this section, any stationary source which emits, or has the potential to emit, 250 tons per year or more of a regulated NSR pollutant; or

(c) Any physical change that would occur at a stationary source not otherwise qualifying under paragraph (b)(1) of this section, as a major stationary source, if the changes would constitute a major stationary source by itself.

(ii) A major source that is major for volatile organic compounds or NO_x shall be considered major for ozone.

(iii) The fugitive emissions of a stationary source shall not be included in determining for any of the purposes of this section whether it is a major stationary source, unless the source belongs to one of the following categories of stationary sources:

(a) Coal cleaning plants (with thermal dryers);

(b) Kraft pulp mills;

(c) Portland cement plants;

(d) Primary zinc smelters;

(e) Iron and steel mills;

(f) Primary aluminum ore reduction plants;

(g) Primary copper smelters;

(h) Municipal incinerators capable of charging more than 250 tons of refuse per day;

(i) Hydrofluoric, sulfuric, or nitric acid plants;

(j) Petroleum refineries;

(k) Lime plants;

(l) Phosphate rock processing plants;

(m) Coke oven batteries;

(n) Sulfur recovery plants;

(o) Carbon black plants (furnace process);

(p) Primary lead smelters;

(q) Fuel conversion plants;

(r) Sintering plants;

(s) Secondary metal production plants;

(t) Chemical process plants—The term chemical processing plant shall not include ethanol production facilities that produce ethanol by natural fermentation included in NAICS codes 325193 or 312140;

(u) Fossil-fuel boilers (or combination thereof) totaling more than 250 million British thermal units per hour heat input;

(v) Petroleum storage and transfer units with a total storage capacity exceeding 300,000 barrels;

(w) Taconite ore processing plants;

(x) Glass fiber processing plants;

(y) Charcoal production plants;

(z) Fossil fuel-fired steam electric plants of more that 250 million British thermal units per hour heat input, and

(aa) Any other stationary source category which, as of August 7, 1980, is being regulated under section 111 or 112 of the Act.

(2)(i) *Major modification* means any physical change in or change in the method of operation of a major stationary source that would result in: a significant emissions increase (as defined in paragraph (b)(40) of this section) of a regulated NSR pollutant (as defined in paragraph (b)(50) of this section); and a significant net emissions increase of that pollutant from the major stationary source.

(ii) Any significant emissions increase (as defined at paragraph (b)(40) of this section) from any emissions units or net emissions increase (as defined in paragraph (b)(3) of this section) at a major stationary source that is significant for volatile organic compounds or NO_x shall be considered significant for ozone.

(iii) A physical change or change in the method of operation shall not include:

(a) Routine maintenance, repair and replacement. Routine maintenance, repair and replacement shall include, but not be limited to, any activity(s) that meets the requirements of the equipment replacement provisions contained in paragraph (cc) of this section;

NOTE TO PARAGRAPH (b)(2)(iii)(a): By court order on December 24, 2003, the second sentence of this paragraph (b)(2)(iii)(a) is stayed indefinitely. The stayed provisions will become effective immediately if the court terminates the stay. At that time, EPA will publish a document in the FEDERAL REGISTER advising the public of the termination of the stay.

(b) Use of an alternative fuel or raw material by reason of an order under sections 2 (a) and (b) of the Energy

Environmental Protection Agency   **§52.21**

Supply and Environmental Coordination Act of 1974 (or any superseding legislation) or by reason of a natural gas curtailment plant pursuant to the Federal Power Act;

(c) Use of an alternative fuel by reason of an order or rule under section 125 of the Act;

(d) Use of an alternative fuel at a steam generating unit to the extent that the fuel is generated from municipal solid waste;

(e) Use of an alternative fuel or raw material by a stationary source which:

(1) The source was capable of accommodating before January 6, 1975, unless such change would be prohibited under any federally enforceable permit condition which was established after January 6, 1975 pursuant to 40 CFR 52.21 or under regulations approved pursuant to 40 CFR subpart I or 40 CFR 51.166; or

(2) The source is approved to use under any permit issued under 40 CFR 52.21 or under regulations approved pursuant to 40 CFR 51.166;

(f) An increase in the hours of operation or in the production rate, unless such change would be prohibited under any federally enforceable permit condition which was established after January 6, 1975, pursuant to 40 CFR 52.21 or under regulations approved pursuant to 40 CFR subpart I or 40 CFR 51.166.

(g) Any change in ownership at a stationary source.

(h) [Reserved]

(i) The installation, operation, cessation, or removal of a temporary clean coal technology demonstration project, provided that the project complies with:

(1) The State implementation plan for the State in which the project is located, and

(2) Other requirements necessary to attain and maintain the national ambient air quality standards during the project and after it is terminated.

(j) The installation or operation of a permanent clean coal technology demonstration project that constitutes repowering, provided that the project does not result in an increase in the potential to emit of any regulated pollutant emitted by the unit. This exemption shall apply on a pollutant-by-pollutant basis.

(k) The reactivation of a very clean coal-fired electric utility steam generating unit.

(iv) This definition shall not apply with respect to a particular regulated NSR pollutant when the major stationary source is complying with the requirements under paragraph (aa) of this section for a PAL for that pollutant. Instead, the definition at paragraph (aa)(2)(viii) of this section shall apply.

(v) Fugitive emissions shall not be included in determining for any of the purposes of this section whether a physical change in or change in the method of operation of a major stationary source is a major modification, unless the source belongs to one of the source categories listed in paragraph (b)(1)(iii) of this section.

(3)(i) *Net emissions increase* means, with respect to any regulated NSR pollutant emitted by a major stationary source, the amount by which the sum of the following exceeds zero:

(a) The increase in emissions from a particular physical change or change in the method of operation at a stationary source as calculated pursuant to paragraph (a)(2)(iv) of this section; and

(b) Any other increases and decreases in actual emissions at the major stationary source that are contemporaneous with the particular change and are otherwise creditable. Baseline actual emissions for calculating increases and decreases under this paragraph (b)(3)(i)(b) shall be determined as provided in paragraph (b)(48) of this section, except that paragraphs (b)(48)(i)(c) and (b)(48)(ii)(d) of this section shall not apply.

(ii) An increase or decrease in actual emissions is contemporaneous with the increase from the particular change only if it occurs between:

(a) The date five years before construction on the particular change commences; and

(b) The date that the increase from the particular change occurs.

(iii) An increase or decrease in actual emissions is creditable only if:

(a) The Administrator or other reviewing authority has not relied on it in issuing a permit for the source under this section, which permit is in effect when the increase in actual emissions from the particular change occurs; and

(b) The increase or decrease in emissions did not occur at a Clean Unit except as provided in paragraphs (x)(8) and (y)(10) of this section; and

(c) As it pertains to an increase or decrease in fugitive emissions (to the extent quantifiable), it occurs at an emissions unit that is part of one of the source categories listed in paragraph (b)(1)(iii) of this section or it occurs at an emission unit that is located at a major stationary source that belongs to one of the listed source categories.

(iv) An increase or decrease in actual emissions of sulfur dioxide, particulate matter, or nitrogen oxides that occurs before the applicable minor source baseline date is creditable only if it is required to be considered in calculating the amount of maximum allowable increases remaining available.

(v) An increase in actual emissions is creditable only to the extent that the new level of actual emissions exceeds the old level.

(vi) A decrease in actual emissions is creditable only to the extent that:

(a) The old level of actual emissions or the old level of allowable emissions, whichever is lower, exceeds the new level of actual emissions;

(b) It is enforceable as a practical matter at and after the time that actual construction on the particular change begins.

(c) It has approximately the same qualitative significance for public health and welfare as that attributed to the increase from the particular change; and

(vii) [Reserved]

(viii) An increase that results from a physical change at a source occurs when the emissions unit on which construction occurred becomes operational and begins to emit a particular pollutant. Any replacement unit that requires shakedown becomes operational only after a reasonable shakedown period, not to exceed 180 days.

(ix) Paragraph (b)(21)(ii) of this section shall not apply for determining creditable increases and decreases.

(4) *Potential to emit* means the maximum capacity of a stationary source to emit a pollutant under its physical and operational design. Any physical or operational limitation on the capacity of the source to emit a pollutant, including air pollution control equipment and restrictions on hours of operation or on the type or amount of material combusted, stored, or processed, shall be treated as part of its design if the limitation or the effect it would have on emissions is federally enforceable. Secondary emissions do not count in determining the potential to emit of a stationary source.

(5) *Stationary source* means any building, structure, facility, or installation which emits or may emit a regulated NSR pollutant.

(6) *Building, structure, facility, or installation* means all of the pollutant-emitting activities which belong to the same industrial grouping, are located on one or more contiguous or adjacent properties, and are under the control of the same person (or persons under common control) except the activities of any vessel. Pollutant-emitting activities shall be considered as part of the same industrial grouping if they belong to the same "Major Group" (i.e., which have the same first two digit code) as described in the *Standard Industrial Classification Manual, 1972*, as amended by the 1977 Supplement (U. S. Government Printing Office stock numbers 4101–0066 and 003–005–00176–0, respectively).

(7) *Emissions unit* means any part of a stationary source that emits or would have the potential to emit any regulated NSR pollutant and includes an electric utility steam generating unit as defined in paragraph (b)(31) of this section. For purposes of this section, there are two types of emissions units as described in paragraphs (b)(7)(i) and (ii) of this section.

(i) A new emissions unit is any emissions unit that is (or will be) newly constructed and that has existed for less than 2 years from the date such emissions unit first operated.

(ii) An existing emissions unit is any emissions unit that does not meet the requirements in paragraph (b)(7)(i) of this section. A replacement unit, as defined in paragraph (b)(33) of this section, is an existing emissions unit.

18

Problem 1.3: Applying Regulatory Language

(A) Based on the definition of "stationary source" contained at 40 CFR §52.21(b)(5), would you say that Buildings #1 and #2 should be treated together or separately for the purpose of determining whether their VOC emissions exceed the PSD threshold? (B) Does the definition of the term "building, structure, facility or installation," located at 40 CFR §52.21(b)(6), alter your view on this?

d. Case Law

As was mentioned above, parties occasionally challenge EPA regulations as being in conflict with the statute. The PSD regulations that you have just read are an example of this. The EPA first promulgated final PSD regulations in 1978. Both industry and environmental groups challenged these regulations in the D.C. Circuit Court of Appeals. The court, in Alabama Power Company v. Costle, 636 F.2d 323, 395 (D.C. Cir. 1979), rejected the definition of "source" that EPA had adopted in these initial regulations as being inconsistent with the Clean Air Act and required the agency to alter its rules. The regulations that you have just read are EPA's revised rules issued in the aftermath of the Alabama Power decision. Pages 394–98 of the D.C. Circuit's opinion are reproduced below.

Alabama Power Company, et al. v. Costle

636 F.2d 323, 394–98 (D.C. Cir. 1979) (footnotes omitted)

Petitions were filed seeking review of Environmental Protection Agency's final regulations embracing prevention of significant deterioration of air quality in "clean air areas," which PSD regulations implemented Clean Air Act Amendments of 1977. Preliminary issues were decided by initial per curiam opinion, 196 U.S.App.D.C. 161, 606 F.2d 1068. Subsequently, a three-part opinion was issued. In an opinion for the Court, Leventhal, Circuit Judge, held, among other things, that: (1) it was error to define "potential to emit" by discounting beneficial effect of air pollution control equipment designed into a facility; (2) EPA may exempt de minimis situations; and (3) authority other than PSD permit requirements permit resolution of problem of interstate pollution. In an opinion for the Court, Robinson, Circuit Judge held, among other things, that: (1) statutory method for establishing baseline concentrations was controlling; (2) modeling regulations would not be overturned; and (3) tall-stack policy, for purpose of PSD program, applies to nonbaseline emissions of nongrandfathered stacks. In an opinion for the Court, Wilkey, Circuit Judge, held, among other things, that: (1) NSPS definition of "source" applies to PSD provisions; (2) a "bubble concept" may be applied in determining a covered "increase"; and (3) visible emission standards may be considered by PSD permitting authority in applying BACT. Affirmed in part and remanded in part.

...

WILKEY, Circuit Judge:

This part of our opinion reviews several interrelated regulatory provisions promulgated by the Environmental Protection Agency under the Clean Air Act, as amended in 1977. These provisions fall within five topical categories: I. EPA's definition of pollution-emitting "sources" subject to rules governing the Prevention of Significant Deterioration (PSD) of air quality ("source definition" issue); II. EPA's definition of the term "modification" of stationary sources for the purposes of PSD, and the right of industries to offset pollution-increasing changes against pollution-decreasing changes in a single source without PSD review ("major modification" and "bubble" issues); III. the applicability of PSD to pollutants other than sulfur dioxide and particulate matter, and EPA's 100 and 250-ton per year emission threshold for each pollutant (pollutants subject to PSD and EPA's "major emitting facility" threshold); IV. EPA's inclusion of visible emission standards among emission limitations subject to best available control technology; and V. administrative conditions imposed by EPA on each stage of a multi-phase construction project for which EPA issues a comprehensive construction permit (the definition of "commerce [sic] construction" for phased projects).

I. SOURCE DEFINITION

Pollution control measures enacted under the Clean Air Act's PSD program apply to major pollution-emitting facilities, which are defined as certain types of "stationary sources" that emit or could emit 100 tons of pollutants per year, or "any other source" that could emit 250 tons. The terms "stationary source" and "any other source," however, are not specifically defined in the PSD provisions of the Act. To fill this statutory definitional breach, EPA as part of comprehensive Clean Air Act regulations promulgated for the purposes of PSD the following definition:

> "Source" means any structure, building, facility equipment, installation or operation (or combination thereof) which is located on one or more contiguous or adjacent properties and which is owned or operated by the same person (or by persons under common control).

EPA also provided by regulation that:

> Notwithstanding the source sizes specified in [the first sentence of Clean
> Air Act § 169(1), 42 U.S.C. § 7479(1) (Supp. I 1977), "major stationary
> source" means] any source which emits, or has the potential to emit,
> 250 tons per year or more of any air pollutant regulated under the Act.

In this section of our opinion we consider three separate issues pertaining to
the above regulatory definitions.

A. *Inclusion of "Equipment," "Operation," and "Combination Thereof" within
EPA's Definition of "Source."*

We consider first whether EPA erred in defining "source" to include "any
structure, building, facility, *equipment,* installation *or operation (or combination
tion thereof)....*"

Petitioning Industry Groups argue that by introducing the above italicized language into the regulatory definition of "source," EPA has subjected a wider range
of pollution-emitting activities to the Act's PSD requirements than Congress intended. Industry groups fear that EPA will capitalize on its expansive definition
of "source" by subjecting to PSD review every type of productive enterprise ranging from mining and forestry to commercial trains and ships. There is a risk of
an unlimited scope of PSD regulation which could follow from literal application of PSD to any "equipment" or "operation," and to any "combination" of, for
example, equipment and operations, that meets minimum emission standards.

EPA, however, argues that Congress did not intend to confine PSD to a class
of pollution-emitting entities so narrow as the four nonitalicized terms above.
EPA considers it prudent to "err on the side of inclusiveness," in order to extend PSD to the range of activities it claims Congress intended, and in order
to give notice to those who must apply for PSD permits.

We find this definitional issue to be governed by the definition of "source"
provided in Clean Air Act section 111(a)(3), pertaining to the Act's new source
performance standards (NSPS). Section 111(a)(3) provides that for the purposes
of NSPS "(t)he term 'stationary source' means any building, structure, facility,
or installation which emits or may emit any air pollutant." In addition, section
111(a)(2) provides that for NSPS "(t)he term 'new source' means any stationary
source, the construction or modification of which is commenced after (a specified time)," thus incorporating into the term "source" the components of the term
"stationary source." For NSPS the two terms become essentially interchangeable.

We find no support in the statute for the notion that Congress intended its
definition of the term "source" as used in the PSD provision of the Act to dif-

fer from that provided for NSPS in section 111(a)(3). Though "stationary source" is not defined expressly for PSD in the Act, it had at the time of the 1977 Amendments a well-established meaning, which included the four terms "structure," "building," "facility," and "installation," but not "equipment," "operation," or "combination thereof."

Given no expression of any contrary intent in the Act or in the legislative history regarding these definitions, we must assume that the meaning of a particular term is to be consistent throughout the Act. This is especially true under present circumstances, where the subject term prior to enactment of the controversial language had assumed a particular definition under closely related statutory provisions.

In support of this conclusion we note that Clean Air Act section 169, which defines certain terms expressly for PSD, states in subsection (2)(C) that "[t]he term 'construction' when used in connection with any source or facility, includes the modification (as defined in section 111(a)) of any source or facility." Section 111(a)(4), in turn, provides that the term "modification" means "any physical change in, or change in the method of operation of, a stationary source ..." as that term is defined in section 111(a)(3). Since several key sections of the Act apply PSD to the construction of new facilities, those sections thereby incorporate the definition of "stationary source" used in section 111, at least with regard to source "modification." The PSD provisions thus indirectly incorporated the section 111 definition of "source" concerning modifications; we find it implausible to assume that the same definition of source does not apply to construction as well. Therefore, we hold that the term "source" retains a consistent meaning in all PSD provisions of the Act and that the applicable definition is provided in section 111.

EPA contends that the words "equipment," "operation," and "combination thereof" must be included in the definition of "source" for PSD, because the full range of industrial entities specifically made subject to PSD in section 169(1) cannot be comprehended within the definition of "source" provided in section 111(a)(3). We do not agree. The four terms encompass all of the types of entities specified in the first sentence of section 169(1), as well as all entities and activities included on a longer list compiled by EPA from which the statutory list was drawn. Thus, for example, the components of the term "source" provided in section 111(a)(3) need not be interpreted so narrowly as to comprehend only those sources that emit pollutants through industrial "point" sources (such as smokestacks and chimneys). EPA has discretion to define the terms reasonably to carry out the intent of the Act, but not to go clear beyond the scope of the Act, as it has done here. Section 169(1) clearly does mean that a plant is to be viewed as a source; the section lists many types of plants as stationary sources. But EPA has discretion to define statutory terms reasonably so as to carry out the expressed purposes of the Act. We view it as reasonable, for instance, to define "facility" and "installation" broadly enough to encompass an entire plant.

In ASARCO Inc. v. Environmental Protection Agency, this court struck down the agency's defining source for NSPS as, inter alia, a combination of facilities. But that case allowed EPA broad discretion to define the statutory terms for "source," so long as guided by a reasonable application of the statute. The agency has the same reasonable discretion here to refashion its regulations.

B. *Extension of EPA's Definition of "Source" to Include Industrial Units Joined by Contiguity and Common Ownership*

EPA regulations provide that the term "source" shall mean any industrial unit "which is located on one or more contiguous or adjacent properties and which is owned or operated by the same person (or by persons under common control)."

Industry Groups contend that Congress intended PSD review to apply only to "major industrial process facilities at specific plant sites" without grouping of such process facilities according to proximity or ownership, and that EPA's contiguity and common ownership language has expanded unlawfully the potential scope of PSD. In ASARCO, this court held that EPA had no authority to attach a similar provision to the definition of "source" for the NSPS program, as defined in section 111 of the Act. That definition, however, was not expanded by any other part of the NSPS provisions or their legislative history. For this reason, the court in ASARCO concluded that the definition of "stationary source" in section 111(a)(3) as "any building, structure, facility, or installation which emits or may emit any air pollutant" could not be administratively expanded to include an entire plant.

With regard to PSD, however, Congress clearly envisioned that entire plants could be considered to be single "sources." Clean Air Act section 169(1) expressly provides that for the purposes of PSD the term "major emitting facility" means "any of the following stationary sources of air pollutants ...: fossil-fuel fired steam electric plants..., Portland Cement plants, ... iron and steel mill plants." In fact, fourteen different types of industrial "plants" are specifically cited in section 169(1) as types of "stationary sources" to which PSD is to apply. By the terms of the PSD provisions, then, the ASARCO holding does not prevent aggregation of individual units of a plant into a single source.

Because of the limited scope afforded the term "source" in section 111(a)(3), however, EPA cannot treat contiguous and commonly owned units as a single source unless they fit within the four permissible statutory terms. To allow an entire plant or other appropriate grouping of industrial activity to be subject as a single unit to PSD, as Congress clearly intended, EPA should devise regulatory definitions of the terms "structure," "building," "facility," and "installation" to provide for the aggregation, where appropriate, of industrial activities according to considerations such as proximity and ownership. We have no doubt that the term installation, for instance, is susceptible in its common usage to a reasonable interpretation that includes all the types of sources specified in the first sentence of section 169(1), as well as those intended by Congress to be reached in the second sentence of section 169(1).

EPA's new definitions should also provide explicit notice as to whether (and on what statutory authority) EPA construes the term source, as divided into its several constituent units, to include the unloading of vessels at marine terminals and "long-line" operations such as pipelines, railroads, and transmission lines. We agree with Industry Groups that EPA has not yet given adequate notice as to whether it considers those industrial activities to be subject to PSD.

EPA has latitude to adopt definitions of the component terms of "source" that are different in scope from those that may be employed for NSPS and other clean air programs, due to differences in the purpose and structure of the two programs. The reasonableness of EPA's contiguity and common ownership criteria, in light of the new source definitions required, must await review until their application in specific circumstances....

Problem 1.4: Judicial Review of Regulations

After you have read the above selection from Alabama Power Company v. Costle, *answer the following questions: (A) How did EPA define the term "source" in its 1978 PSD final rule? What is the significance, in this definition, of EPA's inclusion of the words "or combination thereof"? (B) Why did the D.C. Circuit reject EPA's initial definition? (C) What did the court require EPA to do on remand with respect to the definition of "source" for the PSD program? How did the court require EPA to incorporate into the regulations the "plantwide" definition of "source"?*

---

e. Regulatory Preambles: The Federal Register

Under the PSD regulations reproduced above (Figures 1.7a–1.7e), Buildings #1 and #2 must be considered a single "stationary source" if they meet the following three criteria: (1) the activities that take place in the two buildings must "belong to the same industrial grouping" as defined in the *Standard*

Industrial Classification Manual; (2) the two buildings must be "located on one or more contiguous or adjacent properties; and (3) they must be under "common control." (If you do not see why this is so, go back and do Problem 1.3 again.) In the case of the Fab Furniture operation, the first and third criteria are clearly satisfied. The *Standard Industrial Classification Manual* (a government-issued book that groups all industrial activities into categories) contains an industrial grouping entitled "Furniture and Fixtures," which includes all "establishments engaged in manufacturing household, office, public building, and restaurant furniture; and office and store fixtures." Executive Office of the President, Office of Management and Budget, Standard Industrial Classification Manual (1987) (SIC Major Group 25, "Furniture and Fixtures"). The activities in Building #1 and Building #2 would both fit within this category and so both belong to the same "industrial grouping." Since both operations are owned and operated by Fab Furniture, they qualify as being under "common control." If the two buildings satisfy the final criteria—*i.e.*, if they are "located on one or more contiguous or adjacent properties"—then they *would* qualify as a single "stationary source" and Fab Furniture would have to obtain a PSD preconstruction permit.

Carol has told you that the buildings are a mile and a half apart and that they are connected by a rail line that transfers production materials between them. Does this qualify as "contiguous or adjacent"? The regulation does not define these terms. A standard dictionary definition would indicate that buildings located a mile and a half apart are neither "contiguous" nor "adjacent," but you are beginning to understand that administrative agencies have their own ways of thinking about things and that the dictionary definition might be misleading (as was true in the case of the word "building" in the definition of "stationary source").

To get a sense of what *the agency* thinks its regulations mean you need first to review the regulatory preambles in the *Federal Register*. As was mentioned above, when an agency promulgates a rule it usually publishes in the *Federal Register* a proposed version of the rule accompanied by a preamble explaining the regulation, followed by a final version which is also accompanied by a preamble. The preambles explain, in a narrative form, the reasoning behind and objectives of the regulation. While the final rule is eventually codified in the CFR, the regulatory preambles are not. To interpret the regulation published in the CFR it is therefore helpful to look back in time to the *Federal Register* notices in which the regulation first appeared. It is in the preamble to these initial notices that the agency usually provides a comprehensive introduction to the regulation.

The *Federal Register* is a daily publication that contains all the proposed and final rules and other administrative documents promulgated by federal agencies that day. To find *Federal Register* notices that correspond to a specific Section of the CFR you should look first to the table of contents of the CFR Part in which that Section is located (here, Part 52). At the end of the table of contents you will find a cite to a *Federal Register* notice and a notation that the notice is the "Source" of each of the Sections in that Part "unless otherwise noted." The second place to look is at the conclusion of the specific CFR Section that you are interested in (in the present case, Section 52.21). There, you will find a listing of the *Federal Register* notices, other than the "Source" document, that created or amended that Section.

Practice Tip: Locating the Proposed Rule

The CFR will point you only to the "final" versions of the rules as they appeared in the Federal Register. To find the proposed version of one of these final rules, you should look to the Federal Register version of the final rule. In the section of the preamble labeled "Background" you will find a cite to the Federal Register notice in which the proposed rule was published.

We have done this bit of research for you. Reproduced on the following pages are the relevant portions of the preambles to the proposed and final PSD permitting regulations as they appeared in the *Federal Register* after the *Alabama Power* decision. Notice that at the beginning of each preamble there is an "Outline" that functions as a table of contents for the preamble.

51924   Federal Register / Vol. 44, No. 173 / Wednesday, September 5, 1979 / Proposed Rules

ENVIRONMENTAL PROTECTION AGENCY

[40 CFR Parts 51 and 52]

[FRL 1300–6]

Requirements for Preparation, Adoption, and Submittal of SIP's; Approval and Promulgation of State Implementation Plans

AGENCY: Environmental Protection Agency.

ACTION: Proposed Rules.

SUMMARY: EPA proposes to amend its regulations for the prevention of significant deterioration 40 CFR 51.24, 52.21 (1978) in response to a court decision that overturned those regulations in major respects. EPA also proposes changes to its regulations affecting new source review in nonattainment areas, including restrictions on further major source growth and requirements under EPA's Emission Offset Interpretative Ruling, 40 CFR Part 51 App. S, and section 173 of the Act, to conform those rules to the court decision.

DATES: The deadline for submitting written comments is October 5, 1979.

ADDRESSES: *Comments.* Comments should be sent (in triplicate if possible) to Central Docket Section (A–130), Washington, D.C. Atten: Docket No. A–79–35.

Docket: In accordance with section 307(d) of the Clean Air Act, 42 U.S.C. 7607(d). EPA has established a docket for this rulemaking. It bears Docket No. A–79–35. The docket is an organized and complete file of all significant information submitted to or otherwise considered by EPA during this rulemaking. The contents of the docket will serve as the record in the case of judicial review under section 307(b) of the Act, 42 U.S.C. 7607(b). The docket is available for public inspection and copying between 8 a.m. and 4 p.m., Monday through Friday, at EPA's Central Docket Section, Room 2903B. A reasonable fee may be charged for copying.

PUBLIC HEARINGS: EPA intends to hold public hearings on the proposals in this notice in September in San Francisco, California, and Washington, D.C. The exact times and places will be announced in due course.

FOR FURTHER INFORMATION CONTACT: Michael Trutna, Standards Implementation Branch (MD–15), Office of Air Quality Planning and Standards, Research Triangle Park, N.C. 27711. 919/541–5292.

SUPPLEMENTARY INFORMATION:

Outline

I. Background:
  A. Prevention of Significant Deterioration.
  B. Requirements Relating to Nonattainment Areas.
II. Highlights.
III. Transition:
  A. PSD Part 52 Regulations.
  B. Nonattainment Regulations.
  C. PSD and Nonattainment SIP Revisions.
IV. Potential To Emit.
V. Fifty-Ton Exemption.
VI. Fugitive Emissions.
VII. Fugitive Dust Exemption.
VIII. Source/Facility/Installation:
  A. Definition of Source.
  B. Sources Subject to PSD Requirements.
  C. Sources Subject to Nonattainment Requirements.
  D. Summary.
IX. Modification:
  A. No Net Increase.
  B. Restrictions on Construction.
  C. Accumulation.
X. "De Minimis" Exemptions.
XI. Geographic Applicability:
  A. Designated Nonattainment Areas.
  B. Designated Clean Areas.
  C. VOC Sources.
  D. Interstate Pollution.
XII. Pollutant Applicability.
XIII. Baseline Concentration:
XIV. Best Available Control Technology.
XV. Ambient Monitoring.
XVI. Notification.
XVII. PSD SIP Revisions:
  A. Equivalent State Programs.
  B. Baseline Area.
  C. State Monitoring Exemption.
XVIII. Additional Issues:
  A. Innovative Control Technology.
  B. Modified Permits.
  C. Non-profit Institutions.
  D. Portable Facilities.
  E. Secondary Emissions.
  F. Economic Impact Assessment.
  G. Comments.

I. Background

A. *Prevention of Significant Deterioration.* In 1974, EPA promulgated regulations to prevent emissions of sulfur dioxide (SO_2) and particulate matter (PM) from significantly deteriorating air quality in areas where concentrations of those pollutants were lower than the applicable national ambient air quality standards (NAAQS). 39 FR 42510 (codified at 40 CFR 52.21 (1977)). EPA made those regulations part of the State Implementation Plan (SIP). The prevention of significant deterioration (PSD) regulations prohibited the construction of any new source or modification in certain categories, unless EPA or a delegate state had issued a permit evidencing that the source or modification would apply "best available control technology" (BACT) for SO_2 and PM, and that emissions of those pollutants from the source or modification would

not cause significant deterioration of air quality in any area.

On August 7, 1977, the President signed the Clean Air Act Amendments of 1977 (1977 Amendments) into law. Pub. L. No. 9595, 91 Stat. 685. Those amendments established a new set of PSD requirements as Part C of Title I of the Clean Air Act (Act). *See* Sections 160–169, 42 U.S.C. 7470–79. The new requirements follow the outline of the old regulations, but are more elaborate and in many ways more stringent. The 1977 Amendments also directed that each SIP was to contain the new requirements. *See* Sections 161, 110(a)(2)(D) and (J), 42 U.S.C. 7471, 7410(a)(2)(D) and (J).

In response to that mandate, EPA promulgated two sets of PSD regulations on June 19, 1978. One set specified the minimum requirements that a PSD SIP revision would have to contain in order to warrant EPA approval. 43 FR 26380 (codified at 40 CFR 51.24 (1978)) (hereinafter, the "Part 51 regulations"). The other set comprehensively amended the old PSD regulations and incorporated into them the new PSD requirements. 43 FR 26388 (codified at 40 CFR 52.21 (1978) (hereinafter, the "Part 52 regulations")). EPA intended that, until it had approved a PSD SIP revision for a state, the permitting of new sources and modifications to be constructed in its clean areas would continue under the new Part 52 regulations. The United States Court of Appeals for the District of Columbia Circuit subsequently affirmed that approach. *Citizens To Save Spencer County* v. *EPA*, 12 ERC 1961 (March 27, 1979).

Many industrial and environmental groups petitioned the same court for review of the substantive provisions of both the Part 51 and Part 52 regulations. On June 18, 1979, the court issued a decision that upheld some of those provisions and overturned others. *Alabama Power Company* v. *Costle*, 13 ERC 1225. In its opinion the court merely summarized its rulings, but promised supplemental, comprehensive opinions in due course, probably by "the end of this summer." *Id.* at 1227 n.7. The court also invited the parties to file petitions for reconsideration, several of which were filed but have not yet been acted upon. In an order that accompanied the summary opinion, the court stayed the effect of its decision until it had issued the supplemental opinions. The purpose of this procedure, the court explained, was "to enable EPA to proceed as soon as possible to commence rulemaking or other proceedings necessary to promulgate those revisions in the PSD regulations required by [the court's]

Figure 1.8 Preamble to proposed PSD regulations, Sept. 5, 1979.

Federal Register / Vol. 44, No. 173 / Wednesday, September 5, 1979 / Proposed Rules   51931

included in determining whether a source of modification is "major." The actions described below apply to regulations both PSD and nonattainment NSR.

First, EPA is proposing to define "fugitive emissions" as those emissions which do not pass through an opening which the owner or operator uses for ventilation, such as a stack, chimney, roof vent or roof monitor. *See* proposed §§ 51.24(b)(20) and 52.21(b)(20). EPA would also delete the existing definition of "fugitive dust" at 40 CFR 51.24(b)(6) and 52.21(b)(6) (1978).

Second, EPA is proposing to incorporate into the existing regulations the principle that rulemaking must precede the inclusion of "fugitive emissions" in an applicability determination by adding the following line to the definitions of "potential to emit": "Fugitive emissions shall not be included in determining potential, except with respect to the following stationary sources: * * *."

Finally, the Agency is proposing to list the following stationary sources whose fugitive emissions are to be taken into account: (1) Coal cleaning plants, (2) kraft pulp mills, (3) portland cement plants, (4) primary zinc smelters, (5) iron and steel mill plants, (6) primary aluminum ore reduction plants, (7) primary copper smelters, (8) municipal incinerators, (9) hydrofluoric, sulfuric, or nitric acid plants, (10) petroleum refineries, (11) lime plants, (12) phosphate rock processing plants, (13) coke oven batteries, (14) sulfur recovery plants, (15) carbon black plants, (16) primary lead smelters, (17) fuel conversion plants, (18) sintering plants, (19) secondary metal production plants, (20) chemical process plants, (21) fossil fuel-fired boilers, (22) petroleum storage and transfer units, (23) taconite ore processing plants, (24) glass fiber processing plants, (25) charcoal production plants, (26) fossil fuel-fired steam electric plants, and any other stationary source category which, at the time of the applicability determination, is being regulated under section 111 or 112 of the Act.

EPA believes that there is no reason why a source of a particular pollutant regulated under the Act should escape review because the emissions of the pollutant are fugitive, when a source of the same pollutant has to get a permit if the emissions are not fugitive. In both cases, the emissions would deteriorate air quality regardless of how they emanate. Thus, it serves the purposes of NSR to scrutinize the one as well as the other. EPA is focusing first on the sources listed above because its experience in quantifying the "fugitive

emissions" from such sources is, in general, greater than its experience in quantifying such emissions from other sources. *See, e.g.,* U.S. EPA, *Compilation of Air Pollutant Emission Factors* (AP-42) (3d ed., August 1977). The Administrator over the next several months will consider the need for additional source types to be added to the list beyond those which would be newly regulated under 40 CFR Parts 60 and 61, including strip mines.

VII. Fugitive Dust Exemption

The existing PSD regulations provide that any "fugitive dust" from a major stationary source or major modification is to be ignored in determining what the effect of the source or modification on air quality would be. 40 CFR 51.24(k)(5), 52.21(k)(5) (1978). Because of its decision on "fugitive emissions" and apparently because it thought EPA had no authority to establish the exemption, the court remanded it to the Agency for further consideration. 13 ERC at 1231. In response, EPA is proposing to delete the provisions which embody the exemption. The Agency is also proposing to delete a parallel provision in the offset ruling, 44 FR 3274.

VIII. Source/Facility Installation

A. *Definition of "Source".* In its existing PSD regulations and the offset ruling, EPA has defined "stationary source" as "any structure, building, facility, equipment, installation, or operation (or combination thereof) which is located on one or more contiguous or adjacent properties and which is owned or operated by the same person (or by persons under common control)." EPA also defined "facility" as an "identifiable piece of process equipment." 40 CFR 51.24(b)(4), (5), 52.21(b)(4), (5); 40 CFR Part 51, Appendix s. sections II.A.1 and 2, as amended 44 FR 3282.

In *Alabama Power* the court said that the definition of "stationary source" in section 111(a)(3) governs PSD review. Slip op. at 11. Section 111(a)(3) defines "stationary source" as "any building, structure, facility, or installation which emits or may emit any air pollutant." 42 U.S.C. 7411(a)(3). The court stated that EPA may not add items to this list, Slip op. at 11. In conformance with the court's opinion EPA is proposing to delete the terms "equipment", "operation" and "combination thereof" from the definition of stationary source in both the PSD and nonattainment regulations. The court also found that EPA exceeded its statutory authority in the way in which it tried to apply preconstruction review to both a *single* building, structure, facility or

installation, which is permitted by section 111(a)(3), and a *combination* of such units. Slip op. at 12. EPA therefore proposes to delete the term "combination thereof" from the definition of stationary source.

The court did, however, state that EPA has substantial discretion to define the terms in the definition of source— that is, building, structure, facility, or installation—to include a wide range of pollution-emitting sources. Slip op. at 11. The components of "source" could be defined differently for PSD purposes than for the purposes of other provisions of the Act. Slip op. at 12, note 13. The key constraint on EPA's discretion is that "the definitions applicable to each set of provisions must be reasonably appropriate for the purposes of those sections." *Id.* The same court has earlier stated that, in defining the components of source, "EPA is guided by a reasoned application of the terms of the statute it is charged to enforce, not by an abstract 'dictionary' definition." *ASARCO, Inc.* v. *EPA,* 578 F.2d 319, 324 note 17 (D.C. Cir. 1978). These two court opinions instruct the Agency to analyze the statutory purposes of the various PSD and nonattainment NSR provisions and define the terms "building," "structure," "facility," and "installation" to carry out best the statutory intent of the provisions.

B. *Sources Subject to PSD Requirements.* One of the fundamental purposes of PSD is to maintain air quality better than the ambient standards. This purpose can best be served if NSR applies to the largest industrial grouping that, as a practical matter, industry and the reviewing authorities can reasonably deal with as a single unit. EPA believes the appropriate grouping is all emitting activities on contiguous or adjacent property and under common control— typically an industrial plant.

For PSD, EPA believes that a large industrial grouping is the appropriate unit for review of both construction of new plants and new and modified pieces of process equipment at existing plants. Applying PSD review to large groupings rather than separate pieces of process equipment ensures adequate review of new plants. EPA believes that unit-by-unit review, without plant-wide review, would fail to protect air quality standards and increments. Large new plants could be constructed at one site as a collection of individual process units, each below the potential-to-emit threshold, and thereby escape review altogether. If clustering of new growth were permitted without preconstruction

51932   **Federal Register** / Vol. 44, No. 173 / Wednesday, September 5, 1979 / Proposed Rules

review, increments and even standards could easily be violated.

While increased protection of air quality might be achieved by reviewing groupings even bigger than a plant, review of larger groupings is infeasible. New units not on adjacent property or under common control would be an awkward grouping to evaluate and regulate. Therefore, PSD review will apply to groupings of new construction no larger than a plant.

Plant-wide review also serves the basic purposes of PSD when pieces of equipment are being built or modified at existing plants. With plant-wide review, industry can construct new and modified equipment without a permit, by reducing emissions enough that net emissions at the plant do not increase. (Allowing use of offsetting emission reductions within the source to avoid NSR is called the "bubble" approach. For discussion of the bubble, see "Modification"). The purposes of PSD are served, because assuring that there will be no net increase in emissions from the plant also assures that the construction will not interfere with maintaining good air quality.

Permitting offsets only within individual process units would go beyond maintaining the status quo. While increased emission reductions beyond existing levels are needed to attain standards in nonattainment areas (see discussion in the next section), such reductions are ordinarily unnecessary to meet the purposes of the PSD program. In addition, the review itself would not make sense relative to RSD goals, if new units at sources with offsetting plant-wide decreases were forced to undergo review. Sources might be required to model and monitor increment consumption when air quality is expected to improve or stay the same. In addition, application of the bubble on a plant-wide basis encourages voluntary upgrading of equipment, and growth in productive capacity.

Since obtaining offsets is often less expensive and less time-consuming than obtaining a PSD permit, providing industry with the offset option will facilitate upgrading of productive capacity, and encourage application of improved controls to obtain offsets. Permitting plant-wide use of offsets provides the greatest opportunity for both of these desirable results. Thus, plant-wide review is the preferred approach under PSD for reviewing construction of both new plants, and new and modified pieces of equipment at existing plants.

For these reasons, EPA proposes that PSD review apply to a large grouping of pollutant-emitting activities, like an

industrial plant. To accomplish this, EPA proposes to define "building, structure, facility, or installation" to mean a grouping of activities on contiguous or adjacent properties and under common control. The term "grouping" is intended to include a plant consisting of a single isolated activity, as well as a plant consisting of many activities.

C. *Sources Subject to Nonattainment Requirements.*

1. *Purpose to be Served by Nonattainment NSR Definitions.* Unlike the PSD provisions, the nonattainment provisions are primarily intended not merely to prevent excessive increases in emissions, but to reduce emissions. This fundamental difference in purpose requires a different approach to defining the sources that will be subject to NSR. To assure adequate review, EPA believes that both entire plants and individual pieces of equipment must be subject to NSR. The one exception under EPA's proposal is for areas subject to fully complete SIPs satisfying Part D requirements. In these areas, where attainment is assured, NSR need apply only to entire plants.

To assure adequate review of new plants, a large grouping must be subject to nonattainment NSR for the reasons discussed above for PSD. To do otherwise would allow a new plant that is divided into separate process units, each below the potential emission threshold, to escape review. New emissions could thus be added to the existing violation, without review, making attainment virtually impossible. Therefore, EPA believes that nonattainment programs, like PSD programs, must apply NSR to entire plants.

EPA believes that pieces of process equipment within plants should also be subject to NSR under nonattainment programs. This would prevent use of plant-wide offsets for increases from construction or modification of major pieces of process equipment. The plant-wide bubble is less appropriate for nonattainment programs than for PSD programs because it only holds emissions constant. Nonattainment programs, in contrast to PSD programs, must positively reduce emissions.

If increases from construction of new or modified pieces of process equipment could be offset on a plant-wide basis the construction would make attainment of the standards substantially more difficult. For each nonattainment area, there are only a limited number of cost-effective ways to reduce existing emissions enough to attain standards. If the cost-effective opportunities to reduce emissions are used to offset

equally large increases from new construction, then other, less cost-effective ways to reduce emissions must be found to achieve attainment.

Therefore, to ensure that construction within existing plants does not make attainment of the standards more difficult, nonattainment programs must provide for NSR new and modified pieces of equipment. The NSR requirements will assure that the most stringent controls are applied to new and modified equipment, and that more than offsetting reductions in existing emissions are obtained to assure adequate continued progress toward attainment. The nonattainment requirements also ensure that other sources in the state, owned or operated by the same owner, are in compliance with SIP requirements needed for attainment.

This policy argument is strongly supported by the legislative history. Even where demolition of obsolete equipment reduces emissions, Congress indicated that construction of replacement equipment should be subject to NSR under nonattainment programs without regard to the offsetting reductions:

> Thus, [under the offset ruling and Part D NSR requirements,] a new source is still subject to such requirements as "lowest achievable emission rate" even if it is constructed as a replacement for an older facility resulting in a net reduction from previous emission levels.[4] [Statement of Senator Muskie, 123 Cong. Rec. at S 13702 col. 2 (daily edition, August 4, 1977)].

2. *Proposed Definitions.* To implement this specific expression of Congressional intent, as well as the general purposes of the nonattainment provisions discussed above, EPA is proposing to define "source" to include not only plant-wide groupings of activities, but also individual pieces of process equipment. "Building, structure or facility"[5] would be defined as a large grouping of activities (a plant) and "installation" would be defined as an "individual piece of process equipment."

These definitions would prevent use of plant-wide bubble for all new and modified major pieces of process equipment. ("Major" means having high enough potential emissions to be a major stationary source. "Minor" means having less than that.) The plant-wide bubble would still serve to avoid NSR, when emissions from a new or modified *minor* piece of equipment (or from some activity like a coal pile that is not an installation) are offset by enough

---

[4] Then, as now, "facility" was defined in EPA's offset ruling as a piece of process equipment.
[5] Referred to hereafter as "facility."

52676   **Federal Register** / Vol. 45, No. 154 / Thursday, August 7, 1980 / Rules and Regulations

ENVIRONMENTAL PROTECTION AGENCY

40 CFR Parts 51, 52, and 124

[FRL 1538-2]

Requirements for Preparation, Adoption, and Submittal of Implementation Plans; Approval and Promulgation of Implementation Plans

AGENCY: Environmental Protection Agency.

ACTION: Final rules.

SUMMARY: In response to the decision of the U.S. Court of Appeals for the D.C. Circuit in *Alabama Power Company* v. *Costle*, EPA is today amending its regulations for the prevention of significant deterioration of air quality, 40 CFR 51.24, 52.21. Today's amendments also include regulatory changes affecting new source review in nonattainment areas, including restrictions on major source growth (40 CFR 52.24) and requirements under EPA's Emission Offset Interpretative Ruling (40 CFR Part 51, Appendix S) and Section 173 of the Clean Air Act [40 CFR 51.18 (j)].

DATES: The regulatory amendments announced here come into effect on August 7, 1980. State Implementation Plan revisions meeting today's regulatory changes are to be submitted to EPA within nine months after this publication.

FOR FURTHER INFORMATION CONTACT: James B. Weigold, Standards Implementation Branch (MD-15), Office of Air Quality Qualtiy goals and Standards, Research Triangle Park, N.C. 27711, 919/541-5292.

SUPPLEMENTARY INFORMATION: The contents of today's preamble are listed in the following outline. A section entitled Summary of PSD Program has been added to provide a concise narrative overview of this program.

I. Summary of PSD Program

The purpose of this summary is to help those people who are unfamiliar with the PSD program gain an understanding of it. Because this summary seeks to condense the basic PSD rules, it may not precisely reflect the amendments announced in this notice. Should there be any apparent inconsistency between the summary and the remainder of the preamble and the regulations, the remaining preamble and the regulations shall govern.

A. PSD Allows Industrial Growth Within Specific Air Quality Goals

The basic goals of the prevention of significant air quality deterioration (PSD) regulations are (1) to ensure that economic growth will occur in harmony with the preservation of existing clean air resources to prevent the development of any new nonattainment problems; (2) to protect the public health and welfare from any adverse effect which might occur even at air pollution levels better than the national ambient air quality standards; and (3) to preserve, protect, and enhance the air quality in areas of special natural recreational, scenic, or historic value, such as national parks and wilderness areas.

States are required to develop SIP revisions for PSD pursuant to regulations published today. *See* 40 CFR 51.24, "Requirements for Preparation, Adoption and Submittal of Implementation Plans." If EPA approves the proposed PSD plan, the state can then implement its own program. In the absence of an approved state PSD plan, another portion of today's regulations will govern PSD review. *See* 40 CFR 52.21, "Approval and Promulgation of Implementation Plans." EPA will implement this regulation itself if the state does not submit an approvable PSD program of its own.

States can identify in their SIPs the local land use goals for each clean area through a system of area classifications. A "clean" area is one whose air quality is better than that required by the National Ambient Air Quality Standards. Each classification differs in the amount of growth it will permit before significant air quality deterioration would be deemed to occur. Significant deterioration is said to occur when the amount of new pollution would exceed the applicable maximum allowable increase ("increment"), the amount of which varies with the classification of the area. The reference point for determining air quality deterioration in an area is the baseline concentration, which is essentially the ambient concentration existing at the time of the first PSD permit application submittal affecting that area. To date, only PSD increments for sulfur dioxide and particulate matter have been established. Increments or alternatives

Figure 1.9 Preamble to final PSD regulations, August 7, 1980.

Federal Register / Vol. 45, No. 154 / Thursday, August 7, 1980 / Rules and Regulations   **52693**

functionally equivalent opening." This change will ensure that sources will not discharge as fugitive emissions those emissions which would ordinarily be collected and discharged through stacks or other functionally equivalent openings, and will eliminate disincentives for the construction of ductwork and stacks for the collection of emissions. Emissions which could reasonably pass through a stack, chimney, vent, or other functionally equivalent opening will be treated the same as all other point emissions for threshold calculation purposes.

In addition, in light of EPA's action today deleting the fugitive dust exemption (see Fugitive Dust Exemption), EPA is finalizing the proposed deletion of the existing definition of "fugitive dust" at 40 CFR 51.24(b)(6) and 52.21(b)(6) (1979).

VIII. Fugitive Dust Exemption

The 1978 PSD regulations provided that "fugitive dust" from a major stationary source or major modification be excluded from air quality impact assessment, 40 CFR 51.24(k)(5), 52.21(k)(5)(1979). Because of its decision regarding inclusion of fugitive emissions in threshold calculations, and because it questioned EPA's authority to establish the exemption in the manner in which it did, the court in *Alabama Power* vacated EPA's generalized excemption for fugitive dust and remanded it to the Agency for further consideration. 13 ERC at 1231 and 13 ERC at 2017.

In response to the court's opinion, EPA proposed deletion of the fugitive dust exemption. It also proposed to delete a parallel provision in the Offset Ruling (44 FR 3274). The majority of the public commenters directly opposed this proposal. The primary reasons were that fugitive dust allegedly has little impact on health and that techniques of evaluating its air quality impacts are unreliable.

As indicated above, the *Alabama Power* court vacated EPA's partial exemption of fugitive dust from the requirements of section 165 because the exemption was premised on the erroneous assumption that "the statute of its own momentum subjects major sources of fugitive emissions to PSD preconstruction review and permit requirements" 13 ERC at 2017. However, the court also expressed serious doubt that EPA had the statutory authority to establish such an exemption by regulation, because (1) section 165 does not distinguish between fugitive emissions and point emissions, but applies "with equal force" to both types of emissions, 13 ERC at 2016, and (2) in the absence of explicit statutory

exemption authority, EPA's "general" exemption authority is narrow in reach. 13 ERC at 2005–2010.

The court did outline, though, a mechanism which it indicated is available under the statutory scheme for acccomplishing the objective of partially exempting fugitive dust emitted by major emitting facilities from the requirements of section 165. That approach would involve defining the pollutant "particulate matter" "to exclude particulates of a size or composition determined not to present substantial health or welfare concerns," 13 ERC at 2018, n. 134, and then regulating such "excluded particulates" under section 111. Pursuant to section 109, EPA is currently reviewing the criteria document for the particulate matter NAAQS, and particle size is a factor being considered in this review. If the standard is revised, the rulemaking requirements of section 307(d) will apply.

EPA today is adopting its proposed deletion of the existing "fugitive dust exemption" and is deferring further action on any such "exemption" pending completion of the standard review process.

IX. Source

A. Proposed Definitions of "Source"

In the 1978 PSD regulations, EPA defined "source" as "any structure, building, facility, equipment, installation, or operation (or combination thereof) which is located on one or more contiguous or adjacent properties and which is owned or operated by the same person (or by persons under common control)." The Offset Ruling contained the same definition of "source."

In its June 1979 opinion in *Alabama Power*, the Court of Appeals rejected the definition of "source" in the PSD regulations. It concluded that Congress intended section 111(a)(3) of the Act to govern the definition of "source" for PSD purposes. That section defines "source" as "any building, structure, facility, or installation which emits or may emit any air pollutant." In defining "source," EPA used the terms "building," "structure," "facility," and "installation," but then added "equipment," "operation," and "combination thereof." The court held that EPA, in adding those terms, exceeded its authority. It stated, however, that the Agency has substantial discretion to define one or more of the four terms in section 111(a)(3) to include a wide range of pollutant-emitting activities.

In its June opinion, the court also focused on the clause "which is located on one or more contiguous or adjacent properties and which is owned or operated by the same person (or persons under common control)." The court held that the approach, which that clause embodied, of grouping pollutant-emitting activities on the basis of proximity and control is generally acceptable, since the Agency had "evidenced an intention to refrain from unreasonable literal applications of the definition and instead to consider as a single source only common sense industrial groupings." 13 ERC at 1230.

In September 1979, EPA proposed to define "building, structure, facility and installation" for PSD purposes as "any grouping of pollutant-emitting activities which are located on one or more contiguous or adjacent properties and which are owned or operated by the same person (or by persons under common control)." As the preamble to the September proposal explains in detail, EPA concluded that the proposed definition would serve the purposes of PSD adquately by requiring review of those major projects that would cause air quality deterioration. At the same time, the definition would operate to avoid review of projects that would not increase deterioration significantly. In EPA's view, the dominant purpose of PSD review is to maintain air quality within the applicable increments.

In September, EPA proposed to define the four component terms differently for nonattainment purposes. Specifically, the Agency proposed to define "building, structure and facility" as it had proposed to define them for PSD purposes, and "installation" as "an identifiable piece of process equipment." One effect of that proposal would be the application of nonattainment requirements to a new piece of equipment that would emit significant amounts of a pollutant for which the area had been designated nonattainment, regardless of any accompanying emissions offsets at the plant. The preamble to the proposal explained: "Unlike the PSD provision, the nonattainment provisions are primarily intended not merely to prevent excessive increases in emissions, but to reduce emissions. This fundamental difference in purpose requires a different approach to defining the sources that will be subject to NSR." 44 FR 51932. EPA proposed to apply this definition to "incomplete" SIPs, i.e., those which did not demonstrate attainment based exclusively on currently approved requirements. Fully

52694   Federal Register / Vol. 45, No. 154 / Thursday, August 7, 1980 / Rules and Regulations

"complete" SIPs could, under EPA's proposal, use the PSD definition.

In December 1979, the court issued its final opinion on the 1978 PSD regulations, which opinion superseded the June 1979 opinion. In the December opinion, the court reaffirmed its earlier conclusions that EPA must adhere to section 111(a)(3) in defining "source" for PSD purposes and that EPA has discretion to define the component terms "reasonably to carry out" the purposes of PSD. 13 ERC at 2039. The court added that "a plant is to be viewed as a source" and that the Agency "should" provide for the aggregation of polluting-emitting activities "according to considerations such as proximity and ownership." *Id.* at 2039 and 2040. But it warned that "EPA cannot treat contiguous and commonly owned units as a single source unless they fit within the four permissible statutory terms." Finally, the court said that any new definitions "should also provide explicit notice as to whether (and on what statutory authority) EPA construes the term source, as divided into its constituent units, to include the unloading of vessels at marine terminals and 'long-line' operations such as pipelines, railroads, and transmission lines. We agreed with Industry Groups that EPA has not yet given adequate notice as to whether it considers those industrial activities to be subject to PSD." *Id.* at 2040.

In January 1980, EPA solicited comment on the September proposals in light of the December opinion of the court. 45 FR 6803. EPA specifically asked for comment on whether factors other than proximity and control, such as the functional relationship of one activity to another, should be used. The Agency also asked for specific examples of cases where a literal application of the proposed definition would be unreasonable.

B. PSD: Comments on Proposal and Responses

Most commenters agreed that for PSD purposes EPA should adopt definitions of "building," "structure," "facility," and "installation" that would aggregate pollutant-emitting activities, instead of definitions that would restrict one or more of those terms to an individual activity. One commenter, however, argued that EPA should adopt for PSD purposes the same definitions of those terms that it had proposed to adopt for nonattainment purposes. The commenter asserted that the decision of the court in *ASARCO v. EPA*, 578 F.2d 319 (D.C. Cir. 1978), required the Agency to impose BACT on a new unit at a plant, even if the unit would result in no

net increase in emissions. The commenter also asserted that the "all-encompassing definition * * * destroys the intent of the PSD program by letting opportunities for *reducing* increment consumption disappear before control technology standards (*i.e.*, NSPS) can be in place." (Emphasis added.)

EPA has decided to adopt for PSD purposes the sort of "all-encompassing" definitions that the commenter opposed. First, in its December 1979 opinion in *Alabama Power*, the court explicitly held that *ASARCO* "does not prevent aggregation of individual units of a plant into a single source." 13 ERC at 2040. Second, the dominant purpose of PSD review is not to reduce increment consumption, but rather to maintain air quality deterioration below an applicable increment. A definitional structure that aggregates pollutant-emitting activities into one "source" would serve that purpose, since it would allow only those changes at the "source" that would not significantly worsen air quality to escape review.

Some of the commenters who agreed that each of the component terms of "source" should aggregate pollutant-emitting activities also supported the use of proximity and control as the sole criteria for aggregating them. Most of those commenters, however, objected to the use of proximity and control as the sole criteria, some on the ground that the proposed definitions would be too inclusive and others on the ground that the definitions would not be inclusive enough.

The commenters who thought the definitions would be too inclusive asserted that they would group sets of activities at one site and under common control that are functionally or operationally distinct. Typical of the examples they gave are the following activities at one site and under common control: (1) a surface coal mine and coal-burning electrical generators that the mine supplies with coal; (2) a rock quarry and the portland cement plant that the quarry supplies with raw material; (3) a primary aluminum ore reduction plant, an aluminum fabrication plant and an aluminum reclamation plant; (4) a refinery, a service station, a research laboratory, a fertilizer factory, and a pesticide factory; and (5) a uranium mill and an oil field. With the language of the June 1979 opinion in mind, the commenters contended generally that to group the nominally different activities in each of those examples would violate any common sense notion of "plant."

The commenters who thought the proposed definitions would be too inclusive suggested a wide range of

alternative definitions. For example, one group proposed that activities at one site and under common control should be combined only if: (1) they share the first three digits under the Standard Industrial Classification Code of the U.S. Department of Commerce, (2) they are dependent upon or affect the process of each other, (3) they use a common raw product or produce a common product, and (4) the proponent of the project in question does not show that the activities have entirely separate air quality impacts.

The commenters who thought the proposed definitions would not be inclusive enough urged the Agency to abandon control as a factor and adopt function in its place. Some of them described a plan by a group of independent companies to construct jointly a single coal-burning power plant to replace oil-burning power plants at various manufacturing sites belonging to those companies near to the site of the coal-burning plant. The commenters contended that EPA should treat the old plants and the new plant as being within one "source," so that the new plant might escape PSD review. They argued that the new plant would not deteriorate air quality, since presumably the decrease in emissions from the shutdown of the old plants would offset the increase from the new plant, and that to allow it to escape review would facilitate the national switch from oil to coal.

After considering the comments of those who objected to the use of proximity and control only, EPA has decided to adopt for PSD purposes a definition of "building, structure, facility, and installation" that is different from the one it proposed in September. The final definition provides that those component terms each denote "all of the pollutant-emitting activities which belong to the same industrial grouping, are located on one or more contiguous or adjacent properties, and are under the control of the same person (or persons under common control). Pollutant-emitting activities shall be considered as part of the same industrial grouping if they belong to the same 'Major Group' (*i.e.*, which have the same two-digit code) as described in the *Standard Industrial Classification Manual, 1972*, as amended by the 1977 Supplement (U.S. Government Printing Office stock numbers 4101–0066 and 003–005–00176–0, respectively)."

In EPA's view, the December opinion of the court in *Alabama Power* sets the following boundaries on the definition for PSD purposes of the component terms of "source": (1) it must carry out

Federal Register / Vol. 45, No. 154 / Thursday, August 7, 1980 / Rules and Regulations   52695

reasonably the purposes of PSD; (2) it must approximate a common sense notion of "plant"; and (3) it must avoid aggregating pollutant-emitting activities that as a group would not fit within the ordinary meaning of "building," "structure," "facility," or "installation."

The comments on the proposed definition of "source" have persuaded EPA that the definition would fail to approximate a common sense notion of "plant," since in a significant number of cases it would group activities that ordinarily would be considered as separate. For instance, a uranium mill and an oil field would ordinarily be regarded as separate entities, yet the proposed definition would treat them as one.

In formulating a new definition of "source," EPA accepted the suggestion of one commenter that the Agency use a standard industrial classification code for distinguishing between sets of activities on the basis of their functional interrelationships. While EPA sought to distinguish between activities on that basis, it also sought to maximize the predictability of aggregating activities and to minimize the difficulty of administering the definition. To have merely added function to the proposed definition as another abstract factor would have reduced the predictability of aggregating activities under that definition dramatically, since any assessment of functional interrelationships would be highly subjective. To have merely added function would also have made administration of the definition substantially more difficult, since any attempt to assess those interrelationships would have embroiled the Agency in numerous, fine-grained analyses. A classification code, by contrast, offers objectivity and relative simplicity.

EPA has chosen the classification code in the *Standard Industrial Classification Manual, 1972,* as amended in 1977 ("*SIC*"), because it is both well-known and widely-used. EPA has also chosen to use just one set of categories in the manual, those that describe each "Major Group" in the classification system and that bear a two-digit classification number, although the commenter who suggested that EPA use such a code also suggested that the Agency use the categories at the three-digit level. On the one hand, the two-digit categories are narrow enough to separate sets of activities into common sense groupings. In fact, most of the nominally different sets of activities in the examples given above would fall into a different two-digit

category; only the fertilizer factory and the pesticides factory would fall into the same category. On the other hand, the categories are broad enough to minimize the likelihood of artificially dividing a set of activities that does constitute a "plant" into more than one group and the likelihood of disputes over whether a set of activities falls entirely into one category or another.

Each source is to be classified according to its primary activity, which is determined by its principal product or group of products produced or distributed, or services rendered. Thus, one source classification encompasses both primary and support facilities, even when the latter includes units with a different two-digit SIC code. Support facilities are typically those which convey, store, or otherwise assist in the production of the principal product. Where a single unit is used to support two otherwise distinct sets of activities, the unit is to be included within the source which relies most heavily on its support. For example, a boiler might be used to generate process steam for both a commonly controlled and located kraft pulp mill and plywood manufacturing plant. If the yearly boiler output is used primarily by the pulp mill, then the total emissions of the boiler should be attributed to the mill.

In adopting the new definition of "source," EPA rejected the requests of those commenters who thought that the proposed definition would not be inclusive enough. As noted above, they urged that EPA formulate a definition that looked only to proximity and *function.* But such a definition by looking to function would unnecessarily increase uncertainty and drain the Agency's resources. In addition, such a definition would present groupings, such as the example the commenters gave, that would severely strain the boundaries of even the most elastic of the four terms, "building," "structure," "facility," and "installation."

Many commenters urged EPA to clarify the extent to which the final definition of those terms encompasses the activities along a "long-line" operation, such as a pipeline or electrical power line. For example, some urged EPA to add to the definition provision that the properties for such operations are neither contiguous nor adjacent. To add such a provision is unnecessary. EPA has stated in the past and now confirms that it does not intend "source" to encompass activities that would be many miles apart along a long-line operation. For instance, EPA would not treat all of the pumping stations

along a multistate pipeline as one "source."

EPA is unable to say precisely at this point how far apart activities must be in order to be treated separately. The Agency can answer that question only through case-by-case determinations. One commenter asked, however, whether EPA would treat a surface coal mine and an electrical generator separated by 20 miles and linked by a railroad as one "source," if the mine, the generator, and the railroad were all under common control. EPA confirms that it would not. First, the mine and the generator would be too far apart. Second, each would fall into a different two-digit SIC category.

Three commenters focused on whether and to what extent the emissions from each ship that would dock at a proposed marine terminal should be taken into account in determining whether the terminal would be "major" for PSD purposes. One commenter argued in effect that the emissions of each such ship that are quantifiable and occur while the ship is coming to, staying at or going from the terminal should be taken into account. In the view of that commenter, all of those activities would be "integral" to the operation of the terminal. Another commenter asserted that none of the emissions of any such ship should be taken into account, because ships are mobile sources. The remaining commenter contended that only the emissions that: (1) come from a ship which is under the proprietary control of the owner or operator of the terminal and (2) occur while the ship is at the dock should be included in an applicability determination. That commenter viewed the ability of the terminal owner or operator to regulate the behavior of a ship as the critical consideration.

The permit requirements of the final Part 52 PSD regulations apply to a collection of pollutant-emitting activities according to the "potential to emit" of just those activities in that collection which constitute a "stationary source." Whether and to what extent the emissions of ships that would dock at a terminal are to be taken into account in determining PSD applicability depends, therefore, on whether and to what extent the term "stationary source" in the final regulations encompasses not only the activities of the terminal itself, but also the activities of the ships while they are coming to, staying at, or going from the terminal.

The final definition of "building, structure, facility, and installation" resolves that question. EPA intends the term "stationary source" under that

Problem 1.5: Using Regulatory Preambles

(A) What does the preamble to the proposed PSD regulation tell you about the meaning of "stationary source" and of "contiguous or adjacent" and the applicability of these terms to the Fab Furniture project? (B) What does the preamble to the final PSD regulation tell you about the meaning and applicability of these terms? (C) How does the final definition of "building, structure, facility and installation" differ from the definition as initially proposed? Why did EPA make this change?

After completing Problem 1.5 it should be clear to you that the regulations do not establish any hard and fast rules about what it means for two properties to be "contiguous or adjacent." Rather, the agency has determined that it will handle this question on a "case-by-case" basis. Given this lack of clarity, how are you to determine whether the two Fab Furniture buildings are, or are not, "contiguous or adjacent"? How are you going to advise your client?

When the regulations and regulatory preambles do not answer a question, environmental lawyers generally look to agency "guidance documents." Perhaps these sources will answer Carol Client's question.

f. Agency Guidance Documents

With some frequency, a company or a local environmental official will encounter a compliance question that it cannot answer simply by looking to the statute or regulations (Fab Furniture's question about the PSD permitting regulations is an example). Rather than forge ahead blindly, the company or official may write to EPA headquarters seeking the agency's view of what the law requires. The EPA generally responds by way of a written memo setting forth its interpretation of the relevant statute or regulation. These memoranda are known as "agency guidance."[20]

Guidance documents exist in a strange legal "netherworld." On the one hand, EPA frequently includes a written qualification in these memoranda stating that the document is only intended to provide "guidance" and is not legally binding on the agency. On the other, EPA and state agencies almost always follow the policies and interpretations set forth in their guidance documents. Most environmental lawyers consider EPA guidance in giving advice to their clients.

---

20. The term "guidance" also refers to other agency policy documents that are not promulgated through the notice-and-comment rulemaking process, *e.g.*, certain intra-agency communications.

Practice Tip: Finding Agency Guidance Documents

Good environmental lawyers are adept at finding relevant agency guidance documents that speak to a particular issue. The EPA will occasionally circulate its guidance documents to parties other than the one that initially asked for the advice. In addition, EPA has recently begun to collect and publish its guidance documents. At the time of the writing of this Third Edition of ENVIRONMENTAL LAW PRACTICE, EPA published collected guidance documents at the following Web sites:

- EPA Significant Guidance Documents, http://www.epa.gov/lawsregs/ guidance/index.html (extensive set of agency guidance organized by topic or by EPA office)

- New Source Review Policy and Guidance Database, http://www.epa. gov/region7/air/nsr/nsrpg.htm (searchable database of policy and guidance documents related to the Clean Air Act's Nonattainment New Source Review and Prevention of Significant Deterioration programs)

- EPA Office of Air and Radiation Policy and Guidance Information, http://www.epa.gov/ttn/oarpg/, (USEPA Office of Air and Radiation rules, policies and guidance)

- RCRA Online, http://www.epa.gov/epawaste/inforesources/online/ index.htm (EPA Office of Solid Waste (OSW) letters, memoranda and publications interpreting RCRA regulations).

- Superfund Policies and Guidance, http://www.epa.gov/superfund/ policy/guidance.htm (collection of Superfund policies and guidance)

- Office of Water Laws, Policy, Guidance and Legislation, http://www. epa.gov/OW/laws.html (water pollution-related legal and regulatory materials)

At the time that you read this book, some of these Web addresses may have changed. But the above listing should give you a sense of what the agency has historically provided and provide you with a good starting point for accessing these resources. In addition to these governmental offerings, some private companies have published sets of EPA guidance. For example, both Westlaw and Lexis currently offer databases of EPA guidance. The Bureau of National Affairs (BNA) occasionally publishes agency guidance in its Environment Reporter, a weekly publication that chronicles current developments in environmental law and policy. Finally, some entities have published books of EPA guidance that may be available in your local law library.

For the present purposes, your authors have located two relevant guidance documents. We reproduce them below. The first is a 1981 memorandum from a high-ranking official at EPA headquarters (the Director of the Division of Stationary Source Enforcement) to an official at an EPA regional office. The regional official has encountered a question quite similar to the one that Carol Client has posed to you, and has asked EPA headquarters for its advice. The resulting memorandum provides important insight into the meaning of "contiguous or adjacent." We reproduce first the regional official's letter asking for guidance, and then the resulting guidance document. The second guidance document is a 2001 memorandum from the Manager of Air Programs at EPA Region 10 to the Manager of the Region's NPDES Permits Unit. This second guidance document, written twenty years after the first, also focuses on how to interpret "contiguous or adjacent." It reflects the way in which EPA had refined its thinking on this topic over time.

UNITED STATES ENVIRONMENTAL PROTECTION AGENCY

DATE: JUN [sic] 8, 1981
SUBJECT: Defining Two Separate Plants as One Source
FROM: Steve Rothblatt, Chief
          Air Programs Branch
TO: Edward E. Reich, Director
          Stationary Source Enforcement Division, (E341)

Region V has been asked by the State of Michigan and the General Motors Corporation to make a determination as to whether or not two plants on different sites constitute a single source. The purpose of this memo is to describe the circumstances related to this request and seek your counsel before we respond to the State and GM. We request your recommendation on our tentative position by June 12, 1981 at which time we will be responding to the State.

During the assembly of some vehicles in Lansing, Michigan, auto bodies are made in the Fisher Body plant and then are transported by truck to an Oldsmobile plant one mile away. At the Olds plant the bodies are placed on frames and the fenders and hoods are attached. At the present time the bodies are painted at the first location and the fenders and hoods are painted at the second location. GM is proposing to move the painting operations to one of the locations ...

The issue of concern for GM is whether or not these two plants which are separated by approximately 4,500 feet can be considered as one source.

Our investigation has revealed that both plants come under the same SIC code. Additionally, the two plants are the only facilities served by a special spur of the C&O Railroad for raw material delivery and in the future the spur will be used to move unpainted parts from one plant to another when the painting is done at one location. Furthermore, at other locations in the State where vehicles are assembled in this two step body/frame fashion, the two plants are under one roof or are connected by a conveyor for transporting bodies.

It is our opinion that these Lansing plants are functionally equivalent to a source and that the U.S. EPA has the flexibility to arrive at that conclusion. The Federal Register of August 7, 1980, on page 52695 states the following when discussing proximity of PSD activities: "EPA is unable to say precisely at this point how far apart activities must be in order to be treated separately. The agency can answer that question only through case-by-case determinations." With the distance between the two plants less than one mile and the plants being connected by a railroad used only for GM, we believe that the plants meet the requirement of being adjacent and therefore can be considered one source.

UNITED STATES ENVIRONMENTAL PROTECTION AGENCY

MEMORANDUM

DATE: June 30, 1981
SUBJECT: PSD Definition of Source
FROM: Director
            Division of Stationary Source Enforcement
TO: Steve Rothblatt, Chief
            Air Programs Branch, Region V

This is to respond to your memo of June 8, 1981, in which you requested a determination of whether two General Motors facilities, located in Lansing, Michigan, should be considered one "source" as that term is applied under PSD review. Specifically, the two facilities are approximately one mile apart, have a dedicated railroad line between them and are programmed together to produce one line of automobiles.

The PSD regulations define stationary source as any building, structure, facility or installation which emits or may emit any pollutant regulated under the Clean Air Act. The regulations go on to define "building, structure, facility or installation" as:

> all of the pollutant-emitting activities which belong to the same industrial grouping, are located on one or more contiguous or adjacent properties, and are under the control of the same person (or persons under common control). Pollutant-emitting activities shall be considered as part of the same industrial grouping if they belong to the same "Major Group" (i.e., which have the same first two digit code) as described in the Standard Industrial Classification Manual, 1972, as amended by the 1977 Supplement (U.S. Government Printing Office stock number 4101-0066 and 003-005-00176-0, respectively) (40 CFR 52.21(b)(6)).

The two General Motors facilities without question meet the criteria of common ownership and same industrial grouping. The remaining test is one of adjacency. Based on the unique set-up of these facilities as described above and previous EPA determinations ... this office agrees that the two facilities can be considered adjacent, and therefore, may be treated as one source for the purpose of PSD review.

UNITED STATES ENVIRONMENTAL PROTECTION AGENCY
REGION 10

1200 Sixth Avenue
Seattle, WA 98101
(Attachments not included)

AUG 21 2001

MEMORANDUM

SUBJECT: Forest Oil Kustatan Facility and Osprey Platform Construction Permitting Applicability Determination

FROM: Douglas E. Hardesty, Manager
Federal & Delegated Air Programs Unit (OAQ-107)

TO: Robert R. Robichaud, Manager
NPDES Permits Unit (OW-130)

The purpose of this memorandum is to communicate the Office of Air Quality's position regarding the air quality construction permitting of Forest Oil's Kustatan Facility (Kustatan) and Osprey Platform (Osprey). Both Kustatan and Osprey play vital roles in the Redoubt Shoal Unit Development Project in central Cook Inlet. In preparation for issuing an NPDES permit to Forest Oil for Osprey, Matthew Harrington of your staff is currently developing an environmental assessment (EA) to address potential environmental consequences associated with the development of the Redoubt Shoal Unit. In addition, the environmental assessment identifies the specific federal and state agencies under whose permit authorization mitigation measures for environmental impacts may be applicable.

Mr. Harrington has asked Dan Meyer of my staff to identify the applicable air quality construction permit requirements enabling the Alaska Department of Environmental Conservation (ADEC) to implement the mitigation measures related to air quality impacts. Specifically, Mr. Harrington asks whether or not Kustatan and Osprey should be permitted as one facility or two under the Alaska State Implementation Plan (SIP)-approved Prevention of Significant Deterioration (PSD) program....

Based upon information provided..., the Alaska SIP-approved PSD regulations, and EPA's PSD guidance documents, it is the position of the Office of Air Quality that the Kustatan and Osprey projects are one facility under the Alaska SIP-approved PSD regulations. Given that the development of the Redoubt Shoal Unit is intended to progress swiftly to production in a relatively short period of time, Kustatan and Osprey should be permitted together consistent with rule requirements and so as to avoid potential PSD circumvention.

Discussion

The scope of the proposed Redoubt Shoal Unit development, according to the April 12, 2001, draft EA, includes the following components:

- Conversion of the Osprey Platform from a manned exploratory platform to a minimally-manned production platform.
- Production drilling operations using freshwater-based and oil-based drilling fluids. Drilling muds and cuttings will be disposed of with on-platform grind and injection facilities.
- Construction of a new oil production facility located at Kustatan on the West Forelands for oil separation, platform power generation, and produced water treatment for reinjection offshore.
- Transportation of crude oil and natural gas from the Redoubt Shoal Unit to the new oil production facility.
- Transportation of the crude oil from the new oil production facility to existing facilities onshore (through the Trading Bay Production Facility).

Osprey is located 1.8 miles southeast of the tip of the West Forelands off-shore in central Cook Inlet. Formerly an exploratory drilling operation, Osprey will soon be converted to an oil and gas production platform. The oil and gas produced by Osprey will be processed on-shore at Kustatan approximately 4.5 kilometers (2.8 miles) away.

> According to the July 2001 Revised Application for an Air Quality Construction Permit for Kustatan,
>
> *No industrial activity currently occurs at the [Kustatan] facility location. Exploratory drilling was conducted in November and December 2000. One well was drilled. Production quantities of petroleum were not found and the drilling operation was discontinued.*
>
> *The proposed operation will collect produced liquids and gas from Forest Oil's Osprey Platform, separate the oil, produced water, and natural gas, and transfer the oil and natural gas to Forest Oil's West MacArthur River Production Facility.*

According to 18 Alaska Administrative Code (AAC) 50.900(21) and (41) of the Alaska SIP, approved February 16, 1995, 60 Fed. Reg. 8943,

> *"Facility" means pollutant-emitting sources or activities which are located on one or more contiguous or adjacent properties and which are owned or operated by the same person or by persons under common control; and "source" means a structure, building, installation, or other part of a facility which emits or may emit a regulated air pollutant.*

Both Kustatan and Osprey are individually considered "sources" given that each will contain equipment that emits regulated air pollutants. In order for Kustatan and Osprey to be considered one facility, two elements of the "facility" definition must be satisfied. Namely,

1. Kustatan and Osprey must be located on one or more contiguous or adjacent properties, and
2. Kustatan and Osprey must be owned or operated by the same person or by persons under common control.

It is our understanding that ADEC has not yet made a formal determination whether or not to classify the two sources as one facility. ADEC reviewed the March 2001 Application for an Air Quality Construction Permit for the Forest Oil Corporation Kustatan Production Facility, and ADEC provided comments to Forest Oil in a May 15, 2001, letter. As indicated in the letter, the application did not include emissions from Osprey. ADEC noted,

> *It appears that the Kustatan Facility and Osprey platform are a single fa-*
> *cility as defined in AS 46.14.990.(9) As such, Forest Oil should determine*
> *facility classification based on combined emission rates.*

Forest Oil responded to these comments in a July 20, 2001, letter to ADEC accompanying its July 2001 Revised Application for an Air Quality Construction
Permit for the Forest Oil Corporation Kustatan Production Facility. Forest Oil
stated,

> *Forest Oil is the owner of both the proposed Kustatan Production Facility*
> *and the. Osprey Platform. Pipeline and electrical and communications*
> *cables will span the distance between the two facilities. However, the two*
> *properties are approximately 4.5 kilometers distant from each other. For-*
> *est Oil does not own the land between the Osprey Platform and the Kus-*
> *tatan Production Facility. The intervening terrain is Cook Inlet. The State*
> *of Alaska owns the land under that water body.*

There is no dispute that Kustatan and Osprey are under the common control of Forest Oil and thus satisfy the "common control" element of the "facility" definition. However, Forest Oil disputes that Kustatan and Osprey are
"contiguous or adjacent" as noted in its response to ADEC.

> *The "common sense" notion of plant dictates that these two facilities are*
> *not contiguous or adjacent and should be treated independently for per-*
> *mitting purposes."*

Forest Oil refers to a "common sense" notion of plant, which is a reference
to the preamble to EPA's August 7,1980, final PSD rulemaking in the Federal
Register, 45 Fed. Reg. 52695; however, Forest Oil, does not evaluate how this
"common sense" notion applies to the different elements of the Kustatan-Os-
prey relationship (ie. the distance between Kustatan and Osprey, or the support facility relationship between the two.) The preamble to the August 1980
FR, in addition to other EPA guidance documents, however, do provide further guidance related to the "common sense" notion of whether two facilities
are contiguous or adjacent. With respect to the definition of source [facility
for purposes of the Alaska SIP], EPA states,

> *(1) it must carry out reasonably the purposes of the PSD; (2) it must ap-*
> *proximate a common sense notion of "plant"; and (3) it must avoid ag-*
> *gregating pollutant-emitting activities that as a group would not fit within*
> *the ordinary meaning of "building," "structure," "facility," or "installa-*
> *tion." Each source is to be classified according to its primary activity, which*
> *is determined by its principle product or group of products produced or*
> *distributed, or service rendered. Thus one source classification encompasses*

*both primary and support facilities, even when the latter includes units
with a different two-digit SIC code. (emphasis added)*

45 Fed. Reg. 52694 and 52695.

More specifically, with respect to the concept of "contiguous or adjacent", EPA
states,

> *EPA has stated in the past and now confirms that it does not intend "source"
> to encompass activities that would be many miles apart along a long-line op-
> eration. For instance, EPA would not treat all of the pumping stations along
> a multistate pipeline as one "source." EPA is unable to say precisely at this
> point how far apart activities must be in order to be treated separately. The
> Agency can answer that question only through case-by-case determinations.*

45 Fed. Reg. 52695.

EPA Region 8, with the assistance of EPA's Office of Air Quality Planning and
Standards and Office of General Counsel, provided guidance to the State of
Utah concerning multi-source aggregation for purposes of air quality construction permitting. The May 21, 1998, guidance document (Utility Trailer)
utilizes previous EPA determinations to assist Utah in determining whether or
not to aggregate two sources under common control but separated by about
a mile. The guidance suggests that the determination include an evaluation of
whether the distance between the two facilities is sufficiently small to enable
them to operate as a single source. The evaluation questions proposed by Region 8 are transposed here with responses specific to the facts surrounding
Kustatan and Osprey:

> *1. Was the location of the new facility chosen primarily because of its prox-
> imity to the existing facility, to enable the operation of the two facilities
> to be integrated? In other words, if the two facilities were sited much fur-
> ther apart, would that significantly affect the degree to which they may be
> dependent on each other?*

Forest Oil chose to construct the Kustatan production unit at the former
Tomcat drill site in West Foreland, 2.8 miles from Osprey, for a number of
reasons. Utilization of the old Tomcat drill site avoids any further disturbance
of wetlands, archaeological sites, and other surrounding properties while uti-
lizing existing assets. Regardless of the specific location of the production facility in West Foreland (or outside West Foreland for that matter), the platform and production unit operate as one facility as each is exclusively
dependent upon the other as illustrated in response to item 4, below.

> *2. Will materials be routinely transferred between the facilities? Support-
> ing evidence for this could include a physical link or transportation link*

between the facilities, such as a pipeline, railway, special-purpose or public road, channel or conduit.

To enable such an integrated operation, Kustatan and Osprey are physically connected by the following equipment: a) pipelines to transport the oil/gas/produced water from Osprey to Kustatan and to transport the treated produced water from Kustatanto Osprey, b) electrical cables to provide Osprey with power generated at Kustatan, and c) communication cables to coordinate efforts between the two.

> *3. Will managers or other workers frequently shuttle back and forth to be involved actively in both facilities? Besides production line staff, this might include maintenance and repair crews, or security or administrative personnel.*

During the production phase of the project (20 years), the project will support 10-full time employees according to the draft EA (page 4-50). It is anticipated that Osprey will require up to 5 employees per hitch, and onshore personnel from Kustatan will also work at the West McArthur River Unit (West McArthur). Personnel from Kustatan and West McArthur will be utilized at Osprey to perform maintenance activities as required.

> *4. Will the production process itself be split in any way between the facilities, i.e., will one facility produce an intermediate product that requires further processing at the other facility, with associated air pollutant emissions? For example, will components be assembled at one facility but painted at the other?*

Osprey relies upon Kustatan to process all the platform's product into marketable oil and gas while separating and treating the produced water. Once treated, the produced water is piped back to Osprey and is then reinjected offshore by Osprey. Kustatan also provides power generation to Osprey. Thus, after considering the factors relevant to determining whether Kustatan and Osprey are "contiguous or adjacent," we conclude that they are adjacent facilities within the federal definition of "source" and consequently under the definition of "facility" under the Alaska SIP-approved PSD regulations.

Conclusion

The Office of Air Quality concludes that because Kustatan and Osprey are located on adjacent properties and are owned or operated by the same person under common control, they should be considered one facility under the Alaska SIP-approved PSD regulations. If you have any questions regarding this determination, please contact Dan Meyer of my staff at 206.553.4150.

cc: Marcia Combs, AOO
       Matthew Harrington, OW-130
       Jeff Kopf, ORC-158
       Dan Meyer, OAQ-107
       John Pavitt, AOO
       Theodore Rockwell, AOO

Problem 1.6: Using Agency Guidance

(A) Based on your review of the above guidance documents, would you say that the two Fab Furniture buildings should be treated as a single "stationary source," or as separate "stationary sources"? (B) Does Fab Furniture have to apply for a PSD permit prior to commencing construction of its new plant?

Practice Tip: Using EPA Hotlines

The EPA operates several hotlines that can sometimes provide quick answers to your environmental law questions. These hotlines are generally staffed by private contractors that provide the service under EPA's direction. They are usually quite helpful and will answer "hypothetical" questions so that you do not have to reveal any client confidences. However, their answers do not bind the agency. You should use the hotlines only as a resource. You should not rely on them as authority. Do not attempt to use the above-listed hotlines for the problems and exercise that follow. It is important that you learn how to work through the process of environmental law research for yourself.

The principal EPA hotlines are:

The Acid Rain Hotline (answering questions about the Clean Air Act's Acid Rain Program): (202) 343-9620.

The RCRA, Superfund and EPCRA Hotline (answering questions about RCRA, Superfund, the Emergency Planning and Community Rights-to-Know Act, and the Risk Management Program under the Clean Air Act): (800) 424-9346.

The Toxic Substances Control Act Hotline (answering questions on TSCA, including questions on PCBs and Asbestos): (202) 554-1404.

The Safe Drinking Water Hotline (answering questions about the Safe Drinking Water Act): (800) 426-4791.

The Wetlands Help Hotline (answering questions about wetlands and wetlands protection issues): (800) 832-7828.

The Environmental Justice Hotline (providing information about environmental justice issues): (800) 962-6215.

The Endangered Species Hotline (answering questions about the Endangered Species Act): (800) 447-3813.

Practice Tip: Online Resources for Environmental Law Research

This chapter has focused on the use of books to conduct statutory and regulatory research. It has done so for several reasons. First, most lawyers will always have access to a law library but may not have access to pay-as-you-go online resources. Second, books often provide more comprehensive coverage than online resources. Finally, books offer some research aids (e.g. a detailed index) that you may not be able to find online.

That said, online resources can prove very useful. Below, we have provided information on some such resources that environmental lawyers find particularly helpful. While this is not an exhaustive list, it should give you a good start on finding environmental legal materials online.

- **Westlaw and Lexis**. These leading commercial services contain many resources relevant to environmental law practice. You can use them to find environmental statutes, legislative history, regulations, Federal Register notices, guidance documents, law journals and much more. Given the speed with which Westlaw and Lexis change their offerings and formats, this book will not attempt to describe in any detail the resources that they currently offer. However, it is worth pointing out that each service has for some time provided collections of databases organized by area of practice (Westlaw currently refers to these collections as "Topical Materials by Area of Practice," and Lexis calls them "Area of Law-By Topic"). Both include environmental law as one of the featured areas of practice. A good way to start doing environmental law research on Westlaw or Lexis is to locate the area of practice page devoted to environmental law and review the many relevant databases offered there.

- **GPO Access**. This free service, provided by the U.S. Government Printing Office and available at www.gpoaccess.gov, offers wide access to federal statutory and regulatory materials. For example, it provides searchable databases of federal statutes, legislative history, regulations, Federal Register notices, and Executive Orders.

- **U.S. Environmental Protection Agency Web Site**. Available at www.epa.gov, EPA's Web Site provides user-friendly access to a great deal of legal, regulatory and environmental information. The EPA designs its Web site for the public at large, and not just for environmental lawyers, so it may take a bit of looking to find the materials most relevant to environmental law practice. But it is worth the effort. Among other useful materials EPA's Web site provides online versions of all the major environmental statutes, regulatory materials organized by environmental topic (e.g. air pollution, water pollution, etc.), and extensive, searchable databases of agency guidance documents.

- **Regulations.gov**. This Web site (www.regulations.gov) provides U.S. government regulatory materials from nearly 300 agencies, including U.S. EPA. Among other features, it allows users to search for agency regulations and Federal Register notices, submit comments on particular proposed regulations, read comments submitted by others, review agency rulemaking dockets, sign up for e-mail alerts about emerging regulations, and view agency regulatory agendas.

- **HeinOnline**. Many law libraries make HeinOnline available to students. Among other offerings, this service presents Federal Register and Code of Federal Regulation documents in .PDF format and is particularly useful for locating past editions of these key sources of regulatory law.

2. Complying with the Clean Air Act's New Source Performance Standard Program

Complete the following problems which test your ability to conduct environmental statutory and regulatory research under the Clean Air Act.

Problem 1.7: Finding and Applying Statutes

The Prevention of Significant Deterioration program is not the only Clean Air Act program dealing with newly constructed sources of air pollution. Under the New Source Performance Standard (NSPS) program (also referred to as the "Standards of Performance for New Stationary Sources" program), EPA establishes nationally-uniform technology-based emission lim-

itations for "new sources" that fall within certain listed industrial categories
(e.g., all new glass manufacturing plants). Locate the NSPS provisions of
the Clean Air Act. Based on these statutory provisions, answer the following questions:

(A) What actions does the statute "prohibit" owners and operators of stationary sources from taking?

(B) What is a "standard of performance"?

(C) To whom does Congress delegate the task of identifying categories of air
emission sources and of establishing standards of performance for new sources
in these categories?

(D) How do the NSPS provisions define the term "new source"?

(E) How do the NSPS provisions define the term "modification"? Does a
change at a source have to result in an increase of air pollutants beyond a
threshold amount in order to qualify as a "modification"?

Problem 1.8: Finding and Applying Legislative History

The New Source Performance Standard program applies to "new sources."
Why does it focus on new sources and not on existing ones? Find the legislative history for the New Source Performance Standard provisions of the Clean
Air Act Amendments of 1970. Using only this legislative history, explain why
Congress decided to focus the program on new sources of air pollution, rather
than on existing sources. [Hint: The answer can be found in the 1970 committee reports. You need not look any further than this].

Problem 1.9: Finding and Applying Regulations

Locate EPA regulations in the Code of Federal Regulations that implement the
NSPS provisions. Based on these regulations, answer the following questions:

(A) How do the regulations define the applicability of the NSPS program?
(Note that the term "affected facility," as used in the regulations, means the
specific equipment at a plant to which a given performance standard applies).

(B) What are the Title, Part and Section numbers of the regulation that establishes the performance standard for Glass Manufacturing Plants? How do
these regulations define the "affected facility" at such plants? What is the date
after which all "new" and "modified" glass manufacturing plants must comply with the standard?

(C) Under the NSPS regulations, what is the definition of "stationary source"? Is this definition the same as that under the PSD regulations?

Problem 1.10: Applying Case Law

The NSPS definition of "stationary source" that you have just read represents EPA's second attempt at defining this term for the purposes of the NSPS program. The D.C. Circuit struck down the first attempt in ASARCO, Inc. v. U.S. EPA, 578 F.2d 319 (D.C. Cir. 1978) which is reproduced in relevant part below. Read the ASARCO decision and then answer the following questions: (A) How did EPA define "stationary source" in the regulations that were challenged in the ASARCO decision? Why did EPA initially define the term this way? (B) Why did the court believe that EPA's definition of "stationary source" conflicted with the plain language of the statute? (C) Why did it believe that the definition conflicted with the purposes of the statute?

ASARCO Inc. v. U.S. Environmental Protection Agency

578 F.2d 319 (D.C. Cir. 1978) (footnotes omitted)

J. Skelly Wright, Circuit Judge:

These cases involve challenges by ASARCO Incorporated, Newmont Mining Corporation, and Magma Copper Company (hereinafter referred to collectively as ASARCO) and the Sierra Club (Sierra) to regulations issued by the Environmental Protection Agency (EPA). The challenged provisions modify previous regulations implementing Section 111 of the Clean Air Act ... which mandates national emission standards for new stationary sources of air pollution, by introducing a limited form of what the parties call the "bubble concept." ...

I.

A. Section 111 and the "Bubble Concept"

The 1970 amendments to the Clean Air Act were passed in reaction to the failure of the states to cooperate with the federal government in effectuating the stated purposes of the Act, especially the commitment "to protect and enhance the quality of the Nation's air resources so as to promote the public health and welfare and the productive capacity of its population." Clean Air Act s 101(b)(1), 42 U.S.C. s 1857(b)(1) (1970). See generally W. Rogers, Environmental Law s 3.1 (1977). The 1970 changes were designed "to improve the quality of the nation's air," 84 Stat. 1676 (1970), by increasing the federal government's role in the battle against air pollution....

[T]he 1970 amendments added Section 111, which is the focus of this litigation. This section directs EPA to set specific and rigorous limits on the amounts of pollutants that may be emitted from any "new source" of air pollution. The New Source Performance Standards (NSPSs) established under Section 111 are designed to force new sources to employ the best demonstrated systems of emission reduction. Since the NSPSs are likely to be stricter than emission standards under State Implementation Plans, plant operators have an incentive to avoid application of the NSPSs.

The basic controversy in the cases before us concerns the determination of the units to which the NSPSs apply. Under the Act the NSPSs apply to "new sources." A "new source" is defined as *any stationary source, the construction or modification of which*" begins after the NSPS covering that type of source is published. Section 111(a)(2), 42 U.S.C. s 1857c-6(a)(2) (1970) (emphasis added). Further statutory definitions explain the terms used in this one. A "'stationary source' means any building, structure, facility, or installation which emits or may emit any air pollutant." Section 111(a) (3), 42 U.S.C. s 1857c-6(a)(3) (1970). A "'modification' means any physical change in, or change in the method of operation of, a stationary source which increases the amount of any air pollutant emitted by such source or which results in the emission of any air pollutant not previously emitted." Section 111(a)(4), 42 U.S.C. s 1857c-6(a)(4) (1970). The statute thus directs that the NSPSs are to apply to any building, structure, facility, or installation which emits or may emit any air pollutant and which is either (1) newly constructed or (2) physically or operationally changed in such a way that its emission of any air pollutant increases.

The "bubble concept" is based on defining a stationary source as a combination of facilities, such as an entire plant, and applying the NSPSs only when a new plant is constructed or when an existing plant is physically or operationally changed in such a way that net emissions of any pollutant from the entire plant increase. If applied consistently, the bubble concept would allow the operator of an existing plant to avoid application of the strict NSPSs by offsetting any increase in pollution caused by a change in the plant (e.g., modification or replacement of an existing facility, or even addition of a new facility) against a decrease in pollution from other units within the plant as a whole.

B. History of the EPA Regulations

[The court summarizes EPA's initial NSPS regulations, promulgated in 1971, which did not include the "bubble" concept. It then explains that] in September 1974, the agency ... propos[ed] new regulations incorporating a limited version of the bubble concept. After an additional concession further extending the bubble concept in response to a submission by DOC, the proposed regulations were adopted by EPA.

The new regulations would classify an entire plant as a single stationary source by embellishing the statutory definition of a stationary source as follows:

> "Stationary source" means any building, structure, facility, or installation which emits or may emit any air pollutant *and which contains any one or combination of the following*:
> *(1) Affected facilities.*
> *(2) Existing facilities.*
> *(3) Facilities of the type for which no standards have been promulgated in this part.*

40 C.F.R. s 60.2(d) (1976) (emphasis added). The italicized language is not included in the statutory definition of "stationary source" ("any building, structure, facility, or installation which emits or may emit any air pollutant"), nor was it included in the prior regulations. See 40 C.F.R. s 60.2(d) (1975). Thus the present regulations, instead of limiting the definition of "stationary source" to one "facility" as the statute does, make it cover "any one or combination of" facilities. The preamble to the new regulations makes it clear that the purpose of this change is to define a statutory source as an entire plant.

Relying on this new definition of a statutory source, EPA applies the bubble concept to allow a plant operator who alters an existing facility in a way that increases its emissions to avoid application of the NSPSs by decreasing emissions from other facilities within the plant. The regulations provide that "(a) modification shall not be deemed to occur" unless the change in an existing facility results in a net increase in the emission of a pollutant from the whole "source"....

In its petition ... Sierra argues that the Act defines a "source" as an individual facility, as distinguished from a combination of facilities such as a plant, and that the bubble concept must therefore be rejected in toto. For the reasons stated below we agree with Sierra and remand to EPA for further proceedings consistent with this opinion.

II

A. Scope of Review....

B. Sierra's Challenge to the Regulations

The Sierra Club's basic contention is that the new regulations are inconsistent with the plain language of Section 111. The statute defines a stationary source as "any building, structure, facility, or installation which emits or may emit any air pollutant." Section 111(a)(3), 42 U.S.C. s 1857c-6(a)(3) (1970) (emphasis added). In contrast, the new regulations define stationary source to include "any * * * *combination of* * * * facilities * * *." 40 C.F.R. s 60.2(d) (1976) (emphasis added).

This change in the definition of a stationary source is essential to EPA's adoption of the bubble concept. By treating a combination of facilities as a single source, the regulations allow a facility whose emissions are increased by alterations to avoid complying with the applicable NSPS as long as emission decreases from other facilities within the same "source" cancel out the increase from the altered facility. Sierra argues forcefully that this result is incompatible with the statute's mandate that NSPSs should be applied to "any structure, building, facility, or installation" that undergoes "any physical change * * * or * * * change in the method of operation * * * which increases the amount of any air pollutant emitted by such (structure, building, facility, or installation)." 42 U.S.C. ss 1857c-6(a)(3), 1857c-6(a)(4) (1970) (emphasis added). See brief for petitioner Sierra Club at 25–33.

EPA responds that the "broad" statutory definition of stationary source gives it "discretion" to define a stationary source as either a single facility or a combination of facilities. Brief for EPA at 13–16. We find this response unpersuasive. The regulations plainly indicate that EPA has attempted to change the basic unit to which the NSPSs apply from a single building, structure, facility, or installation — the unit prescribed in the statute — to a combination of such units. The agency has no authority to rewrite the statute in this fashion. See, e. g., Ass'n of American Railroads v. Costle, supra; Lubrizol Corp. v. EPA, supra.

Our conclusion that the regulations incorporating the bubble concept must be rejected as inconsistent with the language of the Act is reinforced when we consider the purpose of the Clean Air Act and Section 111, the confusion generated by the present regulations, and the weakness of EPA's arguments in favor of the bubble concept.

"(T)he goal of the Clean Air Act," as EPA admits in its brief, "is to enhance air quality and not merely to maintain it." Brief for EPA at 17 (emphasis added). See Clean Air Act s 101(b)(1), 42 U.S.C. s 1857(b)(1) (1970). Section 111's provisions mandating New Source Performance Standards were passed because Congress feared that the system of state plans designed to keep air pollution below nationally determined levels was insufficient by itself to achieve the goal of protecting and improving air quality. The New Source Performance Standards are designed to enhance air quality by forcing all newly constructed or modified buildings, structures, facilities, or installations to employ pollution control systems that will limit emissions to the level "achievable through application of the best technological system of continuous emission reduction which * * * the Administrator determines has been adequately demonstrated." 42 U.S.C. s 1857c-6(a)(1) (1970), as amended, Pub.L.No. 95-95 s 109(c)(1), 91 Stat. 699–700. The bubble concept in the challenged regulations would undercut Section 111 by allowing operators to avoid installing the best pollution control technology on an altered facility as long as the emissions from the entire plant do not increase. For example, under the bubble concept an operator who alters one of its facilities so that its emission of some pollutant increases might avoid application of the NSPS by simultaneously equipping other plant facilities with additional, but inferior, pollution control technology or merely reducing their production. Applying the bubble concept thus postpones the time when the best technology must be employed and at best maintains the present level of emissions....

We therefore agree with the Sierra Club that EPA's regulations incorporating the bubble concept are inconsistent with the language and purpose of the statute and cannot be justified by any alleged need for flexibility.... Accordingly, we remand to the EPA for further proceedings not inconsistent with this opinion.

So ordered.

Problem 1.11: Finding and Applying Regulatory Preambles

Find the NSPS regulations dealing with the "reconstruction" of stationary sources. Now locate the Federal Register notices in which the proposed and final "reconstruction" regulations appeared. Based on these materials, answer the following questions:

(A) Under the NSPS regulations, what is a "reconstruction"?

(B) How is a "reconstruction" different from a "modification"?

(C) Why did EPA find it necessary to address "reconstructions" in the regulations? What loophole was the agency trying to close? [Hint: see the preambles to the proposed and final "reconstruction" rules.]

(D) How did the definition of "reconstruction," as it is appears in the final regulation, differ from the definition as initially proposed? Why did EPA make this change?

In the following exercise, you will be asked to counsel a client with respect to a question under the New Source Performance Standards (NSPS) provisions of the Clean Air Act. To answer the question, you will need to examine the statute, the legislative history, the Code of Federal Regulations and, finally, the regulatory preambles in the Federal Register. You should not need agency guidance in order to answer the questions posed.

Exercise 1.1: Counseling a Client on a New Source Performance Standard Issue

You are the junior in-house counsel to Limeco, one of the nation's largest manufacturers of lime. Limeco's manufacturing process is relatively simple. The typical Limeco plant consists principally of a quarry, crushing operations, a "rotary lime kiln" and a packaging area. The company mines limestone from the quarry, crushes it, and then heats it in the rotary lime kiln. The heat calcines (chemically changes) the raw limestone and turns it into lime. The lime is then further crushed, packaged and shipped to Limeco's customers. The main air pollutant associated with the lime manufacturing process is particulate matter (PM), fine grains of dust that are emitted from the kiln. Health studies have shown that high concentrations of PM in the ambient air can result in premature mortality and in the aggravation of respiratory diseases among the elderly and those with cardiovascular disease, and can increase the respiratory problems experienced by children and individuals with asthma. In addition, the kiln emits small amounts of two other pollutants, nitrogen oxides (NOx) and carbon monoxide (CO), that result from the burning of fossil fuel to heat the kiln.

One morning, you receive a call from Limeco's general counsel, Carl Counsel, who asks you to please come see him. You gather your pen and legal pad and head up to his office. Carl tells you that the company needs advice on an environmental law issue. The situation is as follows. Back in March 1977, Limeco signed a contract with a construction firm to build a new lime manufacturing plant in Hoboken, New Jersey. The project broke ground in June, 1977 and was completed a year later, in June 1978. The plant began operating in July, 1978. Limeco has always believed that the plant was not subject to the New Source Performance Standard for lime manufacturing plants, and has never complied with this regulation.

In 1982, there was a surge in the demand for lime in New Jersey and surrounding areas. To meet this demand, Limeco did away with its old equipment for loading the limestone into the rotary lime kiln and installed new machines capable of blowing the crushed stone into the kiln. This allowed the company to inject the limestone more quickly and so to increase the production of lime. The blowers also increased the volume and intensity of the air flow through the kiln, resulting in more particulate matter being carried up through the kiln. The addition of the blowers would have led to an increase in the rate at which PM was emitted from the kiln (whether measured on an hourly basis, or per unit of limestone feed) but for the fact that, at the same time that it deployed the blowers, Limeco also installed a pollution control device on the kiln. Due to the control technology, the installation of the blowers did not result in an increase in the rate of PM emissions from the kiln.

Recently, demand for lime in the New Jersey area has been growing again. Limeco is contemplating taking two actions to boost its production at the Hoboken plant. First, the company is going to begin operating the rotary lime kiln 16 hours per day rather than the 12 hours per day that it had been operating previously. This will increase the amount of raw limestone that the kiln is able to process. It will also result in an increase in the overall emissions of PM over time from the kiln, although it will not increase the rate at which pollutants are emitted. Secondly, the company is going to install a new piece of equipment in the kiln known as a "pre-heater." The pre-heater will draw heat (but not pollutants) from the gases being emitted at the top of the kiln and transfer it down to the crushed limestone at the bottom that is waiting to be blown into the main kiln chamber. When limestone is pre-heated for a period of time it becomes more susceptible to calcination. The addition of the pre-heater will therefore increase the "yield" of lime generated from each ton of limestone feed, allowing Limeco to produce product at a faster rate. Limestone that has been pre-heated also generates more particulate matter when it is further cooked in the kiln than does limestone that has not been pre-heated. The installation of the pre-heater will accordingly increase by twenty percent the amount of particulate matter that is generated per ton of limestone feed, resulting in an increase in the kiln's PM emission rate (whether measured on an hourly basis, or per unit of limestone feed). Finally, the installation of the pre-heater will allow the company to burn ten percent less fuel since the limestone will already be quite hot at the time that it enters the main kiln chamber. The company is not planning to install any new pollution control technology when it makes these changes.

Carl Counsel wants to know: (1) whether the Hoboken plant became subject to the NSPS for lime manufacturing plants when it was initially constructed back in 1977–78; (2) whether it became subject to the NSPS regulation at the time of the 1982 installation of the blowers and additional control technology; and (3) whether either of the two contemplated actions (the shift from 12- to 16-hour days, or the installation of the pre-heater) will subject the plant to the

NSPS for lime manufacturing plants. Write him a memo answering these questions and explaining the reasons behind your conclusions. Your memo should cite relevant statutory provisions, regulations and regulatory preambles, where appropriate. You will not need to use agency guidance to answer these questions.

C. Counseling Clients When the Law Is Ambiguous

Thus far, we have assumed that your research, if performed correctly, will yield clear answers to your client's questions. But what if the language of the statute, regulation and/or guidance can be read in two different ways, one of which is consistent with your understanding of the document's underlying purpose[21] and the other of which is most favorable to your client's purposes? Should you choose one of these interpretations for your client? Should you give the client both views and let the client decide? If you give both, how should you present the different views?

In the following excerpt, Professor David Dana argues that environmental attorneys should construe ambiguous statutes and regulations in accordance with the public purposes that underlie these provisions.

* * *

Dana, *Environmental Lawyers and the Public Service Model of Lawyering*[22]

In one of the dominant models of the private lawyer as counselor, the "client service model," the sole task of the lawyer is to assist the client in maximizing the client's welfare within the constraints of the legal system. In this model, the lawyer presents the client with options and assesses the possible risks and rewards for the client associated with each option; the lawyer's role is not to encourage the client to pursue those options that best comport with the lawyer's understanding of the public welfare.

In a second major model of the private lawyer as counselor, the "public service model," the lawyer's role is to encourage her clients to act in accordance with the public purposes underlying statutes, even where other options exist

---

21. This discussion will assume that the document's purpose is not itself ambiguous.

22. 74 Or. L. Rev. 57, 58–62 (1995) (footnotes omitted). Reprinted by permission. Copyright 1995 by University of Oregon.

that have greater expected value for the client. In this model the private lawyer is, at least in part, an agent for the public good....

In a world of unambiguous laws and regulations, immediate detection and vigorous prosecution of every violation, and automatic draconian penalties, the client service and public service models of environmental counseling would be essentially the same—every lawyer simply would inform her clients of plainly applicable requirements. In fact, environmental statutes and regulations often contain ambiguities and inconsistencies, and regulators often remain unaware of arguably unlawful conduct by regulated entities....

Given these realities, one might expect client service counseling to differ from public service counseling in several fundamental respects. First, client service lawyers might help their clients identify advantageous interpretations of regulatory requirements and evaluate the likelihood that regulators would accept or reject such interpretations....

By contrast, a public service lawyer might decline to inform her clients of statutory and regulatory interpretations that she believes are contrary to the public purpose of the statutory or regulatory framework. At a minimum, such a lawyer would probably downplay the attractiveness of those options.

Second, one might expect a client service lawyer to help her clients assess the risk that regulators will discover particular courses of conduct and, assuming they do, the risk that they will bring an enforcement action challenging the conduct....

A public service lawyer, by contrast, might believe that clients should act as if regulators will detect and respond to all questionable conduct. Consequently, the public service lawyer might decline to discuss the probabilities of non-detection and non-enforcement, at least where she believes those probabilities to be high....

Finally, a client service lawyer might assist clients by predicting the magnitude of informal penalties (*e.g.*, loss of regulators' good will) and formal civil or criminal penalties that might be imposed at different points in the process....

The public service lawyer, on the other hand, might decline to offer a realistic assessment of penalties if she believes that her client, if fully informed, would conclude that the benefits of pursuing a dubious course of conduct outweigh the risks. Such a lawyer might highlight the worst possible outcomes for a client or, at a minimum, might exhort the client that compliance with regulatory requirements is the "right thing to do" regardless of the magnitude of possible penalties.

* * *

Problem 1.12: Role as Counselor

Why does Professor Dana advise environmental attorneys to interpret statutes and regulations in light of their underlying purpose when counsel-

ing clients? What other steps does Dana urge environmental lawyers to take with respect to client counseling? Which of these steps would you take if you were in private practice?

Problem 1.13: Prevalence of Public Service Model

Do you think most environmental lawyers in private practice follow the "client service" model or the "public service" model of lawyering? Which do you think they should follow, and why?

Problem 1.14: Effectiveness of Public Service Model

Do you think that it is possible to follow a "public service" model of lawyering and still maintain a successful private law practice? Are there any ways in which this approach might make you a more effective lawyer in a regulatory field such as environmental law, and thereby help you to gain business?

Assume that you are outside counsel to a company. Further assume that, in a situation of regulatory ambiguity, your client's general counsel insists on adopting an interpretation that would serve the company's bottom line but would, in your view, significantly undermine the regulatory purpose. Must you abide by the general counsel's wishes? If you do not want to go along, what steps can you ethically take to avoid doing so? Can you raise the issue with higher-level executives in the company? Can you withdraw from the representation? Can you tell EPA what the company is doing? Consider these questions as you read the following excerpt from ABA's Model Rules of Professional Conduct.

* * *

American Bar Association, *Model Rules of Professional Conduct* (2008)[23]

Preamble: A Lawyer's Responsibilities

[1] A lawyer, as a member of the legal profession, is a representative of clients, an officer of the legal system and a public citizen having special responsibility for the quality of justice....

---

23. The following selections of the Model Rules are excerpted from American Bar Association Center for Professional Responsibility, Model Rules of Professional Conduct, 2008 Edition, Copyright 1983, 1989–2008 by the American Bar Association. All rights reserved.

[8] A lawyer's responsibilities as a representative of clients, an officer of the legal system and a public citizen are usually harmonious. Thus, when an opposing party is well represented, a lawyer can be a zealous advocate on behalf of a client and at the same time assume that justice is being done. So also, a lawyer can be sure that preserving client confidences ordinarily serves the public interest because people are more likely to seek legal advice, and thereby heed their legal obligations, when they know their communications will be private.

[9] In the nature of law practice, however, conflicting responsibilities are encountered. Virtually all difficult ethical problems arise from conflict between a lawyer's responsibilities to clients, to the legal system and to the lawyer's own interest in remaining an ethical person while earning a satisfactory living. The Rules of Professional Conduct often prescribe terms for resolving such conflicts.
....

Rule 1.2 Scope of Representation and Allocation of Authority Between Client and Lawyer

(a) Subject to paragraphs (c) and (d), a lawyer shall abide by a client's decisions concerning the objectives of representation and ... shall consult with the client as to the means by which they are to be pursued....

(b) A lawyer's representation of a client, including representation by appointment, does not constitute an endorsement of the client's political, economic, social or moral views or activities.

(c) A lawyer may limit the scope of the representation if the limitation is reasonable under the circumstances and the client gives informed consent.

(d) A lawyer shall not counsel a client to engage, or assist a client, in conduct that the lawyer knows is criminal or fraudulent, but a lawyer may discuss the legal consequences of any proposed course of conduct with a client and may counsel or assist a client to make a good faith effort to determine the validity, scope, meaning or application of the law.
....

[Comment 2] On occasion ... a lawyer and a client may disagree about the means to be used to accomplish the client's objectives. Clients normally defer to the special knowledge and skill of their lawyer with respect to the means to be used to accomplish their objectives, particularly with respect to technical, legal and tactical matters. Conversely, lawyers usually defer to the client re-

Reprinted by permission of the American Bar Association. Copies of the ABA *Model Rules of Professional Conduct* (2008) are available from Service Center, American Bar Association, 750 North Lake Shore Drive, Chicago, IL 60611-4497, 1-800-285-2221.

garding such questions as the expense to be incurred and concern for third persons who might be adversely affected....

Rule 1.6 Confidentiality of Information

(a) A lawyer shall not reveal information relating to the representation of a client unless the client gives informed consent, the disclosure is impliedly authorized in order to carry out the representation or the disclosure is permitted by paragraph (b).

(b) A lawyer may reveal information relating to the representation of a client to the extent the lawyer reasonably believes necessary:

(1) to prevent reasonably certain death or substantial bodily harm....

[Comment 2] A fundamental principle in the client-lawyer relationship is that, in the absence of the client's informed consent, the lawyer must not reveal information relating to the representation.... The client is thereby encouraged to seek legal assistance and to communicate fully and frankly with the lawyer even as to embarrassing or legally damaging subject matter. The lawyer needs this information to represent the client effectively and, if necessary, to advise the client to refrain from wrongful conduct....

[Comment 6] Although the public interest is usually best served by a strict rule requiring lawyers to preserve the confidentiality of information relating to the representation of their clients, the confidentiality rule is subject to limited exceptions. Paragraph (b)(1) recognizes the overriding value of life and physical integrity and permits disclosure reasonably necessary to prevent reasonably certain death or substantial bodily harm. Such harm is reasonably certain to occur if it will be suffered imminently or if there is a present and substantial threat that a person will suffer such harm at a later date if the lawyer fails to take action necessary to eliminate the threat. Thus, a lawyer who knows that a client has accidentally discharged toxic waste into a town's water supply may reveal this information to the authorities if there is a present and substantial risk that a person who drinks the water will contract a life-threatening or debilitating disease and the lawyer's disclosure is necessary to eliminate the threat or reduce the number of victims....

[Comment 14] Paragraph (b) permits disclosure only to the extent the lawyer reasonably believes the disclosure is necessary to accomplish one of the purposes specified....

Rule 1.13 Organization as Client

(a) A lawyer employed or retained by an organization represents the organization acting through its duly authorized constituents.

(b) If a lawyer for an organization knows that an officer, employee or other person associated with the organization is engaged in action, intends to act or refuses to act in a matter related to the representation that is a violation of a legal obligation to the organization, or a violation of law that reasonably might be imputed to the organization, and that is likely to result in substantial injury to the organization, then the lawyer shall proceed as is reasonably necessary in the best interest of the organization. Unless the lawyer reasonably believes that it is not necessary in the best interest of the organization to do so, the lawyer shall refer the matter to higher authority in the organization, including, if warranted by the circumstances, to the highest authority that can act on behalf of the organization as determined by applicable law.

(c) Except as provided in Paragraph (d) [concerning representations of an organization for the purpose of investigating or defending against an alleged crime], if,

(1) despite the lawyer's efforts ... the highest authority that can act on behalf of the organization insists upon or fails to address in a timely and appropriate manner an action, or a refusal to act, that is clearly a violation of law and

(2) the lawyer reasonably believes that the violation is reasonably certain to result in substantial injury to the organization, then the lawyer may reveal information relating to the representation whether or not Rule 1.6 permits such disclosure, but only if and to the extent the lawyer reasonably believes necessary to prevent substantial injury to the organization....

[Comment 3] When constituents of the organization make decisions for it, the decisions ordinarily must be accepted by the lawyer even if their utility or prudence is doubtful. Decisions concerning policy and operations, including ones entailing serious risk, are not as such in the lawyer's province. Paragraph (b) makes clear, however, that when the lawyer knows that the organization is likely to be substantially injured by action of an officer or other constituent that violates a legal obligation to the organization or is in violation of law that might be imputed to the organization, the lawyer must proceed as is reasonably necessary in the best interest of the organization. As defined in Rule 1.0(f), knowledge can be inferred from circumstances, and a lawyer cannot ignore the obvious.

Rule 1.16 Declining or Terminating Representation

(a) Except as stated in paragraph (c), a lawyer shall not represent a client or, where representation has commenced, shall withdraw from the representation of a client if:

(1) the representation will result in violation of the rules of professional conduct or other law ...

(b) Except as stated in paragraph (c), a lawyer may withdraw from representing a client if:

(1) withdrawal can be accomplished without material adverse effect on the interests of the client;

(2) the client persists in a course of action involving the lawyer's services that the lawyer reasonably believes is criminal or fraudulent ...

(4) the client insists upon taking action that the lawyer considers repugnant or with which the lawyer has a fundamental disagreement ...

(7) other good cause for withdrawal exists.

(c) ... When ordered to do so by a tribunal, a lawyer shall continue representation notwithstanding good cause for terminating the representation.
...

[Comment 7] A lawyer may withdraw from representation ... if the client persists in a course of action that the lawyer reasonably believes is criminal or fraudulent, for the lawyer is not required to be associated with such conduct even if the lawyer does not further it.... The lawyer may also withdraw where the client insists on taking action the lawyer considers repugnant or with which the lawyer has a fundamental disagreement.
...

Rule 2.1 Advisor

In representing a client, a lawyer shall exercise independent professional judgment and render candid advice. In rendering advice, a lawyer may refer not only to law but to other considerations such as moral, economic, social and political factors, that may be relevant to the client's situation....

[Comment 2] Advice couched in narrow legal terms may be of little value to a client, especially where practical considerations, such as cost or effects on other people, are predominant.... It is proper for a lawyer to refer to relevant moral and ethical considerations in giving advice. Although a lawyer is not a moral advisor as such, moral and ethical considerations impinge upon most legal questions and may decisively influence how the law will be applied.

* * *

Problem 1.15: Questionable Interpretation

Under the Model Rules must an attorney follow a client's instruction to pursue a legal course that, while arguably consistent with ambiguous regulatory language, is at odds with the rule's intent? When can an attorney withdraw from a representation? When must she do so?

Problem 1.16: Going Over the Client's Head

Under the Model Rules, when can an outside attorney go over the head of inside counsel at a client corporation and raise an issue with higher-level executives or the Board of Directors?

Problem 1.17: Confidentiality

As set out in the Model Rules, what are the policy reasons underlying an attorney's duty of confidentiality with respect to communications received from a client? Under what circumstances might the Rules allow an attorney to disclose confidential client information to EPA? When must a lawyer do so?

Problem 1.18: Moral/Ethical Considerations

Under the Model Rules, is it permissible for an attorney in private practice to engage a client in a discussion of environmental ethics in order to influence the client to act in ways that are more protective of the environment? In your personal view, should attorneys do this, or should they focus on explaining the law, leaving the moral and ethical decisions up to the client?

Now that you have become acquainted with the Model Rules, do you think that they provide sufficient guidance for the practice of environmental law? Does environmental practice require more in the way of ethical guidelines and standards than other fields of practice? Consider the following excerpt from an article by J. William Futrell, the former President of the Environmental Law Institute.

Futrell, *Environmental Ethics, Legal Ethics, and Codes of Professional Conduct*[24]

* * *

The United States has built up a complex regime of laws and regulations designed to protect public health and the environment. But this system is not

---

24. The excerpt that follows this footnote is drawn from J. William Futrell, *Environmental Ethics, Legal Ethics, and Codes of Professional Responsibility*, 27 Loy. L.A. L. Rev. 825, 834–35 (1994). Reprinted by permission. Copyright 1994 by the Loyola of Los Angeles Law Review. For further discussion of these and related issues see Douglas R. Williams, *Loyalty, Independence and Social Responsibility in the Practice of Environmental Law*, 44 St. Louis U.

self-implementing. Achievement of the environmental protection goals envisioned by these statutes requires not only concerted enforcement efforts on the part of the government, but also the consistent cooperation of the private environmental bar, the lawyers representing regulated industries.

The key role of the private bar is due to the unique characteristics of environmental law. Environmental law, with its mixture of science and policy, operates through a complex system of regulations that relies for its effectiveness on massive inputs of information and self-reporting by those regulated.... [Environmental] lawyers are essential players in providing the information on which the whole system's performance depends.

Consistent compliance by the regulated community with ongoing regulatory requirements—the most important aspect of which is full and accurate reporting—is crucial to the smooth functioning of the environmental protection system. The lawyer's duty in advising their clients on compliance and reporting is key for the system to function and to serve the public interest in both environmental protection and the rule of law.

Current codes of attorney conduct do not directly address the heightened duties of environmental lawyers to assist their clients in implementing the new self-reporting schemes of the regulatory state. The current codes are based on a tradition of advising the client to offer as little information as possible in order to avoid self-incrimination. Under such codes discreet silence—not open disclosure—is the norm. This approach runs counter to the operation of our environmental law.

... The paradigm case on which most of the rules were modeled is that of the lone criminal defendant, for whom a lawyer is the only means of asserting innocence and who seeks to prevail against the system by stonewalling the government. Although the rules have been supplemented to respond to problems unique to corporate clients, government lawyers, and other specialized practice groups, the underlying premise remains: Lawyers should subsume their personal ethical beliefs and moral stances to the positions that zealous advocacy of their clients' interests require.

* * *

Problem 1.19: Adequacy of Rules

Do you agree with Futrell that the Model Rules are inadequate as applied to the practice of environmental law? If you could re-draft the Rules, what other

L.J. 1061 (2000); Jill Evans, *The Lawyer as Enlightened Citizen: Towards a New Regulatory Model in Environmental Law*, 24 Vt. L. Rev. 229 (2000).

professional and/or ethical obligations would you require for environmental lawyers?

Exercise 1.2: Counseling a Client with Respect to an Ambiguous Regulation

The facts for this exercise are the same as those in Exercise 1.1 (page 62) except that, instead of being in-house counsel to Limeco, you should assume that you are now a partner at a law firm that the company employs. Carl Counsel, the General Counsel of Limeco, has received a memo from a junior attorney in his office that concludes (as a result of working through Exercise 1.1) that the installation of the pre-heater would subject the facility to NSPS requirements. Instead of accepting this report, Carl has called you, his outside counsel, and asked for your view.

Carl tells you that it would cost Limeco $1 million to bring the Hoboken plant into compliance with the NSPS requirements and that he is not inclined to advise the company to do this. Rather, he has looked at the NSPS regulations himself and believes that the installation of the pre-heater would fit within the exception for "[t]he addition or use of any system or device whose primary function is the reduction of air pollutants." 40 CFR 60.14(e)(5) (2009). Carl explains that, as a result of the pre-heating, the kiln will be able to burn ten percent less fuel in order to heat the limestone in the main chamber to the optimal temperature for calcination to occur. This will lead to a corresponding ten percent reduction in the amount of nitrogen oxides (NOx) and carbon monoxide (CO) (the pollutants that result from the burning of fossil fuel) emitted from the kiln. Carl maintains that the pre-heater functions to reduce these air pollutants. As such, its installation should not constitute a "modification" and should be exempt from NSPS requirements. See 40 CFR 60.14(e)(5) (2009). Carl would like to meet with you next week at which time he would like to know whether you concur in his analysis.

In preparation for the meeting, answer the following questions: (1) Do you agree with Carl that the pre-heater is a "system or device whose primary function is the reduction of air pollutants" so that, under 40 CFR §60.14(e)(5), it is exempt from NSPS requirements? In answering this question, assume that there are no cases or agency guidance on point; (2) If, in the meeting, you were to disagree with Carl's analysis but he were to insist on advising the company that it does not need to comply with the NSPS requirements, how would you respond? Would you: (a) Accept Carl's view since he is your client's General Counsel? (b)

Write him a memo reiterating your view and leave it at that? (c) Talk to him about the possible environmental and health consequences of his planned course of action? (d) Go above Carl's head to the CEO or Board of Directors and advise it that the Hoboken facility needs to comply with the NSPS requirements? (e) Withdraw from the representation? (f) Inform EPA about Limeco's plans to add the pre-heater without complying with the NSPS requirements? (g) Take some other step? Which of these actions would be consistent with your duties of confidentiality and of loyalty to your client as defined by the ABA Model Rules?

CHAPTER II

ENVIRONMENTAL ENFORCEMENT

A. Introduction: The Lawyer's Role in Environmental Enforcement

Vigilant enforcement of environmental laws is necessary to achieve compliance. Enforcement serves several functions: it deters violations of the law, punishes wrong-doers, and levels the playing field for businesses that are in compliance. State and federal authorities annually file thousands of administrative, civil and criminal complaints for environmental violations resulting in millions of dollars in penalties, in addition to injunctive relief and prison sentences. In addition, to supplement the government's enforcement authority, environmental groups use the "citizen suit" mechanism to enforce environmental laws. The role of the environmental lawyer, either in enforcing the law or in defending the entity accused of a violation, is therefore an extremely important one, requiring skills beyond those you learned in the compliance context.

Figure 2.1 2008 EPA Enforcement Statistics

Inspections	20,000
Administrative Complaints	over 2000
Administrative Compliance Orders	1370
Civil Judicial Referrals to Dep't of Justice	280
Criminal cases initiated	319
Criminal defendants charged	176
Pollution reduced (among other benefits)	3.9 billion lbs.

Source: 2008 EPA Annual Report, avail. at: www.epa.gov/oecaerth/resources/reports/endofyear/eoy2008/2008numbers.html

---

Enforcement generally occurs when the government agency charged with administering an environmental statute discovers a potential violation and decides to use one of its enforcement powers in response. The federal Environmental Protection Agency, the structure of which is discussed below, is charged with primary enforcement authority for many important federal environmental laws, such as the Clean Air Act, RCRA, and most of the Clean Water Act. However, many other federal agencies also have environmental enforcement responsibility. The killing of an endangered gray wolf would be handled by the Fish and Wildlife Service (FWS) in the Department of Interior, charged with enforcing the Endangered Species Act. Enforcement of the Marine Mammal Protection Act depends on the type of mammal: the killing of a sea lion would be handled by the National Marine Fisheries Service of the National Oceanic and Atmospheric Administration, while the killing of a sea otter would fall to the FWS.

As Figure 2.2 illustrates, several different agencies may be involved with a single environmental issue, depending on the context:

Figure 2.2 Federal Environmental Enforcement Examples

Environmental Area	Statute	Agency
WATER POLLUTION		
- NPDES Permits, CWA	33 USC § 1342	EPA
- Dredge and Fill Permits, CWA	33 USC § 1344	Army Corps of Engineers
- Prevention of Pollution from Ships	33 USC § 1907	U.S. Coast Guard
WILDLIFE		
- Endangered Species Act	16 USC § 1538	DOI, Fish & Wildlife Service
- Marine Mammal Prot. Act	16 USC § 1377	
- Cetatia/Pinnipedia		NOAA
- all other marine mammals		DOI
- illegally taken plants/animals (Lacey Act)	16 USC § 3372	DOI & Commerce (animals) USDA (plants)
CHEMICALS		
- pesticide registration, FIFRA	7 USC § 136j	EPA
- toxic chemical registration, TSCA	15 USC § 2615	EPA
- biological agents and toxins	7 USC § 8401	USDA
- Hazardous Materials Transp. Act	49 USC § 5122	Dept. of Transportation
- prevention of worker exposure	29 USC § 659	OSHA

As discussed below, EPA has delegated the primary enforcement authority for many federal environmental laws to individual state authorities. Thus, it is important to understand the relationship between the state and federal agencies. Of course, some state environmental laws cover areas in which there is no equivalent federal law. For example, some states have enacted their own environmental quality statutes that supplement NEPA. *See, e.g.*, California's Env. Quality Act, Calif. Public Res. Code §21000. Other states have environmental laws that expand on the protections of federal laws. *See, e.g.*, Iowa Code §459.313A (limiting application of manure on frozen ground). For these laws, state agencies have plenary authority regarding enforcement. We will concentrate on EPA enforcement, but note that the process is similar when the state or another federal agency is involved.

The litigating arm of the government also plays a significant role in the enforcement process. While EPA (or other federal agency) attorneys handle most administrative enforcement actions, any federal case that reaches the courts will also involve an attorney from the Department of Justice. In essence, the agency at that point becomes "the client" of the Justice Department attorney. Unlike most lawyers, however, the Justice Department has a larger say in how the case is handled, because it must also ensure that the positions of various agencies do not conflict with the overall goals of the administration. At the state level, the state Attorney General's office serves the same role, representing the state environmental agency. Environmental attorneys who deal with these agency attorneys must fully understand the nature of their role and authority.

Enforcement may also occur through citizen suit actions. Many federal environmental laws allow persons who are injured in some way by a statutory violation to sue for enforcement. *See. e.g.*, Clean Water Act Section 505, 33 U.S.C. §1365. Some state laws have similar provisions. Citizen suits may be brought only when the enforcement agency has failed to "diligently prosecute" a violation. The citizen suit may result in penalties and injunctive relief (i.e., a compliance order); however, no damages may be awarded (for example, for personal injury or property damage) through this mechanism. Nevertheless, a successful plaintiff in a citizen suit may recover the costs of the litigation, including attorney's fees.

This chapter will describe the administrative enforcement process, including the various enforcement options available to the enforcement agency. Often, an administrative penalty may be assessed after an administrative hearing; this chapter will discuss the hearing procedure. We will also outline the sources of law, in addition to those discussed in the compliance chapter, that the environmental lawyer may find useful in the enforcement context. The next chapter will discuss practice issues relating to citizen suit enforcement. Throughout these chapters, we will refer primarily to the federal agency, the federal administrative system, and federal laws; the enforcement process under any given state's system is usually very similar.

Two sets of exercises are included. The exercises at the end of this chapter involve a company charged with violating the Emergency Planning and Community Right-to-Know Act (EPCRA). Your job will be to apply the practice considerations learned in this chapter while representing the agency or the regulated entity in the enforcement process. The next chapter includes a set of exercises involving a citizen suit brought to enforce the Clean Water Act.

B. Agency Enforcement

The first order of business is to understand the structure of the agency in charge of enforcement. EPA, like most agencies, divides its administrative functions between headquarters, in Washington, D.C., and various regional offices. EPA policy is developed at headquarters, where regulations to implement statutory directives are promulgated and guidance documents are drafted. Find the organization chart for EPA headquarters at:

http://www.epa.gov/epahome/organization.htm

As you can see, "program" offices deal with the administration of specific environmental areas. For example, for a question concerning FIFRA interpretation, you would have to consult with the Office of Pesticide Programs, while a Clean Air Act problem would fall under the auspices of the Assistant Administrator for Air and Radiation. Which office would handle a CERCLA (Superfund) issue? If you had a question regarding a new guidance document for industrial wastewater discharges, which office within EPA's Office of Water would you call? Lawyers can be found both in the Office of General Counsel and distributed throughout the program offices.

Overall enforcement policy originates in the Office of Enforcement and Compliance Assurance (OECA) at EPA headquarters. Actual day-to-day enforcement, however, occurs at the regional level, under the oversight of OECA. There are ten regional offices across the country (see Figure 2.3). Find the Regional Office covering your state. You can find the organization chart for that region on EPA's website.[1] Again, the regions divide responsibility for environmental areas among various program offices, although the office categories do not necessarily match the headquarters divisions. Let's say you have an issue concerning a PSD permit in Massachusetts—what program office would you call?

---

1. Usually, the organization chart is located in a section of the website entitled "About Us."

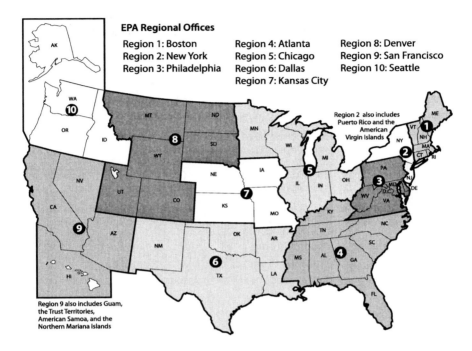

EPA Regional Offices

Region 1: Boston	Region 4: Atlanta	Region 8: Denver
Region 2: New York	Region 5: Chicago	Region 9: San Francisco
Region 3: Philadelphia	Region 6: Dallas	Region 10: Seattle
	Region 7: Kansas City	

Region 2 also includes Puerto Rico and the American Virgin Islands

Region 9 also includes Guam, the Trust Territories, American Samoa, and the Northern Mariana Islands

Figure 2.3 EPA Regional Office Locations.

The program office staff consists of scientific and technical experts trained in that particular environmental area. Each program division includes an enforcement section, whose staff monitor compliance and determine when a violation merits enforcement action. At that point, the matter is referred to the Regional Counsel's office and an EPA attorney then works with program staff in pursuing enforcement. Keep in mind that the program staff and, ultimately, the Regional Administrator comprise the "client" in these cases and will make the final decision about the conduct of the matter. EPA headquarters typically delegates settlement authority to the region; the authority to resolve a case may reside with the branch chief, division director, or the Regional Administrator, depending on the program and specific delegation. Headquarters may also require consultation before decisions are made on matters of national significance.

As noted above, if a case is filed in court, the Department of Justice will act as counsel for the agency. Under a Memorandum of Agreement (MOA)[2] between the EPA and the DOJ, unless the DOJ specifically declines to handle a civil or criminal action, Justice Department attorneys are responsible for handling the case. Their authority may include decisions that in a normal case would be made by the client. The Justice Department claims a larger responsibility in these matters, because of the necessity of ensuring consistency on a nationwide basis in the positions of the various regional offices and in the positions of the various client agencies the DOJ serves.

DOJ is organized into divisions, including the Environment and Natural Resources Divison (ENRD), which handles all environmental matters. The ENRD is in turn divided into ten sections: attorneys in the Environmental Enforcement Section handle civil environmental enforcement cases, while the Environmental Crimes Section attorneys handle criminal matters.[3]

The local United States Attorney will also be involved, at least nominally, in these civil or criminal cases. However, due to the specialized expertise of DOJ environmental attorneys, the U.S. Attorney's role often will be limited (sometimes performing tasks that local counsel undertake in the private practice context).

1. The Federal-State Relationship

In many cases, the state will have the primary enforcement authority, even for federal laws. In fact, one study estimates that up to 80% of enforcement actions for federal environmental laws are undertaken by state authorities.[4] Therefore, understanding the federal-state relationship is critically important.

---

2. The relationship between federal agencies with overlapping responsibilities regarding a particular issue is often delineated in a "memorandum of agreement." Similar agreements are entered into between EPA regional offices and each state environmental agency. For example, EPA may agree to review state NPDES permits only when discharges reach a certain level, or may agree about how to apply RCRA to sites cleaned up under the state's voluntary cleanup program.

3. *See* www.usdoj.gov/enrd. Cases involving the defense of EPA regulations are handled by the Environmental Defense Section.

4. ECOS, State Enforcement Agency Contributions to Enforcement and Compliance, at 11 (April 2001).

First, states take on the primary role through the "delegation" process. Many federal acts are "delegable" to the states, at least in part, if the state enacts its own statutory authority that is deemed substantially equivalent to the federal scheme. For example, EPA may delegate the issuance and enforcement of point source (NPDES) permits under §402 of the Clean Water Act.[5] However, dredge and fill permits under CWA §404 are not delegable. The Title V permit program under the Clean Air Act also may be delegated, but only certain decisions with regard to NESHAPS are subject to delegation.[6] Pesticide use enforcement may be delegated under the Federal Insecticide Fungicide and Rodenticide Act (FIFRA) but of course the federal government retains enforcement authority for labeling violations.[7] Some federal laws, such as the Emergency Planning and Community Right to Know Act (EPCRA) and the Toxic Substances Control Act (TSCA),[8] do not provide for delegation to state authorities.

In addition to requiring the state's laws and regulations to be substantially equivalent to federal law, delegation provisions also require the state's program to have adequate personnel and funding to administer and enforce the program requirements.[9] Federal funding and technical assistance is often available to help ensure sufficient state enforcement capacity. If EPA determines that the state's program falls short of federal minimum requirements or is being inadequately enforced, EPA may "pull the program" from the state and enforce the federal statute itself.[10] Pulling the program is a drastic remedy, however, to which the agency does not resort unless all attempts at bringing the state's program into compliance have failed.

Short of pulling the program, EPA oversight may also involve permit veto authority, as under Clean Water Act Section 402(d). 33 U.S.C. §1342(d) (EPA may object to state-issued NPDES permit as outside CWA requirements). EPA also may be able to override certain state decisions on permit requirements.

---

5. Clean Water Act §402, 33 U.S.C.§1342.

6. National Emissions Standards for Hazardous Air Pollutants. *Compare* Clean Air Act §502, 42 U.S.C.§7661a, *with* 40 CFR Part 63, Subpart E.

7. FIFRA Section 26, 7 U.S.C. §136w-1.

8. Certain parts of the TSCA lead paint abatement program may be delegated to the states. 15 U.S.C. §2684.

9. *See, e.g.*, Clean Air Act §502(b)(4).

10. *See, e.g.*, Clean Air Act §502(d)(3); Clean Water Act §402(c) ("Whenever the Administrator determines after public hearing that a state is not administering a program approved under this section in accordance with requirements of this section, he shall so notify the State and, if appropriate corrective action is not taken within a reasonable time, not to exceed ninety days, the Administrator shall withdraw approval of such program.").

See Alaska, Dep't of Envt'l Conserv. v. EPA, 540 U.S. 461 (2004) (EPA could override state's determination of Best Available Control Technology for permit under Clean Air Act).

Most states have taken advantage of the delegation option. A recent survey indicated that over 96% of delegable federal environmental programs have been delegated as of 2007.[11] State authorities may want control over environmental enforcement, because they believe they understand the circumstances of their environmental problems better than the federal agency. When a major employer is the violator, for example, the state wants to be in a position to decide on the appropriate penalty. For example, the state may be more willing to enter into a compliance schedule with the company, rather than immediately jump to penalties or other sanctions.

When a program has been delegated, may the federal government still take its own enforcement action against a violator if it believes that the state has not responded sufficiently? Consider the following case involving improper disposal of hazardous waste under RCRA:

* * *

Harmon Industries, Inc. v.
Carol M. Browner, Admin., U.S. EPA
191 F. 3d 894 (8th Cir. 1999)

HANSEN, Circuit Judge.

Harmon Industries, Inc., (Harmon) filed this action pursuant to the Administrative Procedure Act, 5 U.S.C. §706 (1994), seeking judicial review of a final decision of the United States Environmental Protection Agency (EPA). The district court granted summary judgment in favor of Harmon and reversed the decision of the EPA. The EPA appeals. We affirm.

I. FACTS AND PROCEDURAL BACKGROUND

Harmon Industries operates a plant in Grain Valley, Missouri, which it utilizes to assemble circuit boards for railroad control and safety equipment. In November 1987, Harmon's personnel manager discovered that maintenance workers at Harmon routinely discarded volatile solvent residue behind Harmon's Grain Valley plant. This practice apparently began in 1973 and contin-

---

11. Environmental Council of the States (ECOS) www.ecos.org/section/states/enviro_actlist. The ECOS website shows the state-by-state breakdown of delegations for each Act.

ued until November 1987. Harmon's management was unaware of its employees' practices until the personnel manager filed his report in November 1987. Following the report, Harmon ceased its disposal activities and voluntarily contacted the Missouri Department of Natural Resources (MDNR). The MDNR investigated and concluded that Harmon's past disposal practices did not pose a threat to either human health or the environment. The MDNR and Harmon created a plan whereby Harmon would clean up the disposal area. Harmon implemented the clean up plan. While Harmon was cooperating with the MDNR, the EPA initiated an administrative enforcement action against Harmon in which the federal agency sought $2,343,706 in penalties. Meanwhile, Harmon and the MDNR continued to establish a voluntary compliance plan. In harmonizing the details of the plan, Harmon asked the MDNR not to impose civil penalties. Harmon based its request in part on the fact that it voluntarily self-reported the environmental violations and cooperated fully with the MDNR.

On March 5, 1993, while the EPA's administrative enforcement action was pending, a Missouri state court judge approved a consent decree entered into by the MDNR and Harmon. In the decree, MDNR acknowledged full accord and satisfaction and released Harmon from any claim for monetary penalties. MDNR based its decision to release Harmon on the fact that the company promptly self-reported its violation and cooperated in all aspects of the investigation. After the filing of the consent decree, Harmon litigated the EPA claim before an administrative law judge (ALJ). The ALJ found that a civil penalty against Harmon was appropriate in this case. The ALJ rejected the EPA's request for a penalty in excess of $2 million but the ALJ did impose a civil fine of $ 586,716 against Harmon. A three-person Environmental Appeals Board panel affirmed the ALJ's monetary penalty. Harmon filed a complaint challenging the EPA's decision in federal district court on June 6, 1997. In its August 25, 1998, summary judgment order, the district court found the EPA's decision to impose civil penalties violated the Resource Conservation and Recovery Act and contravened principles of res judicata. *See Harmon Indus., Inc. v. Browner,* 19 F. Supp.2d 988 (W.D.Mo.1998). The EPA appeals to this court.

The Resource Conservation and Recovery Act (RCRA), 42 U S.C. §6901-6992K (1994), permits states to apply to the EPA for authorization to administer and enforce a hazardous waste program. *See* 42 U.S.C. §6926(b). If authorization is granted, the state's program then operates "in lieu of" the federal government's hazardous waste program. *Id.* The EPA authorization also allows states to issue and enforce permits for the treatment, storage, and disposal of hazardous wastes. *Id.* "Any action taken by a State under a hazardous waste program authorized under [the RCRA] [has] the same force and effect as action taken by the [EPA] under this subchapter" 42 U.S.C. §6926(d). Once authorization is granted by the EPA, it cannot be rescinded unless the EPA finds that (1) the state program is not equivalent to the federal program, (2) the state program is not consistent with federal or state programs in other states, or (3) the state program is failing to provide adequate enforcement of compliance in accordance with the requirements of federal law. *See* 42 U.S.C. §6926 (b). Before withdrawing a state's authorization to administer a hazardous waste program, the EPA must hold a public hearing and allow the state a reasonable period of time to correct the perceived deficiency. *See* 42 U.S.C. §6926(e).

Missouri, like many other states, is authorized to administer and enforce a hazardous waste program pursuant to the RCRA. Despite having authorized a state to act, the EPA frequently files its own enforcement actions against suspected environmental violators even after the commencement of a state-initiated enforcement action.

The EPA contends that the district court's interpretation runs contrary to the plain language of the RCRA. Specifically, the EPA cites section 6928 of the RCRA, which states that:

> (1) Except as provided in paragraph (2), whenever on the basis of any information the [EPA] determines that any person has violated or is in violation of any requirement of this subchapter, the [EPA] may issue an order assessing a civil penalty for any past or current violation, requiring compliance immediately or within a specified time period, or both, or the [EPA] may commence a civil action in the United States district court in the district in which the violation occurred for appropriate relief, including a temporary or permanent injunction.
>
> (2) In the case of a violation of any requirement of [the RCRA] where such violation occurs in a State which is authorized to carry out a hazardous waste program under section 6926 of this title, the [EPA] shall give notice to the State in which such violation has occurred prior to issuing. an order or commencing a civil action under this section.

42 U.S.C. §6928(a)(1) and (2).

The EPA argues that the plain language of section 6928 allows the federal agency to initiate an enforcement action against an environmental violator even in states that have received authorization pursuant to the RCRA. The EPA contends that Harmon and the district court misinterpreted the phrases "in lieu of" and "same force and effect" as contained in the RCRA.

According to the EPA, the phrase "in lieu of" refers to which regulations are to be enforced in an authorized state rather than who is responsible for enforcing the regulations. The EPA argues that the phrase "same force and effect" refers only to the effect of state issued permits. The EPA contends that the RCRA, taken as a whole, authorizes either the state or the EPA to enforce the state's regulations, which are in compliance with the regulations of the EPA. The only requirement, according to the EPA, is that the EPA notify the state in writing if it intends to initiate an enforcement action against an alleged violator.

An examination of the statute as a whole supports the district court's interpretation. The RCRA specifically allows states that have received authorization from the federal government to administer and enforce a program that operates "in lieu of" the EPA's regulatory program. 42 U.S.C. §6926(b). While the EPA is correct that the "in lieu of" language refers to the program itself, the administration and enforcement of the program are inexorably intertwined.

The RCRA gives authority to the states to create and implement their own hazardous waste program. The plain "in lieu of" language contained in the RCRA reveals a congressional intent for an authorized waste program in all respects including enforcement. Harmonizing the section 6928(a)(1) and (2) language that allows the EPA to bring an enforcement action in certain circumstances with section 6926(b)'s provision that the EPA has the right to withdraw state authorization if the state's enforcement is inadequate manifests a congressional intent to give the EPA a secondary enforcement right in those cases where a state has been authorized to act that is triggered only after state authorization is rescinded or if the state fails to initiate an enforcement action. Rather than serving as an affirmative grant of federal enforcement power as the EPA suggests, we conclude that the notice requirement of section 6928(a)(2) reinforces the primary of a state's enforcement rights under RCRA. Taken in the context of the statute as a whole, the notice requirement operates as a means to allow a state the first chance opportunity to initiate the statutorily-permitted enforcement action. If the state fails to initiate any action, then the EPA may institute its own action. Thus, the notice requirement is an indicator of the fact that Congress intended to give states that are authorized to act, the lead role in enforcement under RCRA.

Without question, the EPA can initiate an enforcement action if it deems the state's enforcement action inadequate. Before initiating such an action, however, the EPA must allow the state an opportunity to correct its deficiency and the EPA must withdraw its authorization. *See* 42 U.S.C. §6926(b) and (e). Consistent with the text of the statute and its legislative history, the EPA also may initiate an enforcement action after providing written notice to the state when the authorized state fails to initiate any enforcement action. *See* 42 U.S.C. §6928(a)(2); 1976 U.S.C.C.A.N. 6270. The EPA may not, however, simply fill the perceived gaps it sees in a state's enforcement action by initiating a second enforcement action without allowing the state an opportunity to correct the deficiency and then withdrawing the state's authorization.

A contrary interpretation would result in two separate enforcement actions. Such an interpretation, as explained above, would derogate the RCRA's plain language and legislative history. Companies that reach an agreement through negotiations with a state authorized by the EPA to act in its place may find the agreement undermined by a later separate enforcement action by the EPA. While, generally speaking, two separate sovereigns can institute two separate enforcement actions, those actions can cause vastly different and potentially contradictory results. Such a potential schism runs afoul of the principles of comity and federalism so clearly embedded in the text and history of the RCRA.

III. CONCLUSION

For the reasons stated herein, we affirm the judgment of the district court.

The Tenth Circuit, in *United States v. Power Engineering*, 303 F.3d 1232 (10th Cir. 2002), *cert. denied*, 538 U.S. 1012 (2003), disagreed with *Harmon* and held that RCRA does allow EPA to "overfile" (i.e., take action in addition to the state's enforcement action). The court applied *Chevron* deference,[12] and held that because the statute was ambiguous on the issue, EPA's reasonable interpretation of the "in lieu of" delegation provision should be upheld. *Id.* at 1240.

In *United States v. Elias*, 269 F.3d 1003 (9th Cir. 2001), a defendant charged with federal criminal violations under RCRA argued that, because the state (Idaho) had been delegated the authority to enforce RCRA, the federal government had no authority to bring a criminal action. The court disagreed, however, and distinguished *Harmon*, noting that the Eighth Circuit held only that the state had *primary*, rather than *sole*, enforcement authority. Where the state has not taken action, the federal government certainly can institute enforcement action. *Id.* at 1011. *See also United States v. Hudson*, 522 U.S. 93 (1997) (imposition of a civil penalty and other sanctions did not preclude a later criminal prosecution under the Double Jeopardy clause).

Would the reasoning of *Harmon* extend to overfiling under the Clean Water Act or the Clean Air Act? *See United States v. City of Rock Island*, 182 F.Supp.2d

---

12. *Chevron v. NRDC*, 467 U.S. 837 (1984).

690, 694 (C.D. Ill. 2001) (*Harmon* relied on unique RCRA "in lieu of" language and is therefore inapplicable to Clean Water Act); *United States v. City of Youngstown*, 109 F. Supp. 2d 739, 741 (N.D. Ohio 2000) (same). In *United States v. LTV Steel Co.*, 118 F.Supp.2d 827 (N.D. Ohio 2000), the court held that the language of the Clean Air Act "seems to anticipate overfiling":

> [EPA's] interpretation is neither unreasonable nor particularly surprising. As the EPA explains, dual enforcement helps ensure effective enforcement without the need to publicly declare the state in derogation of its enforcement duties or displace the state entirely in the enforcement scheme. *See* 42 U.S.C. § 7413(a)(2) (permitting EPA to take over state's enforcement actions). It accomplishes this end, moreover, without extreme prejudice to those subject to enforcement. While the need to "respond to two masters" is never pleasant, penalties paid to one enforcement arm may be used to offset those otherwise payable to another. *See* 42 U.S.C. § 7413(e). Thus, despite LTV's protestations, the language of the Clean Air Act itself ameliorates the sting of overfiling.

Id. at 835.

If overfiling is allowed to enforce a particular statute, how would you advise your client concerning a proposed settlement with the state enforcement agency? Would the state's Memorandum of Agreement with the EPA regarding enforcement be relevant?

Problem 2.1: Quality Wood Products: RCRA Overfiling

Quality Wood Products, Inc., a facility in Oregon, treats wood with creosote for use as railroad cross ties, bridge structures, and utility poles. The treatment helps to preserve the wood, making it less vulnerable to weather, fungus, and insects. In the treatment process, creosote is mixed with a solvent and then forced into the wood using a pressure chamber. The preservative formulation is continually re-used, so eventually a sludge forms in the bottom of the treatment tank and in other holding tanks. This sludge is periodically scraped from the tanks and stored on-site, until it can be hauled to a treatment facility or burned in the plant's boiler as fuel.

Creosote sludge is a listed hazardous waste regulated under RCRA. See 40 C.F.R. § 261.32 (K001 waste). Therefore, Quality Wood is required, as a generator, to comply with a variety of regulations regarding storage, labeling, and record-keeping. RCRA § 3002, 42 U.S.C. § 6922. In particular, a generator is allowed to accumulate waste on-site for only 90 days, unless certain requirements are met. 40 C.F.R. § 262.34.

Quality Wood has historically been quite lax in its compliance with these requirements. Although it has applied for and received an EPA identification number, as required, it has often allowed sludge to accumulate on site for long periods of time without following the requirements of Section 262.34.

EPA has delegated enforcement of RCRA to the Oregon Department of Environmental Quality (ODEQ). ODEQ has been monitoring the Quality Wood situation for several years and has issued numerous notices of violation to the company. After much negotiation, the two sides have reached a tentative settlement agreement: Quality Wood will send its waste on a more frequent basis to a nearby factory, which will burn the sludge in its incinerator. This will cost Quality Wood slightly more than its current practice, but will comply with the 90-day storage rule. ODEQ will issue an administrative order on consent, setting out a six-month compliance schedule and assessing a $30,000 penalty for the past violations.

Quality Wood has hired you to represent them in this enforcement action. You believe Quality Wood may fall under the recycling exemption to the RCRA regulations, but the law is so unclear that you intend to advise your client that it would not be worth litigating the issue, given the relatively low penalty. However, EPA Region X has notified ODEQ that it is also looking into the Quality Wood case.

What should you advise your client regarding the proposed settlement with ODEQ?

2. The Enforcement Process

The following is a description of the steps in the agency enforcement process. Again, we will use the federal system as the model, but most state enforcement processes are very similar.

a. Self-Reporting Obligations

Most environmental laws are at least partially self-enforcing. First, the regulated entity must determine for itself whether it falls within the requirements of a particular statutory obligation. An industry that produces waste must test it to determine whether the hazardous waste mandates of RCRA apply. A company discharging pollutants into navigable water must determine whether it needs a permit under the Clean Water Act. The entity cannot just sit back and wait until EPA tells them to comply.

Second, the environmental laws are somewhat like the tax code in that they require the regulated entity to monitor its discharges, emissions or disposal of wastes, keep records, and submit periodic reports of compliance. Each statutory pollution control scheme gives the EPA Administrator the authority to require monitoring, recordkeeping, and reporting. Section 308 of the Clean Water Act, 33 U.S.C. § 1318, for example, gives the Administrator broad discretion to require point sources to test their effluent and make periodic reports of results. These requirements are typically built into the permit for the source. See an example of a point source (NPDES) permit and a monthly discharge monitoring report, Figures 3.1, 3.2, & 3.3, in Chapter 3.A. The Clean Air Act requires monitoring to provide "reasonable assurance of compliance with emissions limitations or standards." 40 CFR § 64.3; 40 CFR § 70.6(a)(3) (CAA permits shall contain required monitoring and record-keeping conditions). Violations of these record-keeping obligations account for many of the penalties the EPA imposes each year.

The costs of these monitoring requirements can be significant. For example, in 2007 the State of Washington's Department of Ecology estimated first-year monitoring costs for NPDES Phase 1 stormwater permits for large and medium cities to be about $175,000, including equipment, lab costs, and personnel.[13] While a lab test for pH may cost only $10 per sample, tests for heavy metals may be over $200 per sample, and NPDES permits generally require multiple sample locations for multiple parameters at various frequencies (monthly, weekly, or sometimes daily). Air monitoring equipment can cost hundreds of thousands of dollars initially, plus significant annual costs for operation and maintenance.[14] In some cases under the CAA, regulators may allow the use of "predictive emissions monitoring systems" (PEMS), which rely on models, rather than actual sampling, to estimate pollutant concentrations, resulting in considerable savings to the permittee.[15]

Increasingly, electronic reporting is becoming the norm. EPA has issued a Cross-Media Electronic Reporting Regulation (CROMERR), which provides standards for electronic submittals, designed to ensure they have the same level

---

13. www.ecy.wa.gov/programs/wq/stormwater/municipal/phase1permit/phipermit.html.

14. *See* Continuous Emissions Monitoring Cost Model spreadsheet, avail. at: www.epa.gov/ttn/emc/cem.html. While a CO analyzer may cost less than $10,000, a mercury system costs around $100,000, and monitoring of several parameters before and after pollution control can easily cost several hundred thousand dollars.

15. *See* Performance Specification 16 for Predictive Emissions Monitoring Systems, 74 Fed. Reg. 12575 (Mar. 25, 2009).

of dependability as the paper they replace. 40 C.F.R. Ch. I, pt. 3. However, the state or Indian tribe that has been delegated enforcement authority may not yet be prepared to accept electronic submissions.

Problem 2.2: Self-Incrimination

Under RCRA § 3002, Quality Wood is required to keep records of how much waste it generates and how long that waste is stored on-site. In the enforcement action described in Problem 2.1, assume EPA decides to seek civil penalties of $100,000 for violations of RCRA storage limits. EPA relies primarily on the company's own records to establish these violations.

May the EPA introduce into evidence the records that the violator has turned over to it or would this implicate the Fifth Amendment's prohibition against forced self-incrimination? See United States v. Ward, 448 U.S. 242 (1980). Does your answer change if the government is seeking to impose criminal penalties against Quality Wood? See Braswell v. United States, 487 U.S. 99, 102 (1988). Would the President of Quality Wood, seeking to avoid prosecution for falsifying these records, have a stronger Fifth Amendment claim? Assuming she had to turn over the documents, could she at least refuse to answer questions regarding storage practices?

How would the privilege apply in the context of CERCLA Section 104(e), 42 U.S.C. § 9604(e), which gives EPA the authority to require any person to furnish information regarding a release of hazardous substances, including the nature and quantity of such substances that were transported to the site?

---

b. Self-Audits and Environmental Management

EPA has worked hard to give companies strong incentives to discover and correct environmental violations themselves, before EPA finds them. EPA's Office of Enforcement and Compliance Assurance (OECA), for example, has developed a series of guidelines, which it calls "Protocols for Conducting Compliance Audits," which detail how a regulated facility should determine its state of regulatory compliance under each Act.[16] The manuals provide managers, or attorneys advising them, with a wealth of information about what EPA will look for in an inspection.

Under EPA's "Audit and Self-Policing Policy," an entity that comes forward with information about its environmental violations is eligible for a substan-

---

16. *See* cfpub.epa.gov/compliance/resources/policies/incentives/auditing/.

tial reduction of penalties and for immunity from criminal prosecution.[17] EPA touts the public benefits of this "amnesty" program, because facilities will be brought into compliance more quickly, while government enforcement costs are reduced. From the industry perspective, the policy has been popular. In 2007, for example, 491 companies used the policy to resolve violations at 728 facilities.[18] The financial incentives for voluntary disclosure can be substantial.[19]

As you might expect, not every violation qualifies for this program. EPA's Audit Policy states that an entity must meet the following conditions:

- **Systematic discovery** of the violation through an environmental audit or a compliance management system [an entity can still get a 75% penalty reduction and no criminal prosecution without this condition].
- **Voluntary discovery**, that is, not through a legally required monitoring, sampling or auditing procedure.
- **Prompt disclosure** in writing to EPA within 21 days of discovery or such shorter time as may be required by law. Discovery occurs when any officer, director, employee or agent of the facility has an objectively reasonable basis for believing that a violation has or may have occurred.
- **Independent discovery and disclosure**, before EPA likely would have identified the violation through its own investigation or based on information provided by a third-party.
- **Correction and remediation** within 60 calendar days, in most cases, from the date of discovery.
- **Prevent recurrence** of the violation.
- **Repeat violations are ineligible**, that is, those that have occurred at the same facility within the past 3 years or those that have occurred as part of a pattern of violations within the past 5 years at another facility(ies) owned or operated by the same company; if the facility has been newly

---

17. EPA, Audit and Self-Policing Policy, 65 FR 19, 618 (April 11, 2000); *see also* epa.gov/compliance/resources/policies/incentives/auditing/auditpolicy51100.pdf.

18. EPA, FY 2007 Annual Report, p. 24.

19. "EPA Region III Waives $539,000 in Penalties After Six Firms Disclose Violations to Agency," BNA Daily Environment Report, at A-3 (April 26, 2002); "EPA Waives $1.5 Million in Potential Fines Against Companies Reporting Own Violations," 71 U.S.L.W. 2551 (March 4, 2003) (11 companies; EPCRA violations); "Auto Parts Firm to pay $20,619 Penalty; Nearly $900,000 in Punitive Fines Waived," 80 BNA Daily Environment Report, at A-6 (Apr. 27, 2004). Many universities have taken advantage of the audit privilege. *See, e.g.*, U.S. EPA, Self-audits, www.epa.gov/region2/capp/cip/agreeex.htm (discussing audit agreements EPA Region II signed with 51 hospitals, colleges and universities in New York and New Jersey).

acquired, the existence of a violation prior to acquisition does not trigger the repeat violations exclusion.

- **Certain types of violations are ineligible**—those that result in serious actual harm, those that may have presented an imminent and substantial endangerment, and those that violate the specific terms of an administrative or judicial order or consent agreement.
- **Cooperation** by the disclosing entity is required.[20]

If an entity meets all of the policy conditions, EPA will impose a penalty intended only to recoup the economic benefit gained by noncompliance. The agency reasons that the entity should not be allowed to gain a competitive advantage by its failure to comply with environmental regulations. The policy also indicates that EPA generally will not recommend criminal prosecution for those meeting the audit policy conditions, although the agency will refer cases if high-level corporate officials knew of the violations, or if management concealed or condoned the environmental violations.

Problem 2.3: Audit Policy

Assume that Quality Wood, Inc., from Problem 2.1, discovers its RCRA violations before any inspections have occurred and before the state or federal agencies are aware of the violations. As you know, some of the violations may be reflected in the reports the company must submit to the ODEQ, but some of them are labeling violations or failure to properly store the waste. Can Quality Wood avoid penalties by voluntarily admitting the violations before ODEQ or EPA begins to investigate? If Quality Wood qualifies for complete penalty waiver, would the Audit Policy prevent someone from filing a citizen suit against them based on the self-reported violations? Could the information on environmental violations be used in a tort suit by neighbors?

The last question in Problem 2.3 touches upon the issue of the "audit privilege." As of 2009, over 30 states had enacted some form of law that protects information a company gathers during a voluntary environmental audit from disclosure to the government or to the public, and prohibits the use of such information in administrative or judicial proceedings, including enforcement

---

20. EPA, Audit Policy, available at www.epa.gov/compliance/incentives/auditing/auditpolicy.html.

actions.[21] Typically, an audit privilege law will protect documents and information gathered during an environmental compliance audit from public disclosure, as long as it is not information or a report that is already required by law. The idea is to encourage companies to conduct audits that would otherwise not occur. Regulated facilities argue they have a strong disincentive to conduct voluntary audits of their facilities, if all of the information they discover would be subject to disclosure.

EPA, on the other hand, opposes the idea of an audit privilege. EPA believes that its audit policy provides sufficient incentives for self-policing, without the secrecy allowed by the privilege law. EPA also considers the privilege an undue interference with enforcement needs and an infringement on the public's right to know. *See* John Davidson, "Privileges for Environmental Audits: Is Mum Really the Word?" 4 *S.C. Envtl. L. J.* 111 (1995). Studies on the effectiveness of audit immunity and privilege laws have reached mixed conclusions.[22]

Practice Tip: Environmental Management Systems

Almost every business of substantial size today has adopted some kind of pro-active Environmental Management System (EMS). As EPA says in its position statement encouraging such approaches:

> EMSs can ... facilitate the integration of the full scope of environmental considerations into the mission of the organization and improve environmental performance by establishing a continual process of checking to ensure environmental goals are set and met. A well-designed EMS includes procedures for taking corrective action if problems occur and encourages preventive action to avoid problems.[23]

Many larger companies opt to comply with ISO 14001, a program of environmental management promulgated by the International Organization

---

21. EPA Region V's Office of Regional Counsel maintains a scoreboard of state adoption of audit privilege and self-disclosure laws: www.epa.gov/region5/orc/audits/audit-apil.htm.

22. *See* Jodi L. Short & Michael W. Toffel, "Coerced Confessions: Self-Policing in the Shadow of the Regulator," 24 J.L. Econ. & Org. 45 (2008) (immunity increased likelihood of self-disclosure, especially if active regulatory presence; no evidence that privilege had effect); Nancy K. Stoner and Wendy J. Miller, "National Conference of State Legislatures Study Finds That State Environmental Audit Laws Have No Impact on Company Self-Auditing and Disclosure of Violations," 29 Envtl. L. Rep. 10265 (1999).

23. EPA, Position Statement on EMSs, http://www.epa.gov/EMS/position/position.htm (Dec. 13, 2005).

for Standardization, a non-governmental federation dedicated to promoting uniform standards to facilitate international trade. *See* www.iso.org. The Environmental Management Standard advocates a Plan-Do-Check-Act/Continual Improvement approach. The basic idea is to determine the environmental impacts of the facility and continually work to minimize those impacts. Often, companies find this results in financial savings as well, through greater efficiencies, lower energy costs and lower waste disposal costs.

c. Inspections

Central to the EPA's enforcement authority is the ability to conduct inspections of the regulated entity's facility and records. The EPA has the power, under most environmental acts, to inspect premises, conduct tests, and obtain copies of records. *See, e.g.,* CWA §308(a)(4)(B), 33 U.S.C. §1318(a)(4)(B). Even without specific inspection authority, the agency may rely on its inherent authority to enforce the statutes that it has the responsibility to implement. Agency inspection authority is frequently exercised; in FY 2008, for example, EPA conducted about 20,000 inspections nationwide, while state inspectors conducted many times that number.[24] Inspections may range from "drive-by" reconnaissance to compliance sampling to full-fledged facility evaluations.

However, state and federal inspectors cannot regularly inspect the universe of regulated entities. For example, EPA estimates that there are 22,000 sources of air pollution that have or should have Title V operating permits.[25] There are about 15,000 large quantity generators of hazardous waste, in addition to 1500 treatment, storage, or disposal facilities.[26] If you then consider the thousands of regulated entities under EPCRA, CWA, and TSCA, you begin to understand the enormity of the enforcement task. Thus, while EPA has broad inspection authority, the reality is that inspections at some regulated facilities are uncommon, although the frequency varies by area and type of facility.

Does an agency inspector need a warrant to enter a regulated entity's premises? Although the agency may have statutory authority for an inspection, it

---

24. EPA, FY 2008 Annual Report. ECOS reported that states conducted almost 300,000 inspections in 1999. Report to Congress: State Agency Contributions to Enforcement and Compliance, at 14 (ECOS Sept. 2001).

25. EPA, Air Pollution Operating Permit Update (1998).

26. EPA, Office of Solid Waste and Emergency Response, Biennial RCRA Report, at p.9, 16 (2005).

is still subject to the Constitution's Fourth Amendment prohibition against warrantless searches and seizures. In some cases, the entity's permit under RCRA, the CAA or the CWA will include a specific condition allowing the EPA or state to inspect the premises. Therefore, the entity can be said to have "consented" to a warrantless search. Absent a permit condition, however, the question is closer. In *New York v. Burger*, 482 U.S. 691, 702–03 (1987), the Supreme Court upheld the government's warrantless entry in the case of a "pervasively regulated" business, but only if the "statute's inspection program, in terms of the certainty and regularity of its application, provides a constitutionally adequate substitute for a warrant." Is a facility subject to EPCRA really "pervasively regulated"? How about a hog lot that the state wants to inspect to determine if it is large enough to need a Clean Water Act permit?

In most cases, the regulated entity will gain little by requiring a warrant, so cooperation is usually the best policy. For an administrative warrant, the agency need not establish the "probable cause" a criminal warrant would require, but rather only that the inspection is being conducted pursuant to a neutral plan or that there is a reasonable suspicion of a violation. But there may be instances in which the entity may want to enforce its right to demand a warrant. In some instances, the entity may object to the scope of the inspection and a warrant can be a useful way of delineating what documents or areas are subject to search.

Problem 2.4: Inspection Authority

Carla Murphy, the president and general manager of Quality Wood, Inc., has called you to say that an EPA inspector has arrived at the facility, presented credentials, and requested to be allowed to inspect the facility and its records. Murphy tells you that, because the facility is in the middle of the busy season, their recordkeeping is behind and they have not been properly labeling hazardous waste storage units.

Murphy would like to deny entry to the inspector. Murphy questioned the inspector as to the purpose of the visit and was informed that it was "routine"—EPA does not appear to have any specific evidence of a violation. Even if you can't completely deny entry to the inspectors, but could buy them a little time, Murphy says, the company could probably "clean things up a little" and get their records in order.

Does EPA have the statutory authority to enter the premises? Based on your reading of the following case, does the EPA inspector need a warrant? If so, will he be able to get one, absent "probable cause" to believe a violation has occurred?

Can you ethically advise your client to require a warrant, if you believe the sole purpose is delay? Assume Murphy tells you she thinks some of the waste was illegally dumped in an adjacent field and the delay would allow the company to cover up evidence of this disposal. Does it matter ethically whether the delay is for correcting violations or covering them up? Consult in particular Rules 1.2(d), 1.6, and 1.16(a) of the Model Rules of Professional Conduct.

To determine whether a warrant is required for the inspection in Problem 2.4, consider and apply the following case:

* * *

V-1 Oil Company v. State of Wyoming, Department of Environmental Quality
902 F.2d 1482 (10th Cir. 1990)

STEPHEN H. ANDERSON, Circuit Judge.

Plaintiff-appellant V-1 Oil Company ("V-1") appeals an adverse summary judgment and an award of attorneys' fees rendered by the district court. We affirm.

BACKGROUND

The district court, *V-1 Oil Co. v. Wyoming*, 696 F.Supp. 578 (D.Wyo. 1988), found the following undisputed facts: Defendant-appellee Steven P. Gerber is an official of defendant-appellee the Wyoming Department of Environmental Quality ("DEQ"), an agency of defendant-appellee the State of Wyoming. He was aware that previous investigations of the V-1 Oil Station in Lander, Wyoming revealed that it was a source of groundwater pollution. On April 28, 1988, he noticed, while driving by, that the concrete above the station's underground storage tanks was being removed. Twice he tried to find out what was being done, and twice he was refused permission to enter the property. Informed of this, a senior assistant attorney general tried to obtain a court order allowing Gerber to inspect the premises, but no judge was available. The attorney then advised Gerber that the Wyoming Environmental Quality Act ("the Act") authorized him to conduct a warrantless search. That evening, Gerber, accompanied by a policeman and the Lander City Attorney, returned to the gas station, visually inspected the tanks, and took a soil sample from the exposed area.

On May 27, 1988, V-1 filed suit under 42 U.S.C. § 1983, alleging that the search violated V-1's Fourth Amendment rights. The district court granted summary judgment for each defendant. DEQ and the State were dismissed because of their Eleventh Amendment immunity from suit in federal court. V-1 does not appeal this holding. Gerber was deemed entitled to judgment because the statute authorizes warrantless searches, such searches are constitutional, and Gerber's conduct fell within his qualified immunity because it violated no clearly established right. The judgment in favor of Gerber is the subject of [this appeal].

DISCUSSION
I. WARRANTLESS SEARCH
A. Whether The Wyoming Environmental Quality Act Authorizes Warrantless Searches

Gerber claims that section nine of the Act authorizes warrantless inspections of suspected sources of pollution. That section empowers certain officers, including Gerber, to "enter and inspect any property, premise or place, except private residences, on or at which an air, water or land pollution source is located or is being constructed or installed.... Persons so designated may ... inspect any monitoring equipment or method of operation required to be maintained pursuant to this act ... for the purpose of investigating actual or potential sources of air, water or land pollution and for determining compliance or noncompliance with this act...." Wyo.Stat. § 35-11-109(a)(vi) (1988).

V-1 contends that this section did not authorize the search which took place, either because it does not authorize warrantless searches or because it only authorizes warrantless searches of monitoring equipment and methods of operation required by the Act, and underground storage tanks do not fall into this category. We disagree.

V-1's first contention seems to be "that a warrant was required since the statute nowhere mentions the words 'warrantless search.'" V-1 Oil Co. v. Wyoming, 696 F.Supp. at 581. Courts do not infer a warrant requirement from statutes which authorize inspections but do not discuss the necessity of warrants. Instead, a bare authorization for inspections is construed to authorize warrantless inspections. (citations omitted) We see no reason to believe that the Wyoming Supreme Court would construe this statute any differently.

Second, because the Wyoming Environmental Quality Act should be construed liberally, *People v. Platte Pipe Line Co.*, 649 P.2d 208, 212 (Wyo. 1982); *Roberts Constr. Co. v. Vondriska*, 547 P.2d 1171, 1182 (Wyo. 1976), we hold that underground gasoline storage tanks are a "method of operation required to be maintained pursuant to th[e] act." The phrase "pursuant to" has a broader meaning than the word "by." *See Black's Law Dictionary* 647 (abr. 5th ed. 1983). The statute authorizes the inspection, not only of facilities which the Act specifically requires, but also of any mechanism which is necessary to avoid committing a violation. Without proper storage equipment, gasoline could escape and pollute the surrounding land and groundwater. This is prohibited by, inter alia, Wyo.Stat. § 35-11-301 (1988). Therefore, the Act authorized Gerber to inspect V-1's tanks.

B. Whether a Warrantless Search Pursuant to the Wyoming Environmental Quality Act Is Constitutional

The warrant requirement of the Fourth Amendment applies to commercial premises. *See v. City of Seattle,* 387 U.S. 541, 543 (1967). An exception to this requirement has developed, however, for "pervasively regulated business[es]," *United States v. Biswell,* 406 U.S. 311, 316 (1972), or "'closely regulated' industries," *Marshall v. Barlow's, Inc.,* 436 U.S. 307, 313 (1978) (quoting *Colonnade Catering Corp. v. United States,* 397 U.S. 72, 74 (1970)). To be reasonable, the warrantless inspection of such a business must meet the three-part test enunciated in *New York v. Burger,* 482 U.S. 691 (1987):

> "First, there must be a 'substantial' government interest that informs the regulatory scheme pursuant to which the inspection is made....
>
> Second, the warrantless inspections must be 'necessary to further [the] regulatory scheme.'
>
> Finally, 'the statute's inspection program, in terms of the certainty and regularity of its application, [must] provid[e] a constitutionally adequate substitute for a warrant.' In other words, the regulatory statute must perform the two basic functions of a warrant: it must advise the owner of the commercial premises that the search is being made pursuant to the law and has a properly defined scope, and it must limit the discretion of the inspecting officers. To perform this first function, the statute must be 'sufficiently comprehensive and defined that the owner of commercial property cannot help but be aware that his property will be subject to periodic inspections undertaken for specific purposes.' In addition, in defining how a statute limits the discretion of the inspectors, ... it must be 'carefully limited in time, place, and scope.' United States v. Biswell, 406 U.S., at 315."
> Id. at 702–03 (quoting Donovan v. Dewey, 452 U.S. 594, 600, 602, 603 (1981)).

The two major questions relevant to the constitutionality of Gerber's search are whether V-1 is pervasively regulated and whether the Act provides a constitutionally adequate substitute for a search warrant.[27]

1. Whether V-1 Is Pervasively Regulated

A pervasively regulated industry is one which has "such a history of government oversight that no reasonable expectation of privacy could exist...." *Marshall v. Barlow's, Inc.*, 436 U.S. at 313. "[T]he doctrine is essentially defined by 'the pervasiveness and regularity of the ... regulation' and the effect of such regulation upon an owner's expectation of privacy." *New York v. Burger*, 482 U.S. at 701 (quoting *Donovan v. Dewey*, 452 U.S. 594, 606 (1981)). Pervasively regulated industries "represent the 'exception' rather than the rule." *Marshall v. Horn Seed Co.*, 647 F.2d 96, 99 n. 1 (10th Cir.1981) (quoting *Marshall v. Barlow's, Inc.*, 436 U.S. at 313); *see also McLaughlin v. Kings Island*, 849 F.2d 990, 994 (6th Cir.1988).

Wyoming state law requires a license and payment of a fee before one may do business as a gasoline dealer. Violation of this requirement is a misdemeanor. The price of the gasoline must be displayed conspicuously and gasoline tax must be collected. However, while gasoline wholesalers and refiners must submit reports and keep special records, gasoline dealers face no similar requirement. [citations omitted] Under federal law, owners of underground gasoline storage tanks must furnish substantial and detailed information about the tanks and must permit certain inspections[28] and monitoring. *See* 42 U.S.C. §§6991–6991i.

In *Burger*, the Supreme Court held that New York vehicle dismantlers were pervasively regulated because they were subject to the following circumscriptions: the requirement of a license and payment of a fee; the maintenance and availability for inspection of certain records; the display of the operator's registration number; and the existence of criminal penalties for failure to comply

---

27. The other two parts of the Burger test may be discussed summarily.

V-1 concedes, Appellant's Brief at 18, and we agree, that the protection of the environment and the public from pollution in general, and from leakage from underground gasoline storage tanks in particular, is a substantial governmental interest.

We cannot determine from the record whether warrantless inspections are necessary to the regulatory scheme, i.e., whether there will be times that DEQ cannot obtain a warrant promptly enough for the subsequent search to be effective, *see McLaughlin v. Kings Island*, 849 F.2d 990, 996 (6th Cir.1988); *Blackwelder v. Safnauer*, 689 F.Supp. 106, 139 (N.D.N.Y. 1988). Fortunately, such a determination is not necessary to our disposition of this case.

28. Gerber has not claimed that he was acting pursuant to the federal inspection provision, 42 U.S.C. §6991d(a). Also, the constitutionality of that provision is not before us.

with these provisions. *Burger v. New York*, 482 U.S. at 704–05. The aggregation of requirements to which Wyoming gas stations are subject is equally intrusive, so we affirm the district court's holding that V-1 was pervasively regulated.

2. Whether the Statute Provides a Constitutionally Adequate Substitute for a Warrant

The district court concluded, with no explanation, that the Act provided a constitutionally adequate substitute for a warrant. *V-1 Oil Co. v. Wyoming*, 696 F.Supp. at 582. We disagree. The statute is not so " 'comprehensive and defined that the owner of commercial property cannot help but be aware that his property will be subject to periodic inspections undertaken for specific purposes.' " *Burger v. New York*, 482 U.S. at 703 (quoting *Donovan v. Dewey*, 452 U.S. 594, 600 (1981)).

First, because the Act applies to every business in Wyoming, it provides no notice whatsoever to the owner of any particular business that his or her property will be subject to warrantless inspections. The only warrantless administrative searches which have been upheld are those conducted pursuant to narrow statutes which regulate particular industries. *Rush v. Obledo*, 756 F.2d 713, 718–19 (9th Cir.1985); *cf. Marshall v. Barlow's, Inc.*, 436 U.S. at 321. Administrative searches conducted pursuant to statutes of general applicability require search warrants.

Second, the Act provides no "assurance of regularity" of inspections. *Donovan v. Dewey*, 452 U.S. 594, 599 (1981). In both *Burger*, 482 U.S. at 711, and *Dewey*, 452 U.S. at 604, the inspections were conducted on a regular basis. The Wyoming Environmental Quality Act leaves inspectors free to inspect any business as often or seldom as he or she pleases. A warrant is required if searches are "so random, infrequent, or unpredictable that the owner, for all practical purposes, has no real expectation that his property will from time to time be inspected by government officials." *Donovan v. Dewey*, 452 U.S. at 599.

Because the Act does not provide a constitutionally adequate substitute for a warrant, Gerber's warrantless search violated V-1's Fourth Amendment rights.

* * *

Can you apply the *V-1 Oil* court's distinction between "narrow statutes" and "statutes of general applicability" to other environmental acts?

Inspectors may be able to obtain evidence without a warrant, even on private property, if there is a diminished expectation of privacy. In *Riverdale Mills Corp. v. Pimpare*, 392 F.3d 55 (1st Cir. 2004), the First Circuit held that it was not illegal for EPA inspectors to take samples of a company's wastewater without a warrant. Although the manhole location where the samples were taken was still on private property, the court found it significant that the wastewater would "irretrievably" flow into the public sewer, such that it would be exposed to the public, and therefore the company had abandoned its expectation of privacy. The court compared the wastewater to cases where courts have held that there is no reasonable expectation of privacy once trash is left on the curb for collection. Similarly, in *U.S. v. Hajduk*, 396 F. Supp. 2d 1216 (D. Colo. 2005), the court approved of warrantless sampling of wastewater once it entered the sewer line, due to consent and diminished expectation of privacy. However, the court also held that the pervasively regulated exception did not apply merely because an entity holds a wastewater permit. The court held that the Supreme Court did not intend the pervasively regulated exception to apply when only a specific activity, such as wastewater disposal, is regulated. *Id.* at 1234.

For an excellent discussion of the legal and practical aspects of government inspections pursuant to environmental statutes, *see* Arnold W. Reitze, Jr. & Carol S. Holmes, "Inspections Under the Clean Air Act," 1 Env. Lawyer 29 (Sept. 1994).

Practice Tip: Inspections

Attorneys who represent regulated entities should take steps to protect the client's interests during an inspection:

- Ask for split samples. *EPA is required to give the regulated entity a portion of each sample taken of water or waste streams. An independent test can then be done to verify the agency's results. Testing of samples can be unreliable in many cases due to faulty testing procedures, contamination of samples, or even falsification of test results by the lab. See "Contractor Employee Pleads Guilty to Charges of Falsifying Test Results," 21 Env. Rptr. 795 (Aug. 17, 1990) (government Superfund contractor falsified toxicity test results at Superfund sites).*

- Protect confidential information. *Once your client's information becomes part of the EPA's file, it is subject to disclosure under the Freedom of Information Act or other more specific provisions. See, e.g., Clean Water Act Section 308(b), 33 U.S.C. § 1318(b) (records, reports, and data obtained from regulated entity available to public). You can, however, protect trade secret or other confidential business information if you identify confidential documents at the time they are submitted to EPA. 40 C.F.R. § 2.201 et seq. Officials are subject to fine or imprisonment for knowingly disclosing such information and the agency may also be sued for a taking of property if trade secrets are disclosed. See Ruckelshaus v. Monsanto Co., 467 U.S. 986 (1984).*

- Be prepared. *The regulated entity should appoint a person who is knowledgeable about the company and environmental procedures to accompany the EPA inspector and answer questions. The point person should be instructed to fully answer questions but not to volunteer information. EPA has developed compliance inspection manuals for many specific statutory areas, which are now published on the agency's website; these manuals provide a wealth of information about what clients should expect during an inspection.*

- Cooperate if possible. *As you will see in the exercise below, the EPA has a great deal of discretion in enforcement cases. Building a good relationship with the agency is not only a good thing to do from the ethics and civility standpoint, it may also avoid or reduce costly penalties. Sometimes, of course, the agency may be pushing for more than it is entitled to and you may not be able to cooperate; still, if you can assert your position in a reasonable manner and offer alternatives, your client will be better off.*

---

d. Types of Enforcement Actions

Enforcement of environmental laws can come in a variety of forms, ranging from a warning to serious criminal penalties. Here are the tools that the agency may use:

i. Informal Action

The agency may simply orally advise the regulated entity of its obligations under the law or write an informal warning letter. This does not go "on the record" of the entity, but of course could lead to further sanctions if the entity does not come into compliance. Informal warnings may be very effective, especially if the entity was simply unaware of its compliance obligations.[29] State agencies alone issue over 30,000 of these warning letters each year, in addition to countless oral admonitions.[30]

---

29. A study by the Environmental Council of the States (ECOS) found that oral warnings resulted in compliance in 76% of cases. Report to Congress: State Agency Contributions to Enforcement and Compliance, at 14 (ECOS Sept. 2001).

30. *Id.* at 32 (note that ECOS believes the data significantly underestimates the total).

ii. Notice of Violation (NOV)

Notices of Violation are the most commonly used enforcement tool.[31] These citations, also called Notices of Noncompliance (NON) or even Notices of Warning (NOW) by various agencies under a variety of statutes,[32] constitute a formal warning that the agency has found violations of law. No penalty is assessed under these notices and, if the entity remedies the violations, usually no further action will result. The NOV merely constitutes an initial "finding" of a violation, which the agency can modify later based on additional evidence, and is therefore not binding on the agency in later proceedings, such as permit approval. *See Sierra Club v. EPA*, 557 F.3d 401 (6th Cir. 2009).

The NOV can have significant consequences, however. The violation may go "on the record" of the entity, so that it may result in increased penalties for later violations.[33] Thus, the NOV should be taken seriously and challenged if it was issued in error or there is some defense. However, courts typically hold that NOVs are not final agency action, and therefore may not be appealed, because the agency has not yet decided to penalize the violation. *See, e.g., Pacificorp v. Thomas*, 883 F.2d 661 (9th Cir. 1988) (no pre-enforcement review of CAA NOV); *Lloyd A. Fry Roofing Co. v. EPA*, 554 F.2d 885 (8th Cir. 1977) (same).

iii. Administrative Order (AO)

In certain circumstances, enforcement statutes empower the agency to simply order an entity to come into compliance. Section 309 of the CWA, for example, allows the Administrator to issue an administrative order (AO) to any person who is discharging without a permit or in violation of their permit.[34] Similarly, CAA Section 113 allows the Administrator to issue an AO upon a finding of a violation of a State Implementation Plan or permit, but the Administrator must first issue a NOV and allow 30 days for compli-

---

31. ECOS estimates state and federal environmental agencies issue well over 42,000 NOVs annually. *Id.* at 31–33. With the move toward electronic reporting, some systems are now set up to generate automatic NOVs when the system detects a violation, which may increase this number.

32. For example, references to these notices may be found in the EPA's Enforcement Response Policies for EPCRA, FIFRA, and TSCA, along with illustrations of the circumstances in which this type of enforcement may be appropriate.

33. *See, e.g.,* RCRA Civil Penalty Policy, at 37 (upward adjustment for history of violations, including NOVs).

34. 33 U.S.C. § 1319(a).

ance.[35] EPA uses administrative orders "on consent" under CERCLA when an entity agrees to perform required remedial actions and uses unilateral administrative orders under Section 106 in cases of "imminent and substantial endangerment."[36] Some orders can be fairly simple, in the case of plugging or sealing a leaky well to comply with the SDWA, for example, or ceasing an unpermitted discharge. Others, such as an AO ordering the cleanup of a hazardous waste site, can be quite complex, containing the specific work plan for the site, penalty provisions for noncompliance, and reporting requirements.

Unilateral administrative orders may require the installation of expensive pollution control equipment or costly cleanups of contaminated areas; they typically provide for significant penalties for violating the order. Constitutional due process rights would seem to require the opportunity to challenge the basis for these orders before being required to comply. Yet, in most instances courts hold that an AO is not reviewable until EPA decides to enforce the order by seeking penalties or injunctive relief, at which time the entity may challenge the underlying justification and assert defenses. *See, e.g., Laguna Gatuna, Inc. v. Browner*, 58 F.3d 564, 565–66 (10th Cir. 1995) (no pre-enforcement review of CWA compliance order).

However, if the effect of an AO is immediate and "legal consequences will flow" from its violation, some courts have allowed judicial review. *See, e.g., Alaska, Dept. of Envt'l Conserv. v. U.S. EPA*, 244 F.3d 748, 750 (9th Cir. 2001) (order effectively closed facility); *Allsteel, Inc. v. U.S. EPA*, 25 F.3d 312 (6th Cir. 1994) (violation of order would incur additional penalties). *Compare Fairbanks North Star Borough v. U.S. Army Corps of Engineers*, 543 F.3d 586 (9th Cir. 2008) (Corps determination of wetlands jurisdiction was not final agency action from which consequences flowed). Unable to construe the CAA to allow pre-enforcement review of unilateral compliance orders, the Eleventh Circuit held the scheme unconstitutional under the Due Process clause. *Tennessee Valley Auth. v. Whitman*, 336 F.3d 1236, 1258–60 (11th Cir. 2003).

Practice Tip: Model Administrative Orders

> *The EPA has model Administrative Orders for some common situations. See, e.g., Model Administrative Order for CERCLA Remedial Design/Remedial Action, available at: www.epa.gov. Beware that many model AOs contain one-*

---

35. 42 U.S.C. §7413(a)(3).

36. 42 U.S.C. §9606(a). Consent administrative orders are also frequently used as in other circumstances, such as for negotiated settlements under the Safe Drinking Water Act.

sided language regarding the regulated entity's obligations (such as stipulated penalties or responsibility for the agency's oversight costs). Although the agency will not negotiate some of these provisions, if a party is willing to enter into an administrative order on consent, there may be some room to negotiate. Even though the EPA has the power to enforce a unilateral order, it may be willing to make some changes to ensure willing compliance and avoid litigation.

iv. Administrative Penalty

Most environmental acts give the agency the authority to impose administrative penalties for violations. *See, e.g.,* RCRA, 42 U.S.C. §6992d(a)(2) (penalties of up to $25,000 per day for noncompliance).[37] Administrative penalties are imposed through the EPA's internal administrative court system. *See* Administrative Practice, Section 3 below. Administrative penalties are the most common agency response if the situation merits more than an NOV or compliance order, and the fines imposed can be substantial. *See, e.g.,* "DuPont to Pay $16.5 Million to Settle Alleged Violations of EPA Reporting Rules," 240 BNA Daily Env. Rep. A-14 (Dec. 15, 2005) (TSCA/RCRA violations). In FY 2008, EPA assessed over $38 million in administrative penalties in over 2000 administrative cases.[38] Although these penalties are initially imposed by an administrative law judge, the alleged violator can eventually appeal the penalty to federal court, as described below.

v. Civil Suit

The agency can also seek civil penalties or injunctions in federal court. *See, e.g.,* RCRA, 42 U.S.C. §6992d(d). In FY 2008, EPA referred 280 civil cases to DOJ, resulting in over $88 million in civil environmental penalties in addition to injunctive relief.[39] Because courts have greater enforcement powers, such as the contempt order, civil actions may be preferable to administrative proceedings when an entity has not complied with previous agency orders. If the violations are serious and compliance measures will be complex or costly to implement, judicial injunctive relief is the best course. The agency may also

---

37. The Debt Collection Improvement Act of 1996, 31 USC §3701, requires EPA to adjust these penalty amounts once every four years to account for inflation. On January 12, 2009, statutory penalties of $25,000 were raised to $37,500. 40 C.F.R. §19.4. Because these limits continue to increase, this book will refer to the stated statutory penalties rather than the current adjusted amounts.

38. EPA, FY 2008 OECA Accomplishments Report, at 16.

39. *Id.*

use the civil suit remedy in order to seek more substantial penalties than those allowed in the administrative context.

In these cases, the EPA first refers a "request for litigation" to the Department of Justice (DOJ), which will represent the agency in court. Under the current Memorandum of Understanding governing the relationship between the EPA and the DOJ, EPA attorneys may participate along with DOJ attorneys in civil litigation, but the Attorney General retains ultimate control over the conduct of the case. In some instances, DOJ may decline representation and allow EPA attorneys to pursue the matter. *See, e.g.,* CWA § 506, 33 U.S.C. § 1366 (Administrator shall request Attorney General to represent United States in civil or criminal actions brought by the agency; if the Attorney General decides not to appear, EPA attorneys will represent United States).

Practice Tip: Administrative vs. Civil Actions

Whenever possible, the EPA may prefer to handle cases through the administrative penalty system, rather than through a civil suit, for several reasons. The administrative system is more low-key, and therefore may avoid unwanted publicity. Because of limited discovery and expanded motion practice, administrative hearings usually are concluded more rapidly. Thus, in a classic guidance document on CWA remedies, EPA directed the regions to choose "the least resource-consuming enforcement option that will do the job."[40] Finally, handing the case to the DOJ means that the agency's legal staff loses some of its ability to affect how the case is conducted. Obviously, adding additional layers of attorneys to the case will increase its complexity and reduce chances for a quick settlement. Nevertheless, in many cases, filing a civil penalty action may be preferable because of the potential for greater penalty amounts and judicial injunctive authority.

---

vi. Criminal Penalties

Environmental statutes also provide for criminal penalties, including substantial fines and imprisonment. These penalties typically require something beyond the mere violation of the statute, such as a "knowing" or at least a "negligent" violation, or that the violation harmed or threatened harm to the

---

40. EPA, "Guidance on Choosing Among Clean Water Act Administrative, Civil, and Criminal Enforcement Remedies," at 2 (Aug. 28, 1987).

public. *See, e.g.*, CWA § 309(c), 33 U.S.C. § 1319(c) (criminal penalties up to 1 year/$2500 per day for negligent violations; 15 years/$250,000 per day for knowing violations that endanger others); RCRA § 3008(e); 42 U.S.C. § 6928(e) (criminal penalties of $250,000, up to 15 years imprisonment for knowing endangerment violations). When criminal penalties are sought, the case is typically handled by the U.S. Attorney's office (or the state Attorney General in the case of state enforcement) in conjunction with the Environmental Crimes section of the DOJ. The EPA considers incarceration "a key component" of the enforcement program, because violators "cannot pass the sentence on as another 'cost of doing business.' "[41] In FY 2008 alone, EPA criminal referrals resulted in charges against 176 defendants, 215 total years of incarceration, and $86 million in fines, restitution, and mandated environmental projects.[42]

Both corporations and individuals may be charged with these crimes.[43] For example, the Clean Water Act allows criminal charges against the "responsible corporate officer," 33 U.S.C. § 1319(c)(6), which courts have held means the person with the authority to control the corporate activity constituting the violation. *See, e.g., U.S. v. Ming Hong,* 242 F.3d 528, 531 (4th Cir. 2001) (upholding sentence of 36 months and $1.3 million penalty for officer who "bore such a relationship to the corporation that it is appropriate to hold him criminally liable for failing to prevent the charged violations of the CWA"). Some courts, however, require the corporate officer to have actual knowledge of the illegal activity before criminal liability may be imposed. *See, e.g., United States v. MacDonald & Watson Waste Oil Co.,* 933 F.2d 35, 55 (1st Cir. 1991) (requiring proof of knowledge of conduct in question to incur criminal liability under responsible corporate officer doctrine); *United States v. USX Corp.,* 68 F.3d 811, 823 (3d Cir. 1995) (reversing summary judgment for government when genuine issue of fact existed as to whether officers had sufficient knowledge of illegal disposal). For further discussion of the responsible corporate officer doctrine, *see* Susan F. Mandiberg, "Moral Issues in Environmental Crime," 7 Ford. Envtl. L.J. 881 (1996).

---

41. EPA, Enforcement and Compliance Assurance Accomplishments Report, FY 1996, 2-2 (May 1997).

42. EPA, FY 2008 OECA Accomplishments Report, at 18.

43. *See, e.g.,* U.S. DOJ, "Sinclair Tulsa Refining Company, Managers Sentenced for Environmental Crimes" (April 4, 2007) (company sentenced to $5.5 million penalty, probation; two managers received six months home detention, three years probation, in addition to fines and community service), avail. at www.usdoj.gov/opa/pr/2007/April/07_enrd_222.html.

3. Administrative Practice

Before the EPA can assess administrative penalties or revoke or suspend permits, the violator is entitled to a hearing before an Administrative Law Judge (ALJ). EPA administrative enforcement proceedings are conducted according to rules of procedure that differ somewhat from the rules of evidence and procedure used in the judicial court system. *See* Consolidated Rules of Practice Governing the Administrative Assessment of Civil Penalties and the Revocation or Suspension of Permits (Consolidated Rules), 40 C.F.R. pt. 22.[44]

The Consolidated Rules provide that the agency (called the "Complainant") must file an administrative complaint against the alleged violator (called the "Respondent"), who files an answer.[45] The administrative complaint in many ways looks very much like a civil complaint: it begins with a statement of jurisdiction, a description of the parties, and then details the violations in separate counts. In Appendix A, we have included an example of an administrative complaint from an EPCRA case, *GE Precision Corporation*. Notice that, unlike a civil complaint, the administrative complaint proposes a specific penalty, explains how the agency arrived at that proposal, and gives the Respondent notice of an opportunity to request a hearing. It also specifically informs the Respondent of the right to request an informal settlement conference. The agency encourages settlement; over 97% of EPA administrative enforcement cases are settled. Therefore, counsel for both parties should treat the informal settlement conference as an extremely important opportunity to achieve a quick, less costly resolution.

If the case does not settle, the violator is entitled to a formal hearing before an Administrative Law Judge (ALJ).[46] Although the conduct of the hearing is in many ways similar to a civil bench trial, the rules of evidence are more inclusive, in that the ALJ is instructed to consider all relevant evidence. 40 C.F.R. §22.22(a). Even written statements of evidence may be admitted in lieu of oral testimony, although the witness must also appear for cross-examination. 40 C.F.R. §22.22(c). The ALJ makes findings of fact and conclusions of

---

44. Some adjudicative hearings, such as those under Section 120 of the Clean Air Act, are governed by special rules of practice instead of the Consolidated Rules. *See generally* Judge Gerald Harwood, "Hearings Before an EPA Administrative Law Judge," 17 Env. L. Rptr. 10441 (November 1987).

45. Failure to file an answer results in a binding admission of the allegations of the complaint and waiver of the right to a hearing.

46. For certain lower penalties under the CWA and Safe Drinking Water Act, where a hearing "on the record" is not required by the APA, the case is heard by the Regional Judicial Officer under slightly different procedures. 40 C.F.R. §22.50-52.

law and issues an initial decision, which becomes final if not appealed within 45 days.[47]

The Administrator of the EPA has delegated the authority to decide appeals from most penalty and permit decisions to a special administrative appellate body, called the Environmental Appeals Board.[48] The Board may decide, on its own initiative, to review an ALJ's initial decision, even if the parties decide not to appeal.[49] The Board consists of four judges, who sit in panels of three. All of the judges have had extensive environmental experience, including significant EPA experience, before being appointed to the Board by the EPA Administrator. *See* www.epa.gov/eab. The Board's decision represents final agency action and may be appealed to the federal Court of Appeals. 40 C.F.R. § 27.42. Generally, very few cases are appealed to federal court.[50]

As EPA noted in the preamble to revisions of the Consolidated Rules in 1999:

> The EAB is responsible for assuring consistency in Agency adjudications by all of the ALJs and RJOs [Regional Judicial Officers]. The appeal process of the [Consolidated Rules] gives the Agency an opportunity to correct erroneous decisions before they are appealed to the federal courts. The EAB assures that final decisions represent … the position of the Agency as a whole, rather than just the position of one Region, one enforcement office, or one Presiding Officer.… In addition to meeting EPA's institutional needs, this process also offers enormous advantages to respondents who are dissatisfied with an initial decision, in that appeals to the EAB are much quicker and much less expensive than appeals to a federal court.[51]

Practice Tip: Environmental Appeals Board Procedures

Any attorney with a case before the Environmental Appeals Board should obtain the Board's practice manual, which is designed to familiarize the attor-

---

47. 40 C.F.R. § 22.27(c).

48. 57 Fed. Reg. 5320 (Feb. 13, 1992). *See generally* Nancy B. Firestone, *Ensuring the Fairness of Agency Adjudications: The Environmental Appeal Board's First Four Years*, 2 Envtl. Law. 291 (1996).

49. 40 C.F.R. §§ 22.29–30.

50. EPA, Office of Enforcement and Compliance Assurance, Administrative Hearings and Trials, p.4 n.14 (noting that only 6–10 cases each year are appealed to federal court).

51. Consolidated Rules of Practice Governing the Administrative Assessment of Civil Penalties, 64 Fed. Reg. 40138, at 40165 (July 23, 1999).

ney with the Board's responsibilities, rules, and case law. It also includes sample pleadings and orders. See Environmental Appeals Board, U.S. EPA, Environmental Appeals Board Practice Manual (1994).

C. Sources of Law

In addition to the sources of law identified in the compliance section (statutes, regulations, and guidance documents), there are some additional helpful sources of law for enforcement cases.

1. Enforcement Response Policies

For each of the major environmental acts, the EPA has issued a policy regarding how penalties should be assessed. Some state environmental agencies also have adopted uniform penalty policies.[52] The statutes themselves provide little guidance for determining how severe a particular penalty should be. For example, the RCRA statute directs the Administrator, in assessing a penalty, to "take into account the seriousness of the violation and any good faith efforts to comply." 42 U.S.C. § 6992d(a)(2). In the enforcement response policy (also known as the penalty policy), EPA takes this rather vague standard and specifies which violations will be treated most severely and how good faith and other factors will be used to mitigate or, in some cases, enhance the penalty. By applying a firm set of guidelines, the agency hopes to achieve some uniformity among the various regions.[53] In reality, however, there is a great deal of discretion built into each policy.

Counsel for both the EPA and the regulated entity must be aware of the enforcement response policy provisions. The policy will often be the most fruitful basis for arguments on both sides about the appropriate level of penalty for a particular violation. For Exercise 2, at the end of this chapter, you will use the EPCRA Enforcement Response Policy, so you may want to

---

52. *See, e.g.,* N.J.Admin. Code § 7:14-8.5 (matrix for Clean Water Act violations). Other states may use the federal enforcement policy as guidance, *see Barrett Refining Corp. v. Miss. Comm'n on Env. Qual.,* 751 So.2d 1104 (Miss. App. 1999) (state agency used EPA policy to assess CAA violations), but are not bound by the federal penalty policies in determining appropriate penalties under state law. *State v. Elementis Chem., Inc.,* 155 N.H. 299, 306, 922 A.2d 678, 684 (N.H. 2007).

53. *See generally* "Policy on Civil Penalties," EPA General Enforcement Policy #GM-21 (February 16, 1984).

consult that document as we go through the basic format. Policies for the other statutes are very similar. The easiest place to find the penalty policy is probably the Office of Enforcement and Compliance Assurance (OECA) pages on EPA's website (www.epa.gov), which also has some other policies relating to enforcement.

The final penalty will be based on two components: 1) an amount that recaptures the economic benefit the violator gained by its noncompliance, and 2) an amount reflecting the gravity of the violation. The rationale behind the economic benefit portion is simple: EPA does not want the violating entity to gain a competitive advantage by its failure to adhere to the law. Thus, the agency will determine how much it would have cost the facility to comply and make that the starting point for penalty calculations. For example, the facility may have saved money by avoiding or delaying the installation of expensive pollution control equipment, or may have avoided several years of operation and maintenance costs. The agency uses a computer model, called BEN, which takes into account complexities such as present value calculations.[54] Even though the model itself may be difficult to challenge, violators sometimes are successful in challenging the inputs or assumptions made. For example, for CWA violations of suspended solids limits, the agency may base its calculation on the installation of expensive treatment equipment, while the violator may argue it could have complied by simply installing another settling lagoon at a fraction of the cost.

To determine the gravity-based component, the agency first calculates a base penalty, and then makes adjustments up or down based on a variety of factors. Most enforcement response policies proceed as follows:

a. Base Penalty

The base penalty is typically a product of the two most important elements, such as the severity of the violation (how dangerous it was, for example) and the degree of the violation (how far from compliance it was). To determine severity, the agency assigns values such as "Major" or "Minor" to different types of violations. For example, under RCRA, a failure to label a waste drum is categorized as a Minor violation, while improper disposal is a Major violation. The policy also specifies how to determine the degree of the violation:

---

54. *See* www.epa.gov/compliance/civil/programs/econmodels/index.html. The agency also uses computer models for evaluating a company's claim that it cannot afford to pay a particular penalty or cleanup costs (ABEL) or to evaluate a similar claim by an individual (INDIPAY). These models are updated frequently and are readily available, so that the violator's attorney may double-check the agency's calculations.

for example, for a RCRA labeling violation, as we discussed in the problems above, a label that merely contained some incorrect information would be closer to compliance and penalized less severely than not labeling the waste at all. The two base factors are then placed on a matrix and base penalties are assigned for each combination of the two factors.

Under the Emergency Planning and Community Right-to-Know Act, which you will apply in Exercise 2 below, a facility must immediately report the release of hazardous substances to various government emergency response agencies. In the EPA's EPCRA enforcement response policy, as shown in Figure 2.4, the penalty for failure to report the violation is a product of the Extent of the violation (that is, how late the facility was in notifying the appropriate agencies) and the Gravity of the violation (that is, how serious the release was, measured by the amount released).

b. Adjustment Factors

After the agency decides on the base penalty, it may then be adjusted up or down by factors such as cooperation, ability to pay, history of previous violations, or good faith. The policy specifies what type of conduct merits an adjustment and the range of adjustment (by percentage) that can be made. For example, for the "history of violations" factor, the policy will indicate what types of violations count (is an NOV enough, for instance, and what if the previous violation concerned a different Act?) and how recent the previous violations have to be. The agency has a great deal of discretion here, and the decision to reduce the penalty by 10% for good faith or cooperation can be extremely significant in some cases.

c. Per-Day Penalties

Some statutes provide that the violator can be penalized up to $25,000 "per day of violation." *See, e.g.*, RCRA § 11005(a)(2), 42 U.S.C. § 6992d(a)(2). However, the application of this language is confusing. Does the failure to have a RCRA permit for a treatment operation, for example, constitute one violation, justifying a maximum $25,000 penalty, or should it be treated as a violation for every day the facility operated without the permit? Obviously, enormous penalty amounts could be generated quickly if the latter interpretation is used. The penalty policy addresses the circumstances in which per-day penalties should be used, but again, there is some discretion involved. Typically, the policy will specify a much lower value for the per-day penalty, and use it as an incentive for facilities to come into compliance. Because the application of a per-

Figure 2.4

Civil Penalty Matrix for CERCLA Section 103, EPCRA Section 304†, and EPCRA Section 312

GRAVITY (Quantity Released/Stored)

EXTENT (timeliness of notification/timeliness of inventory submission)	LEVEL A (greater than 10 times the RQ/MTL)	LEVEL B (greater than 5 but less than or equal to 10 times the RQ/MTL)	LEVEL C (greater than 1 but less than or equal to 5 times the RQ/MTL)
LEVEL 1 (more than 2 hours/30 days)	$32,500 $24,180	$24,179 $16,120	$16,119 $8,061
LEVEL 2 (between 1 and 2 hours/after 20 but within 30 days)	$24,179 $16,120	$16,119 $8,061	$8,060 $4,032
LEVEL 3 (within 1 hour, but after 15 minutes/after 10 but within 20 days)	$16,119 $8,061	$8,060 $4,032	$4,030 $2,014

†While the penalty amounts in this matrix apply to EPCRA § 304(c), the criteria asociated with the levels do not apply. To determine the appropriate extent level for violations of § 304, *see* pp. 12–13, *supra*.

Note: After calculating the gravity-based penalty for each count, the total applicable gravity-based penalty for all counts in a particular case/matter should be rounded to the nearest unit of $100 as required by the memorandum from Thomas Skinner, dated September 21, 2004, implementing the Civil Monetary Penalty Adjustment Rule as published in the Federal Register on February 13, 2004 (69 FR 7121).

Source: Matrix is from EPA, OECA, "Memorandum re: Penalty Supplements pursuant to the 2004 Civil Monetary Penalty Inflation Adjustment Rule," at 18 (June 6, 2006). "RQ" refers to the Reportable Quantity of that substance.

day penalty can accumulate to large amounts, this may be the most important decision the agency makes, as you will see in Exercise 2 below.

d. Environmentally Beneficial Expenditures or Supplemental Environmental Projects (SEPs)

Most enforcement response policies provide for a discretionary reduction in the penalty amount if the violator agrees to undertake some sort of expenditure that benefits the environment, called either an "Environmentally Beneficial Expenditure" (EBE) or a "Supplemental Environmental Project" (SEP).

The idea behind this policy is that the agency would rather have the money go toward achieving the overall purpose of our environmental regulatory system instead of being dropped into the yawning maw of the government fisc. In some years, the agency has been enthusiastic about this tool—in 1995, for example, the EPA negotiated nearly 350 SEPs, which cost violators over $103 million to implement.[55] In 2002, however, the EPA negotiated only around $56 million in beneficial expenditures. By 2008, only 188 cases included SEPs, resulting in only $39 million in project costs.[56] Nevertheless, in an appropriate case, the use of an SEP may provide a win-win result for the parties and the public.

The EPA's Supplemental Environmental Projects Policy states:

> Supplemental environmental projects are defined as environmentally beneficial projects which a defendant respondent agrees to undertake in settlement of an enforcement action, but which the defendant respondent is not otherwise legally required to perform.[57]

Obviously, not all projects qualify for this penalty reduction: it cannot be a project the entity is already required to do by law or has already done, nor can it be a project that primarily benefits the regulated entity, rather than the public (although many SEPs—such as recycling projects or changes in production processes—actually end up saving the entity money).[58] Moreover, the EPA may balk at projects that require extensive or lengthy agency oversight to ensure their completion.

Finally, the SEP must have an adequate "nexus" to the violation at issue. This relationship exists, for example, if the project "reduces the adverse impact to public health or the environment to which the violation at issue contributes," or if the project "is designed to reduce the likelihood that similar violations will occur in the future."[59] Thus, for a toxic chemical reporting violation in Arizona, the purchase of emergency response equipment for the local Hazmat department would probably qualify, while creating a new wetland in Alaska would not. However, the policy construes the "nexus" requirement broadly—a SEP may qualify even if it addresses a different pollutant in a different medium, as long as it is aimed at reducing the total environmental risk to which this violation contributed.

---

55. EPA, FY 1995 OECA Accomplishments Report, at 3–13.
56. EPA, FY 2008 OECA Accomplishments Report, at 34–35.
57. EPA Supplemental Environmental Projects Policy, 63 Fed. Reg. 24796, 24797–98 (May 5, 1998).
58. EPA has issued a whole series of guidance documents on the use of SEPs, found at: cfpub.epa.gov/compliance/resources/policies/civil/seps/.
59. *63 Fed. Reg.* at 24798.

Many SEPs are undertaken in the areas of pollution prevention or pollution reduction. For example, in settling a TSCA penalty case involving the improper storage of polychlorinated biphenyls (PCBs), generally found in electric transformers, EPA may reduce the penalty in exchange for the violator's agreement to convert to non-PCB transformers, something not required by TSCA. Or in exchange for settling a Clean Air Act violation, the violator might agree to redesign its production process to eliminate the use of certain toxic chemicals. *See, e.g.,* "Georgia-Pacific to Pay $35 million in Fines, Improvements for 11 Southeastern Facilities," 27 Envt. Rptr. 622 (July 26, 1996) (in addition to $6 million penalty, the company agreed to spend $25 million for pollution control technology upgrades).

Other SEPs involve environmental restoration—in the *Ketchican Pulp* case in Alaska, for example, the company was charged with numerous violations of the CWA and the CAA. In addition to paying $3 million in criminal penalties and $3.1 million in civil penalties, the company agreed to spend up to $6 million to clean up damage its discharges caused to the marine habitat of Ward Cove.[60]

The amount of penalty reduction given in exchange for the SEP varies with the "quality" of the project. For example, the EPA favors projects that further the development of innovative pollution control technology or which contribute to "Environmental Justice" (i.e., which "mitigate damage or reduce risk to minority or low income populations which may have been disproportionately exposed to pollution").[61] The penalty may not be reduced more than the net after-tax amount the violator spends on the project and typically does not exceed 80% of the project's cost.[62] In order to achieve deterrence, the SEP cannot reduce the penalty below an amount representing the economic benefit achieved by non-compliance, plus at least some part of the gravity component of the penalty. At a minimum, the penalty must be set at 25% of the gravity-based component.

Supplemental Environmental Projects: Criteria

- Not otherwise legally required to perform project
- Can't primarily benefit regulated entity
- Can't have already been done, must be future project
- Must have adequate nexus to violation at issue
- Can't reduce below the economic benefit amount plus 25% of gravity-based component

---

60. EPA, Enforcement and Compliance Assurance Accomplishments Report, FY 1995, 3–15 (July 1996).

61. *63 Fed. Reg* at 24802.

62. *Id.*

e. Binding Effect of Policy

Although an administrative law judge will generally follow EPA's enforcement response policy, the ALJ may deviate from the policy "where circumstances warrant." *Steeltech, Ltd. v. EPA*, 273 F.3d 652 (6th Cir. 2001) (approving ALJ's close reliance on EPCRA penalty policy, even though it was not a binding regulation); *see also* 40 C.F.R. §22.27(b) (ALJ should consider penalty policy and explain any departure). In a civil action, the effect of the enforcement policy varies with the court. The policies themselves contain language indicating that they are not to be used at trial, and some courts refuse to consider them on that basis. *See Friends of the Earth, Inc. v. Laidlaw Environmental Services, Inc.*, 956 F. Supp. 588, 601 (D. S. Car. 1997) (citizen suit). Other courts have noted that, while the policies are not regulations entitled to *Chevron* deference, the language can be persuasive guidance in determining an appropriate penalty. *See, e.g., Atlantic States Legal Foundation, Inc. v. Tyson Foods, Inc.*, 897 F.2d 1128 (11th Cir. 1990) (while penalty policy may be helpful, the court's focus should be on the statutory language).

2. Case Law

Case law can help identify and bolster defenses to enforcement actions and can provide persuasive authority concerning the appropriate penalty to be imposed. By now you are very familiar with the standard reporting system for case law, and many valuable environmental opinions are contained in the pages of the federal and state reporters. There is also a wealth of authority, however, in harder-to-find sources.

a. Unpublished Opinions

Not all court decisions find their way into the standard reporters. Many opinions are designated "not for publication" by the court or are not selected by the editor for inclusion in a reporter,[63] yet these may contain just the bit of statutory interpretation you are looking for. Although there are limitations on how some of these opinions may be used (the local rules of many federal appellate courts, for example, prohibit parties from citing unpublished opinions in their briefs), the analysis can provide insight into how a court might view the case

---

63. Fewer than half of federal Court of Appeals decisions are now published. See Morris L. Cohen, et al., How to Find the Law 43 (9th ed. 1989). In addition, only a small percentage of U.S. District Court opinions make the Federal Supplement reporter. *Id.* at 42.

and may raise arguments you hadn't thought of before.[64] In addition, even an unpublished opinion of a federal court of appeals can be persuasive authority to an administrative law judge or to opposing counsel in assessing the strength of the case.

b. Administrative Opinions

In addition to unpublished court opinions, you will want to research the opinions of the agency's administrative court, including those of both the ALJ and the Environmental Appeals Board. Because only a few environmental penalty cases are appealed beyond the administrative system each year, these administrative opinions often will be far more helpful to you in the enforcement context than those in the standard reporters.

Practice Tip: Finding Opinions

Many unpublished opinions can be found in computer databases such as WESTLAW and LEXIS. In addition, many environmental opinions not reported in the standard reporters are reported in specialized services such as the Environmental Law Reporter (an ELI publication). You may find references to unpublished opinions in news services such as the Environment Reporter (BNA), which you can then order from the service or access through the court's electronic filing system.

Administrative opinions are easiest to access online, either through specialized databases on WESTLAW and LEXIS (for example, in WESTLAW you can find EPA decisions in the database FENV-EPA) or at the EPA's website (www.epa.gov). Environmental Appeals Board decisions, in particular, are easy to access on the Board's webpage (www.epa.gov/eab). The Administrative Law Judge decisions of state agencies may be harder to find, because in many states they are not widely distributed. The computer databases have many of these decisions, especially the more recent ones, but you may have to make a trip to the agency's headquarters to get them all (and even then, they may not be indexed).

For Problem 2.5, find an Environmental Appeals Board case called *Gordon Redd Lumber Company* and apply it to the facts given. In addition, consider

---

64. Allowing only published decisions to be relied upon as precedent remains controversial. *See* Melissa H. Weresh, "The Unpublished Non-precedential Decision: An Uncomfortable Legality?," 3 J. App. Prac. & Proc. 175 (2001).

whether the Supplemental Environmental Project proposed is appropriate under the EPA's SEP policy described above.

Problem 2.5: Applying Case Law and Policy

On June 1, 2009, EPA sent the State of Oregon (ODEQ) a notice of its intent to seek penalties against Quality Wood, Inc. for violations of RCRA. EPA's notice letter stated: "EPA believes that Quality Wood has improperly stored hazardous waste (creosote sludge) on-site in excess of the time period allowed for generators of waste. EPA intends to seek penalties for these storage violations." On June 10, ODEQ replied to this notice, indicating that it had already issued a compliance order to Quality Wood, which gave the company until the end of 2009 to find another method of waste disposal that would eliminate the storage violations. ODEQ stated that it did not intend to seek further enforcement action at this time against Quality Wood.

On July 1, 2009, pursuant to RCRA Section 3008, 42 U.S.C. §6928, the EPA served Quality Wood with an administrative compliance order directing that it comply with RCRA requirements regarding the storage of hazardous wastes. In addition, EPA served Quality Wood with an administrative complaint, proposing to fine the company $150,000 for violations of RCRA. Specifically, the complaint alleges four counts of improper storage of hazardous wastes, four counts of improper labeling, and two counts of using improper containers.

Quality Wood's counsel has filed a motion with the Administrative Law Judge, seeking to dismiss the penalty counts because the notice to the state was vague and incomplete, in that it failed to state specifically that EPA intended to include the counts regarding improper containers and improper labeling. In addition, Quality Wood argues the complaint should be dismissed because Oregon DEQ's compliance order "excused" the company from compliance until the end of 2009.

In an initial settlement conference today, Quality Wood's counsel suggested that EPA should reduce the penalty by $50,000, the cost of a new groundwater monitoring system that the company plans to install next month. The monitoring system is designed to detect contamination from two underground storage tanks on site, but theoretically would also detect any groundwater contamination from the creosote storage.

You are an attorney representing the EPA in this administrative action. In a memo to EPA Regional Counsel, address the following issues:

1) Was EPA's notice deficient? If so, should the entire proposed penalty be dismissed or only those counts not included in the notice?

2) Does the state's compliance order "excuse" Quality Wood's noncompliance with the RCRA storage requirements?

3) Should the EPA reduce the amount of the penalty for the groundwater monitoring system? Does it meet the requirements of EPA's SEP policy?

Problem 2.6: Administrative Hearings

After settlement negotiations reached an impasse, an Administrative Law Judge heard EPA's RCRA penalty case against Quality Wood. Quality Wood did not deny improperly labeling and storing the creosote sludge. However, it presented an expert, Mr. James Ross, a representative of the creosote supplier, who testified that the environmental dangers of creosote sludge were minimal. The ALJ admitted his testimony over EPA's objection that it did not meet the Daubert standard for scientific evidence.[65] In addition, Quality Wood argued that it could not afford a large penalty, due to a recent downturn in business. EPA objected to this defense, because Quality Wood had failed to provide financial data, including tax returns, despite EPA's request. Quality Wood responded that its financial information was confidential. The ALJ agreed with EPA and declined to consider the ability to pay factor. After submission of post-hearing briefs, the ALJ imposed a penalty of $10,000 for each of ten RCRA violations, for a total penalty of $100,000.

Quality Wood appealed this penalty to the EAB, presenting the following issues:

a) Quality Wood argued first that it had not been properly served with the administrative complaint, because it was simply sent by certified mail, addressed to the company. Although Quality Wood answered the complaint and participated in the hearing, it preserved the ineffective service defense in its pleadings. Quality Wood argues that personal service of a corporate officer or registered agent is required, citing Fed R. Civ. P., Rule 4(d). Under the consolidated rules, 40 CFR § 22.5, does Quality Wood have a valid objection? See Katzson Bros., Inc. v. US EPA, *839 F.2d 1396 (10th Cir. 1988).*

---

65. *Daubert v. Merrell Dow Pharm., Inc.*, 509 U.S. 579 (1993) (setting out standards for the admissibility of scientific evidence under the Federal Rules of Evidence).

b) Quality Wood also asserts that the ALJ incorrectly ruled against the ability to pay defense, based on its failure to provide confidential financial data. How should the EAB hold? See In re Bituma-Stor, Inc., 2000 WL 341010 (EPA ALJ).

c) Finally, EPA cross-appeals, arguing that the ALJ should not have accepted the evidence of James Ross, because it did not meet the Daubert standard. Is EPA correct? See 40 C.F.R. §22.22; In the Matter of Tiger Shipyard, Inc., 1999 WL 1678486 (EAB).

D. Practice Considerations

1. Enforcement Issues

Most enforcement cases revolve around similar types of issues: First, whether a violation in fact occurred, and second, what the size of the penalty should be. The first issue may be contested on both factual grounds (did what the agency says happened really happen?) and legal grounds (how should the regulation/statute be interpreted?). The size of the penalty may also be affected by factual considerations, because larger penalties are assessed for more egregious violations.

a. Defenses

Defenses to enforcement cases usually fall into one of the following categories:

Factual defense—In some cases, the facts may be incontrovertible; *e.g.,* the company's own records may establish a violation. But in many cases, factual disputes can be pivotal: For example, if the allegation concerns a wastewater discharge, respondents[66] may allege faulty testing procedures or conflicting test results. In a case involving failure to notify agency officials about a release of hazardous substances, witnesses may differ as to the extent and timing of notification. In a case alleging violations of a CAA permit, there may be a factual dispute over whether an unavoidable mechanical breakdown caused the violation. Even in cases where the evidence seems

---

66. In administrative cases, the agency is known as the "Complainant" and the alleged violator is called the "Respondent," so we will use those terms here.

to be well established, a good attorney must do a very careful fact investigation.

Statutory/regulatory interpretation—The statutory or regulatory language may be ambiguous and subject to an interpretation that makes it inapplicable to your client's case. Case law showing how courts or administrative law judges have interpreted the language can be very persuasive. For example, whether a pile of mining waste is a "point source" under the Clean Water Act will depend on how the statute and regulations are interpreted. Should the term "waste" under RCRA be interpreted to cover spent shot at a shooting range?

Statutory/regulatory exceptions—Often, the statute or regulation will carve out exceptions to the application of the law. For example, under RCRA, hazardous material may not constitute regulated "waste" if it is being reclaimed in a certain way. 40 C.F.R. § 261.4(a)(8). A NPDES permit is not required for "return flows from irrigated agriculture." CWA § 502(14), 33 U.S.C. § 1362(14). The trigger for CERCLA liability, "hazardous substances," does not include petroleum. CERCLA § 101(14), 42 U.S.C. § 9601(14). Many of these exceptions are found in the "definitions" section of the statute or regulation.

Regulatory validity—Often counsel accepts the agency's regulations as binding authority and, in most cases, that approach is justified. However, counsel should always consider the possibility that an agency's regulations go beyond its statutory authority. As you know, courts allow the agency a great deal of discretion in implementing statutory commands, but the agency's regulations must be at least a reasonable interpretation of the statutory language. *See Chevron U.S.A., Inc. v. Natural Resources Defense Council*, 467 U.S. 837 (1984). In addition, a regulation may not be entitled to deference if it lies outside the agency's expertise or is not within the express or implied delegation of legislative authority. *See, e.g., Mead v. United States*, 538 U.S. 218 (2001) (agency interpretation not entitled to *Chevron* deference if no express or implied legislative delegation); *Kelley v. E.P.A.*, 15 F.3d 1100 (D.C. Cir. 1994) (striking down the EPA's interpretation of CERCLA lender liability exemption; "liability" issues are for the court, not the agency).

However, even if you have a good claim that a regulation exceeds the agency's statutory authority, there are statutes limiting judicial review of regulations. Many environmental acts require that lawsuits to invalidate regulations or other types of agency action must be brought within a short period of time after the regulation is promulgated. If the regulation is not challenged within this time period, or is challenged but upheld, the regulation cannot be challenged later, when it is enforced against your client. *See, e.g.,* CWA §509(b), 33 U.S.C. §1369(b) (limiting challenges to 120 days after regulation is promulgated, unless there are new grounds for review); CAA §307(b)(1), 42 U.S.C. §7607(b)(1) (60-day period for challenges to certain agency actions, absent new grounds).

But what if your client wasn't even in business when the regulation was promulgated and therefore had no way to challenge it within the time period? Or what if the company was in business, but didn't understand the implications of the regulation until it was enforced against them? Does CWA Section 509(b)(2) answer the question? *See also Chevron U.S.A. v. U.S. EPA,* 908 F.2d 468, 470 (9th Cir. 1990) (enforcement action alone does not constitute "new grounds" for review of agency action under Section 509(b)).

Statutory validity—The statute must be constitutionally permissible. All federal statutes must fall under an enumerated power of the Constitution. Most federal environmental statutes can be justified by the Commerce Clause, but *United States v. Lopez,* 514 U.S. 549 (1995), and *United States v. Morrison,* 529 U.S. 598 (2000), indicate that this power is not unlimited; the interstate commerce impacts must be real and substantial to support federal law.

A statute may also impermissibly violate constitutional protections. The enforcement of a statute could raise Fourth Amendment search and seizure issues, for example, or perhaps a statute represents such a significant restriction that it constitutes a taking of property without compensation, in violation of the Fifth Amendment. *See Lucas v. South Carolina Coastal Council,* 505 U.S. 1003 (1992) (beach preservation ordinance could be "taking").

In addition, state or local environmental laws might be pre-empted by federal law, because of an express preemption clause, or because the federal scheme is comprehensive in scope, or because the state or local law is in direct conflict with a federal provision. *See Lorillard Tobacco Co. v. Reilly,* 533 U.S. 525 (2001) (state regulations governing cigarette advertising preempted by federal law); *National Audubon Soc'y v. Davis,* 307 F.3d 835 (9th Cir. 2002) (state law prohibiting certain types of animal trapping preempted by federal law). *See also* Wisc. Stat. §94.701 (state preemption of local pesticide regulation); *Goodell v. Humboldt County,* 575 N.W. 2d 486 (Iowa 1998) (county environmental ordinances regulating animal confinements preempted by state law).

Problem 2.7: Developing Defenses

Royal Koons, an Illinois farmer, owns land containing a seven-acre wetland area, at the edge of his 160-acre parcel. A small, unnamed stream runs next to this wetland. About a mile away, the stream eventually reaches the Middle River, which rarely has sufficient water to float a canoe, and Middle River in turn eventually empties into Lake Darling, a large recreational reservoir located entirely in the state of Illinois. Because it is so wet, Koons has never farmed this parcel, but recently his brother-in-law offered him some fill dirt, which he decided to use to bring this area into production. The United States (Corps of Engineers) has now filed a civil suit against him, seeking an injunction and civil and criminal penalties for violation of the Clean Water Act.

The Clean Water Act requires a landowner to apply for a permit from the Army Corps of Engineers before placing "dredged or fill material" into navigable waters. Read Sections 301, 404 and 502 of the Act and figure out how they combine to require this. 33 U.S.C. §§ 1311, 1344 & 1362. You will note that neither Section 301 nor Section 404 refers to "wetlands" but rather to "navigable waters." How does the Act define that term? See Section 502.

The Corps of Engineers has defined its jurisdiction broadly. See 33 C.F.R. § 328.3(a). An intrastate lake is covered, for example, if it has a sufficient connection with interstate commerce. In addition, tributaries of intrastate lakes are covered, as are wetlands adjacent to such tributaries. Therefore, because Koons' wetland is adjacent to a tributary of a navigable water, the Corps claims it is covered by 33 C.F.R. §§ 328.3(a)(3), (5), & (7).

Assume you represent Koons. Consider possible defenses to this suit under each of the categories outlined above.

1) What sort of factual defense might you have in a case like this?

2) Can you construct an argument that the regulation should be interpreted in a way that does not cover this case?

3) Does the statute or regulation contain any exceptions that Koons could qualify for?

4) Is the Corps' regulation a valid interpretation of the statute, or does it go beyond the agency's authority? In this connection, see the SWANCC and Rapanos cases, below.[67]

5) If the Corps' regulation is a valid interpretation of the statute, does the statute violate the Constitution? Consider a Commerce Clause argument under Lopez and Morrison.

6) You might also explore some procedural defenses such as jurisdiction. What statute authorizes the U.S. to bring this enforcement action and in what court should the case be filed? What are the possible penalties?

---

* * *

Solid Waste Agency of Northern Cook County v. United States Army Corps of Engineers, et al.
531 U.S. 159 (2001)

Chief Justice REHNQUIST delivered the opinion of the Court.

Section 404(a) of the Clean Water Act (CWA or Act) regulates the discharge of dredged or fill material into "navigable waters." The United States Army Corps of Engineers (Corps) has interpreted §404(a) to confer federal authority over an abandoned sand and gravel pit in northern Illinois which provides habitat for migratory birds. We are asked to decide whether the provisions of §404(a) may be fairly extended to these waters, and, if so, whether Congress could exercise such authority consistent with the Commerce Clause, U.S. Const., Art. I, §8, cl. 3. We answer the first question in the negative and therefore do not reach the second.

Section 404(a) grants the Corps authority to issue permits "for the discharge of dredged or fill material into the navigable waters at specified disposal sites." The term "navigable waters" is defined under the Act as "the waters of the United States, including the territorial seas." §1362(7). The Corps has issued regulations defining the term "waters of the United States" to include

> waters such as intrastate lakes, rivers, streams (including intermittent streams), mudflats, sandflats, wetlands, sloughs, prairie potholes, wet

---

67. Does EPA's guidance memorandum, issued in the wake of *Rapanos*, assist you? *See* www.epa.gov/wetlands/guidance/CWAwaters.html.

meadows, playa lakes, or natural ponds, the use, degradation or destruction of which could affect interstate or foreign commerce....

33 CFR § 328.3(a)(3) (1999). In 1986, in an attempt to "clarify" the reach of its jurisdiction, the Corps stated that § 404(a) extends to intrastate waters:

a. Which are or would be used as habitat by birds protected by Migratory Bird Treaties; or
b. Which are or would be used as habitat by other migratory birds which cross state lines; or
c. Which are or would be used as habitat for endangered species; or
d. Used to irrigate crops sold in interstate commerce.

51 Fed.Reg. 41217. This ... promulgation has been dubbed the "Migratory Bird Rule."

The Corps found that approximately 121 bird species had been observed at the site, including several known to depend upon aquatic environments for a significant portion of their life requirements. Thus, on November 16, 1987, the Corps formally "determined that the seasonally ponded, abandoned gravel mining depressions located on the project site, while not wetlands, did qualify as 'waters of the United States'" ... [and] refused to issue a § 404(a) permit.

[Section] 404(a) authorizes respondents to regulate the discharge of fill material into "navigable waters," 33 U.S.C. § 1344(a), which the statute defines as "the waters of the United States, including the territorial seas," § 1362(7). Respondents have interpreted these words to cover the abandoned gravel pit at issue here because it is used as habitat for migratory birds. We conclude that the "Migratory Bird Rule" is not fairly supported by the CWA.

This is not the first time we have been called upon to evaluate the meaning of § 404(a). In *United States v. Riverside Bayview Homes, Inc.,* 474 U.S. 121 (1985), we held that the Corps had § 404(a) jurisdiction over wetlands that actually abutted on a navigable waterway. In so doing, we noted that the term "navigable" is of "limited import" and that Congress evidenced its intent to "regulate at least some waters that would not be deemed 'navigable' under the classical understanding of that term." *Id.,* at 133.

It was the significant nexus between the wetlands and "navigable waters" that informed our reading of the CWA in *Riverside Bayview Homes.* In order to rule for respondents here, we would have to hold that the jurisdiction of the Corps extends to ponds that are not adjacent to open water. But we conclude that the text of the statute will not allow this.

We thus decline respondents' invitation to take what they see as the next ineluctable step after *Riverside Bayview Homes:* holding that isolated ponds, some only seasonal, wholly located within two Illinois counties, fall under § 404(a)'s definition of "navigable waters" because they serve as habitat for migratory birds. As counsel for respondents conceded at oral argument, such a ruling would assume that "the use of the word navigable in the statute ... does not have any independent significance." We cannot agree that Congress' separate definitional use of the phrase "waters of the United States" constitutes a basis for reading the term "navigable waters" out of the statute. We said in *Riverside Bayview Homes* that the word "navigable" in the statute was of "limited import" and went on to hold that § 404(a) extended to nonnavigable wetlands adjacent to open waters. But it is one thing to give a word limited effect and quite another to give it no effect whatever. The term "navigable" has at least the import of showing us what Congress had in mind as its authority for enacting the CWA: its traditional jurisdiction over waters that were or had been navigable in fact or which could reasonably be so made. *See, e.g., United States v. Appalachian Elec. Power Co.,* 311 U.S. 377, 407–408.

[W]e find nothing approaching a clear statement from Congress that it intended § 404(a) to reach an abandoned sand and gravel pit such as we have here. Permitting respondents to claim federal jurisdiction over ponds and mudflats falling within the "Migratory Bird Rule" would result in a significant impingement of the States' traditional and primary power over land and water use. We thus read the statute as written to avoid the significant constitutional and federalism questions raised by respondents' interpretation, and therefore reject the request for administrative deference.

We hold that 33 CFR § 328.3(a)(3) (1999), as clarified and applied to petitioner's balefill site pursuant to the "Migratory Bird Rule," 51 Fed. Reg. 41217 (1986), exceeds the authority granted to respondents under § 404(a) of the CWA. The judgment of the Court of Appeals for the Seventh Circuit is therefore
Reversed.

Justice STEVENS, with whom Justice SOUTER, Justice GINSBURG, and Justice BREYER join, dissenting.

Today the Court takes an unfortunate step that needlessly weakens our principal safeguard against toxic water.

It is fair to characterize the Clean Water Act as "watershed" legislation. The statute endorsed fundamental changes in both the purpose and the scope of federal regulation of the Nation's waters. In § 13 of the Rivers and Harbors Appropriation Act of 1899 (RHA) Congress had assigned to the Army Corps of Engineers (Corps) the mission of regulating discharges into certain waters in order to protect their use as highways for the transportation of interstate and foreign commerce; the scope of the Corps' jurisdiction under the RHA accordingly extended only to waters that were "navigable." In the CWA, however, Congress broadened the Corps' mission to include the purpose of protecting the quality of our Nation's waters for esthetic, health, recreational, and environmental uses. The scope of its jurisdiction was therefore redefined to encompass all of "the waters of the United States, including the territorial seas." § 1362(7). That definition requires neither actual nor potential navigability.

As we recognized in *Riverside Bayview*, the interests served by the statute embrace the protection of " 'significant natural biological functions, including food chain production, general habitat, and nesting, spawning, rearing and resting sites' " for various species of aquatic wildlife. 474 U.S., at 134–135. For wetlands and "isolated" inland lakes, that interest is equally powerful, regardless of the proximity of the swamp or the water to a navigable stream. Nothing in the text, the stated purposes, or the legislative history of the CWA supports the conclusion that in 1972 Congress contemplated—much less commanded—the odd jurisdictional line that the Court has drawn today.

Although it might have appeared problematic on a "linguistic" level for the Corps to classify "lands" as "waters" in *Riverside Bayview*, 474 U.S., at 131–132, we squarely held that the agency's construction of the statute that it was charged with enforcing was entitled to deference under *Chevron*. Today, however, the majority refuses to extend such deference to the same agency's construction of the same statute. This refusal is unfaithful to both *Riverside Bayview* and *Chevron*. For it is the majority's reading, not the agency's, that does violence to the scheme Congress chose to put into place.

Whether it is necessary or appropriate to refuse to allow petitioner to fill those ponds is a question on which we have no voice. Whether the Federal Government has the power to require such permission, however, is a question that is easily answered. If, as it does, the Commerce Clause empowers Congress to regulate particular "activities causing air or water pollution, or other environmental hazards that may have effects in more than one State," *Hodel*, 452 U.S., at 282, it also empowers Congress to control individual actions that, in the aggregate, would have the same effect. *Perez*, 402 U.S., at 154; *Wickard*, 317 U.S., at 127–128. There is no merit in petitioner's constitutional argument.

Because I would affirm the judgment of the Court of Appeals, I respectfully dissent.

*   *   *

John A. Rapanos, et ux., et al. v. United States
547 U.S. 714 (2006)

Justice SCALIA announced the judgment of the Court, and delivered an opinion in which THE CHIEF JUSTICE, Justice THOMAS, and Justice ALITO join.

In April 1989, petitioner John A. Rapanos backfilled wetlands on a parcel of land in Michigan that he owned and sought to develop. This parcel included 54 acres of land with sometimes-saturated soil conditions. The nearest body of navigable water was 11 to 20 miles away. Regulators had informed Mr. Rapanos that his saturated fields were "waters of the United States," 33 U.S.C. § 1362(7), that could not be filled without a permit. Twelve years of criminal and civil litigation ensued.

We need not decide the precise extent to which the qualifiers "navigable" and "of the United States" restrict the coverage of the Act. Whatever the scope of these qualifiers, the CWA authorizes federal jurisdiction only over "waters." 33 U.S.C. § 1362(7). The only natural definition of the term "waters," our prior and subsequent judicial constructions of it, clear evidence from other provisions of the statute, and this Court's canons of construction all confirm that "the waters of the United States" in § 1362(7) cannot bear the expansive meaning that the Corps would give it.

The Corps' expansive approach might be arguable if the CWA defined "navigable waters" as "water of the United States." But "the waters of the United States" is something else. The use of the definite article ("the") and the plural number ("waters") show plainly that § 1362(7) does not refer to water in general. In this form, "the waters" refers more narrowly to water "[a]s found in streams and bodies forming geographical features such as oceans, rivers, [and] lakes," or "the flowing or moving masses, as of waves or floods, making up such streams or bodies." Webster's New International Dictionary 2882 (2d ed.1954). On this definition, "the waters of the United States" include only relatively permanent, standing or flowing bodies of water. Even the least substantial of the definition's terms, namely "streams," connotes a continuous flow of water in a permanent channel—especially when used in company with other terms such as "rivers," "lakes," and "oceans." None of these terms encompasses transitory puddles or ephemeral flows of water.

Therefore, *only* those wetlands with a continuous surface connection to bodies that are "waters of the United States" in their own right, so that there is no clear demarcation between "waters" and wetlands, are "adjacent to" such waters and covered by the Act. Wetlands with only an intermittent, physically remote hydrologic connection to "waters of the United States" do not implicate the boundary-drawing problem of *Riverside Bayview*, and thus lack the necessary connection to covered waters that we described as a "significant nexus" in *SWANCC*. Thus, establishing that wetlands such as those at the Rapanos and Carabell sites are covered by the Act requires two findings: First, that the adjacent channel contains a "wate[r] of the United States," (*i.e.*, a relatively permanent body of water connected to traditional interstate navigable waters); and second, that the wetland has a continuous surface connection with that water, making it difficult to determine where the "water" ends and the "wetland" begins.

Kennedy, J., concurring in the judgment:

These consolidated cases require the Court to decide whether the term "navigable waters" in the Clean Water Act extends to wetlands that do not contain and are not adjacent to waters that are navigable in fact. In *SWANCC*, the Court held, under the circumstances presented there, that to constitute " 'navigable waters' " under the Act, a water or wetland must possess a "significant nexus" to waters that are or were navigable in fact or that could reasonably be so made. *Id.*, at 167, 172. In the instant cases neither the plurality opinion nor the dissent by Justice STEVENS chooses to apply this test; and though the Court of Appeals recognized the test's applicability, it did not consider all the factors necessary to determine whether the lands in question had, or did not have, the requisite nexus. In my view the cases ought to be remanded to the Court of Appeals for proper consideration of the nexus requirement.

The statutory term to be interpreted and applied in the two instant cases is the term "navigable waters." The outcome turns on whether that phrase reasonably describes certain Michigan wetlands the Corps seeks to regulate. Under the Act "[t]he term 'navigable waters' means the waters of the United States, including the territorial seas."§ 1362(7). In a regulation the Corps has construed the term "waters of the United States" to include not only waters susceptible to use in interstate commerce—the traditional understanding of the term "navigable waters of the United States," see, *e.g.*, *United States v. Appalachian Elec. Power Co.*, 311 U.S. 377, 406–408 (1940); *The Daniel Ball*, 10 Wall. 557, 563–564 (1871)—but also tributaries of those waters and, of particular relevance here, wetlands adjacent to those waters or their tributaries. 33 CFR §§ 328.3(a)(1), (5), (7) (2005). The Corps views tributaries as within its jurisdiction if they carry a perceptible "ordinary high water mark." § 328.4(c); 65 Fed.Reg. 12823 (2000). An ordinary high-water mark is a "line on the shore established by the fluctuations of water and indicated by physical characteristics such as clear, natural line impressed on the bank, shelving, changes in the character of soil, destruction of terrestrial vegetation, the presence of litter and debris, or other appropriate means that consider the characteristics of the surrounding areas." 33 CFR § 328.3(e).

Riverside Bayview and *SWANCC* establish the framework for the inquiry in the cases now before the Court: Do the Corps' regulations, as applied to the wetlands in *Carabell* and the three wetlands parcels in *Rapanos,* constitute a reasonable interpretation of "navigable waters" as in *Riverside Bayview* or an invalid construction as in *SWANCC?* Taken together these cases establish that in some instances, as exemplified by *Riverside Bayview,* the connection between a nonnavigable water or wetland and a navigable water may be so close, or potentially so close, that the Corps may deem the water or wetland a "navigable water" under the Act. In other instances, as exemplified by *SWANCC,* there may be little or no connection. Absent a significant nexus, jurisdiction under the Act is lacking.

When the Corps seeks to regulate wetlands adjacent to navigable-in-fact waters, it may rely on adjacency to establish its jurisdiction. Absent more specific regulations, however, the Corps must establish a significant nexus on a case-by-case basis when it seeks to regulate wetlands based on adjacency to nonnavigable tributaries. Given the potential overbreadth of the Corps' regulations, this showing is necessary to avoid unreasonable applications of the statute. Where an adequate nexus is established for a particular wetland, it may be permissible, as a matter of administrative convenience or necessity, to presume covered status for other comparable wetlands in the region. That issue, however, is neither raised by these facts nor addressed by any agency regulation that accommodates the nexus requirement outlined here.

In both the consolidated cases before the Court the record contains evidence suggesting the possible existence of a significant nexus according to the principles outlined above. Thus the end result in these cases and many others to be considered by the Corps may be the same as that suggested by the dissent, namely, that the Corps' assertion of jurisdiction is valid. Given, however, that neither the agency nor the reviewing courts properly considered the issue, a remand is appropriate, in my view, for application of the controlling legal standard.

* * *

b. Penalty Amounts

Even if the existence of a violation is conceded, the amount of the penalty may be hotly contested. The Enforcement Response Policy will be the primary source for negotiations. Counsel's arguments typically fall into two categories: interpretation of the penalty policy and factual circumstances. As you will see in Exercise 2 below, while the penalty policies try to be inclusive, there are many ambiguities. And even if you cannot establish a complete factual defense, even a small change in the circumstances EPA used to calculate the penalty may result in large reductions (e.g., if the violation ends up on a lower level of the matrix). Counsel also may spend a great deal of time trying to establish grounds for the "adjustment factors," because even a 10% adjustment for good faith or ability to pay may make a significant difference.

Because the statutes provide very little guidance on the appropriate penalty amount, courts and administrative law judges will be interested in citations to cases imposing penalties in similar circumstances. The EPA itself strives for uniformity in enforcement actions, so prior penalties can be very persuasive. In *United States v. Ekco Housewares, Inc.*, 62 F.3d 806, 815–817 (6th Cir. 1995), the court considered an appeal of a $4.6 million penalty for RCRA violations. The defendant argued that the penalty was disproportionate to other RCRA penalties and cited numerous cases. The court agreed that information about penalties imposed in other cases was relevant, but carefully distinguished between types of cases, noting that "[t]he reasonableness of a penalty ... is a fact-driven question, one that turns on the circumstances and events peculiar to the case at hand." *Id.* at 816. Administrative penalty cases, for example, would naturally involve lower penalty amounts than civil penalty actions, and the violation at issue presented more serious risks than some of the cases cited.

The EAB has cautioned that evidence of penalties imposed in other cases should rarely be considered by ALJs, due to concerns of judicial economy and the "uniqueness of the penalty inquiry." *ChemLab Products, Inc.*, FIFRA App. No. 02-01, 2002 EPA App. LEXIS 17 (EAB, Oct. 31, 2002). Nevertheless, the Board recognized that "there may be circumstances so compelling as to justify, despite judicial economy concerns and Supreme Court precedent affirming agency penalty discretion, our review of other allegedly similar cases." *Id.* *See also In the Matter of Service Oil, Inc.*, 2006 WL 3406348 (allowing discovery on penalties in other cases).

Exercise 2: Agra Enterprises—EPCRA[68]

Background: In this exercise, an explosion has occurred at a pesticide repackaging facility, Agra Enterprises. Agra did not notify the proper emergency response authorities and, it turns out, did not have the proper reports on file concerning the types and amounts of chemicals at the facility. After an investigation, EPA officials decide to bring an administrative penalty action against Agra. As an attorney for either Agra or the EPA, you will investigate the case, research possible defenses, and attempt to negotiate a settlement of the penalty. First, however, you need some background on the law.

---

68. The authors thank Professors Lee Breckenridge and Maria Savasta-Kennedy for helpful comments on earlier versions of this exercise.

The Emergency Planning and Community Right-to-Know Act: Many federal environmental laws have been inspired by high-profile environmental disasters. In 1986, Congress enacted the Emergency Planning and Community Right-to-Know Act (EPCRA), 42 U.S.C. § 11001 *et seq.*, as a response to the 1984 Union Carbide pesticide plant explosion in Bhopal, India.[69] A leak from a tank of methyl isocyanate released a toxic gas that killed at least 3800 people and injured many more. To help avoid such disasters, EPCRA attempts to ensure that every community is aware of the dangerous chemicals being used or stored there and that they are prepared in the event of an emergency.

Although the Act is shorter than most environmental legislation, the variety of obligations it imposes can become confusing in a hurry. The key is to recognize that there are four separate requirements, each imposed on different subsets of facilities: planning notification, emergency notification, inventory reporting, and release reporting.

Planning Notification: The first obligation applies only to facilities that have chemicals classified as Extremely Hazardous Substances (EHS). Each of the EHS chemicals has a Threshold Planning Quantity (TPQ). If a facility, at any time, has a quantity of an EHS on hand in excess of the TPQ, Section 302 ("planning notification") requires the facility to notify state and local emergency planning groups and to participate in formulating emergency plans. 42 U.S.C. § 11002.

Emergency Notification: In the event of a release of any of the EHS chemicals in excess of certain amounts (called "Reportable Quantities"),[70] Section 304 requires the facility to notify the state and local emergency coordinators. 42 U.S.C. § 11004. This "emergency notification" is also required for releases of chemicals listed as hazardous under CERCLA Section 102.

Inventory Reporting: Another, much broader, group of chemicals is covered under the inventory reporting requirements of Sections 311 and 312. These sections cover any chemical for which the facility is required, under the Occupational Safety and Health Act (OSHA), to prepare or maintain a Material Safety Data Sheet (MSDS). If the chemical is stored in excess

---

69. Because EPCRA was enacted as part of the Superfund Amendments and Reauthorization Act of 1986, it is sometimes called SARA Title III.

70. Pay close attention to these different threshold triggers: the TPQ is the amount of the chemical stored, while the RQ is the amount released, which will be a much smaller amount.

of certain threshold quantities, the facility must provide the MSDS sheets (or a list and description of the chemicals) and a yearly inventory of the chemicals to the state and local emergency authorities and to the local fire department. 42 U.S.C. § 11021–22.

Release Reporting: Yet another list of chemicals, designated as "toxic," is covered by Section 313, 42 U.S.C. § 11023. Under this section, a facility that manufactures, processes, or otherwise uses one of these chemicals in excess of threshold quantities must report each year on the amount of the chemical entering each environmental medium (i.e., released to air, water, or land). These amounts are entered into a public database called the Toxic Release Inventory[71] and the annual results are often reported in the media. Note that these are not, for the most part, accidental releases, but planned and permitted releases of chemicals through air emissions, wastewater discharges, or land disposal.

In sum, the Planning Notification and Inventory Reporting requirements focus on the storage of chemicals, while the Emergency Notification and Release Reporting requirements focus on chemicals entering the environment. Once you have read these statutory provisions, along with their implementing regulations, you are ready to participate in an EPCRA enforcement case.

In re Agra Enterprises:[72] Agra Enterprises, Inc. ("Agra") is a chemical packaging plant, which distributes agricultural pesticides and fertilizers. The plant is located in Paradise, Missouri, a town of 15,000 residents. Agra's parent company, Megra, Inc., headquartered in New Jersey, built the facility in 2002.

Agra repackages agricultural chemicals, which it receives from manufacturers in large bulk quantities, into smaller packages for sale to retail outlets. Repackaging is done in a 20,000 square foot building at the Agra site,

---

71. *See* www.epa.gov/TRI.

72. This problem is modeled on an actual case, the fire and explosion at the BPS facility in West Helena, Arkansas, in May 1997. For more information on that event, see "3 Firefighters Die in Arkansas Chemical Blast," New York Times, May 9, 1997, at A19. Many of the facts have been changed, however, and no representations regarding the BPS case are intended. Unfortunately, this type of accident is fairly common. Some recent examples include explosions at ConAgra Foods (2 killed; June 9, 2009, Garner, North Carolina); T2 Lab (4 killed; Dec. 19, 2007, Jacksonville, Florida); and Synthron, Inc. (14 injured; Jan. 31, 2006, Morgantown, North Carolina).

which is in an industrial corridor near a highway and railroad tracks. The Agra site also contains a storage warehouse and a small office building.

On Thursday, May 9, 2009, about 1:00 p.m., workers unloading a container of pesticide noticed a yellowish-green smoke coming from the repackaging building. Alarms sounded and the entire plant was evacuated. Management called the fire department at 1:10 p.m. and firefighters responded immediately. At approximately 1:30 p.m., as firefighters entered the building, a massive explosion occurred. Three firefighters were crushed and killed by the collapse of a cinder block wall.

Although none of the chemicals stored at the plant is normally flammable, extreme heat can cause one of the chemicals—azinphos-methyl,[73] a pesticide used to fight biting and sucking insects in orchards—to become flammable or explode. EPA officials believe that the fire started in a 300-pound container used to ship bulk chemicals to the plant. The container was nearly empty at the time and contained some waste paper. The fire was probably started by a dock worker discarding an unextinguished cigarette into the container. By the time firefighters arrived, the fire had reached an area containing full chemical drums and had become hot enough to cause the azinphos-methyl to explode.

Fumes from the plant spread to the northeast, a primarily agricultural area in which few houses are located. The Missouri Department of Public Health conducted air monitoring and determined that the fumes contained azinphos-methyl. Several individuals who live nearby were treated at a local clinic for headaches and nausea. A school in the vicinity was evacuated before fumes impacted it. Although the fire was brought under control within twelve hours, smoldering, which emitted mildly toxic fumes, continued at the plant for three days. Officials believe that another chemical present at the site, maneb, caused the smoldering. Maneb is a fungicide used to prevent crop damage and deterioration in harvested crops; it is moderately toxic to humans and is water reactive. The Material Safety Data Sheets for both chemicals, obtained from Agra files, are included in Appendix B at the end of this book.

The local emergency planning committee (LEPC) and the state emergency response commission (SERC) state that Agra filed an emergency planning

---

73. EPA issued a registration cancellation order in 2008 that phases out all uses of azinphos-methyl by 2012. 73 Fed. Reg. 9328 (Feb. 12, 2008). However, the chemical may still be manufactured in the U.S. for use abroad.

notification under EPCRA Section 302 and MSDS sheets for azinphosmethyl and maneb in 2002. The company also filed inventory reports covering the years 2002, 2003 and 2004. As of May 2009, however, the company had not filed any reports or inventory records with either the LEPC or SERC for the past four years. In November 2007, the LEPC sent a letter notifying Agra that it had not received the inventory reports for 2005 or 2006 (see Figure 2.5).

In addition, the LEPC and SERC state that they were not notified of the fire until 2 p.m. At that time, the local fire department dispatcher called both agencies. Agra itself did not notify the LEPC or SERC of the emergency and has not yet filed a written follow-up report.

Warren County Emergency Planning Commission
125 B Street
Paradise, Mo. 64234
(573) 555-HELP

November 6, 2007

Manager
Agra Enterprises, Inc.
400 Industrial Boulevard
Paradise, MO 64234

Dear Manager:

The Warren County Emergency Planning Commission has been established under Section 301 of the federal Emergency Planning and Community Right-to-Know Act, 42 U.S.C. § 11001. Under this law, companies that store hazardous chemicals in excess of certain quantities are required to file annual reports with the Commission and to cooperate in emergency planning activity.

It has come to our attention that you may qualify as a regulated entity under this Act. We have not received an inventory report from your facility covering the years 2005 (report due Feb. 2006) or 2006 (report due Feb. 2007). If your inventory exceeded the applicable threshold levels for those years, you are out of compliance with EPCRA Section 312 and could be subject to significant penalties. Please take steps immediately to comply with this federal law. Seek legal guidance if you have any questions, or call us for additional information.

Sincerely,

Paul Doucette
Chairman

Figure 2.5 EPCRA Working Letter.

The following exercises will take you through some of the steps in a typical environmental enforcement case, including fact investigation, administrative procedure, and settlement negotiations. Half of the class will be assigned to play the role of a staff attorney with EPA Region VII in Kansas City, Kansas. The other half of the class will represent Agra Enterprises, Inc.

Exercise 2.1: Fact Investigation

The first step in the process is fact investigation. Although the police and EPA staff may have conducted preliminary inquiries, this will be a formal interview by counsel. Each attorney will interview Paul Johnson, the Agra plant manager at the time of the explosion. In real life the Agra attorney would conduct an investigation in private and would not interview an Agra employee in front of the EPA attorney. However, your professor may want you to conduct the interview with both counsel present in order to make the exercise work. Your professor will provide the witness with the necessary information.

Note that Rule 4.2, Model Rules of Professional Conduct, prohibits an attorney from communicating with a party known to be represented by counsel without that counsel's consent. May EPA's attorney interview Johnson without the consent of Agra's counsel?[74] Are company employees considered "the party" represented by Agra counsel? A managerial employee such as Johnson should be covered by the ex parte prohibition, but would it apply to the dock worker who threw the cigarette that started the fire? See Smith v. Kansas City Southern Ry. Co., 87 S.W.3d 266, 272 (Mo. App. 2002) *(Prohibition applies to: (1) persons having managerial responsibility on behalf of the organization; (2) persons whose act or omission in connection with the matter may be imputed to the organization for purposes of civil or criminal liability; and (3) persons whose statement may constitute an admission on the part of the organization).[75]*

*You should do background research on the statute and regulations to determine what questions you need to ask to establish whether a violation of EPCRA has occurred. Consider **only** violations of EPCRA 304 and 311–312. Do not con-*

---

74. EPA has limited authority to subpoena witnesses for depositions once an administrtive complaint has been filed. See 42 U.S.C. § 11045(f)(2); 40 C.F.R. § 22.19(e)(3).

75. Other jurisdictions apply the prohibition to all employees of the company, while some apply it more narrowly only to the management "control group."

sider potential violations of EPCRA 302, 313 or other environmental acts. Assume that you are investigating shortly after the accident in 2009.

Practice Tip: Legal Interviewing

Learning how to ask the right questions to elicit information is an important skill for lawyers to master. In law school, you most often get "canned" facts—you read appellate court opinions in which the facts are a given, or answer hypotheticals where the professor gives you the facts. In real life, of course, the "facts" are often contradictory or vague and must be unearthed through the investigative process.

Before you interview the witness in this case, you may want to consult some resources on legal interviewing techniques. *See, e.g.,* Robert M. Bastress and Joseph D. Harbaugh, *Interviewing, Counseling, and Negotiating: Skills for Effective Representation* (Aspen 1990). Helpful techniques include the "funnel" approach: using open-ended questions to generate broad, general information, and then following up with narrow questions to nail down specific facts. If the questioner asks only narrow questions, such as: "Did you have azinphos-methyl in 2008?", he or she runs the risk of missing important information (such as "well, not azinphos, but we had cyanide acid"). On the other hand, using only open-ended questions, such as: "Tell me what chemicals you had in 2008?" runs the risk of failing to find out important details. Keep in mind that the witness has little or no idea, usually, what might be relevant to the legal question involved and may have been instructed not to volunteer information. Thus, you must ask enough general questions to elicit all information that might be relevant, and then ask narrow follow-up questions to focus the inquiry on the relevant details.

Exercise 2.2: Drafting the Administrative Complaint

Based on the above interview and an inspection, the EPA has decided to take enforcement action against Agra Enterprises. EPA attorneys should draft an administrative complaint detailing the violations you allege to have occurred. Again, consider only Sections 304 and 311–12. Assume you are drafting this complaint to be filed October 1, 2009. You should follow the model of the GE Precision complaint in Appendix A (although it is a Section 313 complaint, so should be modified accordingly). In addition to the substantive law— statutes, regulations, and case law—each side should consider how to apply

EPA's enforcement response policy to this case. You should be able to access the EPCRA enforcement response policy on EPA's web site (www.epa.gov). Other EPA policy documents may also apply, but to simplify the problem, consider only the EPCRA enforcement response policy. If you have any trouble locating the policy on the web, remember that EPA's Office of Enforcement and Compliance Assistance (OECA) has responsibility for enforcement activity.

Exercise 2.3: Settlement Negotiation

Every administrative complaint must provide the defendant with the opportunity for a settlement conference. See App. A, para. 41–44. After researching the problem, the EPA and Agra attorneys should meet to determine whether a settlement can be reached in the case. Before the conference, the EPA attorney should provide Agra's counsel with a proposed penalty calculation, using the penalty worksheet provided on the last page of EPA's EPCRA enforcement response policy. The case is set for an administrative hearing two weeks after the date of the settlement conference, so if no settlement can be worked out, your alternative is to proceed before an administrative law judge. Your negotiating position should be based on all of the sources of law we have studied thus far, and you should consider whether Agra has any defenses in the categories outlined in Section II. D.1(a) above.

CHAPTER III

CITIZEN SUIT ENFORCEMENT

Another mechanism for enforcing environmental laws is the citizen suit. Many of the federal environmental acts contain specific authority for an ordinary citizen to bring a lawsuit against a violator for injunctive relief and/or penalties. *See, e.g.,* CWA §505, 33 U.S.C. §1365; CAA §304, 42 U.S.C. §7604; RCRA §7002, 42 U.S.C. §6972. Some states have similar statutes for enforcing state environmental laws.[1] Any penalties imposed in a federal citizen suit will go to the U.S. Treasury—the individual plaintiff does not receive damages, but may be reimbursed for litigation costs. The idea behind citizen suit provisions is to bolster the resources of the government enforcement authorities by, in effect, deputizing a host of "private attorneys general." In most cases, citizen suits have been brought by environmental interest groups rather than individual citizens, presumably because such groups have greater resources.

Citizen suits differ from agency enforcement cases in many particulars. This chapter will take you through the stages of a citizen suit, using problems and exercises to explore these special issues.

A. Information Gathering

Assume your client suspects that the paint factory downwind from where she lives is violating the Clean Air Act by illegally spewing toxic fumes into the air. How can you find information on the facility's compliance record? How can you obtain enough proof to establish a violation?

One of the toughest issues facing would-be citizen suit plaintiffs is how to obtain information on possible environmental violations. Unlike government agencies, the citizen suit plaintiff cannot rely on statutory subpoena or inspection powers. If the EPA sends a company a "request for information," it is

---

1. *See, e.g.,* Cal. Health and Safety Code §25249.7(d) (citizen suit for drinking water contamination); 32 Pa. Stat. §680.15 (citizen suit for stormwater management violations).

likely to be answered quickly and completely, while a similar request from a private individual or citizen's group will probably be ignored.

Nevertheless, there are several good sources of information that can provide the basis for citizen enforcement. The first place to start would be the agency files on your target company. Many environmental statutes require the regulated entity to monitor itself. For example, the Clean Water Act requires permitted point sources to maintain and file Discharge Monitoring Reports (DMRs) that indicate the level of regulated pollutants (such as total suspended solids or the pH level) in effluent samples. These records should be on file with the agency and are available now in online databases. See Practice Tip: On-line Databases, below. Thus, the company's own records contained in the agency's files may establish violations of its permit which the agency has decided not to pursue.[2]

Figures 3.1 and 3.2 show two pages from an actual NPDES Permit for IBP, Inc., a meat-packing plant in Perry, Iowa, discharging from an industrial wastewater treatment unit into the Raccoon River. The first page (Figure 3.1) gives both daily maximum and monthly average effluent limitations for each pollutant. Why both? Can you guess why ammonia nitrogen limitations are different for certain months? Why is the fecal coliform limit more stringent in summer than winter? Why does the permit set both concentration and mass limits for each pollutant? The next page of the permit (3.2) specifies monitoring requirements, which tell IBP how often it must test for each parameter and where the sample should be taken. As you can see, some samples must be taken daily, while others are taken only once a month.

The permit's effluent limitations are based on regulations establishing the best technology limits for this category of industry, if EPA has promulgated them. If EPA has not established technology-based limits for a particular industry or a particular pollutant, the effluent limitations are based on the Best Professional Judgment of the permit issuer. If the discharge is entering a water that is not meeting Water Quality Standards (WQS), or if the discharge will cause a violation of the WQS, the limits are based on the agency's calculation of what levels are necessary to "contribute to the attainment or maintenance" of WQS. CWA § 302, 33 U.S.C. § 1312 (water-quality related effluent limitations).

Figure 3.3 shows the monthly Discharge Monitoring Report for the same IBP plant for March 1998. Does it show any violations?

---

2. Of course, you may believe that the company is falsifying the information contained in these required reports. Proving it may be difficult, however. Citizens may gather their own wastewater data from sampling at the discharge point, for example, to determine whether the discharger's data are accurate, but do not have access to the company's treatment facilities as the agency would.

Facility Name: IBP, INC. - PERRY
Permit Number: 2500100
OUTFALL NO.: 001 OUTFALL FROM ACTIVATED BIO-FILTER. EXTENDED AERATION INDUSTRIAL WWTP.

Effluent Limitations

Page 3

You are prohibited from discharging pollutants except in compliance with the following effluent limitations:

Wastewater Parameter	Season/Type	EFFLUENT LIMITATIONS							
		Concentration				Mass			
		7 Day Average	30 Day Average	Daily Maximum	Units	7 Day Average	30 Day Average	Daily Maximum	Units
FLOW	YEARLY/FINAL		.1200	2.5000	MGD				
BIOCHEMICAL OXYGEN DEMAND (BOD5)	YEARLY/FINAL		40.0000	80.0000	MG/L		399.00	798.00	LBS/DAY
TOTAL SUSPENDED SOLIDS	YEARLY/FINAL		47.0000	95.0000	MG/L		475.00	950.00	LBS/DAY
AMMONIA NITROGEN (N)	JAN/FINAL		7.1000	12.0000	MG/L		144.00	248.00	LBS/DAY
AMMONIA NITROGEN (N)	FEB/FINAL		7.1000	12.0000	MG/L		144.00	248.00	LBS/DAY
AMMONIA NITROGEN (N)	MAR/FINAL		3.0000	5.2000	MG/L		62.00	106.00	LBS/DAY
AMMONIA NITROGEN (N)	APR/FINAL		3.0000	5.2000	MG/L		62.00	106.00	LBS/DAY
AMMONIA NITROGEN (N)	MAY/FINAL		3.0000	5.2000	MG/L		62.00	106.00	LBS/DAY
AMMONIA NITROGEN (N)	JUN/FINAL		3.0000	5.2000	MG/L		62.00	106.00	LBS/DAY
AMMONIA NITROGEN (N)	JUL/FINAL		3.2000	5.4000	MG/L		64.00	110.00	LBS/DAY
AMMONIA NITROGEN (N)	AUG/FINAL		3.2000	5.4000	MG/L		64.00	110.00	LBS/DAY
AMMONIA NITROGEN (N)	SEP/FINAL		3.0000	5.2000	MG/L		62.00	106.00	LBS/DAY
AMMONIA NITROGEN (N)	OCT/FINAL		3.0000	5.2000	MG/L		62.00	106.00	LBS/DAY
AMMONIA NITROGEN (N)	NOV/FINAL		3.0000	5.2000	MG/L		62.00	106.00	LBS/DAY
AMMONIA NITROGEN (N)	DEC/FINAL		3.0000	5.2000	MG/L		62.00	106.00	LBS/DAY
PH (MINIMUM - MAXIMUM)	YEARLY/FINAL	6.0000		9.0000	STD UNITS				
CHLORINE, TOTAL RESIDUAL	YEARLY/FINAL		.0290	.0430	MG/L			.81	LBS/DAY
COLIFORM,FECAL	SUMMER/FINAL			1200.0000	MPN/100M				
COLIFORM,FECAL	WINTER/FINAL			400.0000	MPN/100M				
OIL AND GREASE	YEAR-Y/N/A		15.0000	30.0000	MG/L		152.00	304.00	LBS/DAY
ACUTE TOXICITY, CERIODAPHNIA	YEARLY/FINAL						1.00	1.00	NON TOXIC
ACUTE TOXICITY, PIMEPHALES	YEARLY/FINAL						1.00	1.00	NON TOXIC

NOTE: If seasonal limits apply, summer is from April 1 through October 31, and winter is from November 1 through March 31.

Figure 3.1 NPDES Permit.

Practice Tip: On-Line Databases

The internet is now a fruitful source of monitoring data, which can provide the preliminary information needed to prove environmental violations. Among the most useful sites:

Facility Name: IBP, INC - PERRY

Permit Number: 2500100

Page 4

Monitoring and Reporting Requirements

(a) Samples and measurements taken shall be representative of the volume and nature of the monitored wastewater.

(b) Analytical and sampling methods as specified in 40 CFR Part 136 or Table VII of Chapter 63 of the rules, or other methods approved in writing by the department, shall be utilized.

(c) Chapter 63 of the rules provides you with further explanation of your monitoring requirements.

(d) You are required to report all data including calculated results needed to determine compliance with the limitations contained in this permit. This includes daily maximums and minimums, 30-day averages and 7-day averages for all parameters that have concentration (mg/l) and mass (lbs/day) limits. Also flow data shall be reported in million gallons per day (MGD).

Results of all monitoring shall be recorded on forms provided by the department and submitted to the department by the fifteenth day following the close of the reporting period. Your reporting period is on a monthly basis, ending on the last day of each month.

Outfall Number	Wastewater Parameter	Sample Frequency	Sample Type	Monitoring Location
001	FLOW	7/WEEK	24 HR TOTAL	FINAL EFFLUENT
001	FLOW	7/WEEK	24 HR TOTAL	WASTEWATER FLOW FROM THE ABS TOWER
001	FLOW	7/WEEK	24 HR TOTAL	WASTE DIGESTED SLUDGE TO DISPOSAL
001	FLOW	7/WEEK	24 HR TOTAL	WASTE ACTIVATED SLUDGE
001	FLOW	7/WEEK	24 HR TOTAL	RETURN ACTIVATED SLUDGE
001	FLOW	7/WEEK	24 HR TOTAL	HOLDING POND EFFLUENT (WHEN DISCHARGING)
001	BIOCHEMICAL OXYGEN DEMAND (BOD5)	4/WEEK	24 HR COMP	RAW WASTE
001	BIOCHEMICAL OXYGEN DEMAND (BOD5)	4/WEEK	24 HR COMP	EFFLUENT PRIOR TO DISINFECTION
001	BIOCHEMICAL OXYGEN DEMAND (BOD5)	4/WEEK	24 HR COMP	HOLDING POND EFFLUENT (WHEN DISCHARGING)
001	TOTAL SUSPENDED SOLIDS	4/WEEK	24 HR COMP	RAW WASTE
001	TOTAL SUSPENDED SOLIDS	4/WEEK	24 HR COMP	EFFLUENT AFTER DISINFECTION
001	TOTAL SUSPENDED SOLIDS	4/WEEK	24 HR COMP	HOLDING POND EFFLUENT (WHEN DISCHARGING)
001	AMMONIA NITROGEN (N)	4/WEEK	24 HR COMP	EFFLUENT AFTER DISINFECTION
001	AMMONIA NITROGEN (N)	1/MONTH	24 HR COMP	WASTEWATER FROM THE ABS TOWER
001	AMMONIA NITROGEN (N)	1/MONTH	24 HR COMP	DIGESTER CLARIFIER OVERFLOW
001	AMMONIA NITROGEN (N)	4/WEEK	24 HR COMP	HOLDING POND EFFLUENT (WHEN DISCHARGING)
001	PH (MINIMUM - MAXIMUM)	5/WEEK	GRAB	RAW WASTE
001	PH (MINIMUM - MAXIMUM)	5/WEEK	GRAB	EFFLUENT AFTER DISINFECTION
001	PH (MINIMUM - MAXIMUM)	5/WEEK	GRAB	DIGESTER CONTENTS
001	PH (MINIMUM - MAXIMUM)	1/WEEK	GRAB	DIGESTER CLARIFIER OVERFLOW
001	PH (MINIMUM - MAXIMUM)	5/WEEK	GRAB	WASTE DIGESTED SLUDGE TO DISPOSAL

Figure 3.2 NPDES Permit.

EnviroFacts <www.epa.gov/enviro>: EPA offers a single access point for databases covering air, water, and land pollution. By entering a city, county, or zipcode, you can pull up a map locating the area sources of air pollution, wastewater discharges, and hazardous waste. Some detailed compliance information (e.g., NPDES permit sampling) can be accessed.

I.B.P.inc

OPERATION PERMIT SYSTEM
MONTHLY MONITORING REPORT
MONTH: March 1996

FACILITY NO 2501000
DISCHARGE NUMBER 001

*** TOTAL PLANT DISCHARGE TO THE RIVER - OUTFALL 001 ***

	FLOW MGD	BOD mg/L	BOD lbs	TSS mg/L	TSS lbs	NH3-N mg/L	NH3-N lbs	Oil & Grease mg/L	Oil & Grease lbs	Res. Cl2 mg/L	Res Cl2 lbs	Fecal Coli n/100ml
Monthly Ave Std Limits	1.2000	40	399	47	475	3.0	62	15	152	0.029	0.54	200
Maximum Daily Std Limits	2.5000	80	798	85	850	5.2	106	30	304	0.043	0.81	
1 Sun	0.624											
2 Mon	0.785	12	79	24	157	0.34	2			0.020 <	0.13	
3 Tue	1.047	14	122	33	288	0.14	1			0.020 <	0.17	
4 Wed	1.063	12	109	31	263	0.12	1			0.020 <	0.16	
5 Thu	1.066	14	127	26	235	0.22	2			0.020 <	0.18	
6 Fri	1.110							2	19	0.020 <	0.19	
7 Sat	0.728											
8 Sun	0.643											
9 Mon	0.483	47	163	64	263	0.53	2			0.020 <	0.06	
10 Tue	0.681	33	187	53	301	1.56	9			0.020 <	0.11	
11 Wed	0.772	16	103	29	187	0.13	1			0.020 <	0.13	
12 Thu	0.853	17	121	31	221	0.07	0			0.020 <	0.14	
13 Fri	0.866									0.020 <	0.17	
14 Sat	0.868											
15 Sun	0.719											
16 Mon	0.825	22	151	48	330	0.41	3			0.020 <	0.14	
17 Tue	0.666	16	153	7	57	0.38	3			0.020 <	0.16	
18 Wed	0.666	19	158	26	218	0.47	4			0.020 <	0.17	
19 Thu	1.025	17	145	34	291	0.36	3			0.020 <	0.17	TL
20 Fri	1.049									0.020 <	0.17	
21 Sat	0.669											
22 Sun	0.598											
23 Mon	0.663	12	66	192	1110	0.33	2			0.020 <	0.12	
24 Tue	0.820	12	82	13	89	0.33	2			0.020 <	0.14	
25 Wed	0.939	12	94	24	158	0.53	4	4	31	0.020 <	0.16	
26 Thu	0.962	11	88	19	152	0.38	3			0.020 <	0.16	
27 Fri	0.997							28	233	0.020 <	0.17	
28 Sat	0.667											
29 Sun	0.578											
30 Mon	0.712	12	71	32	190	0.39	2			0.020 <	0.12	
31 Tue	0.780	12	78	32	208	0.12	1	4	26	0.020 <	0.13	
Total	25.866	313	2133	718	4765	6.83	46	38	308	0.440	3.26	
AVG	0.835	17	118	18	265	0.38	3	10	77	0.020	0.15	
MAX	1.110	47	193	192	1110	1.56	9	28	233	0.020	0.19	
MIN	0.483	11	66	7	57	0.07	0	2	19	0.000	0.08	

TL - Test Lost

Signature of Executive Officer _[signature: Mike ____]_   Title PLANT MANAGER

C/413/96

Figure 3.3 Discharge Monitoring Report.

Enforcement and Compliance History Online (ECHO) <www.epa-echo.gov>: EPA database allowing public access to permit, inspection, violation, enforcement action, and penalty information covering the past three years.

STORET <www.epa.gov/storet/>: this EPA database collects water quality monitoring data from a variety of sources, including state agencies and watershed groups. If you suspect an unpermitted discharge, the water quality data may help you confirm it.

National Water Information System (NWIS) <*http://waterdata.usgs.gov/ nwis/*>: USGS maintains chemical and physical water quality data for streams, rivers, lakes and groundwater.

Note: the information in these databases may not always be completely accurate and in any case must be followed up by obtaining the actual permit and monitoring documents through a FOIA or discovery request, or a visit to the agency records department.

For practice, try to find online a NPDES permit from your hometown, figure out what parameters are required to be monitored, and determine if the discharger is "in compliance."

Subject to some exceptions, the EPA's records are public information, which any citizen is entitled to access pursuant to the Freedom of Information Act (FOIA), 5 U.S.C. § 552. In addition to FOIA, some environmental statutes also require disclosure of information. *See, e.g.,* Clean Water Act Section 308(b), 33 U.S.C. § 1318(b).[3] If you are looking for state records, of course, you will need to rely on the state version of FOIA. *See, e.g.,* Iowa Code § 22.2.[4]

Making a FOIA request is fairly simple: the Act requires only that you "reasonably describe[ ] such records" and pay a fee for the costs of the document search and duplication of the records. 5 U.S.C. § 552 (a)(3), (4)(ii).[5] Although the scope of the disclosure duty is quite broad, some matters are exempt from disclosure and the application of these exemptions can be the subject of dispute and litigation. Included are exemptions for documents that contain trade secrets, privileged inter-agency or intra-agency memoranda, and law enforcement records the disclosure of which would interfere with enforcement proceedings. 5 U.S.C. § 552(b). Note that the law enforcement records ex-

---

3. *See Gersh & Danielson v. E.P.A.,* 871 F. Supp. 407 (D. Colo. 1994) (specific disclosure provision of Clean Water Act Section 308 prevails over FOIA).

4. In many states, you may be able to simply visit the state agency, ask to see the regulated entity's file and make copies of it. You should follow up with a formal written request, however, to ensure that you have everything.

5. The fee may be waived if disclosure would "contribute significantly to public understanding" and is not "primarily in the commercial interest of the requester." 5 U.S.C. § 552(a)(4)(A). Because the request may involve many hours of search time and substantial duplication charges, qualifying for this waiver provision can be very important for a public interest requester.

emption applies not only to criminal cases, but also to administrative enforcement proceedings, and therefore could arise quite often in the environmental context. *See, e.g., Cohen v. E.P.A.,* 575 F. Supp. 425 (D.D.C. 1983) (EPA withheld identity of recipients of notice letters at CERCLA cleanup site, citing enforcement concerns). If EPA believes an exemption applies, it is required to provide the requester with a so-called "Vaughn index," which lists each document withheld and the justification for the exemption. *Judicial Watch, Inc. v. FDA,* 449 F.3d 141, 146 (D.C. Cir. 2006).

Practice Tip: Protecting Confidential Information

When dealing with a governmental agency, counsel must constantly keep in mind that anything you submit to the government, such as reports, correspondence, even e-mail, will find its way to a file that may be accessed by the public. In other types of litigation, if you write a letter to opposing counsel, you may assume that it won't be disclosed under normal circumstances. But if you write the same letter to an EPA attorney, that letter may be disclosed (unless it falls under an exemption) and end up on the front page of the newspaper. Therefore, you should keep the possibility of disclosure in mind when drafting all communications with the agency.

Similarly, reports or data a company is required to submit may contain highly confidential information about products or finances. The disclosure laws allow entities to protect "trade secret" information. *See, e.g.,* CWA § 308(b), 33 U.S.C. § 1318(b). FOIA also exempts from disclosure trade secrets and other Confidential Business Information (CBI). 5 U.S.C. § 552(b)(4). Therefore, you should be vigilant in identifying such information as it is submitted. To assert confidentiality, the company is simply required to stamp the words "confidential" or "proprietary" on the document or on a cover sheet attached to the document. If only portions are confidential, they should be marked as such or submitted separately. 40 CFR § 2.203(b).

If information claimed to be CBI is the subject of a FOIA request, the company will be required to substantiate its confidentiality claim, and EPA will refuse to release it if disclosure would be "likely to cause substantial harm to the business's competitive position." 40 CFR § 2.208(e)(1) (criteria for confidentiality determinations).

Delay can be a problem in obtaining records through a FOIA request. FOIA requires the agency to determine whether it will comply with an information request within twenty working days after receiving it. 5 U.S.C. §552(a)(6)(A). The twenty-day limit can be extended in exceptional circumstances, however, as long as the agency is exercising due diligence in responding to the request. *But see Matlack, Inc. v. United States*, 868 F. Supp. 627 (D. Del. 1994) ("bald assertion" that the EPA had large docket of FOIA requests was not sufficient to demonstrate exceptional circumstances). Moreover, this time limit applies only to notifying the requester of the agency's response; the agency does not have to actually release the documents in that time. Although the documents are to be made "promptly available" under the statute, the agency may be able to justify a delay. *Strout v. U.S. Parole Comm.*, 40 F.3d 136 (6th Cir. 1994) (four-month delay reasonable where file unavailable to regional office).

It is very difficult to obtain information directly from the alleged violator. After suit is filed, of course, normal discovery rules allow the citizen suit plaintiff to obtain documents and may permit inspections of the defendant's premises, including sampling and testing. *See* Rule 34, Fed. R. Civ. P. But until you have adequate information to support a claim of violation, you can't file suit. How sure do you have to be? *See* Rule 11, Fed. R. Civ. P. Before suit is filed, is there any way for a private citizen to obtain information or to conduct an inspection, based only on a suspicion that something is wrong?

The exercises in this chapter, based on the following fact pattern, will take you through some of the issues that arise in citizen suit enforcement litigation:

Exercise 3: Citizen Enforcement of the Clean Water Act: Pork Unlimited

Pork Unlimited (PU), a meat processing facility in Leesburg, Minnesota, processes about 7000 hogs per day. Wastewater from the processing plant passes through a dissolved air flotation unit to remove some solids and then is discharged into a storage lagoon, where additional settling occurs. Periodically, this wastewater is discharged into the North Fork River, a tributary of the Mississippi.

The state environmental agency, the Minnesota Pollution Control Authority (MPCA),[6] has issued PU a NPDES permit for this discharge, pursuant to its delegated authority under the Clean Water Act. The permit contains effluent limitations identical to the IBP Permit in Figure 3.1. The

---

6. Note that the use of MPCA in this exercise is entirely hypothetical and is not intended to represent the actual activity or opinions of the agency.

monthly discharge monitoring reports for this facility indicate violations for two effluent parameters. The company violated the monthly average ammonia nitrogen limitations in May, July, and September 2008, and in the same months of 2009. In addition, it violated the fecal coliform daily limit six times during June and July 2009. An agency inspection report attributed these pathogen violations to a mechanical breakdown in the disinfection unit, which was replaced in August 2009.

The MPCA issued Notices of Violation for each of the ammonia nitrogen violations noted. In addition, in October 2009 the MPCA issued an Administrative Order directing PU to come into compliance with its NPDES permit and assessing an administrative penalty of $200 for each of six ammonia violations, for a total of $1200.

The Minnesota Environmental Coalition (MEC), a citizens group with members all over the state, believes that MPCA has not adequately enforced the permit. The MEC members have noticed dead fish and foul odor in the North Fork, downstream from the PU plant, on several occasions. The group believes that PU's waste treatment system is wholly inadequate to properly treat the effluent and that MPCA does not want to force the plant to upgrade because the Governor is afraid the plant will simply close down and move to a nearby state with less stringent standards.

Exercise 3.1: Information Request

Assume the MEC Board of Directors has authorized you to investigate whether action should be initiated against PU. Draft an information request to the MPCA under the Minnesota equivalent of the FOIA, the Minnesota Government Data Practices Act, Minn. Stat. § 13.03. What else can you do to investigate a potential case against PU?

Problem 3.1: FOIA

Assume that you have submitted a FOIA request to EPA Region V to see whether it has any documents relating to PU. Region V has responded with a few records, but has decided not to release one document, listed as an internal memorandum from the Region's NPDES Program Manager to the Branch Chief of the Office of Water Enforcement and Compliance Assurance "re: possible legal action against Pork Unlimited." From EPA's description of the document, you believe it might contain important information about why EPA decided not to pursue this case further and EPA staff opinion on the effects of the pollution on aquatic life in the North Fork. Can you force EPA to disclose the memo? See FOIA Exemption 5, 5 U.S.C. §552(b)(5); NLRB v. Sears, Roebuck, & Co., 421 U.S. 132, 160–61 (1975); Coastal States Gas Corp. v. Dep't of Energy, 617 F.2d 854, 866 (D.C. Cir. 1980) (exemption protects "deliberative process" documents, disclosure of which could "stifle honest and frank communication within the agency" in the future). Are staff statements summarized in this memo about the aquatic impacts "factual" rather than "deliberative" and therefore subject to disclosure? See Petroleum Inform. Corp. v. Dep't of Interior, 976 F.2d 1429, 1434 (D.C. Cir. 1992).

1. Litigation Issues

The following material will identify citizen suit litigation issues, using the Clean Water Act as a model. Most of these issues also arise under the citizen suit provisions of the other environmental laws.

a. Pre-Suit Notice

At least sixty days before a citizen suit is filed against the violator, notice must be given to the violator, to the EPA, and to the relevant state. *See, e.g., CWA §505(b)(1)(A).* The Supreme Court has held that this notice is mandatory to give the court jurisdiction and may not be waived or modified by the court. *Hallstrom v. Tillamook County,* 493 U.S. 20 (1989). The main purpose of the notice requirement is to give government authorities the first opportunity to take enforcement action before courts get involved. *See Ada-Cascade Watch Co. v. Cascade Resource Recovery, Inc.,* 720 F.2d 897, 908 (6th Cir. 1983). It also gives the violator a chance to come into compliance and avoid suit. *See Steel Company v. Citizens for a Better Environment,* 523 U.S. 83 (1998) (reproduced in subsection d below).The drafting of the notice is an important task, because the alleged violator may have a defense if particular violations are alleged later that were not included in the notice.

May a plaintiff sue in federal court under the federal citizen suit provision, even though the state has been delegated enforcement authority? Most courts considering the question have held that, because EPA must approve the state standards and state-issued permit, a citizen suit based on federal law may be brought. *See, e.g., Parker v. Scrap Metal Processors, Inc.,* 386 F.3d 993, 1006–08 (11th Cir. 2004); *Northwest Envtl. Advocates v. City of Portland,* 56 F.3d 979, 985–990 (9th Cir. 1995) (federal citizen suit may enforce state-issued permit).

However, at least one court has held that state requirements that are stricter than or in addition to federal environmental laws may not be enforced by a federal citizen suit. *Atlantic State Legal Found., Inc. v. Eastman Kodak*, 12 F.3d 353, 359–360 (2d Cir. 1993).

Exercise 3.2: Drafting the Notice Letter

On behalf of MEC, draft a 60-day notice letter to PU, the MPCA, and the EPA. In order to do so, you will have to determine precisely what statutes you believe PU is violating. Do you have a citizen suit action against MPCA as well, under Section 505(a)(2)?

You may want to use model notice letters you can find in books such as Jeffrey G. Miller, Citizen Suits: Private Enforcement of Federal Pollution Control Laws*(1987) or Michael D. Axline,* Environmental Citizen Suits*(Michie 1995). You should also note that EPA has promulgated regulations concerning the contents of a notice letter. 40 C.F.R. § 135.3.*

Assume you are drafting this notice letter in December 2009. How far back can you go in asserting violations? In your review of the DMRs for this facility, assume you find a series of ammonia nitrogen violations in 2003. Can you include that in your notice and later citizen suit? See 28 U.S.C. § 2862 (five-year statute of limitations for civil penalty suits); Sierra Club v. Chevron USA, Inc., 834 F.2d 1517, 1524 (9th Cir. 1987) (five-year statute tolled when 60-day notice filed); U.S. PIRG v. Atlantic Salmon of Maine, 257 F. Supp. 2d 407, 426–27 (D. Me. 2003) (older claims not barred if violations are "continuous and ongoing").

What happens if, in the month after you file your notice letter, PU has another violation? Do you need to file another notice letter? What if, after the notice period has expired and you are drafting your complaint, you discover another violation for 2008 in a DMR that you had not previously obtained? Can you add that violation to your complaint even though it was not in your original notice? See Community Ass'n for the Restoration of the Env't v. Henry Bosma Dairy, 305 F.3d 943 (9th Cir. 2002). Can you add a RCRA count to your complaint if you discover PU disposed of hazardous sludge without a permit?

---

b. Pretrial Publicity

Your client may be anxious to go public with the news about the violations they discover, in order to build pressure on state or federal authorities to take more stringent action. They may want you, as their lawyer, to alert the press, or to speak out at public forums, such as meetings of the state regulatory commission, or to send strongly worded letters to the governor or other public officials. They may want to send out letters about the litigation to their members or potential members, in order to raise funds. While a publicity campaign may be a useful adjunct to litigation, and may even obviate the need for litigation if it's successful, there are a couple of important considerations to keep in mind.

First, a lawyer has ethical obligations regarding extrajudicial statements. Under the Model Rules of Professional Conduct, Rule 3.6(a): "A lawyer who is participating or has participated in the investigation or litigation of a matter shall not make an extrajudicial statement that the lawyer knows or reasonably should know will be disseminated by means of public communication and will have a substantial likelihood of materially prejudicing an adjudicative proceeding in the matter."

Second, the client may be concerned about the potential for retaliatory action by the regulated entity, in the form of a SLAPP suit. SLAPP stands for "Strategic Lawsuits Against Public Participation," which consist primarily of civil tort suits based on theories such as defamation or interference with economic advantage. While most such suits are eventually dismissed, the client may incur substantial litigation costs, which may be enough to discourage them from making public statements. Many states have enacted anti-SLAPP statutes, designed to allow defendants in SLAPP suits to obtain expedited dismissal and recovery of litigation costs. To minimize the risk of retaliatory litigation, lawyers may want to review press releases and advise clients to confine their publicity to statements for which there is adequate evidentiary support.

Problem 3.2: The Perils of Publicity

Assume that MEC has posted its PU notice letter on its website and a local newspaper reporter has called you for further comment. MEC wants you to handle publicity because they are not used to dealing with the press and are afraid of SLAPP suits. Would it violate Rule 3.6 for you to tell a newspaper reporter that "PU is a habitual violator of the Clean Water Act and should pay a stiff penalty for its abuse of this precious natural resource, the North Fork River?"

a. How does Rule 3.6 apply to statements made before or during a citizen suit? Does it matter whether the citizen suit will proceed before a jury? Will there be a jury in a citizen suit? *See Tull v. U.S.*, 481 U.S. 412

(1987) (defendant entitled to jury on liability for, but not assessment of, civil penalty; no jury if only injunctive relief sought).

b. Could you draft a press release to be issued by your client, containing the same statement, and avoid the strictures of Rule 3.6?

c. Could you put the same statement in the preamble to your citizen suit complaint and then make the complaint available on your client's website?

d. What if the newspaper reporter tells you that PU put out its own statement suggesting that MEC was "a bunch of loony vegetarians intent on putting law-abiding meat producers out of business with frivolous litigation"? *See* Rule 3.6(c).

e. Does the limitation on extrajudicial statements violate the lawyer's free speech rights? *See Gentile v. State Bar of Nevada*, 501 U.S. 1030, 1075 (1991) ("substantial likelihood of material prejudice" test strikes proper balance between First Amendment and interest in fair trial).

c. Diligent Prosecution

No citizen suit may be brought if the EPA or state has "commenced and is diligently prosecuting" a civil or criminal enforcement action. *See, e.g.,* CWA § 505(b)(1)(B); RCRA § 7002(b)(1)(B); CAA § 304(b)(1)(B). This comports with the overall purpose of the citizen suit mechanism to "supplement, rather than supplant" government enforcement. *Gwaltney v. Chesapeake Bay Found.*, 489 U.S. 49, 60 (1987). However, if the citizen suit is barred by the government enforcement action, the statutes give citizens the right to intervene, thus ensuring they continue to have a voice in the process.

Although timely government enforcement actions filed in court will clearly bar a citizen suit, if they are diligently prosecuted, the effect of an administrative enforcement action depends on the specific statutory language. Both the Clean Water Act and Endangered Species Act, for example, provide that an administrative penalty proceeding will bar a citizen suit. CWA § 309(g)(6)(A)(i), 33 U.S.C. § 1319(g)(6)(A)(i); ESA § 11(g)(2)(A)(ii), 16 U.S.C. § 1640(g)(2)(A)(ii). The Clean Air Act, however, does not contain a similar provision and courts have reached conflicting decisions on the issue. *Compare Texans United for a Safe Econ. Educ. Fund v. Crown Cent. Petroleum Corp.*, 207 F.3d 789 (5th Cir. 2000) (plain language of CAA citizen suit "diligent prosecution" bar requires court action rather than administrative proceeding) *with Baughman v. Bradford Coal Co, Inc.*, 592 F.2d 215 (3d Cir. 1979) (administrative proceeding may be a bar if tribunal empowered to grant meaningful and effective relief).[7] Similarly, the RCRA citizen suit preclusion provision seems to require a judicial proceeding rather than an administrative action before a citizen suit is barred. RCRA §7002(b)(1)(A), 42 U.S.C. §6972(b)(1)(A).

Even though the CWA specifically provides that an administrative proceeding will bar a citizen suit, it also provides an exception to that rule. If EPA begins its administrative enforcement action only *after* the plaintiff files a 60-day notice letter, it will not bar the citizen suit, as long as the suit is filed within 120 days of the notice. 33 U.S.C. §1319(g)(6)(B). Thus, once a notice letter is filed, only a judicial enforcement proceeding will bar a timely citizen suit. However, it is questionable whether this exception to the diligent prosecution bar applies to state administrative actions. See *Black Warrior Riverkeeper, Inc. v. Cherokee Mining, LLC,* 548 F.3d 986 (11th Cir. 2008) (exception applicable to both state and federal enforcement); *Calif. Sportfishing Prot. Alliance. v. City of West Sacramento,* 905 F. Supp. 792 (E.D. Cal. 1995) (exception applies only to federal administrative enforcement). How is this exception consistent with the purpose of citizen suits to supplement rather than supplant the agency enforcement process?

The administrative enforcement bar also raises other questions of interpretation:

- Will administrative enforcement action short of a penalty bar the citizen suit — for example, if the agency issued a Notice of Violation or an administrative compliance order? *See Oregon State PIRG, Inc. v. Pacific Coast Seafoods Co.,* 341 F.Supp.2d 1170, 1176 (D. Ore. 2004) (§309(g) preclusion appropriate only where penalties assessed). *Compare* EPCRA §326(e) (administrative order bars citizen suit).
- What if the agency's suit is not filed until after the citizen suit has been commenced (thereby beyond the 60-day notice period)? *Compare Atlantic States Legal Found. v. Koch Refining Co.,* 681 F. Supp. 609, 614 (D. Minn. 1988) (once court has jurisdiction over citizen suit, later-filed enforcement action cannot deprive court of jurisdiction) *with U.S. EPA v. City of Green Forest,* 921 F.2d 1394, 1404 (8th Cir. 1990) (however, later-filed consent decree bars citizen suit due to res judicata or collateral estoppel).
- State administrative penalties will bar the citizen suit only if they are assessed under a state law "comparable" to Section 309(g). Courts disagree

---

7. For an excellent discussion of the various preclusion statutes, see Jeffrey G. Miller, "Theme and Variations in Statutory Preclusions Against Successive Environmental Enforcement Actions by EPA and Citizens," 28 Harv. Envt'l L. Rev. 401 (2004).

on the extent to which a state statute must be similar to the CWA before it is deemed comparable. In *Lockett v. E.P.A.*, 319 F.3d 678 (5th Cir. 2003), for example, the state agency relied upon a statute that had less stringent notice and comment requirements than the CWA. The court found, however, that the statutory schemes were comparable because the state statute had the same overall enforcement goals as the CWA. *Id.* at 684. Conversely, the court in *McAbee v. City of Fort Payne*, 318 F.3d 1248 (11th Cir. 2003), used a more focused approach to assessing comparability. The court evaluated three separate factors—public participation, penalty assessment, and judicial review—to determine whether the state statute was roughly comparable to the CWA in each category. *Id.* at 1256. Because the statutes' public participation provisions were not comparable, the court ruled that the state's action could not preclude a citizen suit. *Id.* at 1257. *See also Jones v. City of Lakeland*, 224 F.3d 518 (6th Cir. 2000) (Tennessee enforcement provisions not "comparable" to CWA because interested citizens could not participate in the process).

Problem 3.3: Diligent Prosecution

In Exercise 3, the MPCA has fined PU $1200 for its ammonia nitrogen violations and ordered it to come into compliance. Under Minnesota law, this penalty can be forgiven if PU proves that it has corrected the violations. Minn. Stat. § 116.072(5). PU has written a letter to MPCA claiming it has corrected the ammonia nitrogen problem by constructing a wetland to promote the oxidation of nitrogen before the wastewater is discharged. MEC believes this will not solve the problem and that some form of activated sludge treatment is necessary. In any event, MEC believes the assessed penalty is too low. Can MEC intervene in the penalty action or somehow challenge the penalty as inadequate? Does CWA § 309(g) preclude MEC's citizen suit for the ammonia nitrogen violations? Consider the following case:

---

* * *

Comfort Lake Association, Inc. v. Dresel Contracting, Inc.
138 F.3d 351 (8th Circuit 1998)

Comfort Lake Association, Inc. ("Comfort Lake"), filed this citizen suit seeking injunctive relief, civil penalties and costs and attorney's fees against Dresel Contracting, Inc., and Fain Companies ("Dresel and Fain") for alleged violations of … the Clean Water Act. The district court initially denied Dresel and Fain's motion for summary judgment, rejecting their contention that the Minnesota Pollution Control Agency ("MPCA") had commenced and was diligently prosecuting an administrative enforcement action that barred this citizen suit. See 33 U.S.C. § 1319(g)(6)(A)(ii). However, the court later dismissed the action as mooted by MPCA's subsequent enforcement action and denied Comfort Lake an award of costs and attorney's fees.

In the Fall of 1994, MPCA issued Dresel and Fain a National Pollution Discharge Elimination System ("NPDES") permit for construction of a Wal-Mart store in Forest Lake, Minnesota. The permit required erosion and sediment control facilities because run-off of pollutants from the construction site threatened the water quality of nearby Comfort Lake and its tributaries. After investigating complaints, MPCA sent Dresel and Fain a warning letter on December 30, 1994, noting permit violations. Dresel and Fain responded in early January 1995, claiming to have properly addressed these problems.

On January 31, Comfort Lake, a non-profit association dedicated to protecting the lake and its tributaries, issued a notice of intent to sue Dresel and Fain over the same NPDES permit violations noted in MPCA's December 20 letter. Under the Clean Water Act, plaintiff must give such a notice of intent to sue to the Administrator of the Environmental Protection Agency, the affected state agency, and the alleged violator at least sixty days before commencing a citizen suit. On April 3, Comfort Lake filed this citizen suit under 33 U.S.C. § 1365(a)(1).

Meanwhile, on February 12, MPCA again inspected the construction site, found continuing violations, and issued a Notice of Violation to Dresel and Fain. On May 19, Dresel and Fain reported full compliance with the permit. MPCA promptly inspected, and a May 22 internal agency memorandum states that the violations had indeed been corrected.

Dresel and Fain completed store construction in November 1995 and applied for termination of the NPDES permit. MPCA terminated the permit on April 11, 1996. MPCA staff negotiated and then proposed to the agency Board a Stipulation Agreement requiring payment of $12,203 in civil penalties for all past violations of the permit, including $6,100 payable to the City of Forest Lake for "a diagnostic study of Comfort Lake." The Stipulation Agreement recites that it

> covers all alleged NPDES/SDS Permit violations that occurred at the Wal-Mart construction site and that were known by MPCA as of the effective date of this Agreement. The alleged violations are considered past violations that have been satisfactorily resolved or corrected. This Agreement contains no remedial or corrective action requirements because construction at the Wal-Mart site has been completed. The

NPDES/SDS Permit has been terminated; thus, there is no likelihood that NPDES/SDS Permit violations will recur at the Wal-Mart site.

Dresel and Fain then renewed their motion for summary judgment. The district court granted that motion, and in a separate order denied Comfort Lake an award of costs and attorney's fees.

Is the Claim for Civil Penalties Precluded?

Comfort Lake's complaint asked the court to impose civil penalties of $25,000 per day for each Clean Water Act violation. Contending that Dresel and Fain's payment of $12,203 in civil penalties under the MPCA Stipulation Agreement is an insufficient sanction for their permit violations, Comfort Lake argues that its claim for civil penalties should be allowed to proceed even if its claim for injunctive relief is moot.

A Clean Water Act citizen suit, including any claim for civil penalties, must be based upon on-going violations, "that is, a reasonable likelihood that a past polluter will continue to pollute in the future." *Gwaltney*, 484 U.S. at 57. Despite this limitation, a number of circuits have concluded that, even if a polluter's voluntary permanent cessation of the alleged violations moots a citizen suit claim for injunctive relief, it does not moot a related claim for civil penalties.

Because Comfort Lake satisfied *Gwaltney's* on-going violation test when its complaint was filed, there remains an actual controversy over its claim for civil penalties for these violations. Rather, the issue is what effect Dresel and Fain's settlement with MPCA has on that claim for civil penalties. Or, to state the question differently, may Comfort Lake collaterally attack MPCA's decision that civil penalties of $12,203 are appropriate for the very same violations alleged in the citizen suit.

An underlying principle of the Clean Water Act is that "the citizen suit is meant to supplement rather than to supplant" government enforcement action. *Gwaltney*, 484 U.S. at 60. For example, if the EPA or MPCA commences a court enforcement action before or within sixty days after a citizen suit plaintiff's notice of intent to sue, the citizen suit is completely barred. *See* 33 U.S.C. § 1365(b)(1)(B). Even when an agency enforcement action is not commenced until after the citizen suit, final judgment in the agency's court action will be a res judicata or collateral estoppel bar to the earlier citizen suit. *See United States EPA v. City of Green Forest*, 921 F.2d 1394, 1402–05 (8th Cir. 1990).

In addition to court enforcement actions, the EPA and many state agencies have statutory authority to proceed by formal administrative action. When the EPA "has commenced and is diligently prosecuting" such an administrative action under 33 U.S.C. § 1319(g), or when MPCA has commenced and is diligently prosecuting "an action under a State law comparable to this subsection," a subsequent citizen suit for civil penalties is barred. The Stipulation Agreement between MPCA and Dresel and Fain is not a res judicata or collateral estoppel bar, like the judicially approved consent decree in Green Forest. But as a final agency enforcement action, that Agreement is entitled to considerable deference if we are to achieve the Clean Water Act's stated goal of preserving "the primary responsibilities and rights of States to prevent, reduce, and eliminate pollution." 33 U.S.C. § 1251(b). Moreover, respondents like Dresel and Fain will be disinclined to resolve disputes by such relatively informal agreements if additional civil penalties may then be imposed in pending citizen suits, thereby depriving MPCA of this resource-conserving enforcement tool. For these reasons, we conclude that an administrative enforcement agreement between the EPA or MPCA and the polluter will preclude a pending citizen suit claim for civil penalties if the agreement is the result of a diligently prosecuted enforcement process, however informal.

In this case, MPCA began informal action to enforce the NPDES permit in December 1994, before Comfort Lake issued its notice of intent to sue for the same violations. The agency diligently pursued Dresel and Fain to end permit violations until May 1995, when it concluded compliance had been achieved. After construction was complete MPCA terminated the permit and negotiated stipulated penalties for past violations. As the district court noted, MPCA extracted a civil penalty that "exceeds penalties imposed in similar cases [and] was derived by looking at factors substantially similar to those which must be considered by a court imposing penalties under" the Clean Water Act. Because MPCA diligently prosecuted its enforcement demands, the civil penalties it elected to extract in settling those demands may not be reconsidered in this citizen suit. While Comfort Lake might have preferred more severe civil penalties, MPCA has the primary responsibility for enforcing the Clean Water Act.

Should Attorney's Fees Have Been Awarded?

Although Comfort Lake's claims for affirmative relief are foreclosed by the subsequent MPCA enforcement actions, Comfort Lake may still be entitled to an award of costs and a reasonable attorney's fee as a prevailing party under 33 U.S.C. § 1365(d) if its citizen suit was the catalyst for agency enforcement action that resulted in the cessation of Clean Water Act violations. *See Eastman Kodak*, 933 F.2d at 128; *Green Forest*, 921 F.2d at 1402. However, the district court determined that Comfort Lake was not a catalyst, both because MPCA began enforcing the permit before Comfort Lake's notice of intent to sue, and because Comfort Lake "actually impeded" agency enforcement by suing MPCA in state court and then actively opposing the proposed Stipulation Agreement. This finding of fact is not clearly erroneous. Because Comfort Lake was not a prevailing party, the district court properly denied its request for costs and attorney's fees.

* * *

1. *Informal agency action.* Note that the district court in *Comfort Lake* had found that an NOV was not sufficient to preclude a citizen suit, although imposing penalties by an administrative settlement was. The appellate court agreed that an administrative settlement was sufficient, reasoning that the agency shouldn't be precluded from using "informal" enforcement mechanisms that save resources. Under that rationale, shouldn't the NOV have also been sufficient, or would that stretch the language of Section 309(g) too far? Has the state really "commenced" action by issuing an NOV? Does the *Comfort Lake* result mean that the agency remains able to "cut the legs out from under" a citizen suit by imposing an administrative penalty, long after the case has been filed?

2. *Mootness.* In *Friends of the Earth v. Laidlaw Envt'l Serv., Inc.*, 528 U.S. 167 (2000), the Supreme Court held that a citizen suit for civil penalties is mooted when violations cannot "reasonably be expected to recur." 528 U.S. at 193. The Court held that the violator's voluntary modification of its pollution control to achieve substantial permit compliance might not suffice to moot the citizen suit case, nor would the violator's voluntary shutdown of its facility, because the violator would later be "free to return to his old ways." *Id.* at 189 (quoting *City of Mesquite v. Alladin's Castle, Inc.*, 455 U.S. 283, 289 n.10 (1982)).

Under *Laidlaw,* did Comfort Lake's case become moot when MPCA terminated Dresel and Fain's permit? If that is true, could a citizen suit ever be brought for violations of the type of short-term construction permit at issue in Comfort Lake? Might the termination of the permit moot the claim for injunctive relief, but not the penalty claim, due to the need for deterrence of future violations? *See Laidlaw,* 528 U.S., at 193; *Ecological Rts. Found. v. Pacific Lumber Co.*, 230 F.3d 1141, 1153 (9th Cir. 2000) (penalty case not moot despite new permit due to need for deterrence).

In Exercise 2.2, if the PU permit expires during the pendency of the MEC citizen suit litigation and MPCA drafts a new permit with more lenient effluent limits, will this moot the citizen suit?[8] *See, e.g., Mississippi River Revival v.*

---

8. This could happen based on a revised calculation of the pollutant's impact on water quality (for example, allowing a "mixing zone" before determining in-stream quality), or if the North Fork is downgraded (for example, from a high quality resource water to a fishing stream), or if the Water Quality Standard is amended due to new scientific informa-

City of Minneapolis, 319 F.3d 1013 (8th Cir. 2003) (citizen suit seeking penalties for unpermitted discharges became moot once permit issued).

3. *"Diligence" and lenient penalties.* Plaintiffs challenging lenient penalties face an uphill battle in proving lack of diligent prosecution. Courts presume that agency enforcement is diligent and note that a low penalty alone is insufficient to overcome this presumption. *See, e.g., Community of Cambridge Envt'l Health & Comm. Dev. Group v. City of Cambridge*, 115 F. Supp. 2d 550, 554 (D. Md. 2000) (state agency entitled to deference in penalty decisions; $1500 penalty was diligent prosecution where City had limited resources and agency reserved right to seek future penalties).

However, *Friends of the Earth v. Laidlaw Envt'l Serv., Inc.*, 890 F.Supp. 470 (D. S.Car. 1995) (an early opinion in the litigation resulting in the Supreme Court case above), is a notable exception. After plaintiff served its 60-day notice, the violator asked the state environmental agency to file an enforcement action to block the citizen suit. The agency complied by filing suit on the sixtieth day and a consent order was entered the very next day, imposing a fine of less than half of the amount called for in the agency's uniform enforcement policy. The court noted that a lenient penalty may provide evidence of nondiligent prosecution. Another concern was that the quick government settlement prevented the citizen suit plaintiff from intervening and commenting on the proposed penalty. 890 F. Supp. at 489–91. Accordingly, the court found that the state agency's civil penalty did not constitute "diligent prosecution" and allowed the citizen suit to go forward.

4. *Other potential remedies.* As you discovered in Problem 2.1, the EPA may be able to "overfile," that is, take enforcement action on its own, even though the state has already commenced or even completed enforcement proceedings. In problem 3.3, could MEC urge the EPA to overfile? *See* 40 C.F.R. § 123.27(c) (state penalties must be "appropriate to the violation" and the EPA may commence separate action for penalties if amount is "substantially inadequate"). Could MEC urge EPA to "pull the program" (withdraw delegation) if inadequate enforcement continues?

d. Standing

In any environmental citizen suit case, the first question to ask is whether your client has standing to sue. You have probably already read the most im-

---

tion on its probable impact on aquatic life, or if other sources of the pollutant have been eliminated, allowing the Water Quality Standard to be met despite a greater contribution from PU. All of these possibilities are subject to "anti-backsliding" limitations (*see, e.g.,* CWA § 303(d)(4), 33 U.S.C. § 1313(d)(4)).

portant standing cases in your introductory environmental law or administrative law course. In this text, we will ask you to apply those basic concepts to a specific case, in order to explore some of their practical implications. First, we will briefly review the basics of the standing doctrine, in the context of the citizen suit.

Article III of the Constitution gives the judicial branch jurisdiction only over "cases" or "controversies." The Supreme Court has interpreted that language to require that a plaintiff have "standing" to bring suit, which has developed into a three-part test the Court described in *Lujan v. Defenders of Wildlife*, 505 U.S. 555, 560–61(1992) (citations omitted):

> Over the years, our cases have established that the irreducible constitutional minimum of standing contains three elements. First, the plaintiff must have suffered an "injury in fact"—an invasion of a legally protected interest which is (a) concrete and particularized, and (b) "actual or imminent, not 'conjectural' or 'hypothetical.'" Second, there must be a causal connection between the injury and the conduct complained of—the injury has to be "fairly ... trace[able] to the challenged action of the defendant, and not ... th[e] result [of] the independent action of some third party not before the court." Third, it must be "likely," as opposed to merely "speculative," that the injury will be "redressed by a favorable decision."

The first requirement—"injury in fact"—requires that the plaintiff has suffered or will suffer harm from the alleged violation, rather than merely having an abstract interest in the issue. This is usually not a problem as long as the plaintiff (or a member of the plaintiff's organization) regularly uses the resource that is being polluted or threatened by the defendant's actions. Nevertheless, problems can arise if the defendant's actions are geographically remote or if the harm alleged is only tenuously related to the alleged violation. *See Lujan*, 504 U.S. 555 (1992) (plaintiffs alleging harm to endangered species in foreign country suffered no injury in fact where plaintiffs had no concrete plan to visit the area).

Even where the plaintiffs live nearby, "injury in fact" requires a showing of how their use or enjoyment of the resource has been impacted. For example, how will a trout fisherman be affected by increased fecal coliform in the river, since that pollutant impacts human health rather than aquatic life? How would a canoeist be impacted by a pollutant that dissolves and does not alter the beauty of the river?

Merely alleging a violation and use of the resource may not be enough. In *Friends of the Earth v. Laidlaw Envt'l Serv., Inc.*, 528 U.S. 167, 181–85 (2000), the Court addressed this aspect of the injury in fact requirement and accepted plaintiffs' allegations that their use of a river had been adversely impacted, despite the district court's conclusion that the defendant's permit violations had no discernable impact on aquatic life or aesthetics. *See id.* at 198–201 (Scalia, J., dissenting) (discussing lack of harm to resource). The majority concluded that standing depended on injury to the plaintiff, not injury to the resource, and it was reasonable to assume that a person who used a river that was being polluted would be adversely affected.

On the other hand, in *Summers v. Earth Island Inst.*, 129 S.Ct. 1142 (2009), the Court reaffirmed its requirement that a concrete and particularized injury is required to meet the injury-in-fact test. Plaintiffs challenged Forest Service regulations exempting certain projects from environmental assessments. The Court held plaintiffs did not have standing, because they did not allege that any particular project would impact any particular, concrete plan to enjoy the National Forests. *Id.* at 1149–50. Merely alleging frequent use of the National Forests in general was not sufficient to establish injury in fact.

The Constitutional standing requirement also includes two other tests: that the injury be "fairly traceable" to the violation (which some equate with a "proximate cause" inquiry) and that the injury be "redressable." The latter requirement seeks to avoid cases in which the court's decision will not really do anything to remedy the plaintiff's harm. Redressability issues arise infrequently, but *Steel Company v. Citizens for a Better Env.*, 523 U.S. 83 (1998), reproduced below, suggests that courts may apply the test more stringently in the citizen suit context.

Plaintiffs must also have standing under the relevant statute. Citizen suit provisions authorize "any citizen" to bring suit, defined as a "person or persons having an interest which is or may be adversely affected." Clean Water Act § 505(g), 33 U.S.C. § 1365(g). The term "person" under the statute includes groups, *see* Section 502(5), as long as at least some of its members would have standing to sue in their own right and the interests sought to be protected are "germane to the organization's purpose." *Save Our Community v. E.P.A.*, 971 F.2d 1155 (5th Cir. 1992) (establishing requirements for organizational standing).[9] Of course, Congress cannot grant the courts greater jurisdiction than

---

9. In *Steel Company*, reproduced below, the Supreme Court suggests in a footnote that statutory language such as this may allow a group "to vindicate only its own interests as an organization, and not the interests of its individual members." 523 U.S. at 104 n.6. Would this interpretation make a difference in MEC's case?

the Constitution allows and therefore these statutory provisions generally have been construed to be co-extensive with the Constitutional limitations on standing.

e. "In Violation" Issue

The Clean Water Act citizen suit provision allows a suit to be filed only against those alleged to be "in violation" of the applicable standards. The use of present tense in this statute precludes suits based entirely on past violations. *See Gwaltney v. Chesapeake Bay Foundation*, 484 U.S. 49 (1987). This accords with the primary purpose of the citizen suit, which is to bring facilities into compliance. The *Gwaltney* court held that past violations could establish that the entity was "in violation," if it had taken no action to solve the problem, resulting in "a reasonable likelihood that a past polluter will continue to pollute in the future." 484 U.S. at 57.

If the court rules that it has jurisdiction over the case because the violator is "in violation," can the court impose penalties for the violations that occurred prior to the suit? Read Section 505 again and see if it answers that question. *See Public Interest Group v. Yates*, 790 F. Supp. 511 (D.N.J. 1991) (once court has jurisdiction, it can impose penalties for past violations). If plaintiff establishes ongoing violations of one permit parameter, can the court impose penalties for "wholly past" violations of other parameters of the permit? *Compare Yates*, 790 F.Supp., at 515–16 (violations of one parameter may be used to establish likelihood of continuing violation of another parameter), *with Gwaltney v. Chesapeake Bay Found.*, 890 F.2d 690, 698 (4th Cir. 1989) ("in violation" status must be established separately for each parameter).

Not all citizen suit statutes contain the same constraining language. For example, in the Clean Air Act provision, Section 304, suit is authorized against a person "who is alleged to have violated (if there is evidence that the alleged violation has been repeated)." RCRA allows a citizen suit against a past violator (someone who dumped hazardous waste illegally, for example), if the situation presents an "imminent and substantial endangerment."

In Exercise 2, the Agra Enterprises case, assuming that EPA decided not to penalize Agra, could a citizen bring suit against Agra solely for its past violations of EPCRA? Note carefully the differences in language between the CWA citizen suit provision and that of EPCRA, Section 326(a)(1), 42 U.S.C. §11046 (a)(1). Although the Supreme Court didn't reach this issue in *Steel Company*, several of the concurring Justices discussed it:

* * *

Steel Company v. Citizens for a Better Environment

523 U.S. 83 (1998)

Justice Scalia delivered the opinion of the Court.

This is a private enforcement action under the citizen-suit provision of the Emergency Planning and Community Right-To-Know Act of 1986 (EPCRA), 42 U.S.C. § 11046(a)(1). The case presents the merits question, answered in the affirmative by the United States Court of Appeals for the Seventh Circuit, whether EPCRA authorizes suits for purely past violations. It also presents the jurisdictional question whether respondent, plaintiff below, has standing to bring this action.

I

Respondent, an association of individuals interested in environmental protection, sued petitioner, a small manufacturing company in Chicago, for past violations of EPCRA. EPCRA establishes a framework of state, regional and local agencies designed to inform the public about the presence of hazardous and toxic chemicals, and to provide for emergency response in the event of a health-threatening release. Central to its operation are reporting requirements compelling users of specified toxic and hazardous chemicals to file annual "emergency and hazardous chemical inventory forms" and "toxic chemical release forms," which contain, *inter alia*, the name and location of the facility, the name and quantity of the chemical on hand, and, in the case of toxic chemicals, the waste-disposal method employed and the annual quantity released into each environmental medium. 42 U.S.C. §§ 11022 and 11023. The hazardous-chemical inventory forms for any given calendar year are due the following March 1st, and the toxic-chemical release forms the following July 1st. §§ 11022(a)(2) and 11023(a).

Enforcement of EPCRA can take place on many fronts. The Environmental Protection Agency (EPA) has the most powerful enforcement arsenal: it may seek criminal, civil, or administrative penalties. § 11045. State and local governments can also seek civil penalties, as well as injunctive relief. §§ 11046(a)(2) and (c). For purposes of this case, however, the crucial enforcement mechanism is the citizen-suit provision, § 11046(a)(1), which likewise authorizes civil penalties and injunctive relief, see § 11046(c). This provides that "any person may commence a civil action on his own behalf against ... [a]n owner or operator of a facility for failure," among other things, to "[c]omplete and submit an inventory form under section 11022(a) of this title ... [and] section 11023(a) of this title." § 11046(a)(1). As a prerequisite to bringing such a suit, the plaintiff must, 60 days prior to filing his complaint, give notice to the Administrator of the EPA, the State in which the alleged violation occurs, and the alleged violator. § 11046(d). The citizen suit may not go forward if the Administrator "has commenced and is diligently pursuing an administrative order or civil action to enforce the requirement concerned or to impose a civil penalty." § 11046(e).

In 1995 respondent sent a notice to petitioner, the Administrator, and the relevant Illinois authorities, alleging—accurately, as it turns out—that petitioner had failed since 1988, the first year of EPCRA's filing deadlines, to complete and to submit the requisite hazardous-chemical inventory and toxic-chemical release forms under §§ 11022 and 11023. Upon receiving the notice, petitioner filed all the overdue forms with the relevant agencies. The EPA chose not to bring an action against petitioner, and when the 60-day waiting period expired, respondent filed suit in Federal District Court. Petitioner promptly filed a motion to dismiss under Federal Rule of Civil Procedure 12(b)(1) and (6), contending that, because its filings were up to date when the complaint was filed, the court had no jurisdiction to entertain a suit for a present violation; and that, because EPCRA does not allow suit for a purely historical violation, respondent's allegation of untimeliness in filing was not a claim upon which relief could be granted.

The District Court agreed with petitioner on both points. The Court of Appeals reversed, concluding that citizens may seek penalties against EPCRA violators who file after the statutory deadline and after receiving notice. 90 F.3d 1237 (7th Cir. 1996). We granted certiorari.

II

We granted certiorari in this case to resolve a conflict between the interpretation of EPCRA adopted by the Seventh Circuit and the interpretation previously adopted by the Sixth Circuit in *Atlantic States Legal Foundation, Inc. v. United Musical Instruments, U.S.A., Inc.*, 61 F.3d 473 (6th Cir. 1995)—a case relied on by the District Court, and acknowledged by the Seventh Circuit to be "factually indistinguishable," 90 F.3d, at 1241–1242. Petitioner, however, both in its petition for certiorari and in its briefs on the merits, has raised the issue of respondent's standing to maintain the suit, and hence this Court's jurisdiction to entertain it.

IV

[The Court here discusses at length its decision to decide the standing issue first, rather than the merits issue]. Having reached the end of what seems like a long front walk, we finally arrive at the threshold jurisdictional question:

whether respondent, the plaintiff below, has standing to sue. Article III, §2 of the Constitution extends the "judicial Power" of the United States only to "Cases" and "Controversies." We have always taken this to mean cases and controversies of the sort traditionally amenable to and resolved by the judicial process. Standing to sue is part of the common understanding of what it takes to make a justiciable case. *Whitmore v. Arkansas*, 495 U.S. 149, 155 (1990).[10]

The "irreducible constitutional minimum of standing" contains three requirements, *Lujan v. Defenders of Wildlife, supra*, at 560. First and foremost, there must be alleged (and ultimately proven) an "injury in fact"—a harm suffered by the plaintiff that is "concrete" and "actual or imminent, not 'conjectural' or 'hypothetical.' " Second, there must be causation—a fairly traceable connection between the plaintiff's injury and the complained-of conduct of the defendant. And third, there must be redressability—a likelihood that the requested relief will redress the alleged injury. This triad of injury in fact, causation, and redressability comprises the core of Article III's case-or-controversy requirement, and the party invoking federal jurisdiction bears the burden of establishing its existence.

We turn now to the particulars of respondent's complaint to see how it measures up to Article III's requirements. The complaint asserts that respondent's "right to know about [toxic chemical] releases and its interests in protecting and improving the environment and the health of its members have been, are being, and will be adversely affected by [petitioner's] actions in failing to provide timely and required information under EPCRA." The complaint also alleges that respondent's members, who live in or frequent the area near petitioner's facility, use the EPCRA-reported information "to learn about toxic chemical releases, the use of hazardous substances in their communities, to plan emergency preparedness in the event of accidents, and to attempt to reduce the toxic chemicals in areas in which they live, work and visit." The members' safety, health, recreational, economic, aesthetic and environmental interests" in the information, it is claimed, "have been, are being, and will be adversely affected by [petitioner's] actions in failing to file timely and required reports under EPCRA."

As appears from the above, respondent asserts petitioner's failure to provide EPCRA information in a timely fashion, and the lingering effects of that

---

10. EPCRA states that "any person may commence a civil action on his own behalf...." 42 U.S.C. §10046(1) (emphasis added). "Person" includes an association, see §10049(7), so it is arguable that the statute permits respondent to vindicate only its own interests as an organization, and not the interests of its individual members. Since it makes no difference to our disposition of the case, we assume without deciding that the interests of individual members may be the basis of suit.

failure, as the injury in fact to itself and its members. We have not had occasion to decide whether being deprived of information that is supposed to be disclosed under EPCRA—or at least being deprived of it when one has a particular plan for its use—is a concrete injury in fact that satisfies Article III. *Cf. Lujan v. Defenders of Wildlife,* 504 U.S., at 578. And we need not reach that question in the present case because, assuming injury in fact, the complaint fails the third test of standing, redressability.

The complaint asks for (1) a declaratory judgment that petitioner violated EPCRA; (2) authorization to inspect periodically petitioner's facility and records (with costs borne by petitioner); (3) an order requiring petitioner to provide respondent copies of all compliance reports submitted to the EPA; (4) an order requiring petitioner to pay civil penalties of $25,000 per day for each violation of §§ 11022 and 11023; (5) an award of all respondent's "costs, in connection with the investigation and prosecution of this matter, including reasonable attorney and expert witness fees, as authorized by Section 326(f) of [EPCRA]"; and (6) any such further relief as the court deems appropriate. None of the specific items of relief sought, and none that we can envision as "appropriate" under the general request, would serve to reimburse respondent for losses caused by the late reporting, or to eliminate any effects of that late reporting upon respondent.

The first item, the request for a declaratory judgment that petitioner violated EPCRA, can be disposed of summarily. There being no controversy over whether petitioner failed to file reports, or over whether such a failure constitutes a violation, the declaratory judgment is not only worthless to respondent, it is seemingly worthless to all the world.

Item (4), the civil penalties authorized by the statute, *see* § 11045(c), might be viewed as a sort of compensation or redress to respondent if they were payable to respondent. But they are not. These penalties—the only damages authorized by EPCRA—are payable to the United States Treasury. In requesting them, therefore, respondent seeks not remediation of its own injury—reimbursement for the costs it incurred as a result of the late filing—but vindication of the rule of law—the "undifferentiated public interest" in faithful execution of EPCRA. Justice Stevens thinks it is enough that respondent will be gratified by seeing petitioner punished for its infractions and that the punishment will deter the risk of future harm. Obviously, such a principle would make the redressability requirement vanish. By the mere bringing of his suit, every plaintiff demonstrates his belief that a favorable judgment will make him happier. But although a suitor may derive great comfort and joy from the fact that the United States Treasury is not cheated, that a wrongdoer gets his just desserts, or that the nation's laws are faithfully enforced, that psychic satisfaction is not an acceptable Article III remedy because it does not redress a cognizable Article III injury. Relief that does not remedy the injury suffered cannot bootstrap a plaintiff into federal court; that is the very essence of the redressability requirement.

Item (5) the "investigation and prosecution" costs "as authorized by Section 326(f)," would assuredly benefit respondent as opposed to the citizenry at large. Obviously, however, a plaintiff cannot achieve standing to litigate a substantive issue by bringing suit for the cost of bringing suit. The litigation must give the plaintiff some other benefit besides reimbursement of costs that are a byproduct of the litigation itself.

The remaining relief respondent seeks (item (2), giving respondent authority to inspect petitioner's facility and records, and item (3), compelling petitioner to provide respondent copies of EPA compliance reports) is injunctive in nature. It cannot conceivably remedy any past wrong but is aimed at deterring petitioner from violating EPCRA in the future. See Brief for Respondent 36. The latter objective can of course be "remedial" for Article III purposes, when threatened injury is one of the gravamens of the complaint. If respondent had alleged a continuing violation or the imminence of a future violation, the injunctive relief requested would remedy that alleged harm. But there is no such allegation here—and on the facts of the case, there seems no basis for it. Nothing supports the requested injunctive relief except respondent's generalized interest in deterrence, which is insufficient for purposes of Article III.

Having found that none of the relief sought by respondent would likely remedy its alleged injury in fact, we must conclude that respondent lacks standing to maintain this suit, and that we and the lower courts lack jurisdiction to entertain it. However desirable prompt resolution of the merits EPCRA question may be, it is not as important as observing the constitutional limits set upon courts in our system of separated powers. EPCRA will have to await another day.

Justice Stevens, with whom Justice Souter joins as to Parts I, III, and IV, and with whom Justice Ginsburg joins as to Part III, concurring in the judgment.

This case presents two questions: (1) whether the Emergency Planning and Community Right-to-Know Act of 1986 (EPCRA), 42 U.S.C. § 11001 et seq., confers federal jurisdiction over citizen suits for wholly past violations; and (2) if so, whether respondent has standing under Article III of the Constitution. The Court has elected to decide the constitutional question first and, in doing so, has created new constitutional law. Because it is always prudent to avoid passing unnecessarily on an undecided constitutional question, see *Ashwander v. TVA*, 297 U.S. 288, 345–348 (1936) (Brandeis, J., concurring), the Court should answer the statutory question first. Moreover, because EPCRA, properly construed, does not confer jurisdiction over citizen suits for wholly past violations, the Court should leave the constitutional question for another day.

The Court's conclusion that respondent does not have standing comes from a mechanistic application of the "redressability" aspect of our standing doctrine. "Redressability," of course, does not appear anywhere in the text of the Constitution. Instead, it is a judicial creation of the past 25 years.

The Court acknowledges that respondent would have had standing if Congress had authorized some payment to respondent. Yet the Court fails to specify why payment to respondent—even if only a peppercorn—would redress respondent's injuries, while payment to the Treasury does not. Respondent clearly believes that the punishment of the Steel Company, along with future deterrence of the Steel Company and others, redresses its injury, and there is no basis in our previous standing holdings to suggest otherwise.

When one private party is injured by another, the injury can be redressed in at least two ways: by awarding compensatory damages or by imposing a sanction on the wrongdoer that will minimize the risk that the harm-causing conduct will be repeated. Thus, in some cases a tort is redressed by an award of punitive damages; even when such damages are payable to the sovereign, they provide a form of redress for the individual as well.

History supports the proposition that punishment or deterrence can redress an injury. In past centuries in England, in the American colonies, and in the United States, private persons regularly prosecuted criminal cases. The interest in punishing the defendant and deterring violations by law by the defendant and others are sufficient to support the "standing" of the private prosecutor even if the only remedy was the sentencing of the defendant to jail or to the gallows. Given this history, the Framers of Article III surely would have considered such proceedings to be "Cases" that would "redress" an injury even though the party bringing suit did not receive any monetary compensation.

The Court's expanded interpretation of the redressability requirement has another consequence. Under EPCRA, Congress gave enforcement power to state and local governments. 42 U.S.C. § 11046(a)(2). Under the Court's reasoning, however, state and local governments would not have standing to sue for past violations, as a payment to the Treasury would no more "redress" the injury of these governments than it would redress respondent's injury. This would be true even if Congress explicitly granted state and local governments this power. Such a conclusion is unprecedented.

It is, therefore, not necessary to reject the Court's resolution of the standing issue in order to conclude that it would be prudent to answer the question of statutory construction before announcing new constitutional doctrine.

III

EPCRA's citizen-suit provision states, in relevant part:

> [A]ny person may commence a civil action on his own behalf
> against ... [a]n owner or operator of a facility for failure to do any of
> the following: ... Complete and submit an inventory form under sec-
> tion 11022(a) of this title ... [or] [c]omplete and submit a toxic
> chemical release form under section 11023(a) of this title." 42 U.S.C.
> §§ 11046(a)(1)(A)(iii)–(iv).

Unfortunately, this language is ambiguous. It could mean, as the Sixth Circuit has held, that a citizen only has the right to sue for a "failure ... to complete
and submit" the required forms. Under this reading, once the owner or operator has filed the forms, the district court no longer has jurisdiction. *Atlantic
States Legal Foundation v. United Musical Inst., Inc.*, 61 F.3d 473, 475 (1995). Alternatively, it could be, as the Seventh Circuit held, that the phrases "under section 11022(a)" and "under section 11023(a)" incorporate the requirements of
those sections, including the requirement that the reports be filed by particular
dates. *Citizens for a Better Environment v. Steel Co.*, 90 F.3d 1237, 1243 (1996).

Although the language of the citizen-suit provision is ambiguous, other
sections of EPCRA indicate that Congress did not intend to confer jurisdiction over citizen suits for wholly past violations. First, EPCRA requires the
private litigant to give the alleged violator notice at least 60 days before bringing suit. 42 U.S.C. § 11046(d)(1). In *Gwaltney*, we considered the import of
a substantially identical notice requirement, and concluded that it indicated a
congressional intent to allow suit only for on-going and future violations.

> The purpose of notice to the alleged violator is to give it an oppor-
> tunity to bring itself into complete compliance with the Act and thus
> likewise render unnecessary a citizen suit. If we assume, as respon-
> dents urge, that citizen suits may target wholly past violations, the re-
> quirement of notice to the alleged violator becomes gratuitous. In-
> deed, respondents, in propounding their interpretation of the Act,
> can think of no reason for Congress to require such notice other than
> that "it seemed right" to inform an alleged violator that it was about
> to be sued. Brief for Respondents 1. 484 U.S., at 60.

Second, EPCRA placed a ban on citizen suits once the EPA has commenced
an enforcement action. 42 U.S.C § 11046(e). In *Gwaltney*, we considered a
similar provision and concluded that it indicated a congressional intent to prohibit citizen suits for wholly past violations:

This bar on citizen suits when governmental enforcement action is under way suggests that the citizen suit is meant to supplement rather than supplant governmental action.... Permitting citizen suits for wholly past violations of the Act could undermine the supplementary role envisioned for the citizen suit. This danger is best illustrated by an example. Suppose that the Administrator identified a violator of the Act and issued a compliance order ... Suppose further that the Administrator agreed not to assess or otherwise seek civil penalties on the condition that the violator take some extreme corrective action, such as to install particularly effective but expensive machinery, that it otherwise would not be obliged to take. If citizens could file suit, months or years later, in order to seek the civil penalties that the Administrator chose to forgo, then the Administrator's discretion to enforce the Act in the public interest would be curtailed considerably. The same might be said of the discretion of state enforcement authorities. Respondents' interpretation of the scope of the citizen suit would change the nature of the citizens' role from interstitial to potentially intrusive. *Id.*, at 60–61.

* * *

Discussion Questions

1. In Exercise 2 (Agra Enterprises), if EPA had ultimately decided not to penalize Agra for its violation of EPCRA § 304, as long as it agreed to file the required post-release reports, could a citizen suit have been filed for that violation? Substantial litigation costs may be incurred before an EPCRA citizen suit is filed, in finding potential violators and investigating claims against them. If violators can then nullify citizen suit standing by simply filing their late forms, thereby preventing plaintiffs from recovering litigation costs, do plaintiffs have an adequate incentive to conduct this type of investigation? Would you be surprised to find many EPCRA citizen suits after *Steel Company*?

2. Note that the Clean Air Act citizen suit provision does not contain the "in violation" language found in the Clean Water Act; instead it explicitly allows a citizen suit for past violations. CAA § 304, 42 U.S.C. § 7604 (allowing suit for past, repeated violations). If the defendant claims that the past violations were due to faulty equipment that has now been replaced, does *Steel Company* indicate citizens would not have standing to sue, even though the statute allows it? *See, e.g., Cambrians for Thoughtful Dev. v. Didion Milling, Inc.*, 571 F.Supp.2d 972, 977–80 (W.D. Wisc. 2008) (CAA violations not redressable where permit changes eliminated likelihood of recurrence); *Anderson v. Farmland Indust., Inc.*, 70 F.Supp.2d 1218, 1224 (D.Kan. 1999) (despite statutory language, CAA citizen suit standing exists only where defendant in violation at time of suit or future violations imminent).

Problem 3.4: Wholly Past Violations and Standing

In Exercise 3, the DMRs show three violations of monthly ammonia limits in both 2008 and 2009. In addition, the DMRs show six bacteria (fecal coliform) violations in June and July 2009, which PU claims resulted from an equipment malfunction it remedied in August. Assume MEC files a notice letter in September 2009 and files its suit December 1, 2009.

a) Was PU "in violation" of its permit at the time MEC filed suit or does Gwaltney *give PU a defense? Is your answer the same for both ammonia and fecal coliform?*

b) Does MEC have standing to sue PU? Has MEC suffered an "injury in fact?" What exactly will its complaint have to allege? Is MEC's injury redressable?

c) For the ammonia violations, would both the Minnesota Flyfishers Association and the Minnesota Canoeists Association have standing? How about for the fecal coliform violations? Would the Midwest Environmental Group, located in Chicago, have standing?

Exercise 3.3: Drafting the Complaint

Assume that MEC decides to file a citizen suit against PU, seeking injunctive relief and civil penalties for the CWA violations. Draft the complaint. Be sure to have adequate allegations in your complaint to cover the "in violation" and standing issues. In order to draft the complaint, you will need to determine which court has jurisdiction over your case and what the potential penalties are. Again, you may want to use model pleadings you can find on the internet or in guidebooks such as Axline, Environmental Citizen Suits *(Michie 1995).*

f. Potential Recovery

What can plaintiffs hope to gain by bringing a citizen suit? Citizen suit provisions generally give the court the authority to enforce the environmental standard, usually by a compliance order, and to impose "appropriate civil penalties." *See, e.g.,* Clean Water Act § 505(a), 33 U.S.C. § 1365(a). In addition, any "prevailing or substantially prevailing party" can recover the costs of litigation (including "reasonable expert witness and attorney fees") if the court deems it appropriate. CWA § 505(d). Although this provision gives public interest groups the ability to bring suit despite scarce financial resources, it may also cause them to fear a judgment for costs if they lose. Nevertheless, while

courts typically deem it "appropriate" to award prevailing citizen suit plain-
tiffs at least some of their litigation costs, courts do not generally award costs
to prevailing defendants, unless the suit is deemed frivolous or in bad faith.
Should courts use this "double standard" for litigation costs? Kerry D. Florio,
"Attorneys' Fees in Environmental Citizen Suits: Should Prevailing Defendants
Recover?" 27 Boston Coll. Envt'l Aff. L. Rev. 707 (2000).

Of course, attorney fee awards usually do not completely cover the cost of the
litigation. For example, courts may exclude fees for work on motions that were
unsuccessful, *Armstrong v. ASARCO, Inc.*, 138 F.3d 382, 389 (8th Cir. 1998) (fees
denied for unsuccessful opposition to consent decree). Courts may also carefully
scrutinize bills to exclude any duplicative or unnecessary costs. *New Mexico Citizens for Clean Air and Water v. Espanola Merc. Co.*, 72 F.3d 830, 835 (10th Cir.
1996). Moreover, time spent on non-litigation activities, such as preparing press
releases or holding press conferences, will not be reimbursed. *Id.* Court-awarded
fees, unlike contingency fees, will not be increased to account for litigation risk.
City of Burlington v. Dague, 505 U.S. 557 (1992) (federal fee-shifting statutes do
not permit risk enhancement). And of course, fees are not awarded until the litigation is concluded, which can take many years. Therefore, unlike an attorney
billing a corporate client on a monthly basis, attorneys representing citizen suit
plaintiffs need to understand the challenges to fee recovery.[11]

Civil penalties, of course, go directly to the United States Treasury. Although a court does not have the authority to order damages or any other type
of payment (other than litigation costs) to be made to the citizen suit plaintiff, courts have ordered defendants to undertake restoration or other environmentally beneficial projects in addition to or instead of penalties. Settlements are more flexible; citizen suits have been settled by payments made
directly to the plaintiff or to environmental projects the plaintiff favors. Such
a settlement is at issue in *Sierra Club v. ECD*, reproduced below.

Problem 3.5: Settlement

*In the PU litigation, MEC's main objective is to punish PU sufficiently to
deter future violations; however, if possible, MEC would also like to obtain
funding for a water quality monitoring project. In addition, it seeks compensation for its litigation costs. As MEC's attorney, you have taken the case
on a "contingency" basis, knowing that a small nonprofit group has no budget
for your fees; therefore, the fee agreement provides you will receive no compensation for your many hours of work on this case unless the court awards*

---

11. *See generally* Russell E. Lovell, II, Court-Awarded Attorneys' Fees (ABA 1999)

costs under CWA § 505(d). PU has now proposed a settlement that includes the installation of an activated sludge treatment system, which promises to solve the ammonia problem, plus a payment of $40,000 to MEC to support a water quality monitoring project, including regular monitoring of the North Fork River. How would you as the attorney for MEC evaluate a settlement offer that includes such a payment, but no money for litigation costs?

* * *

Sierra Club, Inc. v. Electronic Controls Design, Inc.
909 F.2d 1350 (9th Cir. 1990)

Godwin, Chief Judge:

Sierra Club, Inc. appeals the refusal to enter a proposed consent judgment in its citizens' suit against Electronic Controls Design (ECD) for alleged violations of the Federal Water Pollution Control Act ("Clean Water Act" or "the Act"). We reverse.

On February 23, 1987, the Sierra Club filed a citizens' suit against ECD under section 505 of the Clean Water Act, 33 U.S.C. § 1365. The complaint alleged that ECD violated section 301(a) of the Act by discharging pollutants from its printed circuit board manufacturing plant into the Molalla River via Milk Creek, in violation of the terms of ECD's National Pollutant Discharge Elimination System (NPDES) permit.

On September 30, 1988, the parties filed a Stipulation for Entry of Consent Judgment. In the proposed judgment, ECD agreed to: (1) comply with the terms of its NPDES permit and to terminate all discharges if it violates its permit after June 1, 1989; (2) pay $45,000 to various identified private environmental organizations for their efforts to maintain and protect water quality in Oregon; (3) pay additional sums to these organizations if ECD violates its permit between September 1, 1988, and June 1, 1989; and (4) pay $5000 to the Sierra Club for attorney and expert witness fees. In the consent judgment ECD did not admit any violation, and none was established.

The United States filed an objection to the proposed consent judgment,[12] arguing that the proposed judgment was illegal because it contained no requirement that ECD make payments to the U.S. treasury. The Clean Water

---

12. Section 505(c)(3) of the Clean Water Act, 33 U.S.C. § 1365(c)(3), requires that the United States be given 45 days to review a proposed consent judgment in an action to which it is not a party. If it finds that the proposed judgment is not in accordance with the Act, the United States can object.

Act authorizes the imposition of civil penalties only if paid to the federal treasury. The district court concluded that the payments to be made under the proposed consent judgment were civil penalties within the meaning of the Act and therefore refused to enter the order. *Sierra Club*, 703 F.Supp. at 876–77.

We agree with the district court that if the payments required under the proposed consent decree are civil penalties within the meaning of the Clean Water Act, they may be paid only to the U.S. treasury. We disagree, however, that the payments are civil penalties. No violation of the Act was found or determined by the proposed settlement judgment. When a defendant agrees before trial to make payments to environmental organizations without admitting liability, the agreement is simply part of an out-of-court settlement which the parties are free to make.

The Supreme Court has stated on two occasions that civil penalties imposed by a court in a citizens' suit under the Clean Water Act must be made payable to the U.S. treasury. *Gwaltney*, 484 U.S. at 53 ("If the citizen prevails in such an action, the court may order injunctive relief and/or impose civil penalties payable to the United States Treasury"); *Middlesex County Sewerage Authority v. National Sea Clammers Ass'n*, 453 U.S. 1, 14 n. 25 (1981) ("Under the [Federal Water Pollution Control Act], civil penalties, payable to the Government, also may be ordered by the court). Because the monetary payments required under the proposed consent judgment will not go to the U.S. treasury, the district court was correct in concluding that if they are "civil penalties" they violate the Clean Water Act.

While it is clear that a court cannot order a defendant in a citizens' suit to make payments to an organization other than the U.S. treasury, this prohibition does not extend to a settlement agreement whereby the defendant does not admit liability and the court is not ordering non-consensual monetary relief. "[C]onsent decrees bear some of the earmarks of judgments entered after litigation. At the same time, because their terms are arrived at through mutual agreement of the parties, consent decrees also closely resemble contracts." *Local No. 903, Int'l Ass'n of Firefighters, AFL-CIO v. City of Cleveland*, 478 U.S. 501, 519.

Because of the unique aspects of settlements, a district court should enter a proposed consent judgment if the court decides that it is fair, reasonable and equitable and does not violate the law or public policy. *See Citizens for a Better Environment v. Gorsuch*, 718 F.2d 1117, 1125–26 (D.C. Cir. 1983).

The consent decree agreed to by the Sierra Club and ECD comes within the scope of the pleadings, furthers the broad objectives upon which the complaint was based and does not violate the Clean Water Act. The Sierra Club's complaint was based upon the allegation that ECD was not in compliance with the Clean Water Act and was polluting the Oregon waters. The district court found that compelling ECD to comply with the terms of its permit or cease all discharges is "in the public interest." *Sierra Club*, 703 F.Supp. at 878. It also acknowledged that the environmental organizations that will receive funds under the proposed consent judgment "will apply the money in ways that will help further the goals of the Act." Id. Moreover, as the court noted, "Congress 'encourages' settlements of this type 'which preserve the punitive nature of the enforcement actions while putting the funds collected to use on behalf of environmental protection.'" *Id.* at 877 (quoting H.R. Conf. Rep. No. 1004, 99th Cong., 2d Sess. 139 (1986)).[13]

We therefore find that the proposed consent decree furthers the purpose of the statute upon which the complaint was based and does not violate its terms or policy. Upon remand, the district court should enter the consent decree proposed by the Sierra Club and ECD and award costs and attorney fees pursuant to the decree.

REVERSED and REMANDED.

* * *

1. *Payments to environmental groups.* The *Sierra Club* court believed that a payment to an environmental group, rather than to the U.S. Treasury, comports with the policy behind citizen suit enforcement. If that is true, then why does that policy apply only in the context of a settlement? Why can't a court order a payment to environmental groups? Does that distinction give an environmental group an inordinate incentive to settle, knowing that if the case goes to court any penalties awarded will go to the government? In a similar vein, does the possibility of acquiring funds for nongovernmental projects provide citizen suit plaintiffs with *more* of an incentive to bring a citizen suit than Congress envisioned?

---

13. Consent decrees, such as the one at issue here, are also consistent with current practice. Courts throughout the country have entered consent judgments in civil suits requiring defendants to make payments to various environmental organizations and, in some cases, the defendants have not been required to pay penalties to the U.S. Treasury. *See, e.g., Friends of the Earth v. Eastman Kodak Co.,* 656 F.Supp. 513 (W.D.N.Y.), *aff'd,* 834 F.2d 295 (2nd Cir. 1987) ($49,000 to the Conservation Foundation "for projects reasonably related to the protection of water quality"); *Sierra Club v. Port Townsend Paper Corp.,* Civ. No. C87-316C (W.D. Wash. Oct. 28, 1988) ($137,500 to the Nature Conservancy "to be used directly for purposes of improving environmental and water quality); *Natural Resource Defense Counsel v. Duquesne Light Co.,* Civ. No. 87-0511 (D.Pa. Aug. 14, 1987) ($40,000 to Western Pennsylvania Conservancy with penalties generated by future violations going to state clean water fund); *Natural Resource Defense Council v. Pennsylvania Electric Co.,* Civ. Nos. 87-0512 & 87-0513 (W.D.Pa. Aug. 25, 1987) (monies paid to Pennsylvania Clean Water Fund).

2. *Consent decrees.* In many other types of litigation, a settlement agreement is not filed with the court; the plaintiff simply dismisses the suit with prejudice once the agreement is signed. No judicial approval of the settlement agreement is necessary or appropriate and it is enforced like any other contract. A consent decree, on the other hand, is a judgment of the court and therefore requires the judge to determine whether it is fair, equitable, and consistent with public policy. Why are citizen suits (as well as government enforcement suits) typically resolved by consent decree rather than settlement agreement? The Supreme Court, in *Buckhannon Bd. & Care Home Inc. v. W. Va. Dep't of Health & Human Res.*, 532 U.S. 598 (2001), held that federal fee-shifting statutes that authorize an award to "prevailing parties" require a plaintiff to obtain a favorable court judgment in order to be entitled to fees (a mere settlement agreement would not qualify). What other differences between a consent decree and a settlement agreement can you see?

3. *Overfiling.* If the EPA is not happy with the terms of a citizen suit settlement, can it "overfile" a suit of its own for penalties? Does the "diligent prosecution" of the citizen suit action preclude this agency filing? Or has the EPA waived its right to sue by not filing within the 60-day notice period? What about *res judicata*?

Problem 3.6: Attorneys' Fees

Assume that, after MEC has been litigating its citizen suit for over a year, EPA files its own action against PU and very soon thereafter enters into a consent decree which requires PU to upgrade its pollution control system and pay $40,000 in penalties. The court now dismisses MEC's suit on mootness grounds.

- *Is MEC entitled to attorneys' fees, if it can show that its citizen suit was the "catalyst" for EPA's action?* See Buckhannon, supra.

- *Does it matter whether MEC intervened in EPA's lawsuit?* Compare Environmental Cons. Org. v. City of Dallas, *307 Fed. Appx. 781 (5th Cir. 2008)* with Sierra Club v. Hamilton Cty., *504 F.3d 634 (6th Cir. 2007)*.

- *Would the same result obtain in a CAA citizen suit?* See Sierra Club v. EPA, *322 F.3d 718 (D. C. Cir. 2003) (relying on* Ruckelshaus v. Sierra Club, *463 U.S. 680 (1983))*.

---

g. Suits against the EPA or State Agency

The citizen suit provisions also allow suit against the EPA Administrator when the Administrator has failed "to perform any act or duty under this chapter which is not discretionary." Section 505(a)(2). This type of citizen suit is often brought when the EPA misses deadlines for promulgating certain standards or limitations. *See, e.g., Defenders of Wildlife v. Browner*, 888 F. Supp. 1005 (D. Ariz. 1995) (environmental group alleged that the EPA failed to perform nondiscretionary duty to promulgate water quality standards under the Clean Water Act).

Can a citizen sue the EPA for failing to take enforcement action against a violator? The issue hinges on whether the EPA's enforcement duties are classified as mandatory or discretionary. Look at the Clean Water Act enforcement section, Section 309, and determine whether the duties are stated in mandatory language—is the EPA told it *must* impose a fine or issue a compliance order?

Section 309 seems to say that the Administrator, when he or she finds a violation has occurred, must either issue a compliance order or bring a civil action. 33 U.S.C. § 1319(a)(3). Nevertheless, the mandatory duty kicks in only after the Administrator has made a "finding" of violation—does that give the EPA discretion? Courts have interpreted this language to mean that EPA enforcement powers are discretionary and therefore not subject to citizen suits. *See, e.g., Sierra Club v. Whitman*, 268 F.3d 898, 902–05 (9th Cir. 2001); *Dubois v. Thomas*, 820 F.2d 943, 946–51 (8th Cir. 1987).

What if the state has been delegated the primary enforcement authority and is not exercising it? Remember that the EPA always has supervisory enforcement authority and can use its enforcement powers if the state does not (or even if the state does act, but insufficiently, in the EPA's view). In extreme cases of failure to enforce, the EPA may revoke its delegation to the state. In our problem, MEC may want to consider lobbying the EPA to put pressure on the state agency, MPCA, to enforce the CWA more effectively.

Could MEC sue MPCA for failing to take action against PU? Re-read Clean Water Act Section 505. It is difficult to interpret Section 505 to authorize citizen suits against state agencies. *See Allegheny Cty San. Auth. v. U.S. EPA*, 732 F.2d 1167, 1174 (3d Cir. 1984). Beyond that, allowing the federal government to authorize suits against state officials would be of dubious constitutionality. *See Printz v. United States*, 521 U.S. 898, 928–29 (1997) (striking down provisions of Brady Bill under 10th Amendment because they unconstitutionally imposed obligations on state officials).

Practice Tip: Political Pressure

Politics are inevitably involved in these cases. Just as the facts of the MEC problem suggest that PU may be using political influence, MEC should consider whether to take its case to political figures who can bring pressure to bear on the MPCA or the EPA. Sometimes making one's case to a Senator or Representative can be more useful than pursuing costly litigation. If your Senator happens to sit on the EPA's oversight committee, so much the better. Even though the agency should not allow political considerations to influence its decision making, contact from political representatives may at least encourage a careful look at your concerns. Be aware, however, that playing politics may backfire if the agency resents overbearing pressure by politicians. In addition, political influence in an adjucatory process raises due process concerns. *Pillsbury Co. v. F.T.C.* 54 F. 2d 952 (5th Cir. 1966); *ATX Inc. v. U.S. DOT*, 41 F. 3d 1522 (D.C. Cir. 1994)

Assume MPCA, in its review of the Pork Unlimited matter, obtains new monitoring data for the North Folk River and determines that the water-quality-based effluent limits in PU's permit are unnecessarily strict. It now issues PU a revised permit, with higher limits for ammonia nitrogen and fecal coliform. If MEC wants to challenge the permit on the basis that it does not comport with federal or state law, it would no longer be an enforcement case under the citizen suit provision. Instead, this would be litigation to challenge agency action, and would be brought under the state's version of the Administrative Procedure Act. *See, e.g.,* Ch. 14, Minn. Stat. The nature of this lawsuit would be different, involving issues regarding the record on appeal, the scope of judicial review, and the availability of attorneys' fees. We consider these issues in the next chapter on Environmental Litigation.

CHAPTER IV

ENVIRONMENTAL LITIGATION

A. Introduction: The Lawyer's Role in Environmental Litigation

The enforcement cases covered in the last two chapters were a particular type of environmental litigation. This chapter discusses lawsuits involving environmental problems, filed for purposes other than enforcement. For example, at the end of the last chapter, we discussed the possibility that our client might have to sue the state agency for improperly issuing a NPDES permit. Environmental litigation covers a wide variety of actions, including:

- lawsuits involving environmental statutes applied to individual cases, such as a challenge to the denial of a permit or a challenge to permit conditions;
- facial challenges to environmental regulations or statutes, typically filed by environmental interest groups (such as the Sierra Club or the Natural Resources Defense Council) or groups representing the regulated entities (such as the American Petroleum Institute or the Chemical Manufacturers Association);
- suits claiming that an agency has violated a statutory provision, such as failing to complete an Environmental Impact Statement under NEPA, or improperly funding a project that violates the Endangered Species Act, or failing to regulate greenhouse gases under the CAA;
- common law actions to recover for or enjoin environmental harms, such as toxic tort litigation or nuisance suits; and
- actions, filed by either the government or a private party, to require hazardous substance remediation or to recover the cost of a hazardous substance cleanup under CERCLA (Superfund) or similar laws.

In many ways, environmental litigation is no different from any other type of civil litigation. The rules of civil procedure and evidence are the same, the same motions and discovery requests are made, and the same types of litigation strategies apply. Moreover, the environmental litigator may need to know as much about other areas of law as about the environmental law itself. For example, the environmental lawyer may need to become a constitutional law specialist, when litigating whether the Commerce Clause allows a state to ban hazardous waste imports, or a corporate law expert, when litigating whether a successor corporation is liable for hazardous waste costs under CERCLA when it buys the assets of another corporation.

In other ways, however, environmental litigation requires special expertise. Because the typical environmental case involves a government agency on one side, some specific types of litigation issues arise. *See generally* Gregory C. Sisk, *Litigation with the Federal Government* (2d ed. 2007). Consider the following hypothetical, continued from the last chapter, in thinking through some of these particular problems:

Problems 4.1 through 4.4: Pork Unlimited Permit Appeal

Assume that you represent Pork Unlimited (PU), a meat processor that has been granted a NPDES permit to discharge ammonia and fecal coliform into the North Fork River. The technology-based effluent limitation for fecal coliform for this type of meat processing plant would be 400 CFU/100 mL. 40 C.F.R. §432.12.[1] CFU refers to "colony forming units" and is one way of estimating the bacteria organisms in a sample. Because it is impossible to actually count the millions or billions of bacteria in a wastewater sample, labs must use an estimating technique.

Fecal coliform is one type of indicator bacteria, which may not be harmful itself, but typically indicates the presence of pathogens, the bacterial agents that do cause illness. Water-borne pathogens can cause significant human health problems such as gastroenteritis, dysentery, ear infections, and hepatitis A. Because of the variety of pathogens and their low concentration, regulators must use more common bacteria as indicators. Some water quality standards use total coliforms or a specific subset of fecal coliform—enterococci or *E. coli.*—as the indicator.

PU is discharging into the North Fork River, which is classified as a Class 2 waterbody, designated for both human recreation and aquatic life.

---

1. This regulation specifies the Best Practicable Technology (BPT) for the "Simple Slaughterhouse" subcategory of point source dischargers. You learned in Environmental Law class that dischargers must now meet a higher pollution control level, called Best Available Technology Economically Achievable (BAT) for some types of pollutants and Best Conventional Technology (BCT) for conventional pollutants such as fecal coliform. In this case, BCT limits were identical to BPT. 40 C.F.R. §432.17.

Class 2 waters are required to meet a bacteria standard of 200 organisms of fecal coliform per 100 mL[2] and the North Fork is listed as impaired for bacteria, primarily due to the runoff from some feedlots and cattle grazing further upstream. Therefore, MPCA imposed a water-quality-based effluent limitation (WQBEL) more stringent than the technology-based regulation.

MPCA bases its effluent calculations using a "mixing zone," which allows the effluent to be diluted by the ambient water before measuring its impact on water quality.[3] Typically, the size of the mixing zone depends on the amount of water in the waterbody, how it's used, and the type of pollutant. In this case, MPCA allowed a mixing zone of only 25 yards, because a popular swimming area was nearby. Using this dilution, MPCA determined that a permit limit of 250 CFU/100 mL of fecal coliform would be required to meet the water quality standard at the mixing zone boundary.

PU believes that this fecal coliform effluent limitation is too stringent, because the mixing zone MPCA used was too small. In addition, PU believes the MPCA improperly calculated the volume of river water available for dilution, based on historic flow data that is now out-of-date. You will represent PU in its appeal of this permit, as you work through the problems below.

Administrative Procedure: In many environmental actions, the case may have to work its way through an agency process before it reaches court. The agency process will be governed by the state or federal administrative procedure act, plus any specific procedures provided for that particular action. 5 U.S.C., ch. 5; Minn. Stat., ch. 14. The agency's failure to follow administrative procedures, such as giving proper notice and the opportunity for comment, may provide fertile grounds for challenge. For example, in PU's situation, MPCA is required to issue a draft permit and give public notice with an opportunity for public comment. In some cases, MPCA must also issue a fact sheet providing an explanation of the permit conditions. Minn. Admin. Rules §§ 7001.0100; 7001.1070. The federal procedure is similar. 40 C.F.R. § 124.6.

---

2. Minn. Admin. Rules § 7050.0222. The standard requires the geometric mean of five samples per month to be below 126 org./100 mL of *E. coli*, which is generally equivalent to 200 org./100 mL of fecal coliform. The standard applies only between April 1 and October 31 — do you know why?

3. Minn. Admin. Rules § 7050.0210.

Parties must know how to build or supplement the agency record, because the court's review may be limited to that record. In the case of NPDES permits, for example, federal regulations require "all persons ... who believe any condition of a draft permit is inappropriate or that the Director's tentative decision to ... prepare a draft permit is inappropriate, must raise all reasonably ascertainable issues and submit all reasonably available arguments supporting their position by the close of the public comment period," in order to contest a final permit determination in an evidentiary hearing or to preserve an issue for review by the EAB. 40 C.F.R. § 124.13. Additionally, 40 C.F.R. § 124.76 provides that "[n]o issues shall be raised by any party that were not submitted to the administrative record ... as part of the preparation of and comment on a draft permit unless good cause is shown for the failure to submit them."

Administrative law doctrines, such as ripeness, finality, and exhaustion of remedies, may be crucial. The federal Administrative Procedure Act, 5 U.S.C. § 704, authorizes judicial review only of "final agency action," unless review is specifically authorized by another statute. The related requirement of "ripeness" is designed:

> to prevent the courts, through avoidance of premature adjudication, from entangling themselves in abstract disagreements over administrative policies, and also to protect the agencies from judicial interference until an administrative decision has been formalized and its effects felt in a concrete way by the challenging parties.

Abbott Laboratories v. Gardner, 387 U.S. 136, 148–149 (1967). *See, e.g., Ohio Forestry Ass'n, Inc. v. Sierra Club*, 523 U.S. 726, 733–38 (1998) (forest management plan not ripe for review); *Comm'r of Public Works of City of Charleston v. United States*, 30 F.3d 129 (4th Cir. 1994) (Corps' jurisdictional wetlands determination not ripe for review until enforced). The finality doctrine would require a NPDES permit to be appealed first within the agency, if the state provides such a procedure, before a court could review it.

Problem 4.1: Administrative Procedure

a) Assume that PU is located in a state without a NPDES program, so that EPA is issuing its permit. After EPA issues a final permit decision, an interested party may request an evidentiary hearing to contest the resolution of any questions raised during the public comment period. See 40 C.F.R. § 124.74(a). The Regional Administrator then grants or denies the request for a hearing. See 40 C.F.R. § 124.75(a)(1). Assume EPA issued a draft per-

mit with the fecal coliform limitation of 250 org./100 mL. During the com-
ment period, PU submitted a memo from its consultant, which argued that
a larger mixing zone should be used, based on her review of similar permits.
In its final permit decision, EPA rejected that argument, on the basis that the
North Fork River is used frequently for contact recreation. PU now requests
an evidentiary hearing, in order to submit evidence showing that EPA sig-
nificantly underestimated the volume of water in the North Fork River avail-
able for diluting the effluent in the mixing zone. EPA rejects the request for
a hearing, because PU did not raise this issue during the comment period.
What result? See Adams v. U.S. EPA, *38 F.3d 43 (1st Cir. 1994);* In re
Broward County, Fla., *6 E.A.D. 535 (EAB 1996).*

b) Now assume PU's permit is being issued by MPCA. MPCA informed
PU early in the administrative process that it has tightened its approach to
mixing zones based on an EPA memorandum indicating that the federal
agency planned to object to any state-issued permits containing mixing zones
that exceed EPA guidance without adequate justification. Can PU bring an
action challenging EPA's memorandum as beyond its authority under the
Clean Water Act? See Appalachian Energy Grp. v. EPA, *33 F.3d 319, 322–23*
(4th Cir. 1994); Delaware Cty. Safe Drinking Water Coal'n, Inc. v.
McGinty, *2007 WL 2213516 (E.D. Pa.).*

Statutory Issues: Litigation may be controlled by a specific statute—one that
limits the type of review, when review can be sought and which court has jurisdiction. For example, under the CAA, a challenge to EPA's promulgation
of a National Emission Standard for Hazardous Air Pollutant (NESHAP) must
be brought in the D.C. Circuit Court of Appeals, while a challenge to EPA's
approval of Virginia's State Implementation Plan must be brought in the Court
of Appeals for the Fourth Circuit. *See* CAA §307(b), 42 U.S.C. §7607(b). Why
do you suppose these cases go directly to the court of appeals rather than starting in the district court?

In a case involving review of agency action, such as the denial or issuance
of a permit, the Administrative Procedure Act limits review as follows:

The reviewing court shall—

(1) compel agency action unlawfully withheld or unreasonably de-
layed; and

(2) hold unlawful and set aside agency action, findings, and conclusions found to be—

(A) arbitrary, capricious, an abuse of discretion, or otherwise
not in accordance with law;

(B) contrary to constitutional right, power, privilege, or immunity;

(C) in excess of statutory jurisdiction, authority, or limitations, or short of statutory right;

(D) without observance of procedure required by law;

(E) unsupported by substantial evidence in a case subject to sections 556 and 557 of this title or otherwise reviewed on the record of an agency hearing provided by statute; or

(F) unwarranted by the facts to the extent that the facts are subject to trial de novo by the reviewing court.

5 U.S.C. § 706. Thus, any challenge must be framed in those terms — for example, you may argue that the imposition of a CAA penalty without a pre-enforcement hearing violated your client's due process rights (§ 706(2)(B)), or that the issuance of a draft NPDES permit without a fact sheet violated statutory procedure (§ 706(2)(D)). Often, you may argue that the agency's decision was "arbitrary and capricious," a deferential standard which means that an agency must "examine the relevant data and articulate a satisfactory explanation for its action." *Motor Vehicle Mfrs. Assn. of United States, Inc. v. State Farm Mut. Auto. Ins. Co.*, 463 U.S. 29, 43 (1983).

Judicial review of an agency's regulations will also be limited. In *Chevron U.S.A., Inc. v. NRDC*, 467 U.S. 837 (1984), the Supreme Court clarified the role of the court where an administrative agency has interpreted a statute. The Court held that Congress's clear and unambiguous statutory intent must be followed. However, if any ambiguity exists in the statutory language, the court should accept the agency's interpretation as long as it is reasonable. Similarly, courts give great deference to an agency's interpretation of its own ambiguous regulations. *Gonzales v. Oregon*, 546 U.S. 243 (2006). While not bound by *Chevron* or *Gonzales,* state courts also give deference to state agency interpretations of state statutes and regulations, although the degree of deference may vary. *See, e.g., Adrian School Dist. v. Mich. Pub. Schl. Emp. Ret. Sys.*, 458 Mich. 326, 582 N.W.2d 767, 769 (1998) (agency interpretations given deference "provided they are consistent with the purpose and policies of the statute in question"). This deferential standard of review makes it difficult, but certainly not impossible, to successfully challenge agency regulations or interpretations.

Moreover, the agency may have the ability to affect the litigation through its rule-making power (perhaps even by promulgating an applicable regulation while the case is pending). *Smiley v. Citibank (South Dakota), N.A.*, 517 U.S. 735, 740–41 (1996) (*Chevron* deference due regulation prompted by underlying litigation). Congress or the state legislature also may shift the turf beneath the litigation by amending the statute. *See, e.g., Miccosukee Tribe v. U.S.*, 2008 WL 2967654 (Florida enacted Everglades Forever Act and amendments to resolve pending litigation over phosphorus pollution of Everglades). Thus, unlike an auto accident case where the trial deals only with evidence regarding a historical event, environmental litigation may involve an agency process that continues to evolve while the litigation is pending.

Problem 4.2: Judicial Review

Assume that MPCA originally proposed to issue the PU permit with a higher fecal coliform limit, using a larger mixing zone. Under CWA § 402(d), proposed state NPDES permits must be submitted to EPA, which then has 90 days to object, if it finds the permit is inconsistent with the CWA. 33 U.S.C. § 1342(d). EPA objected to the proposed PU permit, believing that the large mixing zone did not comport with EPA policy and regulations.[4] In response, MPCA revised the permit, resulting in the 250 CFU/100 mL effluent limitation described above. Can PU file suit against EPA, challenging its determination that MPCA's use of a larger mixing zone would violate the CWA? See American Paper Inst., Inc. v. U.S. EPA, 890 F.2d 869, 872–75 (7th Cir. 1989).

Discovery: Parties litigating against the government may find it helpful to use statutory tools, such as the Freedom of Information Act, which are not available in other types of litigation. However, discovery against the government also presents some unique challenges:

- <u>witnesses</u>: depositions of high-ranking agency officials will not be allowed absent "extraordinary circumstances." *U.S. v. Morgan*, 313 U.S. 409 (1941). In *Morgan*, the Court noted that administrative proceedings have "'a quality resembling that of a judicial proceeding'... Just as a judge cannot be subjected to such a scrutiny ... so the integrity of the administrative process must be equally respected." Moreover, it is a fundamental principle of administrative law that a party challenging agency action is forbidden from inquiring into the mental processes of an ad-

---

4. For example, EPA's Water Quality Standards Handbook sets out detailed guidance for the use of mixing zones, including a statement that mixing should not be permitted where it might endanger critical areas, such as recreation areas or drinking water supplies. EPA, Water Quality Handbook, at 5-1 (2d ed. 1994) (avail. at http://www.epa.gov/water-science/standards/handbook/). *See also* 40 C.F.R. § 131.13 (allowing state to include mixing zone policies in water quality standards, subject to EPA approval).

ministrative official, unless there is a showing of bad faith or improper behavior. *See, e.g., U.S. v. Sensient Colors, Inc.*, 2009 WL 303869 (quashing deposition subpoenas issued to former EPA Administrator and former EPA Regional Administrator).

•   privilege: Professor Sisk states that:

> "courts have recognized government privileges in cases where disclosure would seriously impair governmental operations, undermine deliberative candor, or endanger national security. Recognition of a privilege does not necessarily mean that it is absolute. Decisions on claims of privilege for government documents require weighing two conflicting considerations: (1) the public need to keep secret or uninterrupted the particular facet of government operations involved and (2) the right of the private litigant to obtain information in support of his or her claim or defense, that is, the interest of the judicial administration of justice."

Gregory C. Sisk, *A Primer on Civil Discovery Against the Federal Government*, 52 Fed. Law. 28, 31 (June 2005). An excellent example is *Kasza v. Browner*, 133 F.3d 1159 (9th Cir. 1998), in which the court dismissed a RCRA citizen suit alleging that the Air Force and EPA failed to comply with RCRA hazardous waste regulations at a "classified operating location," because the state secrets doctrine would prevent necessary discovery.

•   production of documents: in civil litigation, parties ordinarily obtain documents from non-parties by using a subpoena duces tecum. Federal agencies are authorized by the Federal Housekeeping Statute, 5 U.S.C. § 301, to establish a centralized approach to such requests. EPA regulations provide that EPA employees may not provide testimony or produce documents "concerning information acquired in the course of performing official duties" unless authorized by the General Counsel or his designee (typically Regional Counsel). 40 C.F.R. § 2.402(b). The regulations further provide that no EPA employee may produce subpoenaed documents in cases where the United States is not a party "[u]nless the General Counsel or his designee … determines that compliance with the subpoena is clearly in the interests of EPA." 40 C.F.R. § 2.405. The failure to provide documents, of course, may be challenged by the litigant, and a court may compel production if it rejects EPA claims of privilege and undue burden. *See, e.g., U.S. EPA v. General Elec. Co.*, 197 F.3d 592, 599 (2d Cir. 1999) (in compelling production court must "maintain the appropriate balance between the interests of the government in conserving limited resources, maintaining necessary confidentiality and preventing interference with government functions, and the interests of suitors in discovering important information relevant to the prosecution or defense of private litigation").

Of course, if the case involves an appeal of an agency decision, the court's review may be limited to the administrative record below and discovery disallowed because new evidence would be inadmissible. *Illinois EPA v. Ill. Poll. Cont. Bd.*, 386 Ill. App. 3d 375, 896 N.E.2d 479 (2008). However, on rare occasions the court may permit discovery and evidentiary supplementation of the record upon a "strong showing of bad faith or improper behavior" in the administrative proceeding. *Citizens to Preserve Overton Park, Inc. v. Volpe*, 401 U.S. 402, 420 (1971); *Newton Cty. Wildlife Ass'n v. Rogers*, 141 F.3d 803, 807–08 (8th Cir. 1998).

Problem 4.3: Discovery

In response to MPCA's decision to tighten the fecal coliform limits, PU filed a contested case petition under Minn. Admin. Rules §§ 7000.1750 et seq. In a contested case, an evidentiary hearing is held before an administrative law judge, who issues a report to the agency, which then makes a final decision. Minn. Admin. Rules §§ 1400.8100–8200. Thus, the agency grants permission for a contested case hearing only when there are disputed issues of material fact regarding the permit application. Minn. Admin. Rule § 7000.1900. MPCA granted PU's petition to hold a contested case.

In preparing the case, PU's attorneys discovered a memo in the agency's file indicating that the Governor's office had contacted the Commissioner of the MPCA regarding the permit. PU believes that, because it made substantial contributions to the Governor's political rivals, it is possible that the telephone call improperly influenced MPCA's decision making process. Minnesota rules allow discovery in contested case proceedings, but on a more limited scale than in a judicial trial. Minnesota rules provide that if the other side objects, "the party seeking discovery shall have the burden of showing that the discovery is needed for the proper presentation of the party's case, is not for purposes of delay, and that the issues or amounts in controversy are significant enough to warrant the discovery." Minn. Admin. Rule § 1400.6700.

PU serves a deposition notice on the MPCA Commissioner, the agency's top official, in order to elicit information regarding the telephone call from the Governor's office. MPCA objects. What result? See, e.g., Coleman v. Schwartzenegger, 2008 WL 3843292 (allowing depositions of high-ranking government official when they have personal factual information not available from other sources).

Attorney's Fees: Many environmental lawsuits involve a claim for attorney's fees or other litigation costs. Some statutes specifically provide for the award of litigation costs.[5] For example, the previous chapter dealt with the award of fees under the various citizen suit provisions, such as CWA §505(d). Similarly, statutes authorizing review of administrative action (such as permit denials) may also provide for fee-shifting. *See, e.g.,* CWA §509(b)(3).

Where there is no specific fee-shifting provision, the Equal Access to Justice Act, 28 U.S.C. §2812, may provide an attorney's fees claim.[6] Under EAJA, a party prevailing in a suit against the United States is entitled to a fee award only if the court finds the government's position was not "substantially justified," 28 U.S.C. §2812(d), which the Supreme Court has defined as "'justified in substance or in the main'—that is, justified to a degree that could satisfy a reasonable person." *Pierce v. Underwood,* 487 U.S. 552, 557 (1988). In addition, only parties of limited means are eligible (thereby providing them "equal access to justice").[7] Thus, the fee-shifting provisions of the specific statutes noted above, lacking financial eligibility and "substantial justified" limitations, may be easier to meet. Many states have fee-shifting statutes similar to EAJA, which may provide fees for administrative proceedings as well as court litigation. *See, e.g.,* Minn. Stat. §15.472.

Problem 4.4: Litigation Costs

Assume that, in Problem 4.3, PU was denied a contested case hearing, because the agency believed PU had not adequately raised the stream flow issue

---

5. Under CERCLA, the government may recover its "enforcement" costs, including attorney's fees, in addition to the costs of a hazardous waste cleanup. CERCLA Sections 107(a)(4)(A) & 101(25), 42 U.S. C. §9607(a)(4)(A) & 9601(25). A private party seeking reimbursement of its response costs, however, may not recover attorney's fees. *Key Tronic Corp. v. U.S.,* 511 U.S. 809 (1994).

6. *See generally* Gregory C. Sisk, "The Essentials of the Equal Access to Justice Act: Court Awards of Attorney's Fees for Unreasonable Government Conduct," Part One, 55 La. L. Rev. 219 (1994); Part Two, 56 La. L. Rev. 1 (1995).

7. 28 U.S.C. §2412(d)(2)(B) (defining eligible parties as including individuals with a net worth under $2 million and business entities, organizations, or local governments with a net worth of less than $7 million and fewer than 500 employees).

in its comments on the draft permit. On appeal, the court determined that it was an abuse of discretion not to allow PU to present this evidence. Will PU be entitled to recover its litigation costs for this appeal?

Government attorneys: Another issue unique to agency litigation involves dealing with multiple attorneys within the government. We have already discussed the roles of the agency attorney and the Justice Department (or state Attorney General's office) in the enforcement context. In other litigation matters, their roles are similarly complex.

The U.S. Attorney General is vested with the authority to conduct litigation on behalf of the United States, including the various agencies. 28 U.S.C. §516. That authority is delegated to the Justice Department's various litigating divisions, the U.S. Attorneys' offices and, occasionally, agency attorneys. *See* 28 C.F.R. Part 0 (Organization of the Department of Justice). The Justice Department has six litigating divisions, each headed by an Assistant Attorney General. Almost all environmental cases would be handled by the Environment and Natural Resources Division. *See* 28 C.F.R. §0.65 (jurisdiction of ENRD). Within each division are a number of sections, branches, or offices, which handle different types of cases, each under the supervision of a Deputy Assistant Attorney General. For example, the Environmental Enforcement section would handle a civil penalty action under the Clean Water Act, while the Wildlife section would handle an Endangered Species Act case. These offices are staffed by Section Chiefs and Trial Attorneys.

As a result of these multiple layers of control, decision-making authority in litigation matters is often complicated. A proposed settlement, for example, must be approved at a variety of levels, depending on its nature, size and whether settlement authority has been delegated by the higher official. *See generally,* 28 C.F.R. Subpart Y. Thus, a lawyer representing the other side may think a settlement has been reached with the agency attorney or the Assistant U.S. Attorney, only to find it rejected by the Assistant or Deputy Attorney General. Officials at the higher levels of authority consider broader policy objectives, such as the impact of the settlement on similar cases elsewhere or the need to establish precedent by a test case. *See* Angus MacBeth, *Settling with the Government,* Environmental Law Manual 410 (Theodore L. Garrett, ed. 1992); Richard K. Willard, *How to Settle Your Civil Case with the Government,* 3 Department of Justice Manual §4-3.200A, at 4-48 to 4-48.7 (1994).

The next section will outline some important practice considerations that arise in environmental litigation, using the Superfund area as the primary example.

B. Practice Issues in Superfund Litigation

The Comprehensive Environmental Response, Compensation and Liability Act (CERCLA or "Superfund") was enacted in 1980 to respond to the growing number of hazardous substance disposal sites that had either contaminated or threatened to contaminate the environment. CERCLA gave the federal government broad authority to respond to hazardous substance releases and to recover the response costs from the parties deemed responsible. Superfund litigation for the recovery of hazardous waste cleanup costs may be the most prevalent form of environmental litigation. Stakes are typically high, with the cleanup tab averaging $25–30 million per site. Because the CERCLA liability scheme casts a wide net, it is common to have dozens, or even hundreds, of parties involved in one case.

The complexity of these suits requires lawyers to consider issues such as whether and how to conduct joint litigation endeavors (such as the use of common counsel), whether to use alternative dispute resolution methods, and how to bring in third parties. As a result, Superfund not only provides a good context for issues that can arise in environmental cases, but it also provides an opportunity to explore some of the practical aspects of complex litigation. Note, however, that the federal Superfund process typically focuses on only the worst hazardous substance sites; many contaminated sites are cleaned up under state law regimes or voluntarily, using state "Land Recycling Programs."[8]

1. The Superfund Remediation Process

We will not attempt to re-examine in detail the CERCLA liability scheme you probably covered in your environmental law survey class. What follows is a quick overview of how CERCLA works. For a more detailed explanation, you might wish to consult Topol & Snow, *Superfund Law & Procedure* (West 2005).

Section 104 of CERCLA, 42 U.S.C. §9604, authorizes the EPA (by delegation from the President) to respond to any release or threat of release of a hazardous substance, pollutant, or contaminant. Response actions take two forms. "Removal action" is short-term action, usually taken to prevent the problem from getting worse (e.g., a berm to prevent further run-off) and prevent immediate threats to human health and the environment. "Remedial action" is the long-term solution for the release (e.g., pumping and treating groundwater, or excavation and incineration of the hazardous substances).

---

8. *See, e.g.,* Pennsylvania Land Recycling and Environmental Remediation Standards Act 35 Pa. Stat. §§6026.101 *et seq.*

All government actions undertaken must be consistent with the National Contingency Plan (NCP), which establishes procedures and standards for responding to releases. CERCLA § 105, 42 U.S.C. § 9605. The NCP, set out in the Code of Federal Regulations at 40 C.F.R. Part 300, details such requirements as how the site should be studied, how the remedy should be selected, and how public participation should be ensured. The EPA will not be able to recover any costs that are inconsistent with the NCP. CERCLA § 107(a)(4)(A), 42 U.S.C. § 9607(a)(4)(A).

The EPA has two choices in deciding how to proceed with a site response action. If "imminent and substantial endangerment" exists, it may issue an administrative order to one or more of the parties deemed to be responsible for the release, requiring them to undertake abatement action. CERCLA § 106, 42 U.S.C. § 9606.[9] Alternatively, the EPA may clean up the site itself, using the Hazardous Substance Superfund.[10] The agency may then seek reimbursement from the responsible parties under Section 107, 42 U.S.C. § 9607. In some cases, of course, no responsible parties will be available and, at those "orphan" sites, the Superfund will have to absorb the entire cost of the response.

Hazardous waste problems come to light in a variety of ways—for example, when a water contamination problem is discovered and traced back to its source, or when development activity uncovers an old disposal site. In the typical case, someone notifies the EPA and the remediation process begins. The following discussion outlines a typical EPA-lead Superfund remediation. Keep in mind that many sites are cleaned up voluntarily by private parties or pursuant to state Superfund-type laws. Those sites may follow the same basic process, and indeed, private parties may recover their response costs from other potentially responsible parties (PRPs) under CERCLA as long as they act consistently with the NCP. CERCLA § 107(a)(4)(B), 42 U.S.C. § 9607(A)(4)(13).

a. Removal Action

The EPA may decide to take action right away to respond to immediate threats while long-term remedies are studied. This short-term action, called "removal action" (*see* Section 101(23)), does not require the type of full-scale

---

9. Section 106 also allows a court to order a party to perform abatement action under these circumstances.

10. The Superfund initially received the majority of its funding from a tax on the chemical and petroleum industries and a corporate environmental tax. The Superfund tax expired in December 1995 and has not been reauthorized as of 2009, although Congress is considering legislation that would reinstate it. Meanwhile, the Superfund is being replenished by cost-recovery efforts and annual budget authorizations from general funds.

preliminary study that remedial action requires.[11] The EPA, using its Section 106 authority, may order one of the potentially responsible parties (PRPs) to undertake the removal, or may seek a PRP volunteer. Even though designated "removal," the short-term action may take many forms, such as providing alternative water supplies, building berms, or actually excavating contaminated soil or drums of waste.

At many sites, response actions are divided into "operable units (OU)," depending on the complexity of the site. EPA defines an OU as "a discrete action that comprises an incremental step toward comprehensively addressing site problems…. Operable units may address geographical portions of a site, specific site problems, or initial phases of an action." 40 C.F.R. § 300.5.

b. Site Investigation

The investigation of the site begins with a Preliminary Assessment (PA) — basically a desktop review of the information known about the site situation. This is followed by the Site Investigation (SI), in which the EPA does some preliminary testing of the hazardous substances and the media they are or may be affecting.

c. Information Gathering

There are several ways for the EPA to gather information about the site and to begin identifying responsible parties. First, CERCLA gives the EPA access to the site to conduct testing, including taking samples of soil or water, and other investigation. CERCLA § 104(e)(3), 42 U.S. C. § 9604(e)(3). In addition, the EPA makes use of Section 104(e) information requests, which are sent to those who are suspected of having a connection to the site. Failure to respond to a § 104(e) request may result in an administrative order or a civil penalty. CERCLA § 104(e)(5).

EPA has published a 359-page manual to guide agency staff involved in the search for potentially responsible parties.[12]

d. Hazard Ranking System ("HRS")

The EPA uses the information gathered in the PA/SI to conduct a risk assessment of the site. Risk values are assigned for factors such as the potential

---

11. *See* Jerry L. Anderson, *Removal or Remedial? The Myth of CERCLA's Two-Response System,* 18 Colum. J. of Envt'l L. 103, 108 (1993).

12. EPA, OECA, "PRP Search Manual" (Sept. 2003), avail. at www.epa.gov/compliance/resources/publications/cleanup/superfund/prpmanual/prp-search-man-cmp.pdf.

for contamination of drinking water supplies, the potential for destruction of sensitive ecosystems, and the population potentially affected. CERCLA § 105(a)(8)(A); 40 C.F.R. pt. 300, app. A. These values are then factored into an HRS "score," which is supposed to represent a rough approximation of the risks presented by the site.

e. National Priorities List

CERCLA directs EPA to prioritize the most dangerous sites. EPA lists those sites with the worst HRS scores on the National Priority List (NPL). Current policy is to list every site which scores above 28.5.[13] States also have an opportunity to place their top priority sites on the list. For the complete list, see 40 C.F.R. pt. 300, App. B.[14] The NPL listing is significant; for example, the EPA can use Superfund money to fund remedial action only if the site is listed on the NPL.[15] EPA is required to update the NPL at least once each year. As of July 13, 2009, the NPL listed 1264 sites; a total of 332 sites have been deleted from the list.[16]

f. Remedial Investigation/Feasibility Study

The National Contingency Plan requires that a Remedial Investigation (RI) and Feasibility Study (FS) be conducted at the site before a permanent remedy is selected. The RI is a thorough study of the sources of contamination and the possible pathways of risk. Thus, information is developed on the physical characteristics of the site, including its geology and hydrology; the characteristics of the hazardous substances present, including quantity, toxicity, concentration, and mobility; and potential exposure routes, such as inhalation or ingestion.[17] The Feasibility Study contains a detailed analysis of viable remedial alternatives, which are evaluated according to nine criteria. These criteria include effectiveness, permanence, cost, and implementability.[18]

g. Record of Decision

The EPA selects the remedy in accordance with CERCLA Section 121, 42 U.S.C. § 9621, and issues the Record of Decision (ROD) explaining its rea-

---

13. *See, e.g.,* 74 Fed. Reg. 16126 (April 9, 2009) (revision of NPL).

14. You can also view a state-by-state list of NPL sites at www.epa.gov/superfund/sites/npl.

15. 40 C.F.R. § 300.425(b)(1).

16. EPA, NPL Site Totals, avail. at www.epa.gov/superfund/sites/npl/status.htm.

17. 40 C.F.R. § 300.430(d)(2).

18. 40 C.F.R. § 300.430(e)(9).

soning. At a minimum, the remedy selected must meet state and federal environmental standards that are "applicable or otherwise relevant and appropriate" (ARARs), such as Clean Water Act effluent limitations or Safe Drinking Water Act Maximum Contaminant Levels.[19] Before the EPA selects the remedy, it must allow the public to comment on the proposed plan.

The remediation process is set up as a "shoot first, ask questions later" approach, in order not to delay the site cleanup. Thus, courts cannot review the EPA's choice of remedy or the EPA's issuance of a Section 106 administrative order before the agency seeks to recover its cleanup costs or enforce the administrative order. CERCLA § 113(h), 42 U.S.C. § 9613(h).

h. Remedial Design/Remedial Action (RD/RA)

The project manager will then carry out the remedy selected in the ROD. The NCP states the RD/RA stage "includes the development of the actual design of the selected remedy and implementation of the remedy through construction."[20] While some remedies, such as soil excavation with offsite transport, may be completed relatively quickly, remedies such as groundwater treatment may last for many years. After initial construction, the continuing operation of the remedy is referred to as "Operation and Maintenance" (O & M). For example, a landfill cap with a leachate collection system will require maintenance to prevent erosion of the cover and periodic disposal of the leachate, among other tasks. The RA and O&M may be performed by EPA ("federal-lead"), the state ("state-lead"), or a PRP ("enforcement lead"). In the case of state or PRP actions, EPA will retain oversight responsibility.

If the remedial action will leave any contaminants on-site, Section 121 requires EPA to review the site every five years, to determine if the remedy continues to be protective of human health and the environment. 42 U.S.C. § 9621. The five-year review process may result in additional response action if the initial remedy is found to be deficient.

Practice Tip: The Superfund Cleanup Process

To familiarize yourself with the Superfund process, find an NPL site in or near your community, using EPA's "Superfund Sites Where You Live" feature, found at: www.epa.gov/superfund.

---

19. 42 U.S.C. § 9621(d)(2).
20. 40 C.F.R. § 300.435.

The "Superfund Site Information" link will give you specific information about the status of the site, so you can follow it through the stages
of the process. Many of the important documents, such as the RI/FS
and the ROD, can be accessed on-line through this website.[21] Reading
through those documents will give you a good idea of the complexity
involved in selecting a remedy and the length of time required to
complete remediation. For your selected site, answer the following
questions:

- what are the "contaminants of concern" at the site?
- what media (e.g., soil, surface water, groundwater, air) are contaminated?
- were any short-term "removal" actions undertaken at the site?
- is the response at this site divided into "operable units"? Why?
- what remedy was selected and why?
- what was the length of time between initial action at the site and selection of the remedy? What about the length of time between remedy selection and initial construction? What do you think accounts for
this delay?

If you would like to search a site somewhat similar to the one we will use
in the Superfund exercise below, search for the Davis Liquid Waste site in
Smithfield, Rhode Island.

2. The Superfund Liability Scheme

The parties held liable for response costs (PRPs) under CERCLA fall into
four categories:

- current owners and/or operators of the site—Section 107(a)(1);
- owners and/or operators of the site at the time of disposal of the substances—Section 107(a)(2);
- those who arranged for the disposal of the hazardous substances (usually those who generated the waste)—Section 107(a)(3); and
- transporters of the waste to the site, if they selected the site—Section
107(a)(4).

---

21. EPA is required to maintain a information repository containing the entire administrative record at or near the site, commonly at a public library or city hall. The site team
will also develop a community involvement plan to facilitate public information about the
remedial process.

A party that qualifies as a PRP under one of these four categories is liable for all government response costs incurred consistently with the NCP, plus interest and enforcement costs (including Department of Justice and EPA staff attorney fees). Superfund liability is strict, retroactive, and usually joint and several:

> *Strict Liability:* Although CERCLA itself is silent on this issue, courts have held that Congress intended PRPs to be held strictly liable. *Burlington Northern & S.F. Ry. Co. v. U.S.*, 129 S.Ct. 1870, 1878 (2009). No negligence or recklessness needs to be proved and a PRP's argument that it complied with all applicable laws or that it used state-of-the-art disposal or treatment techniques will be futile. A PRP can escape liability only by establishing one of the limited defenses provided in § 107(b). Those defenses will be discussed in section 3(e) below.

> *Retroactive Liability:* Liability attaches even if the conduct at issue occurred long before CERCLA was enacted and was entirely legal at the time. Although parties have challenged the retroactive aspect of the scheme as unconstitutional, they have never been successful. *See U.S. v. Alcan Alum. Corp.*, 315 F.3d 179, 189 (2d Cir. 2003) (CERCLA retroactivity constitutional); *United States v. Olin Corp.*, 927 F. Supp. 1502 (S.D. Ala. 1996) (retroactivity of CERCLA held unconstitutional), *rev'd*, 107 F.3d 1506 (11th Cir. 1997) (retroactivity constitutional).

> *Joint and Several Liability:* Liability in CERCLA cases is typically joint and several, meaning that each party may be held liable for all of the response costs, not just those it individually caused. Joint and several liability, however, is less of a "given" than strict and retroactive liability. Courts have held that joint and several liability should be imposed using common law standards. Accordingly, joint and several liability is appropriate only when there is no "reasonable basis for apportionment" of the harm. *Burlington Northern*, 129 S.Ct., at 1881. This aspect of the CERCLA liability scheme will be explored in the problems below.

> The parties held jointly liable may sue other PRPs for contribution, of course, *see* Section 113, but typically many potentially liable parties are never sued, either because the evidence against them is weak, because they are impossible to locate, because they are insolvent, or because they are deceased (or if a corporation, dissolved). Thus, imposing joint and several liability means the remaining liable parties will have to absorb this "orphan" share.

The fact scenario below will provide a context for exploring the CERCLA litigation issues. For purposes of the problems and exercises which follow, your professor may assign you to represent one of the parties involved:

* * *

The Shenandoah Superfund Site

This case involves the Shenandoah Industries Superfund site ["the Site"] in Dallas County, Iowa. The Site, outlined in Figure 4.1, is located in a rural area approximately twenty miles from Des Moines. The Site is currently owned and operated by **Shenandoah Industries**, a company that makes parts for farm equipment. Shenandoah bought the 34-acre parcel of land in 1981.

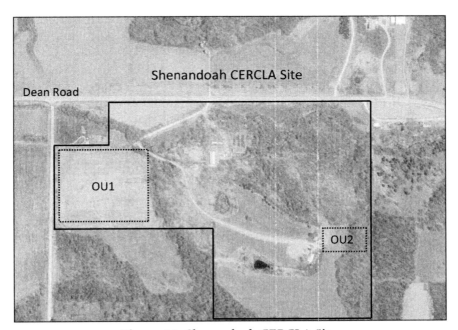

Figure 4.1 Shenandoah CERCLA Site.

From 1965 to 1975, **Carson, Inc.**, owned the Site. Carson also manufactured machine parts and disposed of solvents from its manufacturing process in a large pit located in a remote area of the Site now designated as Operable Unit #1 (OU1). In 1967, **Carrie Carson** inherited all of the Carson, Inc., stock and began serving as the president of the company. In 1968, she raised the possibility of opening up the Site to waste dumpers, although she left it to her general manager, Bart Starr, to carry out this plan.

In 1968, Carson, Inc., opened up the pit for disposal by outside waste transporters, including **Town & Country Sanitation** ["TCS"]. No other transporters to the Site have been identified. TCS paid Carson, Inc., in cash for each load and no written records of the transactions were kept. The customers of TCS were billed each month, but those customer files were destroyed long ago. The disposal activity by Carson and TCS continued until 1974.

Carson, Inc., sold the site in 1975 to **Mittel Corp.**, a developer. Mittel held the property primarily for investment purposes. It did use the Site for disposal of some construction waste in 1976, consisting of concrete from another development. That waste was dumped in the same area as the earlier disposal and the dump trucks ran over some partially exposed drums and buried others in debris. Mittel then sold the property to Shenandoah in 1981.

The main source of information about the waste at the Site has come from Department of Justice interviews of former TCS drivers. The following are summaries of those interviews:

Carl Larson: Larson worked for TCS from 1969 to 1970. During that year, TCS acquired the contract to haul residential garbage for the nearby city of **Maryville**, Iowa, and Larson worked that route almost exclusively. He frequently used the Site for Maryville garbage during that year. He does not remember anything particularly hazardous in the city's garbage.

Paul Opperman: Opperman worked for TCS from 1968–75. He had an industrial route that included several companies near the Site. He remembers hauling toluene waste in fifty-five gallon drums from **Dreck Co.** on a regular basis to the Site. He estimates he made thirty-five to forty trips from Dreck, with around ten drums per load. He also hauled paint waste in drums from a car manufacturer, **General Cars, Inc.** He estimates that he hauled over a hundred drums of General Cars' paint waste to the Shenandoah site.

Foster Grant: Grant worked for TCS as a driver from 1970 to 1975. He is now 78 years old and in poor health. He seems to remember hauling a sludge that "smelled really bad" from **Balsam Corp.**, another nearby company. This substance was identified by plant workers as creosote sludge from a wood treatment process. Balsam was not on his regular route, but he hauled from Balsam five or six times while filling in for other drivers. Each load consisted of a 30-cubic-yard roll-off container of sludge, which would be emptied into a pit. He believes it was hauled on a weekly basis to the Site for around a year in 1974, but the driver who regularly hauled from Balsam cannot be located. It is possible that the Balsam waste was taken to another dump site frequently used by TCS, although that dump is two miles further from the Balsam plant than the Shenandoah Site.

Frank Baines: Baines worked as a driver for TCS from 1965 to 1975. He remembers taking three or four 30-cubic-yard roll-off containers of off-spec phosphate fertilizer waste from **Agro Enterprises** to the Site. He also took a large amount of baghouse dust from an air pollution filter system containing small amounts of aluminum sulfate from **Ferros Industries**. He estimates he hauled two 40-cubic-yard containers of this dust on a weekly basis to the Site for about two years, creating, as he called it, a "little mountain of black dust" in one portion of the dump site.

United Waste, Inc., (UWI) the nation's second largest waste transportation company, purchased the TCS company in 1980. The deal was structured as an asset purchase. UWI took over all of TCS's equipment and customer routes in exchange for $1 million in cash. TCS dissolved soon thereafter and its assets were distributed to its stockholders. Note that UWI itself has never hauled waste to the Site.

Officials of Shenandoah Industries, the current owner of the Site, have asserted that they had no knowledge of the disposal activity when they purchased the property in 1981 from Mittel. The disposal area was covered by trees and dumping activity had ceased more than nine years before. It is possible, however, that a thorough visual inspection of the Site would have revealed evidence of the dumping activity. A few drums were visible on the surface, for example, although they were largely covered by trees, undergrowth, and the construction debris dumped by Mittel.

Shenandoah discovered the contamination in 2002, while making preliminary plans to develop that portion of the property. The company then conducted a preliminary investigation to determine the extent of the problem and held some negotiations with Dreck, in an effort to convince Dreck to clean up the Site. When those efforts proved unsuccessful, Shenandoah asked the Environmental Protection Agency to become involved.

The EPA began to take action with respect to the Site in 2002. First, the agency conducted a PA/SI for the Site. The preliminary tests revealed that a variety of contaminants—including phosphorus, lead, and creosote—had leached into the soil and had contaminated a surficial (near the surface) aquifer. The agency performed some immediate response activities, including the removal of some drums on the surface and the erection of a fence to keep out trespassers (the "initial removal action"). This action was complete as of March 2004. The agency then ranked the Site using the Hazard Ranking System. The Site scored a 31.5; it was proposed for listing on the NPL in late 2004 and was finally listed in 2005.

In 2005, pursuant to its authority under CERCLA Section 106, the EPA issued an administrative order to Dreck, ordering it to perform the RI/FS. Dreck refused to do so, citing its belief that it was not liable. Dreck claims that it believed that TCS was disposing of Dreck's waste at a different site, one that was safe for such disposal. In addition, Dreck claimed that it did not have the financial resources to comply by itself.

In September 2006, the EPA hired a contractor to perform the RI/FS. The RI/FS was completed in June 2007. The RI revealed that the Site contained several "hot spots" containing large concentrations of drums and a fairly large area of relatively low contamination. In addition, the RI located two pools of dense non-aqueous phase liquids (DNAPL), consisting of creosote and solvent wastes. The FS recommended a remedy of excavation and incineration of the hot spots, along with a landfill cap and leachate collection system to minimize further migration of the contamination. On January 1, 2008, the EPA issued its Record of Decision selecting the remedy recommended by the RI/FS. See Figure 4.2. Additional contamination consisting of polychlorinated biphenyls (PCBs) was recently discovered in the area designated as Operable Unit #2 (OU2). The implications of this will be explored in Problem 4.7 below.

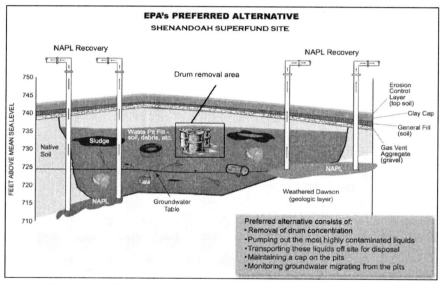

Figure 4.2 Shenandoah Superfund Site Preferred Alternative.

The cost of the remedy is estimated to be $10 million. The cost of the initial removal action was $400,000. The cost of the RI/FS was $500,000. In March 2007, the EPA hired another contractor to perform some additional removal work, because a severe rain storm had exposed more drums on the surface which had to be removed. The cost of this additional removal work was $100,000.

On December 1, 2009, the Department of Justice (DOJ), on behalf of the United States, brought suit against **Agro Enterprises, Balsam, Carson, Inc.,**

Dreck, Ferros Company, and General Cars (known collectively as the "Original Defendants"). The suit seeks recovery of past costs of $1 million under Section 107 of CERCLA, plus interest and enforcement costs, and seeks a declaratory judgment, pursuant to Section 113(g) of CERCLA, for any future response costs at the Site that are not inconsistent with the National Contingency Plan (NCP). In addition, the U.S. seeks the recovery of penalties against Dreck for its failure to comply with the Section 106 administrative order. The original defendants in turn filed a contribution action against third-party defendants **Mittel Corp., City of Maryville, Carrie Carson, UWI, and Shenandoah Industries.**

* * *

The original defendants have met and decided to form a PRP group to coordinate their defense. They initially have confronted the following litigation issues:

Problem 4.5: Hazard Ranking System/NPL Listing

(a) The Shenandoah PRP group hired a consultant geologist who discovered a couple of facts that are not reflected in the Hazard Ranking System scoresheet prepared by the EPA's consultant. First, the geologist believes that the geologic material lying between the contaminated area and the underlying groundwater aquifer should be characterized as silty clay, which has relatively low permeability, as opposed to the sandy silt characterization used in the HRS score. In addition, the geologist found what she believes to be an impermeable rock barrier located less than a mile downgradient from the site, which could prevent any contamination from reaching wells currently being used for drinking water.

Consult the Hazard Ranking System, 40 C.F.R. pt. 300, app. A, to determine whether this could make a difference in the Shenandoah site score. If this error could change the score, is it possible for the group to challenge the scoring? *See Board of Regents of the Univ. of Washington v. EPA,* 86 F.3d 1214 (D.C. Cir. 1996). Remember, NPL listing is a notice-and-comment rulemaking. If the consultant's opinion arrives after the comment period, does EPA have to consider it?

(b) The consultant geologist also believes that the Hazard Ranking System, even if properly applied, significantly overstates the true risks at sites like this one. She believes that the EPA's assignment of values to various factors is fairly arbitrary and results in a meaningless risk calculation.

Can the PRP group use her opinion to mount a challenge to the HRS regulation? Remember from the previous chapter that this falls into the category of a regulatory challenge. Make sure you determine what the exact basis of your challenge would be and whether there are any impediments to it. Consult in particular CERCLA § 105(a)(8) and § 113.

(c) What value is there for the PRP Group in challenging the NPL listing? Will the cleanup at the Site proceed any differently or will the group's liability be affected by taking the Site off of the list? See Mead Corp. v. Browner, 100 F.3d 152, 155 (D.C. Cir. 1996).

Practice Tip: Hiring Consultants

Environmental attorneys deal with consultants in a variety of circumstances. In Problem 4.5, a quick glance at the Hazard Ranking System should convince you that a hydrogeologist would be required to do any meaningful analysis of EPA's groundwater risk scoring. Similarly, the PRP group may hire an environmental consultant to analyze EPA's feasibility study to determine if there are other cleanup methods that would cost less while still achieving remediation goals. If you are representing a purchaser of an industrial site, you will want to hire a consultant to do an environmental audit, both for informational purposes and to meet the due diligence requirements of the innocent purchaser defense under CERCLA. In a citizen suit under the Clean Water Act (such as the Pork Unlimited exercise from Chapter 2), the plaintiff may want to hire a consultant to test the water in the North Fork River to establish the impact of the pollution, or to testify concerning possible alternative pollution control methods. In the EPCRA case, Exercise 2.1, Agra Enterprises may need a consultant to determine how much azinphos-methyl is released during combustion.

Lawyers working with contaminated sites may need to hire consultants to take advantage of the risk-based approach now being used in many states. Rather than simply requiring cookie-cutter cleanup standards to be met at every site, the risk-based approach allows an alternative standard to be established based on site-specific information. This site-specific standard may allow a higher concentration of pollutants than the pre-determined standard, and therefore may be less expensive.[22] For example, assume that

---

22. *See, e.g.*, Arizona Dep't of Env. Qual., "Cleanups: Site Assessment," avail. at www.azdeq.gov/environ/waste/cleanup/site.html (discussing risk-based approach).

your client owns a site where groundwater contamination levels are above the "action" level set for that contaminant, which typically requires an expensive "pump and treat" remedy. If a consultant can prove to the agency that the contamination does not present an unacceptable risk to drinking water aquifers, and will dissipate within a few years, then the agency may allow "monitored natural attenuation" rather than active remediation. To establish your case for this alternative approach, your experts will need to study the aquifer and contaminant plume and prove that it presents an acceptable risk.

In retaining a consultant, you will want to ensure that you select one with sufficient expertise and experience in the relevant area (for example, an air quality consultant may not be qualified to do a hazardous waste evaluation). You and the consultant will develop the scope of work detailing exactly what the consultant is expected to do. You should consider how to preserve confidentiality. Fed. R. Civ. Pro. 26(b)(3) protects the work product of your consultant from discovery by the other side if it is prepared "in anticipation of litigation," which includes administrative investigations. In other cases, if the attorney retains the consultant for the purpose of providing legal advice, communications between the attorney and the consultant, which the attorney then forwards to the client, may qualify for the attorney-client privilege. *See U.S. v. Kovel*, 296 F.2d 918, 921 (2d Cir. 1961) (privilege must include those who assist lawyer in giving advice); *but see U.S. Postal Service v. Phelps Dodge Ref. Corp.*, 852 F. Supp. 156 (E.D. N.Y. 1994) (outside environmental consultants were not attorney's agents for purposes of privilege).

Exercise 4.1: Joint Defense Agreement

You represent one of the PRPs in the Shenandoah case. The PRPs have formed a group to discuss and work together on common interests. There are a number of common goals, such as reducing the cost of the cleanup, asserting common defenses, and finding other liable parties to sue for contribution. Of course, you also have an interest in making sure each of the other parties in your group is held liable to the greatest extent possible. The object of this joint defense exercise is to try to reach an agreement on common items of interest without prejudicing your client's individual interests.

The following is an outline of some of the considerations you should think about when entering into a joint defense agreement. The final agreement may include provisions on all or just some of these points. Remember, there is no require-

ment that you join the defense group (although the court may require some co-ordination among similarly situated defendants). If you can reach agreement, however, there is a great deal to be saved in terms of transaction costs.

1. *Objects of the Agreement.* Many groups decide to hire a common counsel to represent the group on motions and/or in discovery, saving repetitive work by other lawyers. You should think carefully, however, about the extent to which coordination is possible. Other possible objects of agreement include sharing information among the group to avoid costly discovery, hiring an investigator to build up evidence against third parties, and hiring technical consultants to advise the group on ways to cut cleanup costs. The group may also want to agree on an Alternative Dispute Resolution (ADR) method of allocating response costs among those group members found liable.

2. *Common Counsel Duties.* If you do decide to hire a common counsel, you will have to determine the scope of his or her responsibility. Do you want common counsel to conduct depositions, file motions, and make court appearances on behalf of the group? Do you want to reserve the right to take a separate position on certain issues? For example, the group will need to allege UWI is liable as a successor corporation merely because it purchased the assets of TCS. What if your client has engaged in similar acquisitions elsewhere and does not want to be on record favoring liability in those circumstances?

3. *Sharing of Information.* When numerous parties are involved, it would be more efficient if the group could agree on a method of obtaining information from each other without having to file separate sets of virtually identical interrogatories. Is it possible or advisable to share information among group members without releasing it to the EPA?

4. *Investigator or Consultant.* In order to develop information against potential third-party defendants, the group may want to hire an investigator to interview truck drivers, neighbors, landfill employees, etc. A consultant also may be useful to explore technical issues. If an investigator or consultant is hired, the group must determine the proper scope of the work, who will control it, and how to keep the information confidential. What happens if the investigator finds information that inculpates one of the group?

5. *Decision-making.* Many groups establish committees to decide the day-to-day questions: for example, a Technical Committee to choose the consultants and direct their work, and a Steering Committee to direct the work of the common counsel and to take care of billing. Group decisions

may be made by unanimous consent, by majority vote, or by some supermajority percentage. Should each party get an equal vote or should the votes be weighted in some fashion (e.g., by potential liability)?

Suppose, for example, Carson, Inc., suggests that the group hire an investigator to find and interview additional TCS truck drivers, in order to unearth more evidence that might implicate other PRPs to help share the response costs. Would your client be in favor of that? Assume Agro's attorney knows, from confidential client interviews, that Agro produced many more tons of pesticide waste during the relevant time period that it cannot account for. There is a chance that other TCS truck drivers would provide more evidence of Agro waste, thereby increasing Agro's share. Thinking about a potential decision such as that, does Agro want to allocate decision-making on an equal or weighted fashion? What would Carson's position be on the same issue?

6. *Allocation of Group Costs.* The group needs to set up some sort of fund to pay for the costs of the joint defense activities. Deciding how to allocate those defense costs may be just as important as deciding how to allocate response costs among the group, because in some cases the costs of defense can approach or even exceed the costs of the cleanup. Obviously, some parties are smaller and cannot bear an equal share of the cost, and some parties may feel that their potential liability does not merit an equal share. The group may provide that group costs will be divided according to the final assessment of liability; but in the meantime, how do you assess contributions to the joint defense fund? If Dreck agrees to pay a larger share of joint defense costs, should it also have a larger say in how those funds are spent?

7. *Allocation of Cleanup Costs.* Rather than go through a trial on the issue of allocation of liability among PRPs, many groups have tried ADR techniques, such as mediation or arbitration. In some cases, they will hire a "neutral third party" to come up with an allocation based on the parties' submission of evidence and arguments. The question then is whether the arbitrator's allocation should be binding, or whether it should just provide a fruitful basis for settlement discussions.

8. *Ability to Withdraw; Termination.* There are many reasons why a party may wish to withdraw from the group. The costs may become prohibitive, the party may disagree with the group's policy decisions, or the party may just perceive that it is being treated unfairly by other group members. Also, a party may get out of the case on a summary judgment or by a separate settlement with the EPA. Should that party be allowed to withdraw? What

happens to the contributions of that party? Should it remain bound by any of the parts of the agreement after withdrawal? Some agreements terminate automatically when the defense costs have reached a certain limit. In addition, you may wish to include a provision to allow new parties to join later, and set out the conditions for new membership. For example, will the new party need to pay for any of the past costs incurred by the group?

9. *Miscellaneous.* The group will want to provide for confidentiality among group members for all discussions and information shared among them. The agreement should provide that participation does not constitute an admission of liability. The agreement should provide that the group waives any conflict of interest claims that result from common counsel continuing to represent the group after any parties withdraw from it. Finally, you may want some kind of indemnification by the group for any member engaged in the good faith performance of his or her duties under the agreement.

---

3. Superfund Litigation Issues

Assume you are counsel to one of the parties named as a defendant in the EPA's cost-recovery suit for the Shenandoah Site. You are in the difficult position of having to fight a three-front litigation battle. On one front, you need to explore possible defenses against the EPA. On another front, you are interested in building evidence against the other defendants, to minimize your comparative liability. Finally, you want to find evidence against PRPs who have not yet been sued, to expand the number of parties sharing the response costs.

a. Section 107 Liability

Look carefully at Section 107(a) and determine the elements you need to establish in order to hold a defendant liable under each of the four PRP categories. You may need to look up the definitions for each of the elements in Section 101.

Notice that for generators (or "arrangers"), for example, you need to establish the following elements, under Section 107(a)(3):

1) they arranged for
2) the disposal or treatment (or transportation for disposal or treatment)
3) of a hazardous substance (defined in Section 101 (14))
4) owned or possessed by them
5) at the facility
6) which now contains "such hazardous substances" (do you have to prove they are the same hazardous substances, or just some like them?).

Think about the evidence you will need to establish each of these points. What problems might you encounter?

Problem 4.6: Section 107 Elements of Liability

What elements does the Department of Justice need to allege to establish a prima facie case against each of the PRPs identified in the fact pattern? Do you have sufficient evidence to establish a case against each PRP or do you need further information? What factors will go into DOJ's choice of which parties to sue?

If you represent one of the PRPs, consider whether there is adequate evidence against your client or whether you may challenge liability. If you represent an Original Defendant, you should also consider whether you have enough evidence to sue any third-party defendants.

As an example, consider Agro Enterprises. We have evidence that a transporter disposed of Agro's phosphate fertilizer waste at the site. Is that enough? While "phosphorus" is listed as a hazardous substance under CWA and CER-CLA, "phosphate" is not. See City of Tulsa v. Tyson Foods, Inc., 258 F. Supp. 2d 1263 (N.D. Okla. 2003) *(phosphorus contained in phosphate waste is hazardous substance) (vacated by settlement).*

---

* * *

United States v. Alcan Aluminum Corp.
964 F.2d 252 (3rd Cir. 1992)

GREENBERG, Circuit Judge.

I.

FACTS AND PROCEDURAL HISTORY

Virtually all of the facts in this case ... are undisputed. The Butler Tunnel Site (the "Site") is listed on the National Priorities List established by the Environmental Protection Agency ("EPA") under section 105 of CERCLA, 42 U.S.C. § 9605. The Site includes a network of approximately five square miles of deep underground mines and related tunnels, caverns, pools and waterways bordering the east bank of the Susquehanna River in Pittston, Pennsylvania. The mine workings at the Site are drained by the Butler Tunnel (the "Tunnel"), a 7500 foot tunnel which feeds directly into the Susquehanna River.

The mines are accessible from the surface by numerous air shafts or bore-holes. One borehole (the "Borehole") is located on the premises of Hi-Way Auto Service, an automobile fuel and repair station situated above the Tun-nel. The Borehole leads directly into the mine workings at the Site.

In the late 1970's, the owner of Hi-Way Auto Service permitted various liquid waste transport companies, including those owned and controlled by Russell Mahler (the "Mahler Companies"), to deposit oily liquid wastes con-taining hazardous substances into the Borehole. The Mahler Companies col-lected the liquid wastes from numerous industrial facilities located in the northeastern United States and, in total, disposed of approximately 2,000,000 gallons of oily wastes containing hazardous substances through the Borehole. Apparently, it was contemplated that the waste would remain at the Site indefinitely.

From mid-1978 to late 1979, Alcan contracted with the Mahler Companies to dispose of at least 2,300,950 gallons of used emulsion from its Oswego, New York, facility. During that period, the Mahler Companies disposed of ap-proximately 32,500–37,500 gallons (or five 6500–7500 gallon loads) of Alcan's liquid waste through the Borehole into the Site.

In September 1985, approximately 100,000 gallons of water contaminated with hazardous substances were released from the Site into the Susquehanna River. It appears that this discharge was composed of the wastes deposited into the Borehole in the late 1970's.

In November 1989, the Government filed a complaint against 20 defen-dants, including Alcan, for the recovery of costs incurred as a result of the re-lease of hazardous wastes from the Site into the Susquehanna River.

The Government then moved for summary judgment against Alcan, the only non-settling defendant, to collect the balance of its response costs. Alcan cross-moved for summary judgment, arguing that its emulsion did not con-stitute a "hazardous substance" as defined by CERCLA due to its below-am-bient levels of copper, cadmium, chromium, lead and zinc, and further con-tending that its emulsion could not have caused the release or any response costs incurred by the Government.

A. CERCLA FRAMEWORK:

Under section 107, CERCLA liability is imposed where the plaintiff estab-lishes the following four elements:

(1) the defendant falls within one of the four categories of "responsible parties";

(2) the hazardous substances are disposed at a "facility";

(3) there is a "release" or threatened release of hazardous substances from the facility into the environment;

(4) the release causes the incurrence of "response costs."

Finally, and of great significance in this case, CERCLA imposes strict liability on responsible parties, 42 U.S.C. § 9601(32). *See Dedham Water Co. v. Cumberland Farms Dairy*, Inc., 889 F.2d at 1150; *New York v. Shore Realty Corp.*, 759 F.2d 1032, 1042 (2d Cir. 1985) ("Congress intended that responsible parties be held strictly liable, even though an explicit provision for strict liability was not included in the compromise....")

B. CERCLA CONTAINS NO QUANTITATIVE REQUIREMENT IN ITS DEFINITION OF "HAZARDOUS SUBSTANCE":

Alcan argues that it should not be held liable for response costs incurred by the Government in cleaning the Susquehanna River because the level of hazardous substances in its emulsion was below that which naturally occurs and thus could not have contributed to the environmental injury. It asserts that we must read a threshold concentration requirement into the definition of "hazardous substances" for the term "hazardous" to have any meaning.

The Government responds that under a plain reading of the statute, there is no quantitative requirement in the definition of "hazardous substance."

For reasons that follow, we are satisfied that the court was correct in that conclusion.

[T]he statute does not, on its face, impose any quantitative requirement or concentration level on the definition of "hazardous substances." Rather, the substance under consideration must simply fall within one of the designated categories.

Since the statute is plain on its face, we need not resort to legislative history to uncover its meaning. [However], it is difficult to imagine that Congress intended to impose a quantitative requirement on the definition of hazardous substances and thereby permit a polluter to add to the total pollution but avoid liability because the amount of its own pollution was minimal.

In addition, courts that have addressed this issue have almost uniformly held that CERCLA liability does not depend on the existence of a threshold quantity of a hazardous substance. *See, e.g., Amoco Oil Co. v. Borden, Inc.*, 889 F.2d at 669 ("The plain statutory language fails to impose any quantitative requirement on the term hazardous substance and we decline to imply that any is necessary.")

It may be that Congress did not intend such an all-encompassing definition of "hazardous substances," but this argument is best directed at Congress itself. If Congress had intended to impose a threshold requirement, it could easily have so indicated. We should not rewrite the statute simply because the definition of one of its terms is broad in scope.

C. CAUSATION

Alcan maintains that, if we decline to construe the determination of "hazardous substance" to encompass a concentration threshold, we must at least require the Government to prove that *Alcan's emulsion* caused or contributed to the release or the Government's incurrence of response costs. The Government contends, and the district court ... agreed, that the statute imposes no such causation requirement, but rather requires that the plaintiff in a CERCLA proceeding establish that *the release or threatened release* caused the incurrence of response costs; it underscores the difficulty CERCLA plaintiffs would face in the multi-generator context if required to trace the cause of the response costs to each responsible party.

The plain meaning of the statute supports the Government's position. As noted above, section 107 imposes liability upon a generator of hazardous substances who contracts with another party to dispose of the hazardous substances at a facility "from which there is a release, or threatened release which causes the incurrence of response costs." 42 U.S.C. § 9607.

Decisions rejecting a causation requirement between the defendant's waste and the release or the incurrence of response costs are well-reasoned, consistent with the plain language of the statute and consistent with the legislative history of CERCLA. Accordingly, we reject Alcan's argument that the Government must prove that Alcan's emulsion deposited in the Borehole caused the release or caused the Government to incur response costs. Rather, the Government must simply prove that the defendant's hazardous substances were deposited at the site from which there was a release and that the release caused the incurrence of response costs.

D. DIVISIBILITY OF HARM

CERCLA does not specifically provide for joint and several liability in a case involving multiple defendants.... In determining whether the imposition of joint and several liability upon Alcan is proper, so that it may be held liable for the Government's full response costs less what had been recovered from the settling defendants, we turn to the Restatement (Second) of Torts for guidance.... [S]ection 881 [of Restatement (Second) of Torts] sets forth the affirmative defense based upon the divisibility of harm rule of Section 433A: "If two or more persons, acting independently, tortiously cause distinct harms or a single harm for which there is a reasonable basis for division according to the contribution of each, each is subject to liability only for the portion of the total harm that he has himself caused." ... However, where joint tortfeasors cause a single and indivisible harm for which there is no reasonable basis for division according to the contribution of each, each tortfeasor is subject to liability for the entire harm.

These provisions underscore the intensely factual nature of the "divisibility" issue and thus highlight the district court's error in granting summary judgment for the full claim in favor of the EPA without conducting a hearing. For this reason, we will remand this case for the court to determine whether there is a reasonable basis for limiting Alcan's liability based on its personal contribution to the harm to the Susquehanna River.

Our conclusions on this point are completely consistent with our previous discussion on causation, as there we were concerned with the Government's burden in demonstrating liability in the first instance. Here we are dealing with Alcan's effort to avoid liability otherwise established. We observe in this regard that Alcan's burden in attempting to prove the divisibility of harm to the Susquehanna River is substantial, and the analysis will be factually complex as it will require an assessment of the relative toxicity, migratory potential and synergistic capacity of the hazardous waste at issue. *United States v. Monsanto Co.*, 858 F.2d at 172 n. 26. *See also United States v. Chem-Dyne Corp.*, 572 F.Supp. at 811. But Alcan should be permitted this opportunity to limit or avoid liability. If Alcan succeeds in this endeavor, it should only be liable for that portion of the harm fairly attributable to it. Of course, if Alcan cannot prove that it should not be liable for any response costs or cannot prove that the harm is divisible and that the damages are capable of some reasonable apportionment, it will be liable for the full claim of $473,790.18.

* * *

b. Joint and Several Liability

The Restatement test states that apportionment is proper when "there is a reasonable basis for determining the contribution of each cause to a single harm." Restatement (Second) of Torts §433A(1)(b), p. 434 (1963–1964). In many cases, there is no "waste-in" list to provide solid evidence of how much of the contamination each generator was responsible for. Moreover, even being able to prove the amount of waste your client contributed to a site does not necessarily equate to proving a reasonable basis for apportionment.[23] As the *Alcan Aluminum* case makes clear, it can be difficult to apply the Restatement test when there is

---

23. Distinguish carefully between "apportionment," which avoids joint and several liability, and "allocation" of damages among those held jointly and severally liable. In every case, the damages eventually will have to be allocated among the defendants held liable.

commingling of wastes. On remand, Alcan was unsuccessful in its effort to avoid joint and several liability, in part because the synergistic effect of its wastes with the other chemicals at the site made it difficult to assess the amount of harm Alcan was responsible for. *U.S. v. Alcan Alum. Corp.*, 315 F.3d 179, 187 (2d Cir. 2003). *But see Matter of Bell Petrol. Serv., Inc.*, 3 F.3d 889 (5th Cir. 1993) (no joint liability where volume of waste provided reasonable basis for apportionment).

Would the *Burlington Northern* case below change the result in a case like *Alcan Aluminum*? *See* Alfred R. Light, "Restatement for Joint and Several Liability Under CERCLA after *Burlington Northern*," 39 Env. Law Rptr. 11058 (2009).

* * *

Burlington Northern and Santa Fe Railway Company, et al. v. United States et al.
129 S.Ct. 1870 (2009)

Justice STEVENS delivered the opinion of the Court.

In 1960, Brown & Bryant, Inc. (B & B), began operating an agricultural chemical distribution business, purchasing pesticides and other chemical products from suppliers such as Shell Oil Company (Shell). Using its own equipment, B & B applied its products to customers' farms. B & B opened its business on a 3.8 acre parcel of former farmland in Arvin, California, and in 1975, expanded operations onto an adjacent .9 acre parcel of land owned jointly by the [Railroads]. Both parcels of the Arvin facility were graded toward a sump and drainage pond located on the southeast corner of the primary parcel. Neither the sump nor the drainage pond was lined until 1979, allowing waste water and chemical runoff from the facility to seep into the ground water below.

During its years of operation, B & B stored and distributed various hazardous chemicals on its property. Among these were the herbicide dinoseb, sold by Dow Chemicals, and the pesticides D-D and Nemagon, both sold by Shell. Dinoseb was stored in 55-gallon drums and 5-gallon containers on a concrete slab outside B & B's warehouse. Nemagon was stored in 30-gallon drums and 5-gallon containers inside the warehouse. Originally, B & B purchased D-D in 55-gallon drums; beginning in the mid-1960's, however, Shell began requiring its distributors to maintain bulk storage facilities for D-D. From that time onward, B & B purchased D-D in bulk.[24]

---

24. Because D-D is corrosive, bulk storage of the chemical led to numerous tank failures and spills as the chemical rusted tanks and eroded valves.

When B & B purchased D-D, Shell would arrange for delivery by common carrier. When the product arrived, it was transferred from tanker trucks to a bulk storage tank located on B & B's primary parcel. From there, the chemical was transferred to bobtail trucks, nurse tanks, and pull rigs.

Over the course of B & B's 28 years of operation, delivery spills, equipment failures, and the rinsing of tanks and trucks allowed Nemagon, D-D and dinoseb to seep into the soil and upper levels of ground water of the Arvin facility. In 1983, the California Department of Toxic Substances Control (DTSC) began investigating B & B's violation of hazardous waste laws, and the United States Environmental Protection Agency (EPA) soon followed suit, discovering significant contamination of soil and ground water. Of particular concern was a plume of contaminated ground water located under the facility that threatened to leach into an adjacent supply of potential drinking water.

Although B & B undertook some efforts at remediation, by 1989 it had become insolvent and ceased all operations. That same year, the Arvin facility was added to the National Priority List, and subsequently, DTSC and EPA (Governments) exercised their authority under 42 U.S.C. §9604 to undertake cleanup efforts at the site. By 1998, the Governments had spent more than $8 million responding to the site contamination; their costs have continued to accrue.

[In the government's cost-recovery action], the court held that both the Railroads and Shell were potentially responsible parties (PRPs) under CERCLA — the Railroads because they were owners of a portion of the facility, see 42 U.S.C. §§9607(a)(1)–(2), and Shell because it had "arranged for" the disposal of hazardous substances through its sale and delivery of D-D, see §9607(a)(3).

Although the court found the parties liable, it did not impose joint and several liability on Shell and the Railroads for the entire response cost incurred by the Governments. The court found that the site contamination created a single harm but concluded that the harm was divisible and therefore capable of apportionment. Based on three figures — the percentage of the total area of the facility that was owned by the Railroads, the duration of B & B's business divided by the term of the Railroads' lease, and the Court's determination that only two of three polluting chemicals spilled on the leased parcel required remediation and that those two chemicals were responsible for roughly two-thirds of the overall site contamination requiring remediation — the court apportioned the Railroads' liability as 9% of the Governments' total response cost. Based on estimations of chemicals spills of Shell products, the court held Shell liable for 6% of the total site response cost.

The Governments appealed the District Court's apportionment, and Shell cross-appealed the court's finding of liability. The Court of Appeals acknowledged that Shell did not qualify as a "traditional" arranger under § 9607(a)(3), insofar as it had not contracted with B & B to directly dispose of a hazardous waste product. 520 F.3d 918, 948 (C.A.9 2008). Nevertheless, the court stated that Shell could still be held liable under a "'broader' category of arranger liability" if the "disposal of hazardous wastes [wa]s a foreseeable byproduct of, but not the purpose of, the transaction giving rise to" arranger liability. *Ibid.* Relying on CERCLA's definition of "disposal," which covers acts such as "leaking" and "spilling," 42 U.S.C. § 6903(3), the Ninth Circuit concluded that an entity could arrange for "disposal" "even if it did not intend to dispose" of a hazardous substance. 520 F.3d, at 949.

Applying that theory of arranger liability to the District Court's findings of fact, the Ninth Circuit held that Shell arranged for the disposal of a hazardous substance through its sale and delivery of D-D.

On the subject of apportionment, the Court of Appeals found "no dispute" on the question whether the harm caused by Shell and the Railroads was capable of apportionment. *Id.*, at 942. Nevertheless, the Court of Appeals held that the District Court erred in finding that the record established a reasonable basis for apportionment. Because the burden of proof on the question of apportionment rested with Shell and the Railroads, the Court of Appeals reversed the District Court's apportionment of liability and held Shell and the Railroads jointly and severally liable for the Governments' cost of responding to the contamination of the Arvin facility.

We granted certiorari to determine whether Shell was properly held liable as an entity that had "arranged for disposal" of hazardous substances within the meaning of § 9607(a)(3), and whether Shell and the Railroads were properly held liable for all response costs incurred by EPA and the State of California. Finding error on both points, we now reverse.

II

In these cases, it is undisputed that the Railroads qualify as PRPs under both §§ 9607(a)(1) and 9607(a)(2) because they owned the land leased by B & B at the time of the contamination and continue to own it now. The more difficult question is whether Shell also qualifies as a PRP under § 9607(a)(3) by virtue of the circumstances surrounding its sales to B & B.

To determine whether Shell may be held liable as an arranger, we begin with the language of the statute. As relevant here, § 9607(a)(3) applies to an entity that "arrange[s] for disposal ... of hazardous substances." It is plain from the language of the statute that CERCLA liability would attach under § 9607(a)(3) if an entity were to enter into a transaction for the sole purpose of discarding a used and no longer useful hazardous substance. It is similarly clear that an entity could not be held liable as an arranger merely for selling a new and useful product if the purchaser of that product later, and unbeknownst to the seller, disposed of the product in a way that led to contamination. Less clear is the liability attaching to the many permutations of "arrangements" that fall between these two extremes—cases in which the seller has some knowledge of the buyers' planned disposal or whose motives for the "sale" of a hazardous substance are less than clear. In such cases, courts have concluded that the determination whether an entity is an arranger requires a fact-intensive inquiry that looks beyond the parties' characterization of the transaction as a "disposal" or a "sale" and seeks to discern whether the arrangement was one Congress intended to fall within the scope of CERCLA's strict-liability provisions.

Although we agree that the question whether § 9607(a)(3) liability attaches is fact intensive and case specific, such liability may not extend beyond the limits of the statute itself. Because CERCLA does not specifically define what it means to "arrang[e] for" disposal of a hazardous substance, we give the phrase its ordinary meaning. In common parlance, the word "arrange" implies action directed to a specific purpose. See Merriam-Webster's Collegiate Dictionary 64 (10th ed.1993) (defining "arrange" as "to make preparations for: plan[;] ... to bring about an agreement or understanding concerning"); see also *Amcast Indus. Corp.*, 2 F.3d, at 751 (words "'arranged for' ... imply intentional action"). Consequently, under the plain language of the statute, an entity may qualify as an arranger under § 9607(a)(3) when it takes intentional steps to dispose of a hazardous substance.

The Governments do not deny that the statute requires an entity to "arrang[e] for" disposal; however, they interpret that phrase by reference to the statutory term "disposal," which the Act broadly defines as "the discharge, deposit, injection, dumping, spilling, leaking, or placing of any solid waste or hazardous waste into or on any land or water." 42 U.S.C. § 6903(3); see also § 9601(29) (adopting the definition of "disposal" contained in the Solid Waste Disposal Act). The Governments assert that by including unintentional acts such as "spilling" and "leaking" in the definition of disposal, Congress intended to impose liability on entities not only when they directly dispose of waste products but also when they engage in legitimate sales of hazardous substances knowing that some disposal may occur as a collateral consequence of the sale itself.

While it is true that in some instances an entity's knowledge that its product will be leaked, spilled, dumped, or otherwise discarded may provide evidence of the entity's intent to dispose of its hazardous wastes, knowledge alone is insufficient to prove that an entity "planned for" the disposal, particularly when the disposal occurs as a peripheral result of the legitimate sale of an unused, useful product. In order to qualify as an arranger, Shell must have entered into the sale of D-D with the intention that at least a portion of the product be disposed of during the transfer process by one or more of the methods described in §6903(3). Here, the facts found by the District Court do not support such a conclusion.

Although the evidence adduced at trial showed that Shell was aware that minor, accidental spills occurred during the transfer of D-D from the common carrier to B & B's bulk storage tanks after the product had arrived at the Arvin facility and had come under B & B's stewardship, the evidence does not support an inference that Shell intended such spills to occur. To the contrary, the evidence revealed that Shell took numerous steps to encourage its distributors to *reduce* the likelihood of such spills, providing them with detailed safety manuals, requiring them to maintain adequate storage facilities, and providing discounts for those that took safety precautions. Although Shell's efforts were less than wholly successful, given these facts, Shell's mere knowledge that spills and leaks continued to occur is insufficient grounds for concluding that Shell "arranged for" the disposal of D-D within the meaning of §9607(a)(3). Accordingly, we conclude that Shell was not liable as an arranger for the contamination that occurred at B & B's Arvin facility.

III

Having concluded that Shell is not liable as an arranger, we need not decide whether the Court of Appeals erred in reversing the District Court's apportionment of Shell's liability for the cost of remediation. We must, however, determine whether the Railroads were properly held jointly and severally liable for the full cost of the Governments' response efforts.

The seminal opinion on the subject of apportionment in CERCLA actions was written in 1983 by Chief Judge Carl Rubin of the United States District Court for the Southern District of Ohio. *United States v. Chem-Dyne Corp.*, 572 F.Supp. 802. After reviewing CERCLA's history, Chief Judge Rubin concluded that although the Act imposed a "strict liability standard," *id.*, at 805, it did not mandate "joint and several" liability in every case. See *id.*, at 807. Rather, Congress intended the scope of liability to "be determined from traditional and evolving principles of common law[.]" *Id.*, at 808.

Following *Chem-Dyne*, the courts of appeals have acknowledged that "[t]he universal starting point for divisibility of harm analyses in CERCLA cases" is §433A of the Restatement (Second) of Torts. Under the Restatement,

> "when two or more persons acting independently caus[e] a distinct or single harm for which there is a reasonable basis for division according to the contribution of each, each is subject to liability only

for the portion of the total harm that he has himself caused. Restatement (Second) of Torts, §§ 433A, 881 (1976); Prosser, Law of Torts, pp. 313–314 (4th ed.1971).... But where two or more persons cause a single and indivisible harm, each is subject to liability for the entire harm. Restatement (Second) of Torts, § 875; Prosser, at 315–316." *Chem-Dyne Corp.*, 572 F.Supp., at 810.

In other words, apportionment is proper when "there is a reasonable basis for determining the contribution of each cause to a single harm." Restatement (Second) of Torts § 433A(1)(b), p. 434 (1963–1964).

Not all harms are capable of apportionment, however, and CERCLA defendants seeking to avoid joint and several liability bear the burden of proving that a reasonable basis for apportionment exists. See *Chem-Dyne Corp.*, 572 F.Supp., at 810 (citing Restatement (Second) of Torts § 433B (1976)) (placing burden of proof on party seeking apportionment). When two or more causes produce a single, indivisible harm, "courts have refused to make an arbitrary apportionment for its own sake, and each of the causes is charged with responsibility for the entire harm." Restatement (Second) of Torts § 433A, Comment *i*, p. 440 (1963–1964).

Neither the parties nor the lower courts dispute the principles that govern apportionment in CERCLA cases, and both the District Court and Court of Appeals agreed that the harm created by the contamination of the Arvin site, although singular, was theoretically capable of apportionment. The question then is whether the record provided a reasonable basis for the District Court's conclusion that the Railroads were liable for only 9% of the harm caused by contamination at the Arvin facility.

The District Court ... ultimately concluded that this was "a classic 'divisible in terms of degree' case, both as to the time period in which defendants' conduct occurred, and ownership existed, and as to the estimated maximum contribution of each party's activities that released hazardous substances that caused Site contamination." *Id.*, at 239a. Consequently, the District Court apportioned liability, assigning the Railroads 9% of the total remediation costs.

The District Court calculated the Railroads' liability based on three figures. First, the court noted that the Railroad parcel constituted only 19% of the surface area of the Arvin site. Second, the court observed that the Railroads had leased their parcel to B & B for 13 years, which was only 45% of the time B & B operated the Arvin facility. Finally, the court found that the volume of hazardous-substance-releasing activities on the B & B property was at least 10 times greater than the releases that occurred on the Railroad parcel, and it concluded that only spills of two chemicals, Nemagon and dinoseb (not D-D), substantially contributed to the contamination that had originated on the Railroad parcel and that those two chemicals had contributed to two-thirds of the overall site contamination requiring remediation. The court then multiplied .19 by .45 by .66 (two-thirds) and rounded up to determine that the Railroads were responsible for approximately 6% of the remediation costs. "Allowing for calculation errors up to 50%," the court concluded that the Railroads could be held responsible for 9% of the total CERCLA response cost for the Arvin site. *Id.*, at 252a.

The Court of Appeals criticized the evidence on which the District Court's conclusions rested, finding a lack of sufficient data to establish the precise proportion of contamination that occurred on the relative portions of the Arvin facility and the rate of contamination in the years prior to B & B's addition of the Railroad parcel. The court noted that neither the duration of the lease nor the size of the leased area alone was a reliable measure of the harm caused by activities on the property owned by the Railroads, and—as the court's upward adjustment confirmed—the court had relied on estimates rather than specific and detailed records as a basis for its conclusions.

Despite these criticisms, we conclude that the facts contained in the record reasonably supported the apportionment of liability. We are persuaded that it was reasonable for the court to use the size of the leased parcel and the duration of the lease as the starting point for its analysis. Although the Court of Appeals faulted the District Court for relying on the "simplest of considerations: percentages of land area, time of ownership, and types of hazardous products," 520 F.3d, at 943, these were the same factors the court had earlier acknowledged were *relevant* to the apportionment analysis. See *id.*, at 936, n. 18 ("We of course agree with our sister circuits that, if adequate information is available, divisibility may be established by 'volumetric, chronological, or other types of evidence,' including appropriate geographic considerations" (citations omitted)).

Because the District Court's ultimate allocation of liability is supported by the evidence and comports with the apportionment principles outlined above, we reverse the Court of Appeals' conclusion that the Railroads are subject to joint and several liability for all response costs arising out of the contamination of the Arvin facility.

IV

For the foregoing reasons, we conclude that the Court of Appeals erred by holding Shell liable as an arranger under CERCLA for the costs of remediating environmental contamination at the Arvin, California facility. Furthermore, we conclude that the District Court reasonably apportioned the Railroads' share of the site remediation costs at 9%. The judgment is reversed, and the cases are remanded for further proceedings consistent with this opinion.

* * *

Problem 4.7: Joint and Several Liability/Arranger Liability

Assume that EPA discovers polychlorinated biphenyl (PCB) waste at the Shenandoah site in an area designated in Figure 4.1 as OU2, which promises to raise the cost of the response by another $5 million, because large areas of the site will now have to be excavated and incinerated. Unfortunately, the PCB waste came from a scrap metal dealer, which long ago went out of business. The dealer bought old electric transformers, drained and dumped the fluid (containing PCBs) and recycled the metal. Thus, the liability for this contamination represents an "orphan" share that will have to be paid by any PRPs found jointly liable. Given the evidence described in the Shenandoah problem, can your client establish a "reasonable basis for division" under Burlington Northern *in order to avoid joint and several liability? What additional facts would be helpful to your case?*

Assume Midwest Electric was one of the companies who sent the scrap metal dealer its old transformers for "recycling". Can Midwest Electric be held liable as an "arranger" after Burlington Northern?

c. Consistency with the NCP

CERCLA Section 107 states that the United States can recover only those response costs that are "not inconsistent with the National Contingency Plan." 42 U.S.C. §9607(a)(4)(A). Thus, inconsistency with the NCP is one of the few defenses available to PRPs. Examine the National Contingency Plan at 40 C.F.R. Part 300. Can you think of possible ways that the government or a private party seeking cost recovery might fail to follow the plan? *See, e.g.,* "Failure to Comply with Contingency Plan Dooms Cost-Recovery Claim, Court Holds," 28 Env. Rptr. 1658 (Jan. 2, 1998) (PRP seeking to recover response costs failed to involve other PRPs and the public in the remedy selection and performance process).

In *Washington State DOT v. Washington Natural Gas Co.,* 51 F.3d 1489 (9th Cir. 1995), a state agency was denied its cleanup costs under CERCLA because it failed to follow the NCP. The court faulted the agency for failing to undertake an adequate remedial investigation before starting the cleanup, concluding that it "utterly failed to determine the nature or the extent of the threat." *Id.* at 1499. In addition, the agency failed to thoroughly analyze the remedial alternatives, as the NCP requires. Furthermore, the agency did not provide an opportunity for public comment on its proposed action. *Id.* at 1500. *See also U.S. v. Newmont USA Ltd.*, 504 F.Supp.2d 1077 (E. D. Wash. 2007) (unnecessary, duplicative costs not consistent with NCP).

Note, however, that the party raising the NCP defense cannot rely on minor inconsistencies; the actions must be arbitrary and capricious departures from the NCP. Compare the challenges to the action in *Chapman*, below, to those cited in the *Washington DOT* case.

* * *

United States v. Chapman
146 F.3d 1166 (9th Cir. 1998)

Before: GOODWIN, KOZINSKI, and THOMPSON, Circuit Judges.
DAVID R. THOMPSON, Circuit Judge:

This suit arises out of the storage and release of hazardous substances on property in Palomino Valley, Nevada. Harold B. Chapman Jr., who owned the property and operated a business on it, was found liable under the Comprehensive Environmental Response, Compensation and Liability Act of 1980, 42 U.S.C. § 107(a) ("CERCLA"). On appeal, Chapman contends that the district court erred in granting the government's motion for summary judgment because it had failed to demonstrate a release or threatened release of hazardous substances. Chapman further argues that the EPA acted inconsistently with the National Contingency Plan ("NCP") and therefore is precluded from recovering its response costs.

Finally, Chapman appeals the district court's award of attorney fees as part of the government's response costs.

FACTS

Harold B. Chapman, Jr. manufactured small metal collars and stored and resold military and commercial surplus chemicals on his five-acre parcel of land in Palomino Valley, Washoe County, Nevada. In 1989, at the request of Washoe County, the EPA began an investigation of Chapman's facility.

On December 20, 1989, the EPA's Emergency Response Section and Technical Assistance Team conducted a preliminary assessment of the site to determine if a removal action was necessary. They conducted an inventory of all chemical containers and collected samples. There were approximately 2000 5-gallon containers of paint, insulating oil, sulfuric acid, chloroform, alcohols, and other military surplus chemicals on the property. In addition there were 100 55-gallon drums of unknown substances. The majority of the drums were stored outside in an unprotected storage yard. Many of the containers were deteriorated and many of the drums were leaking into the soil. The soil was visibly stained in several areas.

On May 24, 1990, the EPA issued Order 90-10 pursuant to CERCLA § 106, 42 U.S.C. 9506(a). The Order stated that several contamination threats were identified during the preliminary assessment. Four out of the ten samples had flash points less than 140 degrees Fahrenheit and posed a substantial risk of fire and/or explosion. Many of the drums containing hazardous substances were in poor condition, were leaking into the exposed soil and could migrate causing groundwater contamination.

Because Chapman had failed to take steps to comply with the EPA's Order, the EPA decided to initiate a response action. The EPA sent its contractor to visit the site and determine what actions were necessary to remove the hazardous substances. In February 1991, when the EPA was prepared to begin its response action, Chapman finally began to comply with the Order. Under the supervision of the EPA ... Chapman removed the containers from the site and conducted soil samples which were submitted to the EPA.

In April 1992, the EPA sent demand letters to Chapman requesting $33,946.00 for the response costs it had incurred. Chapman refused to pay the EPA's costs and the United States brought this civil action against Chapman to collect them. The district court granted summary judgment in favor of the government, and this appeal followed.

DISCUSSION

A. The EPA's Prima Facie Case

Chapman argues the government failed to establish a prima facie case sufficient for the court to grant summary judgment, because there is a genuine issue of material fact as to whether Chapman caused a release or a threatened release of a hazardous substance on his property.

There is ample evidence in the administrative record to satisfy the government's burden of proof. As the district court stated, the administrative record reflected that

> [t]here were consultant reports. And the facts established that two thousand drums were stored on the property. They were reported to have been reused and corroded, and without tops, and in poor condition. And there was some evidence of visible soil stains, and actual soil sample contamination.

Three samples were flammable, one was a corrosive basic liquid, and four others were combustible. These are hazardous substances under CERCLA....

That evidence established the EPA's prima facie case under CERCLA § 107(a).

B. Consistency with the NCP

The government having established its prima facie case under CERCLA § 107(a), the burden then shifted to Chapman to create a genuine issue of material fact on the question whether the EPA's response action was inconsistent with the National Contingency Plan ("NCP"). Chapman failed to do so.

The potentially responsible party has the burden of proving inconsistency with the NCP. *Washington State DOT*, 59 F.3d at 800. "To prove that a response action of the EPA was inconsistent with the NCP, a defendant must prove that the EPA's response action was arbitrary and capricious." *Id.*; 42 U.S.C. § 9613(j)(2).

Documentation

The NCP requires:

> During all phases of response, the lead agency shall complete and maintain documentation to support all actions taken under the NCP and to form the basis for cost recovery.

42 C.F.R. § 300.16(a)(1) (1990).

Contrary to Chapman's argument, the EPA adequately documented its response action and the costs incurred. The government submitted detailed cost summaries to the district court documenting the costs incurred by the EPA. The district court record contains declarations from EPA staff, attorneys, accountants, and supervisors attesting to the work they performed and the time spent on the Chapman site. Additionally, the record contains extensive documentation of costs in the form of timesheets and payroll documents.

Current Site Evaluation

> In determining the appropriate extent of action to be taken in response to a given release, the lead agency shall first review the removal site evaluation (preliminary assessment), any information produced through a remedial site evaluation plan, if any has been done previously, and the current site conditions, to determine if removal action is appropriate.

42 C.F.R. § 300.415(a)(1) (1990).

Chapman argues that the EPA failed to review the preliminary assessment and current site conditions before determining that a removal action was appropriate.

The preliminary assessment is contained in the administrative record and it clearly documents the conditions at the site. OSC Bornstein's action memorandum dated January 24, 1991 provides a detailed assessment of the site conditions at that time. Based upon both the preliminary assessment and the action memorandum, the EPA considered all the necessary information in determining a removal action was appropriate.

Mandatory Factors

In determining the appropriateness of a removal action, the EPA must consider the following factors: (1) actual or potential exposure to nearby human populations, animals, or the food chain; (2) actual or potential contamination of the water supply; (3) hazardous substances in drums, barrels or containers that may pose a threat of release; (4) hazardous substances in soils near the surface that may migrate; (5) weather conditions that may cause migration; (6) threat of fire or explosion; (7) the availability of other federal or state response mechanisms; and (8) other factors that may pose threats to public health or welfare.

40 C.F.R. §415(b)(2) (1990).

Chapman argues that the EPA failed to address these factors prior to determining a removal action was necessary. The administrative record refutes this assertion. Order 90-10 reflects consideration of all but one of the specific factors listed in 40 C.F.R. §416(b)(2) (1990). The Order considers: (1) actual or potential exposure of the animals and people at the Bureau of Land Management Wild Horse and Burro Adoption center; (2) the potential contamination of the groundwater that could result in contamination to the domestic and agricultural aquifer endangering residents and crops; (3) the hazardous substances in the drums that pose a threat of release; (4) the substances leaking into the soil that may potentially migrate to the aquifer underlying the site and cause contamination; (5) the many drums stored outside in the elements containing substances with flash points of less than 140 degrees; (6) the risk of fire and/or explosion from drums containing flammable substances.

Community Relations Plan

The NCP specifies the necessary community relations activities to be taken in a removal action. The 1990 NCP requires that in removal action where "on-site action is expected to extend beyond 120 days from the initiation of on-site removal activities," the EPA shall prepare a formal community relations plan. 40 C.F.R. §415(n)(3) (1990). The plan should address the public's concerns and outline any community relations activities that the EPA expects to undertake. *Id.* at (n)(3)(ii).

The EPA's actions were consistent with the NCP because it ordered Chapman to complete the on-site removal within 120 days. Because removal activities on Chapman's property were not to extend beyond 120 days, the EPA was not required to issue a community relations plan.

C. Response Costs

The question we now consider is whether the government can recover, as part of these response costs under section 107(a)(4)(A), its attorney fees attributable to this litigation. The district court held these fees were recoverable. We agree, but conclude the government is not entitled to the actual attorney fees attributable to the litigation, but only to reasonable attorney fees.

* * *

Problem 4.8: NCP Consistency

Assume that the EPA conducted the 2002–2004 removal in the Shenandoah problem without any attempt to locate or consult with the PRPs. Was this consistent with the NCP or might the PRPs mount a challenge to that portion of the response costs? Consult the NCP section on removal action, 40 C.F.R. §300.415. What kind of study should the EPA have done before undertaking the removal? Should a community relations plan have been in place at this point?

d. Insurance Coverage for Cleanup Costs

Many companies have sought coverage for Superfund liability or similar costs under their insurance policies. Standard insurance policies issued to businesses to protect them from bodily injury and property damages claims, either on their premises or as a result of their operations, were called "comprehensive general liability" (CGL) polices before 1986 and are now called "commercial general liability" policies. The standard CGL policy[25] covered only damages caused by an "occurrence," defined as an "accident ... which results in bodily injury or property damage neither intended nor expected from the standpoint of the insured." Certainly, this might be read to cover many Superfund cases, especially if the

---

25. Because the terms of these standard policies are drafted and recommended to the insurance industry by the Insurance Services Office, and then must be approved by state insurance regulators, they are widely used.

company thought its waste was being disposed of safely. Such policies also contained a "pollution exclusion" clause, however, which has evolved over time. From 1973 to 1986, the clause excluded damages caused by pollution, unless the discharge was "sudden and accidental." Thus, the focus of Superfund insurance coverage litigation is often on the precise meaning of that term and whether the particular release of hazardous substances was sufficiently "sudden." In 1986, the insurance industry revised this clause, now called an "absolute pollution exclusion," to more broadly exclude pollution events.[26]

In determining the scope of the "sudden and accidental" language of these older policies, courts have differed on whether the term means "unexpected, unintended, and unforeseen from the viewpoint of the insured" or whether it has an objective, temporal meaning (i.e., happening all at once). *See U.S. Fidelity & Guar. Co. v. Morrison Grain Co.*, 999 F.2d 489, 492–93 (10th Cir. 1993) (discussing split in authority). For example, in *Compass Ins. Co. v. City of Littleton*, 984 P.2d 606, 617–18 (Colo. 1999), the Colorado Supreme Court held that the "occurrence" or relevant pollution event occurred when hazardous wastes placed in an unlined pit were released into the groundwater and neighboring land. Because the insured expected that any contaminants placed in the pit would be either contained or filtered, the pollution event was "sudden and accidental" within the terms of the policy. *Id.*

Problem 4.9 Insurance Coverage

In the Shenandoah case, assume Balsam Corporation had a $1 million CGL policy with National Insurance Company in 1974, the year its creosote sludge was allegedly hauled to the site. Company officials are prepared to testify that they believed the creosote was being hauled to a landfill with a liner that would prevent the spread of any contaminants that did not decompose, and they believed creosote sludge would not migrate once it was buried, in any case. The CGL policy contained the pollution exclusion clause noted above, which provides coverage only if the pollution event was "sudden and accidental." Assuming Iowa law applies, does NIC have a duty to indemnify Balsam for any liability it incurs at the Shenandoah site up to policy limits? See Iowa Comp. Petrol. UST Fund Bd. v. Farmland Mut. Ins., 568 N.W.2d 815 (Iowa 1997). Would the outcome be different in your state?

---

26. In 1988, this language was further broadened to a "total pollution exclusion." *See* James T. O'Reilly & Caroline Broun, 2 RCRA and Superfund: A Practice Guide 3d, §16.3 (2009).

e. Choice of Remedy

CERCLA Section 121 governs the choice of remedy. 42 U.S.C. § 9621. Obviously, this is a crucial choice, because a decision to pump and treat a contaminated groundwater aquifer can cost many millions of dollars more than a decision to simply contain the plume of contamination and await "attenuation." The Feasibility Study explores the potential remedies and analyzes the alternatives in terms of cost and effectiveness. PRPs often complain that the EPA is requiring "a Cadillac cleanup when a Volkswagen would do." Is the EPA bound to consider cost? Consult Section 121(a). Does the use of the term "cost-effective" mean the EPA must choose the cheapest remedy that does the job?

Section 121(b) introduces a number of other considerations the EPA must take into account in choosing the remedy. For example, it expresses a preference for "treatment which permanently and significantly reduces the volume, toxicity or mobility of the hazardous substances, pollutants, and contaminants." Congress was responding here to complaints that the EPA was using too many "containment" remedies, such as landfill caps, which left the hazardous substances in place. On the other hand, the very next sentence cautions the EPA *against* choosing remedies that involve off-site transport and disposal, because of the dangers associated with such transportation. Thus, on-site treatment alternatives appear to have first preference.

But what does "treatment" really mean? In many cases, treatment may mean excavating and incinerating the waste using an on-site incinerator. You can imagine that those remedial actions are often controversial, given the potential air quality impacts, especially in populated areas. If off-site transportation is disfavored and on-site treatment is not feasible, can the EPA choose a containment remedy? Do the factors listed in Section 121(b)(1)(A) through (G) help? In the end, the section states that permanent solutions are to be used "to the maximum extent practicable." Is there any "law to apply" there or is this statute so broadly drawn that it falls under the "committed to agency discretion" exception to judicial review in the APA? 5 U.S.C. § 701(a)(2); *Citizens to Preserve Overton Park v. Volpe,* 401 U.S. 402, 410–14 (1971) (no judicial review if there is "no law to apply").

What level of cleanup must the selected remedy achieve? Section 121(d) states the general rule that any remedy chosen must at least assure "protection of human health and the environment." It goes on to state that, if hazardous substances remain on-site, the cleanup must achieve "legally applicable or relevant and appropriate" standards (known as ARARs) of state and federal environmental laws. For example, if the contaminated water is used as a drinking water source, the Maximum Contaminant Levels established under the Safe Drinking Water Act will probably have to be met and in some cases, the more stringent Maximum Contaminant Level Goals would be considered relevant and appropriate. 40 C.F.R. § 300.430(e)(2)(i)(B).

Must groundwater be cleaned up to meet drinking water standards, even if it is not used for drinking? Should the soil or water be cleaned up beyond naturally occurring levels of contamination? Should land that will be used only for industrial purposes be remediated using residential exposure assumptions? Questions such as these have generated many calls for amendments to the cleanup standards. Some CERCLA reform proposals would eliminate the preference for permanent treatment except for highly toxic and mobile areas ("hot spots"); other proposals would eliminate ARARs entirely. *See* "Superfund: Interested Parties Hail Markup Delay as Talks on CERCLA Reform Resume," 28 Env. Rptr. 843 (Sept. 12, 1997).

The NCP regulations, 40 C.F.R. § 300.430(f), indicate how the EPA intends to factor all of the relevant considerations into its remedy decision. The regulations describe "overall protection of human health and the environment and compliance with ARARs" as "threshold" requirements. Any remedy not meeting those requirements will be discarded. Next, the EPA will consider "balancing" criteria, such as short-term and long-term effectiveness, implementability, and cost. Finally, the agency considers the "modifying" criteria of state and community acceptance of the remedy.

Problem 4.10: Choice of Remedy

In the Shenandoah case, a local community group has been pushing for a more permanent remedy than a landfill cap. They are worried that mere containment of the waste will not work, in the long run, because the cap will deteriorate and there is no barrier, such as a slurry wall, to keep the waste from migrating. They are extremely concerned that, without permanent remediation, the groundwater will be further contaminated in a short period of time. The EPA stated, in the ROD, that a slurry wall was rejected because of high cost without much improvement in efficacy. Furthermore, the alternative of excavating and treating all of the waste would require an on-site incinerator, an expensive and controversial proposition, given air pollution risks. The community group, however, believes that the waste (or at least much of it) could be excavated and trucked to an incineration facility located 200 miles away, thereby eliminating the need for a new incinerator. Can the community group challenge the remedy in court? Does the group have a case?

f. 107(b) Defenses

Section 107(b) provides some limited defenses, if a PRP can prove that the release was actually caused by an Act of God, an Act of War, or the act or omission of a third party. At first glance, many PRPs believe they have a defense under this section. However, Section 107(b) states that one of these sources must have been the *sole* cause of the release. Thus, if the PRP could have taken any action to prevent harm from a foreseeable event (such as a hurricane, tornado, or vandal), the 107(b) defense fails. Courts have been quite strict about that requirement. *See, e.g., United States v. Barrier Industries, Inc.,* 991 F. Supp. 678 (S.D.N.Y. 1998) (unprecedented cold spell led to bursting of pipes; no defense under Act of God because other factors causally contributed to the release); *United States v. Alcan Alum. Corp.,* 892 F. Supp. 648 (M.D. Pa. 1995) (unusual rainfall does not establish Act of God defense). Courts are understandably reluctant to absolve parties who had control over the hazardous substances, even if other factors contributed directly to the release (God, after all, rarely pays cleanup costs).

Problem 4.11: Third Party Defenses

Assume that you represent the owner of a railroad car filled with trichloroethylene, a listed hazardous waste under RCRA being shipped to a disposal facility. While the car was sitting on a side track overnight, a vandal broke open a valve on the car, causing a massive leak of the liquid waste onto the ground. The EPA took immediate response action under CERCLA, and now seeks reimbursement from your client. Under Barrier, Alcan *and the language of Section 107, evaluate whether your client has a defense that the spill was an act of a third party under Section 107.*

g. Statute of Limitations

Section 113 of CERCLA provides a statute of limitations for actions to recover response costs. The statute provides a three-year limitation period for actions to recover removal costs, triggered by the "completion" of the removal. For remedial actions, the period is six years, measured from the time "on-site construction" of the remedial action begins. Thus, the statute of limitations for a remedial action runs from the beginning of the action, while the limitations period for a removal starts at the end of the action. Presumably, this is because remedial actions can last a long time, so waiting until the end would result in an extremely long limitations period, whereas removals are supposed to be "short-term" in nature. The statute also provides that the six-year remedial action time period applies to both types of actions, if the remedial action starts within three years of the removal action's completion. The application of these limitations provisions sounds fairly simple, but in many circumstances it is difficult to determine when a removal action has ended or a remedial action has commenced for purposes of the statute. Moreover, it may be difficult to classify an action as removal or remedial in order to determine the applicable period. *See generally* Jerry L. Anderson, *Removal or Remedial? The Myth of CERCLA's Two-Response System,* 18 Colum. J. of Envtl. L. 103 (1993).

Problem 4.12: Statute of Limitations

In the Shenandoah case, the United States filed its cost-recovery suit on December 1, 2009. Construct an argument under Section 113(g) that certain costs sought by the United States in the Shenandoah case are barred by the statute of limitations. What are the possible arguments to the contrary? Did the "removal action" at the site end in March 2004, or when the additional removal was complete in March 2007, or when the RI/FS was complete in June 2007?

Excerpts from the following law review article outline some of the issues which arise in the CERCLA liability scheme:

* * *

Jerry L. Anderson, *The Hazardous Waste Land*
13 Va. Envt'l L.J. 1 (1993)

I. INTRODUCTION

Twenty-three attorneys gathered in the office of the United States Attorney for the deposition of Paul Kalarski, waste truck driver and landfill worker.[27] Mr. Kalarski, in his mid-sixties, arrived at the deposition in an ambulance. He appeared to be very ill as he began to answer questions, hooked to an oxygen tank and attended by a nurse. Halting every so often for more medication, to catch his breath or regain his strength, Kalarski rambled through his recollections—sometimes very clear, but at other times vague, disjointed, and

---

27. Although this account is based on an actual case, the names of the witness and the site have been changed to protect confidentiality.

often conflicting—of his days at the Hayward dump, now know to the parties as the Bryant Avenue CERCLA site.

The assembled lawyers, representing the likes of a Big Three automaker and a major communications company, as well as the local, state, and federal governments, hung on every word. Kalarski, who had worked as a truck driver and laborer at the site in the 1960's and 1970's, had become the crucial witness in the government's suit to recover the site's cleanup costs, largely because almost everyone else associated with the site had died. Cleanup costs at the site could reach $10 million, and any party might suddenly be in or out of the pool of parties held responsible for the cleanup based on a sentence from this witness's lips.

Although his health worsened throughout the protracted deposition—a two-day session in January and a three-day session in March—Kalarski tried to remember the details of the dump's operations twenty to thirty years before. He struggled to reconstruct which company's waste was hauled where and what it might have been. Was it some sort of acid? Did it smell bad? What color was the powder? How many times a week had he hauled that waste? The memories were now hazy, and progress was slow. Poor health forced a recess, and the deposition was rescheduled and postponed several times. Finally, the United States Attorney sent word that Mr. Kalarski had died. The nightmarish task of deciding who should pay the millions of dollars of cleanup costs had only just begun, however.

Meanwhile, in Toledo, Ohio, negotiations were dragging on over who should pay for the costs to clean up the Dura landfill, run by the city from the 1950's to the 1970's and now an environmental disaster. Located on the banks of the Ottawa River, the dump accepted both residential and industrial wastes for years. A study conducted in 1986 estimated that 5,500 gallons of hazardous leachate from the landfill had been leaking into the river daily. Due to the PCB contamination from the Dura dump, the Ottawa River had to be closed to fishing and swimming in 1991.

The city denied responsibility for the site cleanup and identified a small cadre of major waste generators as the ones who should pay. In response, the generator group began to meet on a monthly basis, with lawyers flying into Toledo from across the country to discuss strategies, peruse studies, and conduct investigations to find more parties to help pay cleanup costs. Negotiations between the group and the city continued sporadically over what should be done to the site and who should pay the estimated $33 million in response costs. City lawyers postured and threatened; generator lawyers gathered and talked. Months became years. The city at last proposed a partial solution: a leachate collection system and a 600-foot-long barrier wall would be constructed to protect the river. The generator group, however, produced a different plan which they believed would accomplish the same thing, while saving a lot of money. While the plans are developed and debated, hazardous substances continue to leak into the Ottawa River.

The hazardous waste cleanup system is in trouble. Not only is the system of assigning liability for cleanup costs manifestly unfair, it simply is not working.[28] The Bryant Avenue case and the Dura dump case are but two examples of the thousands of CERCLA cases mired in the Superfund pipeline,[29] laden with inequities and massive transaction costs for the parties involved and destined for delay by inherent incentives to avoid action.

Like a bureaucratic monster with a life of its own, the Superfund system has resisted a number of attempts to streamline the process and to step up the glacial pace of remediation.[30] Congressional pressure and administrative promises of reform have been as effective as hitting a velociraptor with a fly swatter. The cost-recovery system is also bogged down. Cleanup costs are supposed to be recovered from the parties responsible for the contamination, but the Environmental Protections Agency (EPA) has been forced to write off hundred of millions of dollars of costs because the potential defendants were insolvent or had disappeared, because evidence was insufficient, or because the agency lacked the resources to pursue the case within the statutory limitations period.[31]

---

28. *See, e.g.*, General Accounting Office, Superfund: Issues that Need to Addressed Before the Program's Next Reauthorization, statement of Peter F. Guerrero, Doc. No. GAO/T-RCED-92-15, at 9 (Oct. 29, 1991) [hereinafter Guerrero Statement] ("[D]espite a large investment of resources, Superfund has so far achieved little of its primary purpose: the permanent cleanup of major hazardous waste sites."); Ted Williams, *The Sabotage of Superfund*, Audubon, July–Aug. 1993, at 31 (quoting President Clinton: "We all know it doesn't work ... Superfund has been a disaster.").

29. The National Priorities List (NPL), which is supposed to represent the nation's most dangerous hazardous substance releases, contains 1072 sites. 40 C.F.R. pt. 300, app. B (1992). That list is expected to grow by at least 100 sites per year. Katherine N. Probst & Paul R. Portney, Resources for the Future, Assigning Liability For Superfund Cleanups: An Analysis of Policy Actions 17 (1992). In addition, there are many CERCLA cases involving sites that are not on the NPL, including private party cleanups. Government officials have estimated that it takes an average of fifteen years for an NPL site to be remediated after it is brought to EPA's attention. *Id.* at 20.

30. *See*, e.g., Guerrero Statement, *supra* note 14, at 3 (cleanups complete at only 63 sites, representing 5% of NPL; at 829 sites, remedial action has not even begun).

31. *U.S. Writes Off Cleanup Costs of Toxic Sites: E.P.A. Fails to Collect Money From Polluters*, N.Y. Times, June 21, 1993, at A10 (EPA has collected only $843 million out of the $4.3 billion in costs that could potentially be collected and has written off $270 million).

Delays in cleanups and cost-recovery seem to be tied, at least in part, to CERCLA's liability system. The parties who are responsible for the cleanup costs ("potentially responsible parties" or "PRPs") clog the system by questioning every move the EPA makes and forcing the EPA to spend time building a record to support every decision. For example, the time required for studying sites and developing remedial designs has doubled in recent years, presumably due to the threat of PRP challenge.[32]

In the first years of the Superfund program, courts and commentators, driven by the specter of rampant hazardous contamination, simply glossed over the significant fairness problems in the CERCLA liability scheme in their zeal to achieve environmental progress. One by one, issues like retroactive liability, strict liability, joint and several liability and successor liability were resolved in favor of the government based largely on the slogan that hazardous waste cleanup costs must be placed on those responsible for the problem and that the liability scheme must be "liberally" construed to achieve its goals. But subsequent experience reveals that cleanup costs are often borne by those who are not responsible for the problem at all, and that many other parties are held liable to an extent far exceeding their actual responsibility. The CERCLA liability system has become a black hole that indiscriminately devours all who come near it.

II. THE LIABILITY LOTTERY

The idea behind the CERCLA liability system is deceptively simple: make the polluter pay. By placing the cleanup costs on the generators and transporters of the waste, as well as on those who owned or operated (or who now own or operate) the disposal site, the scheme attempts to reach all parties who had any responsibility for the contamination problem. In many cases, this scheme makes perfect sense and works reasonably well. Some sites involve only one party, perhaps a company which disposed of its own waste on its own property and which has owned the site ever since. It is completely reasonable to hold that party liable for cleanup costs, and few efficiency concerns are raised because allocation of that liability is not an issue. Even at sites where only a handful of parties are responsible, all of whom are still in existence and able to pay, the CERCLA scheme works reasonably well.

The reality, however, is that in many other cases involving multiple parties, what appears on the surface to be a fair distribution of the cleanup costs de-

---

32. *See* Guerrero Statement, *supra note* 14, at 3 (site studies have expanded from two years to over four years; remedial designs have expanded from 18 months to almost three years).

teriorates rapidly into a liability lottery, in which a few randomly-selected parties, many of whom have little or even no connection to the waste disposal activity, bear the entire cost of cleanup.

Much of the delay can be traced directly back to the liability system. When a large group of PRPs, who know they will be required to pay the site cleanup costs, becomes involved with every stage of the cleanup process, the site remediation tends to get bogged down in excessive study and enormous transaction costs. Because the delay is inherent in the liability system no amount of administrative fixes or legislative pressure to speed cleanups will solve the problem — the effects obtained by those devices are like those produced by "pushing on a rope." Rather, the problems must be addressed by fundamental reform of the system itself.

III. SOURCES OF CERCLA'S INEQUITY AND INEFFICIENCY

The paradigm discussed above reveals four primary sources of CERCLA unfairness and inefficiency; (1) joint and several liability; (2) successor liability; (3) the cost allocation mechanism; and (4) the level of cleanup required. Those issues should be critically examined and addressed in any attempt at CERCLA reform.

A. Joint and Several Liability

The imposition of retroactive liability, requiring parties to pay large sums of money for actions that in many cases were deemed proper at the time, is a bitter pill for many parties to swallow. The addition of joint and several liability is enough to make most choke. Parties who might be resigned to paying the cleanup costs for hazardous substances they generated may well object to paying double, triple, or more to cover the shares of those who are dead, dissolved, insolvent, missing or against whom evidence is inadequate.

The dilatory pace of waste cleanups can be traced at least partially to this inequitable distribution of liability. Responsible parties faced with costs greatly exceeding the amount they equitably should pay are likely to dig in their heels, call for more studies, attack the remedy, attempt to reduce the scope of the cleanup and spend significant amounts of time and money arguing over how to split the costs among those left standing in this game of musical chairs. Small companies who may be able to pay cleanup costs of fifty dollars per drum dumped may not be able to pay two hundred dollars per drum to make up for the orphan shares. At some point, parties are likely to find it more desirable to litigate than to pay costs they deem unreasonable or simply unaffordable.

...

C. The Cost Allocation Mechanism

In the typical CERCLA case, the EPA sues a small group of PRPs, usually those against whom there is the most evidence, who had substantial involvement in the site (in terms of ownership or operation of the site, or generation or transportation of significant volumes of hazardous substances), and who have deep enough pockets to shoulder the cleanup costs. Those PRPs then attempt to identify other PRPs to sue for contribution. Often the number of parties drawn into the litigation web reaches ridiculous proportions. As an extreme example, at the Beacon Heights and Laurel Park landfill sites, the original defendants sought to join more than one thousand third-party defendants.

How are the response costs to be divided among the dozens, or even hundreds, of PRPs? CERCLA says only that the court should allocate costs "using such equitable factors as the court determines are appropriate."[33] Many courts have used the so-called "Gore factors" as a guide for cost allocation, looking to the volume and toxicity of hazardous substances contributed and the degree of involvement or culpability of the parties.[34]

The system breeds transaction costs that in some cases outstrip the response costs themselves. Determining a suitable allocation of costs, either by a court or by settlement, is enormously expensive and difficult for two reasons. First, the number of parties involved inevitably increases the difficulty of reaching agreement and increases the costs of bringing the allocation issue before the court. Second, the lack of a firm formula for allocating costs hampers attempts at early settlement. Because there is no way of knowing exactly what factors or what method a court will use to allocate costs, it is difficult for the parties to estimate the alternatives to a negotiated agreement. Who is to say whether a court would hold the owner of the site liable for ten, thirty, fifty, or eighty percent of the response costs? Who is to say whether a generator should be more responsible than a transporter?

---

33. 42 U.S. C. §9613(f)(1) (1988).

34. Then-Representative Albert Gore, Jr., proposed that courts should determine whether to impose joint and several liability in a particular case by weighing these factors. Courts have now borrowed them for the allocation decision. *See, e.g., Environmental Transp. Sys., Inc. v. ENSCO, Inc.,* 969 F.2d 503, 508–509 (7th Cir. 1992) (explaining that "Gore factors" provide a nonexhaustive but valuable roster of equitable apportionment considerations) (citing *United States v. A & F Materials Co., Inc.,* 578 F.Supp. 1249, 1256 (S.D. Ill. 1984)).

Should the generator of 500 tons of low toxicity waste pay as much as the generator of fifty tons of high toxicity waste? Without firm answers to these questions, parties have a difficult time evaluating settlement demands and offers.

Many PRP groups have chosen to use Alternative Dispute Resolution (ADR) techniques, such as arbitration or mediation, to cut transaction costs. It is difficult, however, to get a large number of parties to agree on what form of ADR to use. Significant transaction costs are expended in deciding that issue alone, and most groups can agree only on some "safe" form of non-binding ADR that may not accomplish much in the end. The EPA is supposed to aid the settlement process by producing Nonbinding Preliminary Allocations of Responsibility (NBARs), which are not admissible in court. Unfortunately, very few NBARs have actually been completed.

De minimis settlements, while useful in some cases, are also a limited solution. Under Section 122(g) of CERCLA, the EPA is encouraged to reach early settlements with PRPs whose contributions are minimal. The need for an early resolution of liability is especially acute for small contributors because their transaction costs can quickly become grossly disproportionate to their share of liability. The EPA has been trying for years to motivate the regional branches to make greater use of these settlements, with limited success.

D. Technical Issues: Cleanup Level, Timing and Choice of Remedy

The constant intervention of the PRPs in the current process bogs down the progress of site cleanup. Studies become protracted, and the EPA's flexibility in dealing with sites is limited by the knowledge that every decision will be subject to challenge and review.

To understand how inefficient the Superfund system is, imagine treating the personal injury tort case in a similar fashion. Currently, tort plaintiffs receive a lump sum payment representing the estimated cost of future medical bills. If a Superfund-like tort system were imposed, defendants would instead pay the "necessary costs of the injury" as they are incurred. Thus, the defendants would be involved with every medical decision made for the rest of the plaintiff's life. The defendants would want additional tests done, would want to examine every set of x-rays, would question every choice of procedure and every expenditure. The result would be a totally unacceptable intrusion on the doctor's judgment and a substantial and probably dangerous burden on and delay of the health care process. Transaction costs for all parties would be tremendous. Yet, that is precisely the way the current system handles hazardous waste cleanups.

* * *

Discussion Questions

What reforms of the CERCLA liability system would you advocate on behalf of your client in the Shenandoah case? What reforms, if any, do you personally favor?

C. Substantive Litigation Issues

There are a number of liability issues under CERCLA that remain relatively unsettled in the courts. We have selected some of them to illustrate the complexity of the Superfund liability scheme. The exercises that follow the explanation of each issue will allow you to explore it in-depth in the context of a summary judgment motion in the Shenandoah case. For each summary judgment motion, additional facts to support the motion will be available through the deposition of a witness. Alternatively, your professor may simply provide you with the additional factual information.

1. Successor Liability

Another excerpt from *The Hazardous Waste Land*[35] describes the successor liability problem:

* * *

As a general rule, a corporation ... that purchases assets from another corporation does not thereby become liable for the seller's liabilities. This rule of successor nonliability, established at a time when courts were first grappling with the corporate form itself, arose out of the bona fide purchaser rule; that is, one who takes assets for value and in good faith takes them free of the claims of creditors. The rule promoted the free alienability of property; without it, "commercial transactions could not go on at all."

Corporations could also use the corporate form fraudulently, however, to escape their debts and liabilities. Courts soon developed exceptions that balanced the desire to protect asset purchasers with the need to protect creditors from fraudulent transactions. Thus, liability will be imposed on the purchaser

---

35. 13 Va. Envt'l L.J. 1, 36–39 (1993).

of assets where (1) the asset purchase included an express or implied assumption of liabilities, (2) the transaction operated to defraud creditors, (3) the purchasing corporation was really a "mere continuation" of the seller or (4) the asset purchase was in reality a merger or consolidation of the two corporate entities.

Historically, the exceptions to the rule of nonliability were narrow in scope and based primarily on the need to prevent fraud. The mere continuation exception, for example, attempts to distinguish a bona fide sale of assets between two distinct corporations from a fraudulent reorganization by a single corporation. As one court put it, the mere continuation case is one where the predecessor attempts to "escape liability by merely changing hats." Thus, the important factor in a mere continuation case is not whether the business operations of the seller continued, but whether the corporate identity remained the same because there was a continuation of the same ownership and management. Likewise, under the "de facto merger" exception, courts require an exchange of stock for the assets purchased, thereby merging the ownership of the two companies; otherwise, the two corporate entities "remain distinct and intact."

Recently, some courts have developed another exception—the continuity of enterprise exception—that threatens to engulf the general rule of successor nonliability. Instead of focusing on whether the seller's corporate entity continued in the buyer, as the traditional exceptions do, the continuity of enterprise exception focuses on whether the buyer continued the seller's business operation. Thus, liability will be imposed if the purchaser used the same location as the seller, retained the same employees, produced the same product, retained the same name and held itself out as the continuation of the previous enterprise. Continuity of ownership, so crucial under the traditional mere continuation exception, is not required for liability here. Instead, liability is imposed under a "common sense" approach that ignores the traditional restrictions.

In most areas of the law, this modern extension of successor liability has been rejected by a majority of courts. In the CERCLA context, however, some courts have become enamored with the continuity of enterprise exception as a way to enlarge the pool of parties available to pay cleanup costs. Invoking the now-familiar rationale that expanding liability will "further the goals of CERCLA," courts are now imposing liability on successors who would be not be liable under traditional rules. For example, the district court in *United States v. Western Processing*[36] refused to reject the continuity of enterprise ex-

---

36. 751 F. Supp. 902 (W.D. Wash. 1990).

ception, stating that "[a] more expansive view of successor liability under CERCLA fosters a more equitable sharing of remediation costs."[37] The Eighth Circuit in *United States v. Mexico Feed & Seed Company*[38] applied the continuity of enterprise exception because it wanted to "prevent[] those responsible for the wastes from evading liability through the structure of subsequent transactions."[39]

Expanding the scope of the successor liability, however, could also place response costs on those who are not in any way responsible for the waste problem. A purchaser of assets who has paid full value in cash, in good faith, to an unrelated seller in an arms-length transaction should not be held liable for the seller's past waste disposal activities. While the seller may have reaped a profit from improper disposal practices, the asset purchaser has not benefited, assuming the purchaser paid full fair market value for the assets. When the selling corporation dissolves shortly after the sale, as it often does, the real beneficiaries are the seller's stockholders, who received the profits from the sale of company assets that appreciated in value as a result of using inexpensive waste disposal. It is only because the law limits suits against dissolved corporations or their stockholders that courts have had to seek a surrogate for the responsible party.

* * *

The first issue in a successor liability case under CERCLA is whether the state or federal common law of corporate liability applies. Some early courts held that, because CERCLA was a federal statute, federal common law should apply.[40] Using federal common law allowed the courts to fashion the broader "continuity of enterprise" test, unencumbered by narrower state law precedent. However, the Supreme Court in *U.S. v. Bestfoods, Inc.*, 524 U.S. 51, 63 (1998), stated that "CERCLA is [ ] like many other congressional enactments in giving no indication that 'the entire corpus of state corporation law is to be replaced simply because a plaintiff's cause of action is based upon a federal statute.'" Although the Court in *Bestfoods* declined to decide whether to apply state or federal common law, courts applying this case to CERCLA successor

---

37. *Id.* at 905.

38. 980 F.2d 478 (8th Cir. 1992).

39. *Id* at 488.

40. *See* Gregory C. Sisk & Jerry L. Anderson, "The Sun Sets on Federal Common Law: Corporate Successor Liability Under CERCLA After *O'Melveny & Myers*," 16 Va. J. Envt'l L. 505 (1997).

liability issues have found that state law should apply, unless there is evidence it would frustrate Congress's objectives. *See, e.g., U.S. v. Davis*, 261 F.3d 1, 54 (1st Cir. 2001).

Exercise 4.2(a): Summary Judgment Motion — Successor Liability

You represent United Waste, Inc., in the Shenandoah problem. UWI did not dispose of any waste at this Site; it merely purchased the assets of the company that did. File a summary judgment motion and brief arguing that UWI is not liable under principles of corporate successor liability. This motion will be opposed, on behalf of the original defendants, by Carson, Inc. Your fact witness is M. Victoria (or Victor) Dominguez, Regional Manager, United Waste, Inc., who was in charge of the asset purchase for the company.

---

2. Municipal Solid Waste

Studies of municipal solid waste (MSW) streams have shown that residential garbage generally contains a small percentage of hazardous substances. We all know what these are: the almost-empty cans of insecticide, the half-full can of paint, the rags soaked with motor oil from the garage, and the old bottle of weed-killer. It is also clear that there is no "de minimus" exception to CERCLA liability; even a generator of a small amount of hazardous substances can qualify for PRP status. *See Alcan Aluminum*, reproduced above. In some cases, MSW is a major portion of the waste present at a site. Sites with at least some MSW are very common; EPA estimates that about 17% of the hazardous substances found at Superfund sites came from municipalities and that about 23% of the sites on the NPL are "co-disposal" sites where both MSW and industrial wastes were dumped.

Early on, municipalities tried to avoid CERCLA liability by using the exception for household waste under the Resource Conservation and Recovery Act (RCRA). *See* 40 C.F.R. §261.4(b)(1). The municipalities argued that CERCLA liability should not attach to waste not deemed hazardous enough to be controlled under the RCRA system. Courts, however, decided that the RCRA exclusion did not carry over to the CERCLA definition of hazardous substances. *See B.F. Goodrich Co. v. Murtha*, 958 F.2d 1192 (2d Cir. 1992). Moreover, because there is no threshold amount of hazardous substance required to trigger CERCLA liability, MSW is not exempt merely because it is mostly non-hazardous.

CERCLA does require specific evidence of hazardous substances in the waste stream. *See, e.g., B.F. Goodrich v. Murtha*, 840 F. Supp. 180, 187–88 (D. Conn. 1993); *Dana v. American Standard*, 866 F. Supp. 1481 (N.D. Ind. 1994).

Thus, studies showing hazardous constituents in MSW in general may be insufficient to establish liability; instead, there must be evidence of a particular hazardous substance in a particular municipality's waste. Obtaining that evidence may be more difficult than it sounds, especially if the dumping occurred years ago and witnesses are few. *See, e.g., American Special Risk Ins. v. City of Centerline*, 2001 WL 1218551 (E.D. Mich) (plaintiff gathered affidavits from citizens to establish that hazardous wastes were disposed of by city garbage trucks).

Municipalities argue that holding them liable imposes the costs of Superfund cleanups on the general public, a result Congress surely could not have intended. At least partly because of those arguments, EPA adopted a policy under which it rarely sued a municipality for response costs, unless there was specific evidence that the municipality disposed of commercial, institutional, or industrial hazardous waste as well as MSW. That policy, however, did not prevent PRPs from suing municipalities (and their transporters) for contribution.[41]

Thus, in 1998, EPA developed a policy that allowed municipalities that either owned or operated waste sites, or that generated MSW, along with their transporters, to settle with EPA, thereby gaining contribution protection from the other PRPs. Under the policy, the government will settle with municipal owner/operators of waste disposal sites for between 20 and 35 percent of total site cleanup costs. At sites not owned or operated by the municipality, the EPA will settle with generators and transporters of municipal solid waste for $5.30 per ton of waste.[42] *See* Policy on Municipal Waste Settlements, 63 Fed. Reg. 8197 (Feb. 18, 1998). Does this policy shift too much of the remaining liability to the other, non-municipal PRPs? *See Industry Group Sues EPA Over Policy on Municipal Solid Waste Settlements*, 66 Env't Rptr. 2771 (June 16, 1998).[43] Is limiting liability to a narrow range realistic, given the variety of circumstances presented by these sites? *See, e.g., United States v. Alliedsignal, Inc.*, 62 F. Supp. 2d 713, 723 (N.D.N.Y. 1999) (PRPs successfully challenged $5.30 per ton settlement; court found it did not represent fair share of the remedial action costs).

Although the municipalities who arranged for the disposal of MSW and the transporters who selected the disposal site remain at least minimally liable

---

41. EPA, "Interim Policy on CERCLA Settlements Involving Municipalities and Municipal Wastes" (December 12, 1989).

42. The 1998 base amount will be adjusted for inflation.

43. The industry group's challenge to the MSW settlement policy was dismissed, because the court found the policy did not constitute "final agency action" on the issue. *Chemical Mfg. Ass'n v. EPA*, 26 F. Supp. 2d 180 (D.D.C. 1998).

under this approach, Congress did act, in the Small Business Liability Relief and Brownfields Revitalization Act of 2001 (actually enacted in January 2002), to exempt the individuals and entities who generated the garbage in the first place. The Brownfields Amendments added CERCLA Section 107(p), which exempts from liability any residential property owner (or lessee), small business entity, or small tax-exempt organization that generated MSW, unless EPA determines the MSW "contributed significantly" to the cost of the response, or unless the person/entity fails to cooperate in the site investigation. 42 U.S.C. §9607(p). The provision bars not only EPA cost-recovery actions against those generators, but also contribution suits by PRPs. 42 U.S.C. §9607(p)(6).

Exercise 4.2(b): Summary Judgment Motion—Municipal Waste

You represent the City of Maryville in the Shenandoah problem. The United States has not yet settled with your client under the Municipal Settlement Policy and, of course, there is always the chance that the other PRPs could successfully challenge such a settlement. File a summary judgment motion and brief on behalf of your client, arguing that the City is not liable for arranging for the disposal of MSW at the Site. This motion will be opposed, on behalf of the original defendants, by General Cars. Your fact witness will be the truck driver, Carl Larson, who hauled the City's waste to the Site.

---

3. Interim Landowner Liability

CERCLA Section 107(a)(1) imposes liability on the current owner or operator of the facility, while Section 107(a)(2) imposes liability on the facility owner/operator at the time the hazardous substances were disposed of. Those who owned or operated the facility in between those two time periods do not fall neatly into a liability category. Attempts have been made to hold these interim landowners liable under the theory that they were owners at the time of "disposal" of hazardous substances, because the definition of "disposal" includes "leaking."[44] A CERCLA plaintiff may be able to prove that hazardous substances were leaking, perhaps from drums buried underground, for example, during the interim landowner's ownership. Even if no one actually saw the drums leaking, an expert witness may be able to establish the approximate time

---

44. CERCLA §101(29), 42 U.S.C.§9601(29), defines "disposal" by reference to RCRA§1004, 42 U.S.C.§6903, which provides that it means "the discharge, deposit, injection, dumping, spilling, leaking, or placing" of hazardous wastes into the land or water so that they may enter the environment.

the drums started to leak, by analyzing the current condition of the drums or the extent of the contaminant migration. The interim landowners, on the other hand, argue that "disposal" under Section 107(a)(2) requires a positive action to have occurred during their ownership rather than merely passive migration.

The "passive disposal" theory has met with limited success in the courts. *See* Rita H. McMillen, *Liability for Passive Disposal of Hazardous Substances under CERCLA,* 42 Drake L. Rev. 255 (1993). For example, in *Carson Harbor Village Ltd. v. Unocal Corp.,* 270 F.3d 863 (9th Cir. 2001), the court stated that, in most instances, passive migration of contaminants would not fit the definition of "disposal" required to trigger liability; however, the court acknowledged that, in certain circumstances, failing to examine property for decaying tanks and prevent them from leaking could meet the definition. The court examined the cases from other circuits, finding a broad range of views that "depend[] in large part on the factual circumstances of each case." *Id. At* 875. *See also ABB Indus. Syst., Inc. v. Prime Tech., Inc.,* 120 F.3d 351, 359 (2d Cir. 1997) ("mere passive migration" does not constitute disposal); *U.S. v. CDMG Realty,* 96 F.3d 706, 716 (3d Cir. 1996) (same).

Of course, if the interim owner disturbed the hazardous substances in a way that caused additional dispersal, that action could constitute a new "disposal" triggering Section 107(a)(2) liability. *See U.S. v. Honeywell Intern., Inc.,* 542 F.Supp.2d 1188, 1199 (E.D. Ca. 2008); *United States v. CDMG Realty,* 96 F.3d 706, 719 (3d Cir. 1996).

Exercise 4.2(c): Summary Judgment Motion — Interim Landowner

Mittel Corp. purchased the Shenandoah Site after the hazardous substances were initially deposited there. Although Mittel did not allow any additional hazardous substances to be disposed at the Site during its ownership, it did allow nonhazardous construction waste to be dumped there. An expert consultant has stated that much of the hazardous waste at the site, such as the aluminum sulphate, and the DNAPL pools, started leaching into the soil almost immediately after disposal. He has also established that some of the drums, e.g, those containing toluene waste, probably began leaking around 1975, while others, such as those containing paint waste, probably would not have deteriorated to the point of leaking until the mid-1980s. You represent Mittel Corp. in the Shenandoah problem and should file a summary judgment motion and brief arguing that your client is not liable under Section 107. This motion will be opposed, on behalf of the original defendants, by Agro Enterprises. Your fact witness will be Sam Hodge, a truck driver for Hodge Trucking Company, who dumped construction materials at the Site during Mittel's ownership.

4. Innocent Landowner

Under Section 107(a)(1), the current owner of the facility is liable regardless of fault. Liability may be imposed even though the current owner had nothing to do with the hazardous substances disposal and had no knowledge of it. Because, in many cases, the disposal activity occurred years ago, it is quite common for the contamination source to be hidden from observation, making the purchase of property a risky undertaking.

Under Section 107(b), however, the truly innocent current landowner may claim that the contamination was caused by "the act or omission of a third party," typically the owner or operator of the land at the time hazardous substances were disposed there. The third party on whom the blame is placed must not be in a direct or indirect contractual relationship with the one claiming the defense. Because the definition of "contractual relationship" includes title transactions, former owners would generally not qualify as third parties under this defense. However, the contractual relationship definition also includes what has become known as the "innocent purchaser" defense. *See* Section 101(35), 42 U.S.C. §9601(35).

The innocent purchaser defense provides that a defendant who purchased the property after the hazardous substances were disposed is not liable if the defendant can establish that she did not know and had no reason to know that the substances were there.[45] *Id.* In order to establish "no reason to know," the defendant must be able to show that she undertook "all appropriate inquiries ... into the previous ownership and uses of the property in accordance with generally accepted good commercial and customary standards and practices." Section 101(35)(B).[46] In other words, willful or even negligent ignorance of the contamination will not establish the defense. In addition, the innocent purchaser must have taken reasonable steps to stop any further release, prevent threatened future releases, and prevent exposure to the released hazardous substances.

---

45. The statute also provides a defense to government entities that acquired property by escheat, by other involuntary acquisition, or by eminent domain. Defendants who acquired the property by inheritance or bequest are also protected. 42 U.S.C. §9601(35)(A)(iii).

46. In addition, a prospective purchaser who has knowledge of contamination at the site may limit their liability to the increase in property value attributable to EPA's response action. CERCLA 107(r), 42 U.S.C. §9607(r). However, this liability protection is available only if the prospective purchaser undertook "all appropriate inquiry." Likewise, a contiguous property owner who had no knowledge of the contamination and no reason to know of it, is excluded from liability as an owner as long as they conducted "all appropriate inquiry." CERCLA §107(q), 42 U.S.C. §9607(q).

The statute specifies a number of factors that the court should take into account in determining whether the defendant's inquiry was sufficient, such as the price of the property in relation to its value, the specialized knowledge or experience of the defendant, and the obviousness of the presence of the contamination. *Id.* The uncertainty inherent in the application of these factors made it difficult for a purchaser to know how much inquiry would suffice in a given case. In 2002, the Brownfields Act clarified the situation by stating explicitly that, for ordinary residential purchases, a title search and a visual inspection that reveal "no basis for further investigation" will satisfy the "all appropriate inquiry" standard. Section 101(35)(B)(v) 42 U.S.C. § 9607(35)(B)(v). For nonresidential property, the Brownfields Act required EPA to develop standards for "appropriate inquiry" that detail exactly what a purchaser must do to qualify. Those standards, found at 40 CFR Part 312, require an investigation by an environmental professional within one year prior to the property acquisition.

For property purchased before these standards were developed, however, the courts must still decide what level of inquiry was appropriate at the time. You can imagine that the standard will vary widely with circumstances such as the date of purchase, the type of land acquired, and what kind of parties are involved. A visual inspection might be all that would be required for the purchase of residential property in 1970, but the purchase of industrial property in 1985 might require a fairly thorough environmental audit. Knowledge that the property was formerly owned, for example, by "Acme Chemical Company" might also expand the duty of inquiry. Establishing what was good commercial or customary practice at the time will probably require expert testimony. Can "no inquiry" satisfy the inquiry standard, if it was consistent with the practice at the time? *See United States v. Serafini*, 706 F. Supp. 346 (M.D. Pa. 1988) (lack of visual inspection not fatal to innocent landowner defense if it was consistent with customary practice). For a case discussing in detail the appropriate inquiry standard for a 1986 purchase, *see Goe Eng'ring, Inc. v. Physicians Formula Cosmetics, Inc.*, 1997 WL 889278 (C.D. Cal.).

Exercise 4.2(d): Summary Judgment Motion— Innocent Landowner

Shenandoah bought the Carson Industries site in 1980, just about the time CERCLA was enacted. The facts show that Shenandoah officials did a fairly cursory visual inspection; they were not told about nor did they discover the presence of contamination before they purchased the property. On behalf of Shenandoah, file a summary judgment motion and brief based on the inno-

*cent purchaser defense. This motion will be opposed, on behalf of the origi-
nal defendants, by Ferros Industries. Your fact witness will be Nelson or Nel-
lie Kreitman, VP-Acquisitions for Shenandoah Industries, Inc., who was in
charge of the site purchase in 1980. Can this witness also act as an expert as
to what constituted "generally accepted good commercial and customary
standards and practices" in 1980?*

---

5. Individual Liability

Stockholders of a corporation, under corporate law, generally are not liable for the actions of the corporation beyond the value of their investment.
Individual shareholders can be held liable under CERCLA, however, in a couple of situations. First, under indirect or derivative liability, the court may
"pierce the corporate veil" if it finds that the corporate form is being used
fraudulently or is so undercapitalized and dominated by the stockholder as to
be merely the "alter ego" of the individual. Thus, the individual stock owner
would be deemed the real "person" liable under CERCLA. Second, a share-
holder may become directly liable if his or her involvement in the business
qualifies as "operating" the facility under Section 107(a)(1) or (2). Courts have
been divided, however, as to what actions are sufficient to trigger individual
"operator" liability.

In *United States v. Bestfoods*, 524 U.S. 51 (1998), the Supreme Court clarified "operator" liability in the context of a parent corporation's liability for the
operation of its subsidiary. The Court stated: "[U]nder CERCLA, an operator is simply someone who directs the workings of, manages, or conducts the
affairs of a facility. To sharpen the definition for purposes of CERCLA's concern with environmental contamination, an operator must manage, direct, or
conduct operations specifically related to pollution, that is, operations having
to do with the leakage or disposal of hazardous waste, or decisions about compliance with environmental regulations." *Id.* at *67. See also New York v. Shore
Realty Corp.*, 759 F.2d 1032 (2d Cir. 1985) (holding officer/stockholder liable
under CERCLA as "operator" because he managed the facility).

Prior to *Bestfoods*, some courts held that those who participated in management to the extent that they had the "capacity to control" hazardous waste
decisions, even if that authority was never exercised, could be deemed "operators" under CERCLA. *Idaho v. Bunker Hill Co.*, 635 F. Supp. 665 (D. Idaho
1986). Other courts, however, required "actual control" over the waste disposal decisions. In *United States v. Northeastern Pharmaceutical & Chem. Co.*,
810 F.2d 726, 743 (8th Cir. 1986), the Eighth Circuit held liable a corpora-

tion's President and Vice-President, who were also major stockholders, where they had the authority to control the disposal of hazardous substances and actively participated in those decisions. *See also Kelley v. Tiscornia*, 827 F. Supp. 1315 (W.D. Mich. 1993) (liability requires direct participation in or control of waste handling practices). Does *Bestfoods* resolve the conflict? *See, e.g., KC 1986 Ltd. Partnership v. Reade Mfg.*, 472 F.3d 1009, 1020 (8th Cir. 2007); *United States v. Green*, 33 F. Supp. 2d 203, 217 (W.D.N.Y. 1998) (after *Bestfoods*, individual must have participated in management of facility's pollution control operations, including decisions regarding disposal of hazardous substances, to trigger operator liability).

Think carefully about what circumstances should lead courts to hold individuals liable as operators. Should any manager of a corporation who made decisions about hazardous substance disposal be liable? Or should liability rest higher up the chain, with the CEO, even if he or she didn't get personally involved in the disposal decisions? What about a majority stockholder who was not really involved in the facility management? Under the *Bestfoods* test, does a corporate officer who negligently or willfully ignores the environmental part of a company's operations unfairly avoid liability?

Exercise 4.2(e): Summary Judgment Motion—Individual Liability

The original defendants sued Carrie Carson for individual liability, either as an "operator" of the facility under Section 107(a)(2), or under some sort of corporate veil-piercing theory. Carrie states that, although she inherited all of Carson, Inc.'s stock, she spent very little time on the company's affairs. She did make some decisions regarding the facility's management, but very few. On behalf of Carrie Carson, file a summary judgment motion and brief seeking to avoid individual liability. Balsam will oppose this motion on behalf of the original defendants. Your fact witness will be Carrie Carson herself.

---

6. Section 106 Penalties

CERCLA Section 106 gives the EPA broad authority to issue "such orders as may be necessary to protect public health and welfare and the environment." In the Shenandoah case, pursuant to its authority under Section 106, the EPA ordered Dreck Industries to undertake certain response actions at the site. As you know, Dreck refused to do so, for two reasons. First, Dreck believed, at the time, that it was not a liable party, because it had information indicating that its waste was being taken to a different disposal facility nearby. In addition, Dreck claimed it did not have sufficient financial resources to comply with the order. The EPA is now seeking penalties against Dreck for its failure to comply.

Section 106(b) provides for a fine of up to $25,000 per day for one who fails, "without sufficient cause," to comply with a Section 106 order. More pertinent to the Dreck case, however, is Section 107(c)(3), which provides for punitive damages of three times the amount of costs incurred by the Superfund as a result of the failure to comply. Thus, because EPA spent $500,000 on the RI/FS after Dreck's refusal, the United States is seeking $1.5 million in punitive damages from the company. Again, these treble damages are imposed only if the party lacked sufficient cause for its noncompliance.

Few courts have dealt with the issue of what constitutes "sufficient cause." Some courts have adopted a "subjective" standard, which requires, before penalties may be imposed, that the PRP had refused to comply in bad faith. Other courts, however, use an "objective" standard, which examines the reasonableness of the PRP's actions. *See Aminoil v. EPA*, 646 F. Supp. 294, 298–99 (C.D. Cal. 1986).

A party such as Dreck who believes it is not liable is faced with a difficult decision. If Dreck turns out to be wrong and the court believes it did not have "sufficient cause" to refuse to comply, it will suffer a significant penalty. Couldn't Dreck challenge the order in court right away and thereby resolve the issue quickly? *See* Section 113(h) (no "pre-enforcement" challenge to EPA orders).

The dilemma is ameliorated somewhat by Section 106(b)(2), which allows a party to obtain reimbursement for the costs of compliance with the order, if it can prove it is not a liable party under Section 107(a). The reimbursement provision is supposed to encourage parties with a doubt about liability to comply with the order and resolve the liability issue later. This after-the-fact reimbursement system, however, appears to shift the burden to the PRP to prove it is *not* liable, rather than having the government prove that it is. Given that reimbursement may be available, can a belief that you are not liable ever constitute "sufficient cause" to refuse compliance?

Exercise 4.2(f): Summary Judgment Motion— Section 106 Liability

As counsel for Dreck Industries, file a summary judgment motion and brief on the issue of penalties for refusing to comply with the Section 106 order. You argue that Dreck's noncompliance was based on a good faith belief that it was not liable and that it could not afford to comply. This motion will be opposed by the United States, represented by the DOJ. Your fact witnesses will be Paul Opperman, truck driver for Town & Country Sanitation Co., who hauled some of Dreck's waste; and Darla Dreck, President of Dreck.

D. Superfund Cost Allocation

CERCLA provides very little guidance on how response costs should be divided among PRPs. Section 113(f)(1) states only that the court should allocate the costs "using such equitable factors as the court determines are appropriate." Some courts have used, as a guide for cost allocation, the so-called "Gore factors," which were proposed by then-Representative Albert Gore, Jr., during the Congressional debate on joint and several liability when CERCLA was enacted in 1980. *See, e.g., Environmental Transp. Sys., Inc. v. ENSCO, Inc.,* 969 F.2d 503, 508–09 (7th Cir. 1992) (explaining that "Gore factors" provide a nonexhaustive but valuable roster of equitable apportionment considerations).

The Gore factors consider some of the things you logically might think would be relevant: the amount and degree of toxicity of the hazardous substances involved; the degree of the party's involvement in the generation, transportation, or disposal activity; the degree of care exercised by the party; and the degree of cooperation by the party with federal, state, or local officials. What other factors do you think should be relevant to the apportionment decision? What if, for example, part of the remedy was necessitated solely by one party's waste? What about ability to pay? How should related parties be treated (for example, are the owner and the operator of a site treated as one or two parties for allocation purposes)?

One of the difficulties in CERCLA allocation is comparing the relative liability of different types of parties. If only those who generated the hazardous substances were involved, the allocation might be a fairly simple task of assessing toxicity and volume. But how should the court compare the liability of a generator versus a transporter? Who should pay more, the owner of the site at the time of disposal or the owner of the site now? Should the disposal site operator pay more than the generators?

Unfortunately, there are few answers to these questions, because allocation decisions turn on a seemingly infinite variety of circumstances. However, a few patterns have emerged to help guide parties in determining their potential liability. For example, allocation decisions tend to emphasize the relative fault of the parties. *See United States v. J.B. Stringfellow, Jr.,* 1993 WL 565393 at 113–114 (C.D. Cal.) (citing numerous CERCLA cases in which comparative fault was the key issue in allocation). Thus, even though CERCLA is a strict liability statute, a party proving a relative lack of culpability may receive a low or even zero allocation of the response costs. *See, e.g., Danella Southwest, Inc. v. Southwestern Bell Tel. Co.*, 775 F. Supp. 1227, 1235 (E.D. Mo. 1991); *United States v. Moore*, 703 F. Supp. 460, 463 (E.D. Va. 1988) (blameworthy party may be allocated 100% of response costs).

A study of allocation decisions found that courts often begin by dividing the parties into categories (owners, operators, generators and transporters) and then allocate a portion of the liability to each category. Robert P. Dahlquist, "Making Sense of Superfund Allocation Decisions: the Rough Justice of Negotiated and Litigated Allocations," 31 Envt'l L. Rep. 11098 (2001). The study found that "site operators who have actively caused the contamination are allocated more liability than owners, particularly if the owner is not culpable or is absent; owners and operators of waste disposal facilities are usually allocated more liability than waste generators and transporters, and waste generators are usually allocated more liability than transporters unless the transporter was responsible for selecting the method of disposal."[47] Among generators, the allocation typically starts with an initial share based on volume, which is then adjusted by factors such as ability to pay, culpability, or excessive response costs attributable to a particular type of waste. *Id.*

In any case, the wide-open nature of the allocation decision and the numerous parties involved make settling Superfund cases extremely difficult. Many PRP groups, therefore, have turned to mediators or arbitrators for assistance. Techniques can range from mediator-led settlement discussions to binding or non-binding arbitration. Any of these alternative dispute resolution mechanisms will usually be more efficient and less costly than a full-fledged trial on allocation issues.[48]

You will attempt to reach an agreement regarding allocation of response costs among the PRPs in the Shenandoah case in Exercise 4.3 below.

---

47. Of course, a transporter must have selected *the site* in order to be liable at all under CERCLA, *see* 42 U.S.C. §9607(a)(4); however, selecting the *method* of disposal implies greater control over the process.

48. Dahlquist notes that courts may be able to resolve these issues without a trial, however, particularly if parties agree to submit the allocation issue to the court on a written record.

E. Settlement

In a CERCLA cost recovery case, the United States seeks to recover its past response costs as well as a declaratory judgment for all future response costs incurred that are not inconsistent with the NCP. 42 U.S.C.§§ 9607, 9613(g)(2) (declaratory judgment). In addition, the United States will seek its enforcement costs (including the expense of litigating the cost-recovery suit). 42 U.S.C § 9601(25) (defining "response" to include enforcement). Because the parties are strictly liable and have to pay the government's litigation costs, the United States in most cases has little incentive to discount the claim for "litigation risk." In some cases, however, a large portion of the response costs are attributable to parties that are bankrupt, corporations that have been dissolved, or waste whose generators cannot be identified. Where there is a significant "orphan share," the United States may be willing, in the interest of fairness and expediting settlement, to enter into mixed funding agreements, which use the Superfund to pay for a portion of the response costs. Section 122(b), 42 U.S.C. 9622(b), specifically authorizes this approach.[49] In addition, as a settlement incentive, EPA may agree to forgive some or all of its past costs in cases where there is a large orphan share.[50]

Typically, the government is unwilling to entertain separate settlement offers from individual PRPs. Because liability is usually joint and several, the more PRPs the U.S. can keep in the pool of parties held responsible for the whole cleanup bill, the better. Under certain circumstances, however, the United States will enter into a "cash-out" settlement which relieves a particular PRP from liability for future response costs. The government's current policy is to entertain that possibility primarily for de minimus parties, for current landowners who demonstrate a potential for innocent purchaser status, for municipal waste generators and transporters, or for municipal landfill owner/operators.[51] Even in these cases, the United States is sometimes reluc-

---

49. *See EPA, The Superfund Progress Report 1980–1997* (October 1998) (over $100 million in mixed funding settlements provided in 1996–97). The failure to reauthorize the Superfund tax, however, may make such a settlement less likely if the Fund resources are scarce.

50. OSWER, Interim Guidance on Orphan Share Compensation for Settlors (June 3, 1996), avail. at www.epa.gov/compliance/cleanup/superfund/neg-incentive.html.

51. Although it has not been a typical approach, it is possible for PRPs who do not fit in these categories to reach separate settlements, particularly by agreeing to perform part of the remedial action (a "carve-out" of the response). An interesting example of a "carve-out" settlement for individual PRPs occurred in *United States v. Davis*, 261 F.3d 1 (1st Cir. 2001), in which EPA settled with a small group of PRPs for approximately 34% of the re-

tant to enter into separate settlements, because it takes time to negotiate and draft them and the government usually does not benefit from a partial settlement when it is seeking a global one.

A party settling with the United States receives "contribution protection" from the other PRPs, under Sections 113(f)(2) and 122(g)(5), and the amount of the settlement is deducted from the liability of the remaining parties. As you will see in the negotiation exercise below, in many cases the remaining PRPs feel that the settling party has received too sweet of a deal, leaving the non-settling PRPs with more than their share of the liability. The United States must publish notice of a proposed settlement and take public comment for a thirty-day period. Although de minimus settlements may be accomplished with an administrative order, other settlements take the form of a consent decree, which the court must approve.[52] The non-settling parties may object and the court will approve the settlement only if it is procedurally fair and represents a reasonable allocation of responsibility for response costs. *United States v. Davis*, 261 F.3d 1, 20 (1st Cir. 2001). The government is given much discretion in allocating liability, however, and almost all settlements have been approved.

Congress explicitly directed the government to settle with *de minimus* contributors early on in the litigation, so these small parties could escape both joint and several liability and the expense of protracted litigation. CERCLA Section 122(g), 42 U.S.C. §9622(g). For a generator to qualify for a *de minimus* settlement, the waste contributed must be comparatively minimal both in terms of amount and toxicity.[53] These settlements will be for cash and will absolve the party from liability for future response costs (subject to certain "reopener" provisions, such as if new information surfaces showing the party does not meet de minimus requirements). Because the party is avoiding litigation costs, orphan share costs, and the risk that future costs at the site will increase, the EPA will add a premium (an amount above the

---

sponse costs at the site (including an agreement to perform soil remediation). The non-settling parties, who faced liability for the remaining costs, objected that the settlement did not fairly apportion liability. The court, however, found the settlement to be fair to all parties and the public.

52. For examples of consent decrees in Superfund cases, *see* www.usdoj.gov/enrd/Consent_Decrees.html.

53. Although the statute does not specify a "cut-off" percentage for purposes of de minimus eligibility, EPA has sometimes limited participation to those contributing not more than 1% by volume. *See, e.g., United States v. Cannons Eng'rg Corp.*, 899 F.2d 79, 86 (1st Cir. 1990).

party's share of the liability) to take into account those cash-out benefits. *See generally* Methodology for Early De Minimus Waste Contributor Settlements, 57 Fed. Reg. 29312 (July 1, 1992).[54] In order for EPA to enter into a de minimus settlement, however, it must have established a "waste-in" list that identifies with some certainty the volume and nature of the hazardous substances contributed by each PRP. Would EPA enter into any de minimus settlements with PRPs at the Shenandoah site, given the current state of the evidence?[55]

Section 122(g)(1)(B) also encourages EPA to settle early with innocent purchaser landowners. Note that even if EPA has decided not to sue the current facility owner, the party may wish to seek a settlement to gain contribution protection from other PRPs. The agency will require a showing that is basically the same as that required to establish the innocent purchaser defense under Section 101(35). As part of the settlement, the government will require assurances of access to the site and continued due care with respect to the hazardous substances. It also may require a cash consideration if there is some chance that the landowner would not have prevailed on the innocent purchaser defense at trial. *See* Guidance on Landowner Liability under Section 107(a)(1) of CERCLA, OSWER Dir. # 9835.9 (June 6, 1989). Remember also that EPA has a policy regarding early settlements with municipal solid waste landfill owner/operators and MSW generators and transporters. *See supra* Section C(2).

The Brownfields Act added another subsection to Section 122, directing EPA to consider "alternative payment methods" if a person demonstrates an inability to pay its total allocated amount at the time of settlement. 42 U.S.C. § 9622(g)(7).

Exercise 4.3: Cost Allocations

In the Shenandoah Superfund litigation the United States is seeking to recover $1 million in past costs, plus interest and enforcement costs. In addi-

---

54. *See, e.g., Action Mfg. Co. v. Simon Wrecking Co.,* 428 F.Supp. 2d 288, 332 (E.D. Pa. 2006) (EPA assessed 50% uncertainty premium for *de minimus* settlements). In addition, EPA will enter into "*de micromus*" settlements with very small volume contributors (usually less than .002% of the total volume of waste). EPA offers to settle for little or no money, simply to provide these parties with contribution protection, so that they can avoid being pulled into expensive litigation by the other PRPs. 61 Fed. Reg. 18411 (April 25, 1996) (97 third and fourth-party defendants settled with U.S. for $1 each).

55. *See* EPA, *De minimus Methodology,* 57 Fed. Reg. 29312, 29313 n.5 (de minimus settlements "probably not feasible" where waste-in information not available).

tion, it seeks a declaratory judgment for all future response costs, which are now estimated at $10 million. Due to the discovery of PCB contamination, the future response costs will likely rise to at least $15 million when EPA issues a new ROD for this operable unit. The PCB contamination represents the orphan share at this site.

The PRPs have scheduled a meeting to discuss whether a settlement can be reached in the Shenandoah case. One student should represent the United States as a DOJ attorney; each of the other students should represent one of the PRPs. Any PRP can attempt to negotiate a separate settlement with the EPA at any time, providing it meets the terms of one of the EPA policy documents on early settlements. Assume, for purposes of this exercise, that the EPA will not entertain any other cash-out settlements. The PRPs as a group may attempt to enter into a mixed funding or orphan share contribution settlement with the United States.

In addition to discussing a settlement with the United States, the PRPs should also discuss how to allocate response costs among themselves. For purposes of this exercise, assume that no ruling has been made on any of the summary judgment motions (see Exercise 4.2), although parties should take into account the probability of prevailing on those motions in deciding whether to settle the case now. The PRPs should discuss what factors are appropriate for the allocation decision and attempt to reach an agreement on allocation. Allocations should be made by percentage of response costs, because although there is an estimate of the total cost of remedial action, the actual cost is of course unknown. Prior to the allocation negotiation meeting, prepare a brief summary (1–2 pages) of your proposed allocation and the reasons supporting it.

Remember that the alternative to reaching a settlement is either agreeing to some sort of ADR (such as arbitration or mediation) or, failing that, having a court decide on allocation.

CHAPTER V

ENVIRONMENTAL POLICY

A. Introduction: The Lawyer's Role in Environmental Policy

Environmental policy pervades the practice of environmental law. You have already seen one way in which this is true: lawyers use their knowledge of policy to perform traditional legal tasks such as litigation, client counseling and enforcement. For example, in deciding whether CERCLA liability extends to a "passive" prior owner of a Superfund site (Chapter IV) a court will consider how its decision might affect CERCLA's policy goals. The lawyer who comprehends the statute's purposes and can craft a strong policy argument will be better able to persuade the court. Lawyers also use their understanding of policy when they construe regulations for a client (Chapter I) or assess how a penalty policy applies to a given violation (Chapter II).

Some attorneys go a step beyond this and participate directly in the formation of environmental policy. Government lawyers on Capitol Hill and in state capitals across the country assist in the drafting of environmental legislation. Attorneys at EPA's Office of General Counsel (OGC) and in many state environmental agencies play a significant role in shaping environmental regulations. Private and public interest attorneys are also heavily involved. They lobby federal and state legislators with respect to environmental legislation. They advocate on behalf of their clients in rulemaking proceedings. They bring lawsuits challenging regulations and argue the policy and legal merits of these rules in court. These activities require a special set of skills that complement those you have been learning with respect to environmental counseling, enforcement and litigation. This chapter will help you to develop these competencies.

It will focus on the attorney's role in the rulemaking process. This aspect of environmental policymaking is especially important for the environmental lawyer. It is here that agencies flesh out the meaning of environmental statutes and decide many of the issues that directly affect clients. Moreover, while it can be difficult to access the legislative process, the Administrative Procedure

Act (APA) and analogous state statutes *guarantee* members of the public *the right* to participate in agency rulemakings. Many clients find that this forum presents them with their best opportunity to get their concerns addressed. Often, they rely on their attorneys—who are trained in the art of effective advocacy—to represent them in these policymaking proceedings.

This chapter will address only federal environmental policymaking, although many of the practical skills it teaches should be applicable to state rulemakings as well. It will begin by introducing you to the federal rulemaking process. It will then ask you to play the role of a lawyer participating in the development of policy in an important area: environmental justice.

B. The Federal Rulemaking Process

A rulemaking is an exercise of agency policymaking authority that usually applies to broad groups of persons and that is prospective in effect. It can be distinguished from an agency *adjudication* which resolves disputes among specific persons and is concerned with the determination of past and present rights and liabilities. *See Attorney General's Manual on the Administrative Procedure Act* 14–15 (1947). For example, when EPA sets out by regulation the EPCRA emergency release notification requirements applicable to all who release a hazardous or an extremely hazardous substance, *see* 40 CFR §355.40 (2009), this constitutes agency rulemaking. When an administrative law judge rules on EPA's enforcement action against an alleged violator of these standards, this is agency adjudication.

1. Administrative Procedure Act Requirements

When a federal agency produces a rule, it must do so in accordance with procedural requirements established by the Administrative Procedure Act (APA).[1] 5 U.S.C. §551, *et seq.* (2006). The APA defines two basic sets of procedures for rulemakings and sets out criteria for when each should be used. The first, known as "formal rulemaking," bears many similarities to a trial proceeding. For example, in a formal or "on-the-record" rulemaking there is a hearing presided over by an impartial decision maker (usually an agency official), and interested parties are entitled to be notified of the hearing and to be

---

1. Some statutes, including some environmental statutes, establish additional procedural requirements for rulemakings promulgated under them. *See, e.g.,* Clean Air Act §307(d), 42 U.S.C. §7607(d)(2006).

given the opportunity to present and cross-examine witnesses. See APA §§556, 557, 5 U.S.C. §§556, 557 (2006).

If formal rulemaking resembles a trial, then "informal rulemaking," the APA's second set of rulemaking procedures and the one that governs most environmental rules, resembles a conversation between the agency and the public. Section 553 of the APA sets out the stages of this conversation—the procedural steps that the agency must pass through before it can finalize a rule.[2]

a. The Notice of Proposed Rulemaking

Under the APA's informal rulemaking procedures the agency must first publish in the Federal Register a Notice of Proposed Rulemaking (NPR).[3] APA §553(b), 5 U.S.C. §553(b) (2006). Failure to publish the NPR may result in a court invalidating a rule or remanding it to the agency. *PPG Industries, Inc. v. Costle*, 659 F.2d 1239, 1249–51 (D.C. Cir. 1981). The intent of the NPR is to give the public sufficient notice of the issues to be addressed in the rule, and of the agency's initial position on these issues, that members of the public will be able to comment on the proposal. To this end, the APA requires the agency to set out either the "substance of the proposed rule" or, at minimum, "a description of the subjects and issues involved." APA §553(b)(3). Courts have also required the agency to identify in the NPR any data on which the proposed rule is based so that the public can evaluate and comment upon this information. *See Ethyl Corp. v. EPA*, 541 F.2d 1, 48–49 (D.C. Cir. 1976); *Portland Cement Assoc. v. Ruckelshaus*, 486 F.2d 375, 393–94 (D.C. Cir. 1973). Usually, agencies include in the NPR both the text of the proposed rule and a narrative preamble that introduces and explains the proposal. You have seen such a preamble in the PSD and NSPS proposed rules that you studied in Chapter I.

Problem 5.1: Publication Requirement

Section 553(b) of the Administrative Procedure Act, 5 U.S.C. §553(b) (2006), requires agencies to publish proposed rules in the Federal Register. However,

---

2. The agency *must* follow these steps. A rulemaking that fails to follow the required procedures is invalid. See *United States v. Goodner Bros. Aircraft, Inc.*, 966 F.2d 380, 384 (8th Cir. 1992). As an attorney, you can bring a lawsuit challenging a rulemaking on the grounds that it did not comply with these requirements. This a powerful legal tool.

3. Alternatively, the agency may give actual notice to interested parties and forego Federal Register publication. Administrative Procedure Act §553(b), 5 U.S.C. §553(b) (2006).The agency may also dispense with the notice requirement altogether "when the agency for good cause finds ... that notice [is] ... impracticable, unnecessary, or contrary to the public interest." *Id.*

the statute creates several exceptions to this broad requirement. Under APA § 553(b), what types of policies can an agency issue without *publishing a proposal in the Federal Register?*

b. Public Comment on the Proposed Rule

After an agency publishes an NPR, it must give interested members of the public a "reasonable" opportunity to submit written comments on the proposal. The APA does not specify how long this comment period should be. Many agencies allow 60 days for complex or controversial rules. Upon receipt, some statutes require the agency to place these comments in an agency "docket," where they are available for public review.[4] In an important EPA rulemaking, the agency can receive hundreds of comments running to thousands of pages. Sometimes, the number of comments can go far higher. For example, EPA received over 50,000 written and oral comments on its proposed revisions to the National Ambient Air Quality Standard for Particulate Matter. 62 Fed. Reg. 38652, 38654 (1997). The first two steps of an informal rulemaking—notice of the proposal and the opportunity to comment on it—have given the process another name: "notice-and-comment" rulemaking.

Problem 5.2: Holding Hearings

Under APA § 553, does an agency that has published a proposed rule have to hold a hearing in which it allows interested parties the opportunity to provide oral responses to the proposed rule? Can an agency hold such a hearing if it wishes to?

c. The Final Rule

After EPA receives and considers comments from the public it develops a final rule and publishes it in the Federal Register.[5] The APA requires that the preamble to the final rule contain a "concise general statement of [the rule's] basis and purpose." APA § 553(c). To satisfy this requirement, the agency must articulate its findings of fact and demonstrate a rational connection between

---

4. *See, e.g.*, Clean Air Act § 307(d)(2), (3), 42 U.S.C. §§ 7607(d)(2), (3).

5. Alternatively, the agency can choose to re-propose the rule, put it on the "back burner" indefinitely, or cancel the rulemaking altogether (unless a statute, court order or other legal authority requires the agency to promulgate the rule).

the facts found and the rule arrived at. *Bowen v. American Hosp. Ass'n,* 476 U.S. 610, 626 (1986). In addition, the statement must identify major issues of policy and explain the agency's conclusions on these issues. *St. James Hosp. v. Heckler,* 760 F.2d 1460, 1469 (7th Cir. 1985). Finally, while the statement need not address every comment made, the preamble must respond to all significant issues that the comments have raised. *Northside Sanitary Landfill, Inc. v. Thomas,* 849 F.2d 1516, 1520 (D.C. Cir. 1988). If it fails to do so, a court can deem the final rule invalid and remand it to the agency. *Action on Smoking & Health v. Civil Aeronautics Board,* 699 F.2d 1209, 1217, *modified* 713 F.2d 795, 802 (D.C. Cir. 1983).

Problem 5.3: Timing of Final Rule

Under APA §553, how much time must elapse between the date that a final rule is published in the Federal Register and the date on which it becomes binding on regulated parties? Why do you think that the APA requires this time delay?

---

2. Optional Procedures Prior to the Proposal

The APA mandates the three steps just described for all informal rulemakings. Agencies have the option of adding at least two more procedures prior to the issuance of the proposed rule: publishing an "advance notice of proposed rulemaking" (ANPR) in the Federal Register; and engaging in a "negotiated rulemaking."

a. Advance Notice of Proposed Rulemaking

An ANPR precedes the NPR and provides notice to the public of an agency's intention to propose a rule on a given subject. Frequently, the ANPR will set out various regulatory alternatives that the agency is considering. It may then seek input from members of the public on the wisdom and/or feasibility of the alternatives presented, on the scope of the rulemaking under consideration (should it be expanded? narrowed? are there additional issues that need to be addressed?), and even on the threshold decision of whether to undertake the rulemaking at all. *See, e.g.,* Advanced Notice of Proposed Rulemaking for Water Quality Standards Regulation, 63 Fed. Reg. 36742 (1998) (seeking input on "what if any changes are needed in the national water quality standards program to improve the effectiveness of water quality standards in restoring and maintaining the quality of the Nation's waters.")

Problem 5.4: When to Employ an ANPR

Assume that you are counsel to EPA and that the Agency is preparing to propose a rule. In which of the following situations would you advise EPA to issue first an Advanced Notice of Proposed Rulemaking: (a) the Agency is considering the issuance of a proposed rule that will regulate a given substance but needs more data on how industry uses the substance and on the possible health effects associated with it; (b) the Agency is considering issuance of a proposed rule that is likely to be highly controversial; (c) the Agency wants to issue a rule to deal with a pressing problem that needs to be resolved as soon as possible; (d) a public interest group has requested that EPA promulgate a rule on a given topic but the Agency is not sure that it makes sense to devote scarce resources to such a rulemaking at this time.

b. Negotiated Rulemaking

In a negotiated rulemaking, the agency invites interested parties to work with it in drafting the proposed rule. If the group can reach consensus, the agency will generally use the group's language as the proposal. The Negotiated Rulemaking Act of 1990, 5 U.S.C. § 561 *et seq.*, expressly authorizes agencies to undertake this process, although it does not require them to do so.[6]

As described in the Negotiated Rulemaking Act, the process begins with an agency determination that a negotiated rulemaking would be "in the public interest." Negotiated Rulemaking Act, 5 U.S.C. § 563(a) (2006).[7] The agency

---

6. The Negotiated Rulemaking Act supplements the APA informal rulemaking requirements. It does not replace or modify them.

7. The statute provides that, in making this determination, the agency should consider whether "(1) there is a need for the rule; (2) there are a limited number of identifiable interests that will be significantly affected by the rule; (3) there is a reasonable likelihood that a committee can be convened with a balanced representation of persons who (A) can adequately represent the interests identified under paragraph (2); and (B) are willing to negotiate in good faith to reach a consensus on the proposed rule; (4) there is a reasonable likelihood that a committee will reach a consensus on the proposed rule within a fixed period of time; (5) the negotiated rulemaking procedure will not unreasonably delay the notice of proposed rulemaking and the issuance of the final rule; (6) the agency has adequate resources and is willing to commit such resources, including technical assistance, to the committee; and (7) the agency, to the maximum extent possible consistent with the legal obligations of the agency, will use the consensus of the committee with respect to the proposed rule as the basis for the rule proposed by the agency for notice and comment." Negotiated Rulemaking Act, 5 U.S.C. § 563(a) (2006).

then publishes in the Federal Register a notice of its intention to proceed by negotiated rulemaking and a tentative list of those who will serve on the negotiation committee. *Id.* at § 564. Interested parties not listed in the notice may apply for membership on the committee. *Id.* at § 564(b). However, the number of people on a given committee may not exceed twenty-five. *Id.* at § 565(b). Often, the agency will appoint a neutral "facilitator" to chair the committee meetings and assist the interested parties in reaching consensus. At the conclusion of its deliberations the committee submits a report to the agency. The report includes a proposed rule (if the committee has agreed upon one) as well as any other information, recommendations or materials that the committee deems appropriate. *Id.* at § 566(f). The committee generally disbands upon the publication of the final rule.

Problem 5.5: Why Use Negotiated Rulemaking

Why do you think Congress added the negotiated rulemaking option to the notice-and-comment rulemaking process? What problems of notice-and-comment rulemaking might the negotiation procedure help to address?

---

3. Statute-Specific Procedures

The APA establishes baseline procedures that must be followed in the promulgation of rules but leaves Congress and, to some extent, the agencies themselves free to prescribe additional procedures where they see fit. Both Congress, and EPA, have done so in the environmental area. Several of the environmental statutes require supplemental rulemaking procedures. *See, e.g.,* Clean Water Act § 101(e), 33 U.S.C. § 1251(e); Safe Drinking Water Act § 300g-1(d), 42 U.S.C. § 300g-1(d); Resource Conservation and Recovery Act § 7004(b), 42 U.S.C. § 6974(b); Clean Air Act § 307(d), 42 U.S.C. § 7607(d). The EPA has, by regulation, established procedures that it will follow in rulemakings under such statutes.

Problem 5.6: Public Hearing Requirement

Section 6 of the Toxic Substances Control Act, 15 U.S.C. § 2605 (2006), authorizes EPA to regulate by rulemaking any chemical substance or mixture that "presents or will present an unreasonable risk of injury to health or the environment." TSCA § 6(a). It gives the agency the power to limit or ban "the manufacture, processing, or distribution in commerce" of such substances or mixtures, to impose labeling and record-keeping requirements on those who manufacture or handle them, and to regulate the manner in which such substances are commercially used or disposed. Id.

Assume that, a month ago, EPA proposed a rule under TSCA §6 that would ban the manufacture and distribution of lead-based fishing sinkers. The EPA believes that these sinkers pose an "unreasonable risk of injury" to water fowl that eat and are poisoned by them. You represent the Environmental Defense Fund's Wildlife Program (EDF) and have submitted comments to EPA supporting the proposed rule. Other commentators, such as the American Sportfishing Association, have filed comments opposing the proposed ban and arguing that EPA should instead require only that the sinkers be labeled as potentially hazardous to water fowl.

Your client has expressed to you that it would like the opportunity to present public, oral testimony to EPA regarding the ways that lead sinkers poison water fowl. EDF believes that the media would report on such testimony, and that this would increase the pressure on EPA to finalize the ban. Does the Toxic Substances Control Act require the agency to hold a public hearing to receive such testimony? If so, which provision mandates this and what, exactly, does it require?

Problem 5.7: Hearing Procedure

Locate EPA regulations governing public hearings on TSCA §6 rulemakings. Based on these regulations, answer the following questions: (A) What steps does EDF have to take in order to gain the opportunity to present testimony at the hearing? (B) The American Sportfishing Association (ASA) believes that EPA has overestimated the number of birds killed each year by lead sinkers. If the ASA presents testimony to this effect at the hearing, will the EDF have an opportunity to cross-examine the ASA witnesses? What procedural steps must it take in order to gain such an opportunity?

C. The Lawyer's Involvement in the Rulemaking Process

There are three principal ways that non-governmental attorneys (both private and public interest) get involved in the rulemaking process: they prompt

EPA to initiate rulemakings; they participate in rulemakings; and they challenge rulemakings. We will introduce you to each of these areas in turn.

1. Initiating Rulemaking

A federal administrative agency such as EPA has jurisdiction to issue regulations reasonably related to the purposes of its enabling statutes. But the fact that EPA has the power to issue regulations in a given area does not mean that it will do so. The EPA faces many competing demands for its limited resources. Rulemakings—which require substantial agency investment—must take their place alongside other EPA priorities.

a. Suing the Agency to Enforce Statutory Deadlines

Attorneys can prompt EPA to initiate a rulemaking in three ways. First, attorneys can sue EPA on behalf of their clients to require the agency to meet statutory deadlines for the promulgation of rules. For example, the Clean Air Act Amendments of 1990 require EPA to promulgate, by November 15, 1994, air pollution regulations for solid waste incinerators that combust industrial or commercial waste. After the statutory deadline had passed without EPA having issued such regulations, the Sierra Club successfully sued the agency to force it to initiate the rulemaking. *See* 117 Daily Env. Rept'r A-6 (June 18, 1997).

Problem 5.8: Forcing EPA to Initiate Rulemaking

Assume that you are counsel to the Sierra Club. The organization has learned that EPA has missed a statutory deadline for the promulgation of a nationally-applicable Clean Air Act regulation. It has asked you to bring a legal action to compel the Agency to fulfill the statutory requirement. Answer the following questions: (A) What statutory provision will you cite as the basis for the court's jurisdiction? (B) In which court must you file the suit? (C) Does the statute require the Sierra Club to take any specific actions before filing suit against EPA?

---

b. Petitioning the Agency for the Issuance of a Rule

The Administrative Procedure Act gives "interested person[s]" the "right to petition for the issuance, amendment or repeal of a rule." APA §553(e), 5 U.S.C. §553(e) (2006). Thus, a second way in which attorneys can prompt EPA to initiate rulemaking is to file such a petition on behalf of their clients. The APA does not prescribe procedures for an agency to follow in handling such petitions. However, where an agency denies a petition for rulemaking the APA requires that it give "prompt notice" of this to the petitioner accompanied by a "brief statement of the grounds for denial." APA §555(e). Courts allow agencies substantial discretion in handling rulemaking petitions. Judicial review of an agency denial is "very narrow" in scope. *WWHT, Inc. v. Fed. Communications Comm'n*, 656 F.2d 807, 814–16 (D.C. Cir. 1981).

Problem 5.9: Petitioning for Issuance of a TSCA Rule

Some statutes prescribe procedures to govern petitions for rulemaking. Locate the Toxic Substances Control Act (TSCA) provision governing citizen petitions. Answer the following questions: (A) Who can file a petition requesting that EPA issue, amend or repeal a rule promulgated under TSCA? (B) Where should the petition be filed? (C) What must the petition contain? (D) How long does EPA have to respond to the petition? (E) Under what circumstances may a court reverse an EPA decision to deny a petition for the issuance of a rule and order the Agency to proceed with the rulemaking?

---

c. Suing the Agency to Enforce Notice and Comment Rulemaking Requirements

A third way in which attorneys can initiate EPA rulemaking—and the one on which we will focus—is to challenge EPA's decision to implement a given policy by "guidance" and to argue that the agency should have proceeded by notice-and-comment rulemaking. For these purposes "guidance" consists of written EPA policies other than those promulgated through informal or formal rulemaking or adjudication. For example, the letter that Edward Reich, Director of EPA's Division of Stationary Source Enforcement sent to Steve Rothblatt, Chief of the Air Programs Branch, EPA Region V, interpreting the meaning of the term "source" in the PSD program (reprinted, above, in Chapter I) is a guidance document. It sets out agency policy and has important implications for a regulated party (it determines whether PSD requirements will apply to a General Motors facility), but an EPA official issued it without following APA procedures of any sort.

From EPA's perspective, the fact that guidance is not subject to APA procedures can be a major advantage. Guidance is far less expensive to produce than a rulemaking would be. The agency does not need to burden itself with Federal Register notices, responses to comments, or any of the other rulemaking steps. In addition, by using guidance EPA gains more control over the final policy since it need not respond to or incorporate comments from the public. Finally, agency guidance documents are often not subject to judicial review. For each of these reasons, agencies such as EPA often prefer to proceed through guidance rather than by rulemaking.

This is where you, the environmental lawyer, come in. By mastering the APA provisions that specify when an agency *must* use notice-and-comment rulemaking you can put yourself in a position to argue, on behalf of your clients, that an agency decision to proceed by guidance is invalid and that the agency *must* include the public in its decision making process.[8] To play this role effectively, environmental lawyers need a clear grasp of when the APA requires agencies to proceed by rulemaking.

The APA rulemaking requirement is structured as a very broad requirement followed by several significant exceptions. It begins by mandating that agencies employ notice-and-comment procedures every time that they adopt, amend or repeal a "rule." APA §553. As was explained above, a rule is an exercise of agency policymaking authority that usually applies to groups of people and that is prospective in effect.[9] This far-reaching definition encompasses virtually all policymaking decisions of an agency other than agency adjudications. The APA accordingly qualifies the broad requirement with several important exceptions.

An agency need not follow notice-and-comment rulemaking procedures with respect to "interpretative rules," "general statements of policy" or "rules of agency organization, procedure, or practice." APA §553(b)(3)(A). In addition, an agency may dispense with notice and comment procedures when "the agency for good cause finds that ... [engaging in notice-and-comment rulemaking would be] impracticable, unnecessary, or contrary to the public interest" APA §553(b)(3)(B).[10] The key to mastering the APA rulemaking requirement is to understand these exceptions.

---

8. Government lawyers also need to understand this area of law so that they can advise their clients (*e.g.* the EPA or a state environmental agency) as to whether they can proceed by guidance or whether they must observe notice-and-comment rulemaking procedures.

9. The Administrative Procedure Act defines a "rule" as "an agency statement of general or particular applicability and future effect designed to implement, interpret or prescribe law or policy, or describing the organization, procedure or practice requirements" of an agency. Administrative Procedure Act, 5 U.S.C. §551(4) (2006).

10. You should be aware of two more exceptions, although we will not deal with them further here. First, APA §553(a) expressly exempts from notice-and-comment rulemaking requirements rules that involve "a military or foreign affairs function of the United states, or ... a matter relating to agency management or personnel or to public property, loans, grants, benefits or contracts." Second, APA §553(c) provides that "[w]hen rules are required by statute to be made on the record after opportunity for an agency hearing" formal rule-

An important Congressional goal underlying the APA notice-and-comment rulemaking requirement is to ensure that those who will be strongly affected by a rule have an opportunity to participate in its formulation. Alfred Aman, Jr. & William T. Mayton, Administrative Law 78 & n.2 (2001) (citing cases). To this end, courts construe the §553(b) exceptions "narrow[ly]," *American Hospital Ass'n v. Bowen*, 834 F.2d 1037, 1044 (D.C. Cir. 1987), and limit them to those "situations where the policies promoted by public participation in rulemaking are outweighed by the countervailing considerations of effectiveness, efficiency, expedition and reduction in expense." *Id.* (quoting *Guardian Federal Savings & Loan Ass'n v. FSLIC*, 589 F.2d 658, 662 (D.C. Cir. 1978)). Courts have further adopted the position that, while an agency's view of whether its own rule fits within one of the exceptions is "'relevant,' [it is] not necessarily dispositive.'" *United Technologies Corp. v. U.S. EPA*, 821 F.2d 714, 718 (D.C. Cir. 1987). These rules of construction apply to all four of the exceptions listed above. In addition, considerable case law has grown up around each of the individual exceptions.

i. The Exception for Interpretative Rules

"Interpretative" rules, which merely describe or clarify existing rules of conduct, can be distinguished from "legislative rules," which create new standards. As the D.C. Circuit has put it, "'legislative rules' are those which create law ... whereas interpretative rules are statements as to what [an] administrative officer thinks the statute or regulation means." *American Hospital Ass'n*, 834 F.2d at 1045. In a democracy, it makes sense to require more public participation when an agency is acting like a legislature and creating new standards than when it is merely describing or clarifying rules that are already in force. Thus, the APA requires notice-and-comment rulemaking for legislative rules, but not for interpretative ones.

Often, courts apply the interpretative rule exception where Congress itself has prescribed the standard of conduct and the agency is merely clarifying and resolving interpretative problems that the Congressional standard presents. Aman & Mayton, *supra* at 82. In such instances courts take the position that Congress, not the agency, is the one that has fashioned the standard and so the agency is not engaged in lawmaking. While this distinction seems clear, it can pose analytical problems. What if Congress passes a broad standard and the agency then elaborates and spells out its more specific meaning? Is the

---

making procedures under APA §§556 and 557, rather than informal notice-and-comment rulemaking procedures, apply.

agency action legislative in nature, or interpretative? Consider the following two cases in which courts explored the question of whether the U.S. Army Corps of Engineers "migratory bird rule" was an interpretative or a legislative rule for the purposes of the APA.

Before reading these cases, you should know that, subsequent to these decisions, the Supreme Court struck down the migratory bird rule on the grounds that it exceeded the regulatory authority granted by the Clean Water Act. *Solid Waste Agency of Northern Cook County v. U.S. Army Corps of Engineers*, 531 U.S. 159 (2001). However, the Court did not address the question that concerns us here, *i.e.* whether the rule should have been promulgated through full notice-and-comment rulemaking. The two district court decisions that follow disagree on this question. Given that the Supreme Court never resolved it, you are free to make up your own mind as to which result is the correct one. For a more recent environmental law decision concerning the interpretative rule exception, see *Appalachian Power Co. v. EPA*, 208 F.3d 1015 (2000) (holding that EPA's Periodic Monitoring Guidance was a legislative, not an interpretative, rule and that EPA should have promulgated it through notice-and-comment rulemaking procedures).

Tabb Lakes, Ltd. v. United States

715 F. Supp. 726 (E.D. Va., 1988)
aff'd 885 F.2d 866 (4th Cir. 1989) (footnotes omitted)

MacKenzie, Senior District Judge:

This matter is before the Court on the plaintiff's and defendants' cross Motions for Summary Judgment. The issue is whether the Army Corps of Engineers (Corps) has jurisdiction to require a permit in this case.

Originally plaintiff, Tabb Lakes, Ltd. (Tabb Lakes), sought a permit under section 404 of the Clean Water Act (CWA), in October, 1986, requesting permission to fill portions of its property for development purposes. 33 U.S.C. § 1344. While a decision was pending, Tabb Lakes withdrew its permit application in August 1987 on grounds that it had determined that the property in question was not subject to the Corps' jurisdiction. After Tabb Lakes had commenced this declaratory judgment action, the Corps, in July, 1988, completed its Quantitative Wetlands Jurisdictional Determination which it alleges is the basis for the Corps' asserted jurisdiction over Tabb Lakes' property.

Tabb Lakes filed this complaint on September 21, 1987 seeking a declaratory judgment that its property did not fall within the jurisdictional parameters of section 404 of the CWA. In January 1988 the United States filed its Motion to Dismiss or for Partial Summary Judgment and in March and May 1988

Tabb Lakes filed its own Motion to Dismiss and for Summary Judgment (Amended).

In its Motion for Summary Judgment, Tabb Lakes challenges, among other things, the failure of the Corps to comply with proper notice and comment procedures under the Administrative Procedures Act (APA) before it issued a memorandum, in effect, rule making, which was subsequently the basis for making the jurisdictional determination in this case, claiming that Corps' jurisdiction stems from the regulations implementing section 404 of the CWA. 33 C.F.R. §§ 320, et seq.

The specific regulations set out at 33 C.F.R. § 328.3(a)(3) provide the definition of waters subject to Corps regulation:

> "For the purpose of this regulation these terms are defined as follows:
> (a) The term 'waters of the United States' means
> (1) [N/A]
> (2) [N/A]
> (3) All other waters such as intrastate lakes, rivers, streams (including intermittent streams), mudflats, sandflats, wetlands, sloughs, prairie potholes, wet meadows, playa lakes, or natural ponds, the use, degradation or destruction of which could affect interstate or foreign commerce including any such waters:
> (i) Which are or could be used by interstate or foreign travelers for recreational or other purposes; or
> (ii) From which fish or shellfish are or could be taken and sold in interstate or foreign commerce; or
> (iii) Which are used or could be used for industrial purpose[s] by industries in interstate commerce; ..."

On November 8, 1985, Brigadier General Patrick J. Kelly, the Deputy Director of Civil Works for the U.S. Army Corps of Engineers in Washington, D.C., issued a memorandum to all district Corps offices listing the seven (7) standards which would indicate a sufficient interstate commerce connection to warrant exercise of jurisdiction by the Corps over isolated waters and wetlands. Specifically, number 5 is the indicator relied on by the Corps in this case and it reads, "Waters which are used or could be used as habitat by other migratory birds which cross state lines."

Before a rule is promulgated or amended, section 553 of the APA requires agencies to afford notice of such impending action and to provide an opportunity for public comment. However, an exemption applies: "(A) to interpretative rules, general statements of policy, or rules of agency organization, or procedure, or practice; ..." 5 U.S.C. § 553(b)(3)(A).

The threshold issue here is whether Brigadier General Kelly's November 8, 1985 Memorandum falls within this exception, which exception, according to Batterton v. Marshall, 648 F.2d 694, 703 (D.C.Cir.1980), is a "narrow one" and to be "only reluctantly countenanced." The United States urges that these are merely interpretive rule changes, or at most policy statements.

The APA's § 553 notice and comment provisions seek to insure public participation and fairness to affected parties where agencies hold governmental authority, and to provide for an input of all relevant facts and alternatives. American Hospital Association v. Bowen, 640 F.Supp. 453 (D.D.C.1986), rev'd, 834 F.2d 1037, 1044 (D.C.Cir.1987). Although the distinction between a substantive and interpretive rule is a gray area, the Courts generally differentiate cases "in which an agency is merely explicating Congress' desires from those cases in which the agency is adding substantive content of its own." Id. at 1045.

"Substantive rules are ones which grant rights, impose obligations, or produce other significant effects on public interests, or which effect a change in existing law or policy. Id. Interpretive rules, by contrast, are those which merely clarify or explain existing law or regulations, are essentially ... instructional, and do not have the full force and effect of a substantive rule but are in the form of an explanation of particular terms." Id. The task is very fact specific, however the Court in American Hospital Association, 834 F.2d at 1046, noted that a typical example of a substantive rule was a parole board's use of guidelines that established factors for determining parole eligibility and were thus critical to the ultimate parole decision. Id. (citing Pickus v. United States Board of Parole, 507 F.2d 1107, 1112–13 (D.C.Cir.1974)).

Beyond any doubt, the memorandum produced a "significant effect on public interests" in a 38 acre tract at Tabb Lakes, most of which is a wetland, but not water, and which is brought into Corps jurisdiction as "water which is used or could be used as habitat by other migratory birds which cross state lines." Incidentally, not ducks or geese, but woodpeckers, songbirds, etc. In this case it is clear that Brigadier General Kelly's Memorandum affected a change in Corps policy intended to have the full force and effect of a substantive rule, and that the Corps relied on the memorandum in reaching its jurisdiction determination. Deposition of W. H. Poore, Jr., pp. 50–51; Memorandum of Brigadier General Patrick J. Kelly, November 8, 1985. Additionally, on February 11, 1986 General Kelly issued a second memorandum in which he noted that his November 8, 1985 memorandum "clarified for the first time the factors which are indicative of a connection to interstate commerce for purposes of the CWA." Kelly Memorandum, February 11, 1986. He further noted that "... you should notify your districts that, effective immediately, all waterbodies which are or reasonably could be used by migratory birds are waters of the United States and should be regulated as such for all ongoing and future discharges of dredged or fill material." Id. General Kelly implies in that memorandum that he disagreed with the Corps' Galveston District Office determination denying jurisdiction in the Pond 12 case and that the District should have asserted jurisdiction if it followed his 1985 Memorandum. Id.; see National Wildlife Federation v. Laubscher, 662 F.Supp. 548 (S.D.Tex.1987).

Accordingly, we find that General Kelly's November 8, 1985 far-reaching Memorandum did not fall within any exceptions but instead required appropriate notice and comment under the APA....

The Kelly Memorandum does not fall within any of the exceptions to § 553 of the APA. This Court must, therefore, set aside any agency action found to be without observance of procedure required by law. 5 U.S.C. § 706(2)(D); Natural Resources Defense Council, Inc. v. U.S. Environmental Protection Agency, 683 F.2d 752 (3rd Cir.1982); Brown Express, Inc. v. United States, 607 F.2d 695, 703 (5th Cir.1979).

Although this Court has grave doubts that a property now so used, or seen as an expectant habitat for some migratory birds, can be declared to be such a nexus to interstate commerce as to warrant Army Corps of Engineers jurisdiction, we do not here decide that issue. Further, it is unnecessary for the Court to make a decision as to Counts II, III and IV.

Determining that the Army Corps of Engineers does not have jurisdiction in this particular case, we enter judgment for the plaintiff. Each side shall bear its own costs and attorneys fees.

An Order will be entered contemporaneously herewith declaring that the Army Corps of Engineers does not have jurisdiction in this particular case.

Solid Waste Agency of Northern Cook County v. U.S. Army Corps of Engineers

998 F. Supp. 946 (N.D. Ill., 1998) (footnotes omitted)
aff'd 191 F.3d 845 (7th Cir. 1999)
rev'd on other grounds 531 U.S. 159 (2001)

MEMORANDUM OPINION AND ORDER

Lindberg, District Judge:

This action concerns the future of a 533-acre parcel of real estate owned by plaintiff Solid Waste Agency of Northern Cook County. Defendant United

States Army Corps of Engineers asserted regulatory jurisdiction over the property after determining that it contained approximately fifty-five acres of navigable waters as defined by the Clean Water Act. 33 U.S.C. § 1362(7). It then denied plaintiff a permit to develop the property under section 404 of that statute. 33 U.S.C. § 1344(a). Plaintiff sought judicial review of these actions under the Administrative Procedure Act, 5 U.S.C. §§ 701 et seq. ("APA"), and the parties filed cross-motions for summary judgment on the issue of jurisdiction. For the reasons below, plaintiff's motion for summary judgment will be denied and defendant's motion for summary judgment will be granted.

I. Factual and Procedural Background

Plaintiff Solid Waste Agency of Northern Cook County ("SWANCC") is a municipal corporation created by intergovernmental agreement under the laws of Illinois. Plaintiff owns a 533-acre parcel of real estate located in Cook and Kane Counties, which, due to its prior incarnation as a gravel mining pit, contains large surface depressions that now hold rainwater and other precipitation. Plaintiff sought to convert approximately 180 acres of the property into a balefill, a repository for non-hazardous solid waste that cannot be recycled or otherwise removed from the waste stream. The Army Corps of Engineers determined that 17.6 acres of the balefill area contained "navigable waters" as defined by the Clean Water Act, 33 U.S.C. § 1362(7), and it therefore required plaintiff to obtain a permit for the project under section 404(a) of that statute, 33 U.S.C. § 1344(a).

Section 404(a) of the Clean Water Act authorizes the Corps to issue permits for the "discharge of dredged or fill material into the navigable waters at specified disposal sites." 33 U.S.C. § 1344(a). The Clean Water Act defines navigable waters as "the waters of the United States." 33 U.S.C. § 1362(7). By regulation, the Army Corps of Engineers has further defined the phrase "waters of the United States" to include "[a]ll other waters such as intrastate lakes, rivers, streams (including intermittent streams), mudflats, sandflats, wetlands, sloughs, prairie potholes, wet meadows, playa lakes, or natural ponds, the use, degradation or destruction of which could affect interstate or foreign commerce." 33 C.F.R. § 328.3(a)(3). In a preamble to this regulation, the Corps has explained that the term "other waters" includes those which "are or would be used as habitat by other migratory birds which cross state lines." 51 Fed.Reg. 41,217 (Nov. 13, 1986). For lack of a better term, perhaps, this language in the preamble has been described as the "migratory bird rule."

... On July 8, 1987, the Illinois Nature Preserves Commission asked the Corps to consider whether the SWANCC property might be subject to federal jurisdiction under 33 C.F.R. § 328.3(a)(3) on the grounds that four different species of migratory birds had been observed there. The agency agreed, and on November 16, 1987 it asserted jurisdiction over the waters on the SWANCC property for the reason that they were used or could be used as a habitat by migratory birds. It explained that its previous denial of jurisdiction "was based on the fact that the water areas did not meet the definition of a wetland or lakes, and not on the broader definition of 'waters of the United States.'" (R. 34,619.) Plaintiff then submitted two successive applications for a section 404(a) permit to begin the balefill project. When those applications were denied, plaintiff filed the instant lawsuit.

… Plaintiff has argued that the Corps lacks jurisdiction because (1) the migratory bird rule exceeds the legislative authority created by the commerce clause, (2) the agency's assertion of jurisdiction over the waters of the proposed balefill was arbitrary and capricious, (3) the migratory bird rule goes beyond the mandate of the Clean Water Act, and (4) the rule was adopted in violation of the notice and comment requirements of the APA. On May 22, 1997, the court heard oral argument on these issues, and it will now address them in turn.

II. Discussion

A. Commerce Clause

* * *

B. Evidentiary Basis for Jurisdiction

* * *

C. Clean Water Act

* * *

D. Administrative Procedure Act

Plaintiff argues that the migratory bird rule was promulgated without public notice and comment in violation of the APA. That statute requires federal agencies to provide notice and an opportunity for public comment before they promulgate or amend administrative regulations, but it creates an exception for interpretive rules and general statements of policy. 5 U.S.C. §553. An interpretive rule is one in which an agency explains what a statute means or reminds parties of existing duties, while a substantive rule creates altogether new rights or duties. Metropolitan School Dist. of Wayne Township v. Davila, 969 F.2d 485, 489–90 (7th Cir.1992); see also American Hospital Ass'n v. Bowen, 834 F.2d 1037, 1045 (D.C. Cir.1987). Because the parties agree that the migratory bird rule was adopted without notice and comment, the court need only decide whether the rule is substantive or interpretive.

This issue was addressed in Tabb Lakes, Ltd. v. United States, 715 F.Supp. 726, 728–729 (E.D.Va.1988). In that case, a landowner sought a declaratory judgment that his property was not subject to federal jurisdiction because it did not contain "other waters" as defined by 33 C.F.R. §328.3(a)(3). Id. at 727. The Army Corps of Engineers argued that it had jurisdiction over the site pursuant to an internal memorandum which explained that the term "other waters" included those which "are used or could be used as habitat by other migratory birds which cross state lines." Id. at 728. The district court held that the memorandum was a substantive rule-making because it had a "significant effect on public interests" and was "intended to have the full force and effect of a substantive rule." Id. at 728–729. Accordingly, the court held that the memorandum was adopted in violation of the notice and comment requirements of the APA and did not confer federal jurisdiction over the property in question. Id. at 729.

In an unpublished opinion, a divided panel of the Fourth Circuit affirmed this holding without explanation. See Tabb Lakes, Ltd. v. United States, 885 F.2d 866 (4th Cir.1989) (per curiam) (text at 1989 WL 106990). In dissent, Judge Hall suggested that the district court had erred by considering the impact of the rule instead of limiting its analysis to the question of whether the memorandum created new rights or duties. Id. at *2 (Hall, J., dis.). He reasoned that the memorandum did not give rise to new law because the statutory term "waters of the United States" was intended to have "the broadest possible constitutional interpretation" under the commerce clause, and the memorandum simply identified "what contacts with interstate commerce are sufficient to bring a given wetland within the jurisdictional reach" of that statute. Id. at *3.

More recently, the Ninth Circuit discussed this question in Leslie Salt IV, 55 F.3d 1388. When the plaintiff first raised this issue on appeal in Leslie Salt II, 896 F.2d 354, the court declined to address it and thus held by implication that the rule was procedurally sound. 55 F.3d at 1393. When the court revisited the issue in Leslie Salt IV, its review was limited to the question of whether its prior holding was clearly erroneous. Id. at 1394. Relying on Hoffman Homes II, 999 F.2d at 261, where the Seventh Circuit held that the term "other waters" in both 40 C.F.R. §230.3(s)(3) and 33 C.F.R. §328.3(a)(3) could be read to include waters used by migratory birds, the Ninth Circuit reasoned by analogy that the migratory bird rule could be viewed as an interpretation of the Clean Water Act rather than a substantive rule-making. Leslie Salt IV, 55 F.3d at 1394. In a somewhat narrow holding, then, the court concluded that it was "plausible" to construe the migratory bird rule as an interpretation of the Clean Water Act. Id.

It is the opinion of this court that the migratory bird rule is interpretive rather than substantive. The Clean Water Act authorizes the EPA and the Army Corps of Engineers to exercise regulatory jurisdiction over the "waters of United States." 33 U.S.C. § 1362(7). Pursuant to this authority, the Army Corps of Engineers adopted a regulation in 1977 which defined the term "navigable waters" to include isolated intrastate waters whose "degradation or destruction could affect interstate commerce." 33 C.F.R. § 323.2(a)(5) (1977), 42 Fed.Reg. 37,144 (July 19, 1977). In 1986, the Corps renumbered this provision as 33 C.F.R. § 328.3(a)(3) but left the substance of the regulation largely unchanged. The "migratory bird rule" appears in the preamble to the 1986 version of the regulations. 51 Fed.Reg. 41,216 (November 13, 1986).

In the preamble, the Corps explained that the purpose of the reorganization was "to clarify the scope of the Section 404 permit program." 51 Fed.Reg. 41,216. Rather than change the existing definitions, it sought to clarify them by putting them in a separate and distinct part of the regulation. 51 Fed.Reg. 41,216–41,217. The agency then explained that the term "waters of the United States" includes those:

a. Which are or would be used as habitat by birds protected by Migratory Bird Treaties; or
b. Which are or would be used as habitat by other migratory birds which cross state lines; or
c. Which are or would be used as habitat for endangered species; or
d. Used to irrigate crops sold in interstate commerce.

51 Fed.Reg. 41,217. For additional clarification, the agency then listed five examples of waters that are not generally considered to be "waters of the United States." 51 Fed.Reg. 41,217. The agency emphasized that the reorganization was not intended to expand or retract the scope of agency jurisdiction, but rather "to clarify the scope of the 404 program by defining the terms in accordance with the way the program is presently being conducted." 51 Fed.Reg. 41,217.

There are at least two reasons why the preamble was not a substantive rulemaking. First, the agency itself intended for the preamble to be interpretive. See Davila, 969 F.2d at 489 (characterization of a rule by an agency is relevant to whether it is substantive or interpretive). The agency expressly stated that it intended to clarify the scope of the existing section 404 permit program rather than to change existing definitions or to expand its jurisdiction. This is corroborated by the structure of the preamble, which sets forth the migratory bird rule in juxtaposition to a list of waters that are not generally considered to be subject to federal regulation.

More importantly, however, the migratory bird rule does not create new legal rights or duties, for it does not expand the jurisdictional reach of the Clean Water Act or the regulations promulgated thereunder. By authorizing the Army Corps of Engineers to regulate the "waters of the United States," the Clean Water Act extended the jurisdiction of these agencies to the outer limits of the commerce clause. Rueth, 13 F.3d at 231. Pursuant to this statutory authority, the Army Corps of Engineers defined the term "navigable waters" to include all intrastate waters whose degradation or destruction could affect interstate commerce. 33 C.F.R. § 328.3(a)(3). In effect, this "catch-all" provision simply reiterates that the jurisdiction of the agency is coextensive with that of the commerce clause. Because the commerce clause permits the Corps to regulate intrastate migratory bird habitats, the bird rule cannot be said to increase the jurisdiction of that agency. Rather than creating new rights or duties, then, the preamble simply clarifies that the regulation of intrastate migratory bird habitats falls within the scope of the agency's commerce clause jurisdiction. Accordingly, the court finds that the migratory bird rule was not subject to the notice and comment requirements of the APA.

On this point, then, the court expressly declines to follow the reasoning of the district court in Tabb Lakes, 715 F. Supp. 726. The fact that the bird rule carries the "force and effect of a substantive rule" or has a "significant effect on public interests" does not, as the court in that case reasoned, imply that the rule creates new substantive rights or duties. Id. at 728–729. For the reasons described above, the court believes that the better position on this issue is represented by Judge Hall's dissenting opinion in Tabb Lakes v. U.S., 885 F.2d 866 (4th Cir.1989) (per curiam) 1989 WL 106990, at *2 (Hall, J., dis.), and the Ninth Circuit's opinion in Leslie Salt IV, 55 F.3d 1388.

III. Conclusion

For the reasons stated above, the court finds that … the migratory bird rule set forth at 51 Fed.Reg. 41,217 was exempt from the notice and comment requirements of the APA, 5 U.S.C. § 553.

Problem 5.10: Legislative/Interpretative Rule

Why does the Tabb Lakes *court conclude that the "migratory bird" rule is a "legislative" rule? Why does the* Solid Waste Agency of Northern Cook

County *court hold that it is an "interpretative" rule? Which decision do you find more convincing? Why?*

---

ii. The Exception for "General Statements of Policy"

"General statements of policy" are also defined in contrast to "legislative" rules. Here, the critical distinction is that general statements of policy merely "announce[] the agency's tentative intentions" and do not constrain the agency's discretion in the future, whereas legislative rules will be used to decide future cases and hence create a binding legal norm. *See American Hospital Ass'n*, 834 F.2d at 1037; *Pacific Gas and Elec. Co. v. Federal Power Comm'n*, 506 F.2d 33, 38 (D.C. Cir. 1974); *see generally* Aman & Mayton, Administrative Law, *supra* at 80. Another distinction is that general statements of policy, because they do not create a binding legal norm, do not have a "substantial impact on existing rights and obligations" of members of the public, whereas legislative rules do. *Iowa Power & Light Co. v. Burlington Northern, Inc.*, 647 F.2d 796, 811 (8th Cir. 1981).

Agencies use general policy statements to provide the public with advance notice of their views and so to provide members of the regulated community with an opportunity to engage in long-range planning. *See generally* Aman & Mayton, Administrative Law, *supra* at 80. These statements are thus intended to be merely "advisory" to the public. As such, the APA does not subject them to notice-and-comment rulemaking requirements.

As with interpretative rules, the distinction between general policy statements and legislative rules is not as clear as it first appears to be. One recurring issue arises when an agency expressly states that it does not consider itself bound by a policy pronouncement, but other circumstances, including other language in the document, make it clear that the agency will, in fact, follow the policy in most cases. Should courts find such a statement to be a general statement of policy or a legislative rule? The following two cases address this situation.

General Electric Power Company v. Environmental Protection Agency
290 F.3d 377 (D.C. Cir., 2001) (footnotes omitted)

Ginsburg, Chief Judge:

General Electric Co. petitions for review of the "PCB Risk Assessment Review Guidance Document" issued by the Environmental Protection Agency. The parties dispute (1) whether this case is ripe for review; (2) whether the

Document is a "rule" within the meaning of § 19(a) of the Toxic Substances Control Act (TSCA), and hence whether the court has jurisdiction to review its promulgation; and (3) whether the Agency should have followed the procedures required for rulemaking in the TSCA and in the Administrative Procedure Act when it promulgated the Document. We conclude that the case is ripe for review, and that the Guidance Document is a legislative rule such that the court does have jurisdiction to entertain GE's petition and the Document should not have been issued without prior notice and an opportunity for public comment.

I. Background

The TSCA prohibits the manufacture, processing, distribution, and use (other than in a "totally enclosed manner") of polychlorinated biphenyls (PCBs) unless the EPA determines that the activity will not result in an "unreasonable risk of injury to health or the environment." *15 U.S.C. § 2605*(e)(2) & (3). The Guidance Document governs the application of two regulations promulgated by the EPA under the TSCA to provide respectively for the cleanup and disposal of PCB remediation waste and for the disposal of PCB bulk product waste. *See 40 C.F.R. §§ 761.61* ("cleanup and disposal options for PCB remediation waste"), 761.62 (how "PCB bulk product waste shall be disposed").

Under subsection (c) of each regulation a party may apply for permission to use a method other than one of the generic methods set out in the regulations for sampling, cleaning up, or disposing of PCB remediation waste, or for sampling or disposing of PCB bulk product waste. The EPA will approve applications under these subsections if the alternative method proposed does "not pose an unreasonable risk of injury to health or the environment." *Id.* The regulations do not, however, tell applicants how to conduct the necessary risk assessment.

That is where the Guidance Document comes in. It "provides an overview of risk assessment techniques, and guidance for reviewing risk assessment documents submitted under the final PCB disposal rule." Guidance Document at 10. Of particular relevance to this case, in the Guidance Document the EPA also explains that an applicant seeking to use an alternative method under § 761.61(c) may take either of two approaches to risk assessment. *Id.* at 21, 42. First, the applicant may calculate cancer and non-cancer risks separately. *Id.*.... The second approach endorsed in the Guidance Document is to use a "total toxicity factor" of 4.0 (mg/kg/day)-1 to account for cancer and non-cancer risks together. *Id.* In its brief, the EPA explains that this approach "provides the applicant an opportunity to reduce the time and expense associated with the risk assessment" because the Agency is willing "to accept this 'default' toxicity value of 4.0 (mg/kg/day)-1[ ] without requiring further justification."

II. Analysis

GE's primary argument is that the Guidance Document is a legislative rule and therefore should have been promulgated only after public notice and an opportunity for comment....

[T]he question before us can be framed as whether the Guidance Document is a legislative rule or a statement of policy.

As GE argues, in cases where we have attempted to draw the line between legislative rules and statements of policy, we have considered whether the agency action (1) "imposes any rights and obligations" or (2) "genuinely leaves the agency and its decisionmakers free to exercise discretion." *Community Nutrition Inst., 818 F.2d at 946; Chamber of Commerce v. Dep't of Labor, 335 U.S. App. D.C. 370, 174 F.3d 206, 212 (1999)....*

The EPA urges the court to consider three factors: "(1) the Agency's own characterization of its action; (2) whether the action was published in the Federal Register or the Code of Federal Regulations; and (3) whether the action has binding effects on private parties or on the agency." *Molycorp, Inc., 197 F.3d at 545; see also Florida Power & Light Co. v. EPA, 330 U.S. App. D.C. 344, 145 F.3d 1414, 1418 (D.C. Cir. 1998); American Portland Cement Alliance v. EPA, 322 U.S. App. D.C. 99, 101 F.3d 772, 776 (D.C. Cir. 1996).* As the EPA concedes, however, the third factor is the most important: "The ultimate focus of the inquiry is whether the agency action partakes of the fundamental characteristic of a regulation, i.e., that it has the force of law." *Molycorp, Inc., 197 F.3d at 545.*

The two tests overlap at step three of the *Molycorp* formulation—in which the court determines whether the agency action binds private parties or the agency itself with the "force of law." This common standard has been well-stated as follows:

> If a document expresses a change in substantive law or policy (that is not an interpretation) which the agency intends to make binding, or administers with binding effect, the agency may not rely upon the statutory exemption for policy statements, but must observe the APA's legislative rulemaking procedures.

Robert A. Anthony, *Interpretive Rules, Policy Statements, Guidances, Manuals, and the Like—Should Federal Agencies Use Them to Bind the Public?, 41 DUKE L.J. 1311, 1355 (1992).*

Our cases likewise make clear that an agency pronouncement will be considered binding as a practical matter if it either appears on its face to be binding, *Appalachian Power, 208 F.3d at 1023* ("The entire Guidance, from beginning to end ... reads like a ukase. It commands, it requires, it orders, it dictates."), or is applied by the agency in a way that indicates it is binding, *McLouth, 838 F.2d at 1321.* As Professor Robert A. Anthony cogently comments, the mandatory language of a document alone can be sufficient to render it binding:

> A document will have practical binding effect before it is actually applied if the affected private parties are reasonably led to believe that failure to conform will bring adverse consequences, such as ... denial of an application. If the document is couched in mandatory language, or in terms indicating that it will be regularly applied, a binding intent is strongly evidenced. In some circumstances, if the language of the document is such that private parties can rely on it as a norm or safe harbor by which to shape their actions, it can be binding as a practical matter.

Interpretive Rules, 41 DUKE L.J. at 1328–29.

GE argues that the Guidance Document is binding both because it facially requires an applicant for a risk-based variance to calculate toxicity by one of two methods—either use a total toxicity factor of 4.0 (mg/kg/day)-1 or use a cancer potency factor and account for the specified non-cancer health risks—and because, considering the cost, delay, and uncertainty entailed in the latter course, "for all practical purposes, the Guidance is a rule that directs PCB toxicity to be measured by a 4.0 (mg/kg/day)-1 CPF."

The EPA counters that the Guidance Document lacks the force of law because it does not purport to be binding and because it has not been applied as though it were binding.... Second, the EPA says that it has not in practice "applied the guidance document inflexibly, as if it were a rule or regulation." ...

We think it clear that the Guidance Document does purport to bind applicants for approval of a risk-based cleanup plan under *40 C.F.R. § 761.61(c).* Consider the principal directives: "When developing a risk-based cleanup application ... both the cancer and non-cancer endpoints must be addressed...." Guidance Document at 21. If an applicant chooses not to use the 4.0 total toxicity factor, then it "must, at a minimum account for the risk from non-cancer endpoints for neurotoxicity, reproductive and developmental toxicity, immune system suppression, liver damage, skin irritation, and endocrine disruption for each of the commercial mixtures found at the cleanup site." *Id.* Although the Guidance Document does, as noted, anticipate and acknowledge that "some risk assessments may have components that require the use of non-standard ... unique ... or unconventional methods for estimating risk," *id.* at 44, that does not undermine the binding force of the Guidance Document in standard cases. *See McLouth, 838 F.2d at 1321* ("such a provision for exceptions ... does not push it much in the direction of a policy statement"). Furthermore, even though the Guidance Document gives applicants the option of calculating risk in either of two ways (assuming both are practical) it still requires them to conform to one or the other, that is, not to submit an application based upon a third way. And if an applicant does choose to calculate cancer and non-cancer risks separately, then it must consider the non-cancer risks specified in the Guidance Document. To the applicant reading the Guidance Document the message is clear: in reviewing applications the Agency will not be open to considering approaches other than those prescribed in the Document....

In sum, the commands of the Guidance Document indicate that it has the force of law. On its face the Guidance Document imposes binding obligations upon applicants to submit applications that conform to the Document and upon the Agency not to question an applicant's use of the 4.0 (mg/kg/day)-1 total toxicity factor. This is sufficient to render it a legislative rule. Furthermore, the Agency's application of the Document does nothing to demonstrate that the Document has any lesser effect in practice. Consequently, we conclude that the Guidance Document is a legislative rule. The Guidance Document is therefore undisputedly a "rule" for purposes of §19(a)(1)(A) of the TSCA, and the manner of its promulgation is subject to review.

C. The Merits

The EPA concedes that it did not comply with the procedural requirements of the TSCA and of the APA. More specifically, as GE points out, it failed to publish a notice of proposed rulemaking, give interested parties an opportunity to comment, and hold an informal hearing. *See 15 U.S.C. §2605(e)(4); 15 U.S.C. §2605(c)(2); 5 U.S.C. §553.* Therefore, having held that the case is ripe for review and that the Guidance Document is a "rule" for purposes of the TSCA, it is clear that GE must prevail on the merits....

III. Conclusion

GE's petition for review is granted because the EPA promulgated a legislative rule without following the procedures required by the TSCA and the APA. The Guidance Document is accordingly
Vacated.

Cement Kiln Recycling Coalition v. Environmental Protection Agency

493 F.3d 207 (D.C. Circuit 2007) (footnotes omitted)

GARLAND, *Circuit Judge*: The Cement Kiln Recycling Coalition petitions for review of an Environmental Protection Agency regulation that governs the permitting process for facilities that burn hazardous waste as fuel. The Coalition also petitions for review of a guidance document, the Human Health Risk Assessment Protocol, that pertains to the same permitting process. For the reasons stated below, we deny the petition for review insofar as it challenges the regulation, and we dismiss the challenge to the guidance document as outside our jurisdiction.

I

Hazardous waste combustors (HWCs) are facilities—such as incinerators, boilers, and industrial furnaces (including cement kilns)—that burn hazardous waste as fuel for their operations. The Cement Kiln Recycling Coalition, the petitioner in this case, is a trade association that includes manufacturers of Portland cement that utilize hazardous waste as an alternative fuel in some of their kilns. The Environmental Protection Agency (EPA) has authority to regulate this activity under both the Resource Conservation and Recovery Act (RCRA), *see 42 U.S.C. §6924*, and the Clean Air Act (CAA), *see id. §7412*.

Subtitle C of RCRA, *see 42 U.S.C. §6921 et seq.*, "establishes a 'cradle to grave' federal regulatory system for the treatment, storage, and disposal of hazardous wastes." *American Portland Cement Alliance v. EPA, 322 U.S. App. D.C. 99, 101 F.3d 772, 774 (D.C. Cir. 1996)* (quoting *Chemical Waste Mgmt., Inc. v. Hunt, 504 U.S. 334, 337 n. 1, 112 S. Ct. 2009, 119 L. Ed. 2d 121 (1992)*). This system operates through a combination of national standards established by EPA regulations, and a permit program in which permitting authorities—either EPA or states that have hazardous waste programs authorized by the agency—apply those national standards to particular facilities. *See 42 U.S.C. §§6924–26*.

The national standards applicable to the petitioner are authorized by RCRA §3004, *42 U.S.C. §6924*, which governs "owners and operators of facilities for the treatment, storage, or disposal of hazardous waste," known as TSDs. *42 U.S.C. §6924(a)*. For RCRA purposes, the burning of hazardous waste is considered "treatment," and thus falls within the statute. *Id. §6903(34)*; *see Horsehead Res. Dev. Co. v. Browner, 305 U.S. App. D.C. 35, 16 F.3d 1246, 1252 & n.2 (D.C. Cir. 1994)*. Section 3004(a), which applies generally to all TSDs, directs

EPA to "promulgate regulations establishing such performance standards, applicable to [TSDs], as may be necessary to protect human health and the environment." *42 U.S.C. §6924(a)*. *Section 3004(q)* specifically applies to facilities that burn hazardous waste as fuel, including cement kilns and other types of HWCs. *Id. §6924(q)(1)(B)*. Like *section 3004(a)*, this section directs EPA to promulgate such standards "as may be necessary to protect human health and the environment." *Id. §6924(q)(1)*.

In addition to the national standards authorized by *section 3004*, section 3005 of RCRA, *42 U.S.C. §6925*, establishes a case-by-case permitting process. *Section 3005(a)* directs EPA to "promulgate regulations requiring each person owning or operating an existing [TSD] or planning to construct a new [TSD] to have a permit issued pursuant to this section." *Id. §6925(a)*. *Section 3005(b)* mandates that "[e]ach application for a permit under this section shall contain such information as may be required under regulations promulgated by [EPA]." *Id. §6925(b)*. And *section 3005(c)(3)*—which EPA refers to as the "omnibus" provision—provides that "[e]ach permit issued under this section shall contain such terms and conditions as the [permitting authority] determines necessary to protect human health and the environment." *Id. §6925(c)(3)*.

Although RCRA gives EPA comprehensive authority to regulate hazardous waste combustors, the fact that HWCs emit air pollutants also gives the agency jurisdiction under the Clean Air Act, *42 U.S.C. §7401 et seq.* Section 112 of the CAA, as amended in 1990, directs EPA to issue national emission standards for hazardous air pollutants. *See id. §7412*. The statute requires EPA to "promulgate technology-based emission standards for categories of sources that emit [such pollutants]. These emission standards are to be based not on an assessment of the risks posed by [hazardous air pollutants], but instead on the maximum achievable control technology (MACT) for sources in each category." *Sierra Club v. EPA, 359 U.S. App. D.C. 251, 353 F.3d 976, 980 (D.C. Cir. 2004)* (citations omitted); *see 42 U.S.C. §7412(d)*. Thus, EPA's jurisdiction under *RCRA §3004* and *§3005* overlaps with its jurisdiction under *CAA §112* when the source of hazardous air pollutants is also a TSD.

Anticipating that EPA's jurisdiction under RCRA would overlap with its jurisdiction under other statutes, Congress enacted RCRA § 1006(b), *42 U.S.C. §6905(b)*. This provision requires EPA to "integrate all provisions of [RCRA] for purposes of administration and enforcement and shall avoid duplication, to the maximum extent practicable, with the appropriate provisions of[, inter alia,] the Clean Air Act." *Id. §6905(b)(1)*.

In 1991, EPA promulgated RCRA regulations applicable to boilers and industrial furnaces (including cement kilns) that treat hazardous waste by burning it as fuel. *See Burning of Hazardous Waste in Boilers and Industrial Fur-*

naces, 56 Fed. Reg. 7,134 (Feb. 21, 1991). The 1991 RCRA rule was "principally designed to establish air emissions requirements" pursuant to *RCRA §3004(q)*. *Horsehead, 16 F.3d at 1251*.

Beginning in 1994, EPA began requiring every HWC that applied for a RCRA permit to undergo a site-specific risk assessment (SSRA). *See* Strategy for Hazardous Waste Minimization and Combustion (1994), *available at* http://www.epa.gov/epaoswer/hazwaste/combust/general/strat-2.txt. EPA intended the SSRA program to give permitting authorities the ability to impose permit conditions beyond national standards in order "to limit emissions on a case-by-case basis as necessary to ensure protection of human health and the environment." *Id.* A human-health SSRA could include a "direct exposure" assessment designed to predict the health impact of breathing air in the vicinity of a facility; it could also include an "indirect" exposure assessment designed to focus on multi-pathway non-inhalation exposures, such as the consumption of crops grown in soil upon which substances emitted into the air are deposited. EPA did not enshrine the SSRA program in specific regulations, maintaining that authority was provided by RCRA's "omnibus" provision, *RCRA §3005(c)(3)*. EPA did, however, issue guidance documents to assist permitting authorities in conducting SSRAs.

In 1999, pursuant to the Clean Air Act, EPA promulgated technology-based MACT standards to control hazardous pollutants emitted by facilities that burn hazardous waste, including incinerators and cement kilns. *See Final Standards for Hazardous Air Pollutants for Hazardous Waste Combustors, 64 Fed. Reg. 52,828 (Sept. 30, 1999)*. This court vacated those standards in 2001, holding that EPA had not adequately demonstrated that they satisfied the requirements of *CAA §112(d)*. *See Cement Kiln Recycling Coal. v. EPA, 347 U.S. App. D.C. 127, 255 F.3d 855, 857 (D.C. Cir. 2001)*.

In 2005, following notice and comment, EPA promulgated revised MACT standards for HWCs. *See National Emission Standards for Hazardous Air Pollutants: Final Standards for Hazardous Air Pollutants for Hazardous Waste Combustors, 70 Fed. Reg. 59,402 (Oct. 12, 2005)* ("Final Rule"). At the same time, EPA announced that the 1991 RCRA standards would "no longer apply once a facility demonstrates compliance with" the relevant 2005 MACT standards. *Id. at 59,523*. EPA issued this "deferral" announcement pursuant to RCRA's integration provision, *42 U.S.C. §6905(b)*, and the agency's finding that the new Clean Air Act MACT standards were generally "protective of human health and the environment," as required by RCRA. *See Final Rule, 70 Fed. Reg. at 59,517, 59,536*. Concluding, however, that "there may be instances where [the agency] cannot assure that emissions from each source will be protective of human health and the environment," *id. at 59,504*, EPA issued regulations that authorize permitting authorities to conduct SSRAs on a case-by-case basis, *see 40 C.F.R. §§270.10(l), 270.32(b)(3).*

Those regulations, and particularly *40 C.F.R. §270.10(l)*, which is set out in full in the appendix to this opinion, are the focus of the petition that is now before us. *Section 270.10(l)* expressly authorizes a permitting authority to conduct an SSRA—that is, to "require the additional information or assessment(s) necessary to determine whether additional controls are necessary to ensure protection of human health and the environment." *Id. §270.10(l).* "This includes information necessary to evaluate the potential risk to human health and/or the environment resulting from both direct and indirect exposure pathways." *Id.* A permitting authority may require an SSRA only if it "concludes, based on one or more of the factors listed in paragraph *(l)(1)* of [the regulation,] that compliance with the [MACT standards] alone may not be protective of human health or the environment." *Id.* Finally, a companion regulation provides that, if the permitting authority "determines that conditions are necessary in addition to those required [by the MACT standards] to ensure protection of human health and the environment, [it] shall include those terms and conditions in a RCRA permit for a hazardous waste combustion unit." *Id. §270.32(b)(3).*

Although the 2005 Final Rule expressly authorized the SSRA program by regulation, EPA declined to promulgate regulations defining how SSRAs must be conducted. EPA explained that "risk assessment—especially multi-pathway, indirect exposure assessment—is a highly technical and evolving field," and that "[a]ny regulatory approach [it] might codify in this area is likely to become outdated, or at least artificially constraining, shortly after promulgation in ways that [it] cannot anticipate now." *Final Rule, 70 Fed. Reg. at 59,512.* Instead, EPA issued a revised guidance document, the Human Health Risk Assessment Protocol for Hazardous Waste Combustion Facilities (HHRAP), containing technical recommendations "for conducting multi-pathway, site-specific human health risk assessments on" HWCs. HHRAP at 1-1 (Joint Appendix (J.A.) 453); *see Final Rule, 70 Fed. Reg. at 59,512–13.*

The Coalition now petitions for review pursuant to RCRA §7006(a)(1), *42 U.S.C. §6976(a)(1)*, which gives this court exclusive jurisdiction over "petition[s] for review of action of the [EPA] in promulgating any regulation, or requirement under [RCRA]." *Id. §6976(a)(1).* The Coalition raises several substantive and procedural challenges to the validity of *40 C.F.R. §270.10(l).* It also challenges the HHRAP guidance document as a de facto legislative rule that was not promulgated through notice-and-comment rulemaking, in violation of the Administrative Procedure Act (APA), *5 U.S.C. §553.* EPA responds that the Coalition's petition is not ripe for review and, in the alternative, defends its actions on a number of other grounds. We consider the ripeness question in Part II, the Coalition's challenge to the regulation in Part III, and its challenge to the guidance document in Part IV.

II

...

EPA contends that neither the Coalition's challenge to § 270.10(l), nor its challenge to the HHRAP guidance document, is ripe for review. We disagree on both counts.

A

[Court determines that the challenge to the regulation is ripe for review] ...

B

[Court determines that the challenge to the guidance document is ripe for review] ...

III

...

IV

Finally, we consider the Coalition's attack on the HHRAP guidance document. The Coalition contends that the HHRAP is invalid because it was not promulgated pursuant to the notice-and-comment procedures of the APA. *See* 5 U.S.C. §553(b), (c). While the "APA exempts from notice and comment interpretive rules or general statements of policy," *Syncor Int'l Corp. v. Shalala,* 326 U.S. App. D.C. 422, 127 F.3d 90, 93 (D.C. Cir. 1997) (citing 5 U.S.C. §553(b)), the Coalition maintains that the guidance document is not a policy statement but a legislative rule that is subject to those procedures.

EPA correctly points out that the merits of this APA challenge are inextricably linked to our jurisdiction to hear it. *RCRA §7006(a)(1)* invests this court with jurisdiction over petitions for review of EPA "action ... in promulgating any regulation, or requirement under [RCRA,] or denying any petition for the promulgation, amendment or repeal of any regulation under [RCRA]." 42 U.S.C. §6976(a)(1). We have held that this provision gives us "jurisdiction over 'only final regulations, requirements, and denials of petitions to promulgate, amend or repeal a regulation.'" *GMC, 363 F.3d at 448* (quoting *Molycorp, 197 F.3d at 545*); *see, e.g., American Portland Cement Alliance, 101 F.3d at 774–76.* Under our precedents, the question of whether an agency document is a final "regulation ... or requirement" under RCRA is substantially similar to the question of whether it is a legislative rule under the APA. Thus, because we must decide whether we have jurisdiction before we may reach the merits, *see Steel Co. v. Citizens for a Better Env't, 523 U.S. 83, 94, 118 S. Ct. 1003, 140 L. Ed. 2d 210 (1998)*, and because there is no dispute that the HHRAP guidance document was not issued pursuant to APA rulemaking procedures, there are only two options: "Either the petition must be dismissed for lack of jurisdiction" because the guidance *is not* a final regulation under *42 U.S.C. §6976(a)(1)*, "or the ... [g]uidance should be vacated" on the merits because it *is* a final regulation but was promulgated in violation of the APA. *General Elec., 290 F.3d at 385* (internal quotation marks omitted).

"Three criteria determine whether a regulatory action constitutes the promulgation of a regulation" for purposes of *RCRA §7006(a)(1)*: " '(1) the Agency's own characterization of the action; (2) whether the action was published in the Federal Register or Code of Federal Regulations; and (3) whether the action has binding effects on private parties or on the agency.' " *GMC, 363 F.3d at 448* (quoting *Molycorp, 197 F.3d at 545*). The first two criteria militate against our jurisdiction here: the HHRAP states that it is not "a regulation itself," HHRAP at ii (J.A. 424), and the document was not published in either the Federal Register or the Code of Federal Regulations. Nonetheless, we have held that these criteria merely " 'serve to illuminate the third, for the ultimate focus of the inquiry is whether the agency action partakes of the fundamental characteristic of a regulation, i.e., that it has the force of law.' " *GMC, 363 F.3d at 448* (quoting *Molycorp, 197 F.3d at 545*).

Under this framework, we have jurisdiction to review the HHRAP only if it "binds private parties or the agency itself with the 'force of law.' " *General Elec., 290 F.3d at 382*. "An agency pronouncement [is] binding as a practical matter if it either appears on its face to be binding, or is applied by the agency in a way that indicates it is binding." *Id. at 383* (citation omitted). As noted in Part II.B, the Coalition has expressly limited its challenge to the face of the document, and makes no argument that the agency has applied it in a way that indicates it is binding. ...

So limited, our disposition of the challenge is straightforward. We see nothing on the face of the HHRAP to suggest that it is binding. To the contrary, the document declares that "this guidance does not impose legally binding requirements on EPA, states, or the regulated community, and may not apply to a particular situation based on the specific circumstances of the combustion facility." HHRAP at ii (J.A. 424). Its pages are replete with words of suggestion: its provisions are described as "recommendations," *id.*, that permitting authorities are "encourage[d]" to "consider," *id.* at 1–8 (J.A. 460). The document states that "EPA and state regulators ... retain their discretion to use approaches on a case-by-case basis that differ from those recommended in this guidance where appropriate." *Id.* at ii (J.A. 424). It further states that "[w]hether the recommendations in this [document] are appropriate in a given situation will depend on facility-specific circumstances." *Id.* Moreover, these statements are fully in accord with EPA's explanation of why "this is an area that is uniquely fitted for a guidance approach, rather than regulation": "[R]isk assessors must have the flexibility to make adjustments for the specific conditions present at the source, and ... should be free to use the most recent [assessment tools] available rather than be limited to those that may be out-of-date because a regulation has not been revised." *Proposed Rule, 69 Fed. Reg. at 21,330.*

The Coalition rests its challenge to the HHRAP almost exclusively on our decision in *Appalachian Power Co. v. EPA*, in which we found that another EPA guidance document was in fact a binding legislative rule. *See 341 U.S. App. D.C. 46, 208 F.3d 1015, 1020–23 (D.C. Cir. 2000).* But the factors that led us to that conclusion in *Appalachian Power* are not present here. Among other things, the agency does not treat the HHRAP as binding, has not "le[d] private parties or ... permitting authorities to believe that it will declare permits invalid unless they comply with [its] terms," *id. at 1021*, does not say that the HHRAP represents the agency's "settled position," *id. at 1022*, and has not issued a document that "reads like a ukase," *id. at 1023*. Unlike the guidance at issue in *Appalachian Power*, the HHRAP does not "command[,]" does not "require[,]" does not "order[,]" and does not "dictate[.]" *Id. at 1023*; *cf. General Elec., 290 F.3d at 380, 384–85* (finding that an EPA risk assessment document was a legislative rule, "because on its face it purports to bind both applicants and the Agency with the force of law"). Moreover, the Coalition has forsaken the contention — also important in *Appalachian Power* — that permitting authorities, "with EPA's Guidance in hand, are insisting on" compliance with the guidance during the site-by-site permitting process. *208 F.3d at 1023....*

In short, having limited itself to a challenge based solely on whether the HHRAP guidance document is binding on its face, the Coalition has failed to point to any evidence suggesting that the document is anything other than what EPA asserts it is: a non-binding statement of EPA policy. Accordingly, we conclude that the HHRAP is not a final "regulation ... or requirement" under *RCRA §7006(a)(1)*, and therefore that we are without jurisdiction to review it.

V

For the foregoing reasons, we deny the Coalition's petition for review with respect to its challenge to *40 C.F.R. §270.10(l)*. With respect to its challenge to the HHRAP guidance document, we dismiss the petition for lack of jurisdiction. *So ordered.*

Problem 5.11: General Statements of Policy Exception

The General Electric *and* Cement Kiln Recycling Coalition *courts each considered a different EPA guidance document concerning risk assessment. The* General Electric *court held that the document before it was a legislative rule. The* Cement Kiln *court held that the document before it was a non-binding statement of general policy. What factors did each court consider in determining whether the policy pronouncement before it was a general statement of policy or a substantive rule? Are these two cases at odds with each other, or can they be reconciled?*

---

iii. The Exception for Rules of "Agency Organization, Procedure or Practice"

Rules of "agency organization, procedure or practice" are those dealing with the organization of internal agency operations or with the manner in which agencies conduct their proceedings. These rules "do not themselves alter the rights or interests of parties, although [they] may alter the manner in which parties present themselves or their viewpoints to the agency [e.g. by establishing the ground rules for agency proceedings]." American Hospital Ass'n, 834 F.2d at 1047; *see generally* Aman & Mayton, Administrative Law, *supra* at 78. They are contrasted with "substantive" rules which do alter the rights or interests of parties. The APA exempts "procedural" rules from notice-and-comment requirements on the grounds that, since they do not alter rights or interests, they do not "merit the administrative burdens of public input proceedings." *U.S. Dep't of Labor v. Kast Metals Corp.*, 744 F.2d 1145, 1153 (5th Cir. 1984).

The challenge in applying this exception arises from the fact that purely procedural requirements (e.g. the time allowed to file an appeal) can dramatically affect a regulated party's interests. The trick is to distinguish between procedural changes that may indirectly affect a parties rights and interests, and agency actions that change the underlying substantive rights or interests themselves. *See* KEITH WERHAN, PRINCIPLES OF ADMINISTRATIVE LAW at 260–62 (2008) (explaining this distinction). Consider the following cases.

Waste Management, Inc. v.
U.S. Environmental Protection Agency

669 F. Supp. 536 (D.D.C. 1987) (footnotes omitted)

Richey, District Judge:

INTRODUCTION

Under the terms of the Marine Protection, Research, and Sanctuaries Act, any American citizen or corporation that wishes to dump hazardous material into ocean waters must first obtain a permit from the Environmental Protection Agency. *See* Marine Protection, Research, and Sanctuaries Act ("MPRSA"), *33 U.S.C. § 1401 et seq.; see also* Convention on the Prevention of Marine Polluting by Dumping of Wastes and Other Matter, August 30, 1975, *26 U.S.T. 2403,* T.I.A.S. No. 8165. In 1977, the EPA promulgated regulations for implementing this permitting authority, *see* 40 C.F.R. §§ 220–233 (1986), and it has consistently interpreted these regulations to cover ocean incineration as well as ocean dumping. *Plaintiff's Statement of Material Facts To Which There Should Be No Dispute* ("Plaintiff's Facts"), paras. 3–4. There is no dispute that plaintiff wishes, and is equipped, to obtain ocean incineration permits and conduct ocean burns in future. *Id.* at paras. 5, 10.

The EPA, however, has long recognized the need to promulgate regulations that do not treat ocean incineration as another form of ocean dumping but address the peculiar problems and ramifications of ocean burning in a more specific fashion. *See, e.g.,* 40 C.F.R. § 220.3(f) (ocean dumping regulations apply to ocean incineration "until specific criteria to regulate this type of disposal are promulgated"). In December, 1983, the Assistant Administrator for Water told Congress that the agency would attempt to promulgate ocean incineration regulations within one year.

On February 28, 1985, the EPA proposed such regulations, *50 Fed. Reg. 8222,* and accepted public comment upon the proposals through June 28, 1985....

Although defendant has long contemplated these new regulations, until recently it did not have a policy of maintaining the *status quo* with respect to ocean burning of hazardous waste until the new rules are in place. Accordingly, in 1981, plaintiff submitted applications for two ocean incineration permits. *Defendant's Statement of Material Facts As To Which There Should Be No Dispute* ("Defendant's Facts"), para. 1. Although lower-level EPA officials viewed these applications favorably, the applications ultimately were rejected after lengthy public hearings and internal EPA consideration. *Id.* at paras. 2–9. Plaintiff did not appeal that rejection. *Id.* at para. 18.

One consequence of plaintiff's applications, however, was that EPA reexamined its policy of issuing ocean incineration permits while writing the new ocean incineration regulations. On May 22, 1984, EPA announced that it would defer issuance of operating permits for ocean incineration until specific ocean incineration regulations were promulgated. *Plaintiff's Motion for Summary Judgment, Affidavit of William Y. Brown,* Director of Government Affairs, Waste Management, Inc. ("Brown Affidavit"), Exhibit B (Assistant Administrator's Determination May 22, 1984). On February 25, 1985, EPA published a "Research Strategy" for ocean incineration that contemplated issuance of research permits. *50 Fed. Reg. 51, 361.* On May 24, 1985, plaintiff applied for a research permit. *Id.* at para. 5. That permit was finally denied on May 28, 1986, *51 Fed. Reg. 20,344* (June 4, 1986), and at that time EPA announced that it would defer consideration of research permits—the only ocean incineration permits then available—until regulations specifically governing ocean incineration were promulgated. *Id.* at 20, 346. Shortly thereafter, plaintiff filed this suit....

EPA'S DEFERRAL OF OCEAN INCINERATION PERMITS WAS A
RULE OF AGENCY PROCEDURE AND THEREFORE EXEMPT
FROM THE NOTICE AND COMMENT REQUIREMENTS OF THE
ADMINISTRATIVE PROCEDURE ACT.

Plaintiff's motion argues that, by deferring all applications for ocean incineration permits, defendant has violated its own rules and the Administrative Procedure Act, *5 U.S.C. §551* et seq. When stripped to their essentials, these contentions amount to a single claim that the agency has effectively and illegally revoked or rewritten the regulations governing ocean incineration by refusing to process permit applications until the forthcoming ocean incineration regulations are in place. Plaintiff's characterization of defendant's actions is incorrect.

There can be no question that defendant's action constituted a rule. The Administrative Procedure Act defines a "rule" as

> the whole or part of an agency statement of general or particular applicability and future effect designed to implement, interpret, or prescribe law or policy or describing the organization, procedure, or practice requirements of an agency ...

5 U.S.C. §551(4). Clearly, an agency statement describing conduct that the agency intends to follow in the future is a statement of "future effect designed to ... prescribe law or policy ... or procedure" and thus a rule. *See, e.g., Thomas v. New York, 256 U.S. App. D.C. 49, 802 F.2d 1443, 1446 (D.C. Cir. 1986).*

In general, the Administrative Procedure Act requires public notice and comment whenever a rule is promulgated. *Id.* at §553(b). The absence of notice and a period for public comment is the basis for plaintiff's contention that defendant's alleged revocation of the ocean incineration rules is illegal. If, however, the agency's action falls within the APA's exception for "interpretive rules, general statements of policy, or rules of agency organization, procedure, or practice," 5 U.S.C. §553(b)(A), it is exempt from the notice-and-comment requirement.

Defendant's deferral of permit applications is obviously not an "interpretive rule," which is a "statement interpreting an existing statute or rule." *Batterton v. Marshall, 208 U.S. App. D.C. 321, 648 F.2d 694 (D.C. Cir. 1980).* Nor is it a "general statement of policy," which is defined as a statement that merely expresses, "without force of law," the agency's "general intentions for the future." *Pacific Gas and Electric Co. v. Federal Power Commission, 164 U.S. App. D.C. 371, 506 F.2d 33, 38 (D.C. Cir. 1974).* The final exemption covers agency procedure and practice; defendant argues that its action falls within that exemption and defendant is right.

Whether a rule is "substantive" or "procedural" requires a Court to make "'legal conclusions which depend upon their settings for definition.'" *Neighborhood Television, Inc. v. Federal Communication Commission, 239 U.S. App. D.C. 292, 742 F.2d 629, 637 (D.C. Cir. 1984), quoting Brown Express, Inc. v. United States, 607 F.2d 695, 701 (5th Cir. 1979).* To determine which category best fits the rule, a Court "must look at [the rule's] effect on those interests ultimately at stake in the agency proceeding." *Neighborhood Television, 742 F.2d at 637.* If a rule does not "substantially affect," *Pickus v. Board of Parole, 165 U.S. App. D.C. 284, 507 F.2d 1107, 1113 (D.C. Cir. 1974),* or "jeopardize," *Environmental Defense Fund v. Gorsuch, 230 U.S. App. D.C. 8, 713 F.2d 802, 815 (D.C. Cir. 1983),* those ultimate interests—it is not "primarily directed … toward a determination of the rights or interests of affected parties," *Batterton v. Marshall, 648 F.2d at 702 n.34,*—the rule is one of procedure, and therefore exempt from the notice-and-comment requirement.

Plaintiff's "ultimate interest" is not acceptance and processing of its applications but an EPA permit to conduct ocean incineration. By deferring acceptance or consideration of the permit applications until new regulations are promulgated, defendant has in no way "substantially affected," "jeopardized," or taken actions "toward a determination" of plaintiff's interest in the permit it seeks. Rather, the agency has altered its method of operations: it has changed its procedures.

As with any change in procedures, this deferral affects agency supplicants and it may conceivably cause plaintiff some difficulty. But both effect and difficulty are temporary. Plaintiff will be able to submit applications for consideration once the new rules are in place, and nothing in this record suggests that the deferral itself will jeopardize plaintiff's ability to obtain ocean incineration permits in the future.

Although the law concentrates on the effect of the agency's decision on plaintiff's interests, it also requires a Court to examine the *purpose* of agency action to ensure that the agency did not intend to affect interested parties in a "substantive" way. *See, e.g., Batterton v. Marshall, 648 F.2d at 703.* The record before the Court reveals not only that plaintiff was affected in a procedural, rather than substantive, capacity, it fully supports the conclusion that the purpose of the deferral was procedural only.

There is no dispute that the defendant agency has been writing regulations designed to cover ocean incineration. *See Plaintiff's Facts* at paras. 6–9. After an initial inclination to continue granting permits while drafting the new ocean incineration regulations, the agency decided to impose a temporary freeze on permits until the new regulations were in place. *See id.* at paras. 6–7. Proposed regulations have been published, *50 Fed. Reg. 8,222* (Feb. 25, 1985); they have been, and continue to be, the subject of extensive public comment, including comments by plaintiff. *See Jensen Affidavit* at paras. 3, 5. The agency has made clear that these regulations will be revised and promulgated in final form after the agency considers the regulations in light of the public's (including plaintiff's) views. *See id.* at para. 6. Thus, the only logical way to view defendant's action is "a temporary suspension [on accepting new ocean incineration permit applications] ... until the outmoded and unsatisfactory old rules could be reexamined" and rewritten after full public participation. *Kessler v. Federal Communications Commission, 117 U.S. App. D.C. 130, 326 F.2d 673 (D.C. Cir. 1963).*

Thus, neither the effect nor the intent of the agency's action touches upon plaintiff's ultimate interest in obtaining an ocean incineration permit. As a result, the Court must conclude that the agency's deferral of consideration of applications for ocean incineration permits is a procedural rule and not subject to the notice-and-comment provisions of the Administrative Procedures Act....

CONCLUSION

Whether ocean incineration of hazardous waste is wise or wicked policy is not for this Court to decide. Whether policy concerns support ocean burning is similarly not an issue before the Court. The *only* issue for the Court to consider is whether the Environmental Protection Agency acted contrary to law when it decided to defer processing applications for ocean incineration permits until new regulations governing ocean incineration are in place. The Court finds that the Agency has fully complied with all relevant legal requirements. As such, the Court will deny plaintiff's motion for summary judgment, will grant defendant's motion for summary judgment, and will order this case dismissed from the docket of the Court....

Batterton v. Marshall

648 F.2d 694 (D.C. Cir. 1980) (footnotes omitted)

Bazelon, Senior Circuit Judge:

This case poses the difficult but familiar problem of whether a particular agency action requires notice by publication and opportunity for comment by interested parties. The State of Maryland (Maryland) alleges that the Department of Labor (DOL) violated procedural requirements in changing its methods for determining unemployment rates while implementing the Comprehensive Employment and Training Act (CETA). CETA, as enacted and as amended, created training and job programs with fund disbursements pegged to unemployment levels determined by DOL's Bureau of Labor Statistics (BLS). We reverse the district court's grant of summary judgment for appellee DOL.

I. BACKGROUND

Appellant Maryland administers the training and job programs funded by CETA and collects its state unemployment statistics for DOL. The amicus, representing the city of Baltimore, Maryland, is part of a combination of local government units established to administer CETA programs. Appellees, officials of DOL, are responsible for administering CETA programs and for supervising the collection and computation of unemployment statistics used in allocating CETA monies.

CETA monies are distributed by the federal government to state and local sponsors of manpower training and services, public employment, and emergency job programs. The emergency job program established by Title VI of CETA disburses funds geographically by a formula in relation to the number of unemployed persons in particular locales. "Unemployed persons" as defined by CETA are to be identified by "criteria used by the Bureau of Labor Statistics of the Department of Labor."

Prior to the enactment of CETA in 1973, DOL generated unemployment statistics by applying a method that had evolved over time since the New Deal. Known as the "Handbook" method, this approach draws on data collected by the nationwide network of state employment security agencies created under the Wagner-Peyser Act of 1933, 29 U.S.C. §§ 49 et seq. (1976). These state agencies maintain unemployment insurance data from which DOL developed unemployment estimates. DOL adopted a new methodology for collecting and computing unemployment statistics. This method, devised by the DOL Bureau of Labor Statistics (BLS) relies on the state unemployment insurance data, collected under the Handbook Method, only where data from a preferred, second source are not available. This second source is the Current Population Survey (CPS) ...

In 1974, Congress added Title VI to CETA which created a nationwide emergency jobs program as a direct response to the nation's "deteriorating economic condition." As these Title VI disbursements were being computed in 1975, DOL, again without formal notice, notified the regional office supervising Maryland that another new procedure in the unemployment statistics methodology would apply to Maryland. Called the "Balance of State" procedure, it adjusts the Handbook Method estimate where its addition to the state's CPS data fails to match a total benchmark figure for the state, set solely by national CPS data. DOL then applied the Balance of State procedure to adjust the unemployment statistics submitted by Maryland and the Fiscal 1976 CETA allotments based on the statistics.

Maryland then filed this suit for declaratory and injunctive relief. For the purposes of this litigation, Maryland estimated that application of the "Balance of State" procedure significantly reduced its share of Title VI CETA monies. Maryland alleged (1) violations of publication requirements set by CETA and by the Freedom of Information Act (FOIA); (2) violations of the Administrative Procedure Act's (APA) notice and comment requirements for rulemaking; and (3) that the new method for computing unemployment statistics is arbitrary and capricious.

On summary judgment motions, the district court ruled that no procedural defect occurred in DOL's adoption of the new method, including the Balance of State procedure....

III. CHARACTERIZING THE AGENCY ACTION

Appellant argues that DOL's methodology for developing unemployment statistics constitutes a "rule," requiring notice and comment....

[Under the APA] [r]ulemaking must be accompanied by (1) advance publication in the Federal Register of the proposed rule or its substance; (2) opportunity for public participation through submission of written comments, with or without oral presentation; and (3) publication of the final rule, incorporating a concise statement of its basis and purpose, thirty days before its effective date.... In keeping with the general commitment to public notice and participation, the APA provides only limited exceptions to these requirements. Advance publication and opportunity for public participation applies to all rules except "interpretative rules, general statements of policy, or rules of agency organization, procedure, or practice." ...

We would be less than candid if we pretended that the labels of "legislative" and "non-binding" rules neatly place particular agency actions within any particular category....

Analysis that improves upon semantic play must focus on the underlying purposes of the procedural requirements at issue. The essential purpose of according §553 notice and comment opportunities is to reintroduce public participation and fairness to affected parties after governmental authority has been delegated to unrepresentative agencies....

B. Is the Methodology a Rule.

[In this section of the opinion, the court holds that the "Balance of State" procedure for developing unemployment statistics is a "rule" for the purposes of the APA. It then goes on to examine the §553(b) exceptions to notice and comment rulemaking requirements.]

...

E. Is It a "Rule of Agency Organization, Procedure, or Practice"?

The final characterization that could remove the statistical methodology from §553 requirements may be the hardest to define. Labeled by the APA as a "rule of agency organization, procedure, or practice," this exception was provided to ensure that agencies retain latitude in organizing their internal operations.

The problem with applying the exception is that many merely internal agency practices affect parties outside the agency-often in significant ways. As Professor Freund explained decades ago, "even office hours ... necessarily require conformity on the part of the public." A useful articulation of the exemption's critical feature is that it covers agency actions that do not themselves alter the rights or interests of parties, although it may alter the manner in which the parties present themselves or their viewpoints to the agency. In this light, the exemption has applied to a freeze placed on the processing of applications for radio broadcast stations, to procedures accelerating the processing of applications for abandoning railroad lines and those for processing discrimination charges, and to a directive specifying that requisite audits be performed by nonagency accountants [citing cases for each of these examples].

The exemption cannot apply, however, where the agency action trenches on substantial private rights and interests. As the case law demonstrates, substantial rights and interests in this light have come into play when railroads are directed to file proposed schedules of rates and tariffs with subscribers; when applicants for food stamps are subject to modified approval procedures; when drug producers are subject to new specifications for the kinds of clinical investigations deemed necessary to establish the effectiveness of drug products prior to FDA approval; and when motor carriers are subject to a new method for paying shippers [citing cases for each of these examples].

Here, recipients of CETA emergency job program monies are subject to a new method for determining the one undefined variable in the statutory fund allocation formula. Although the methodology itself may look procedural, as Judge McGowan noted in a similar context, "(t)he characterizations 'substantive' and 'procedural' no more here than elsewhere in the law do not guide inexorably to the right result, nor do they really advance the inquiry very far." The critical question is whether the agency action jeopardizes the rights and interest of parties, for if it does, it must be subject to public comment prior to taking effect. As that is the case here, the exemption cannot apply.

...

CONCLUSION

For the foregoing reasons, we reverse the district court's grant of summary judgment for DOL and order summary judgment for Maryland, consistent with this opinion.

So ordered.

Problem 5.12: Procedural Rule Exception

What standard did the Waste Management *and* Batterton *courts use to decide when a rule that is procedural on the surface should nonetheless be subject to notice-and-comment rulemaking? How did these courts apply the standard in their respective cases, and what was the outcome?*

---

iv. The "Good Cause" Exception

The "good cause" exception is a narrow one. It is not enough for an agency to believe that avoiding notice-and-comment rulemaking procedures would be preferable from a policymaking point of view. Agencies may only employ this exception where: (1) following rulemaking procedures could completely undermine legitimate agency goals; (2) the rule has only a "technical" or "minor" effect on the public; or (3) due to an emergency, the agency cannot afford the time that a rulemaking would require. *See* Aman & Mayton, Administrative Law, *supra* at 96–97; *Levesque v. Block*, 723 F.2d 175, 184 (1st Cir. 1983). The D.C. Circuit has stated that agencies may only invoke this exception in the most extraordinary circumstances. *Utility Solid Waste Activities Group v. EPA*, 236 F.3d 749 (D.C. Cir. 2001).

2. Participating in the Rulemaking Process

Now that you know your client's rights to participate in the rulemaking process, you are ready to learn effective methods for representing your client in this arena.[11]

Many novice practitioners mistakenly assume that participation begins with the submitting of written comments on the proposed rule. Those who wait this long have squandered an important opportunity. The EPA is most receptive to input from public interest groups and the private sector *before* it has drafted its proposal. At this early stage, the agency is often eager for accurate data or studies from the outside that can help it in formulating the rule. Moreover, in a bureaucracy such as EPA, several high-level officials must "sign-off" on a proposal before the agency makes it public. By the time that it is proposed in the Federal Register EPA is already strongly committed to it. It can be very difficult to convince the agency to undo its prior work. Thus, it is best to get involved at the pre-proposal stage, while the agency is still interested in and open to input from the outside. Eckert, *Representing Private Clients*, *supra* note 11 at 27.

At this early juncture, your client can submit to EPA data, studies, legal arguments and other materials that support its view of the regulation. For example, a public interest group might submit a report showing that a contemplated air pollution regulation is not sufficiently protective of public health. Or, a private company might submit data showing that the way a particular piece of control technology is designed will pose a major obstacle for its operations. While preparing these types of inputs can require a good deal of work on your client's part, the pay-off can be great. If EPA adopts your client's view it will become part of the proposal and will be the starting point from which all other interested parties must work.

---

11. Two excellent articles on this subject, on which the following discussion draws, are Alan W. Eckert's *Representing Private Clients in EPA Rule Making*, 1 Nat. Res. & Env., No. 1 27, and Andrea Bear Field & Kathy E.B. Robb's *EPA Rule Makings: Views from Inside and Outside*, in ABA Section on Natural Resources, Energy, and Environmental Law, The Environmental Law Manual (Theodore L. Garrett, ed. 1992).

Once EPA has published its proposal it becomes harder to influence the agency. Telephone calls, face-to-face meetings, even participation in public hearings are often insufficient. To convince EPA to change directions at this point requires compelling and detailed legal and/or technical arguments that are well-researched and well-supported. Such arguments are best made in writing. Thus, after the publication of the proposal the most effective way to communicate with the agency is through written comments on the proposed rule.

Practice Tip: Making Contact with EPA

Prior to its publication of the proposal EPA does not have a formal system set up for receiving input from the public. You should therefore seek to communicate your client's position through contacts with individual agency officials. If the agency has published an Advanced Notice of Public Rulemaking (ANPR), then the best place to start is with the person listed as the agency contact in the Notice. In the absence of an ANPR, you can either contact the program office at EPA that is responsible for drafting the rule, or call EPA's Office of General Counsel (OGC) and ask to speak to the attorney who is involved in the rulemaking (the lawyers at OGC tend to be knowledgeable and influential). Bear Field & Robb, *EPA Rule Makings*, *supra* note 11 at 9–10. Attorneys who represent public interest environmental groups should not overlook contacting the lower-level EPA employees who are working on the rule. Id. These individuals tend to be sympathetic to the environmentalist point of view and are responsible for much of the formative work on the proposal. If you can reach them, you can influence the document! Remember that EPA officials are public servants who should be willing to talk to you.

Interested parties often have their attorneys draft their comments, even where the comments are of a technical, rather than a legal, nature. They do this because they are looking ahead to a possible legal challenge to the final regulations. Such a challenge can consist of a claim that the information on which the agency relied in developing the regulation, known as the "administrative record," does not support the rule that the agency eventually published. In assessing such claims, courts generally will not look beyond the administrative record. Thus, if a party wants to argue that data or studies exist that reveal flaws in the regulation it must be sure that this information enters the administrative record. One way it can do this is to include the material in its written comments on the proposed regulation. In this way, a party's comments lay the groundwork for its later legal challenge to the regulation. Some of the environmental statutes go even further and preclude parties from raising any issues in a legal challenge that they have not previously advanced in comments. *See, e.g.,* Clean Air Act § 307(d)(7)(B), 42 U.S.C. 7607(d)(7)(B) (2006); *Natural Resources Defense Council v. Thomas,* 805 F.2d 410, 427–28 (D.C. Cir. 1986). These considerations make it imperative that interested parties involve their attorneys in the drafting of written comments on a proposed rule.

Practice Tip: Work Closely with Technical Staff

While parties can assert legal arguments in their comments, they more often make technical and scientific arguments as to why the proposed regulation should (or should not) be changed. Engineers and scientists who work for the client generally develop these arguments. Thus, it is important that attorneys learn to work closely with technical staff. Together the attorneys, who are trained in effective advocacy, and the technical employees, who are trained in the relevant scientific discipline, can make a powerful team. Get to know your client's technical personnel. Do not be afraid to ask them questions about topics that are in their areas of expertise. Most of all, do not condescend to them or treat them as unimportant. They are your best allies in your attempt to participate effectively in the rulemaking process.

When drafting comments, you should bear in mind two general principles. First, to advocate effectively with EPA you need to gain the agency's trust. This means that data and studies you provide to EPA should be accurate and legal arguments should be well-reasoned and sound. If you build credibility in these ways the agency will listen to and consider your contributions. On the other hand, if EPA finds out that your data is self-serving or your legal arguments misleading you will develop a bad reputation that will follow you through the comment phase and beyond. The trustworthy lawyer—the one who argues forcefully but honestly with the agency—is generally the most effective advocate. Eckert, *Representing Private Clients, supra* note 11 at 27, 32.

Second, you should try, wherever possible, to identify EPA's goals in the rulemaking and then phrase your arguments in terms of the *agency's* goals rather than your client's. Id at 30. The EPA's regulations affect many different interest groups. If your principal argument is that the regulation, as proposed, hurts your client, this does not give the agency much reason to modify its position, especially if doing so would only serve to injure some other interested party who would then petition EPA to return to the original proposal. To convince EPA of your position you need to explain why the change that you suggest will serve, not only your client's goals, but EPA's as well. For example, an attorney for a citizen's group might argue that the regulation as proposed does not sufficiently protect human health (an EPA goal). Similarly, a lawyer for a private company might maintain that the regulation as proposed is inefficient, and that the suggested modification will result in greater protection of human health at less cost (another EPA goal).[12]

3. Challenging a Final Rule in Court

Once EPA has finalized a rule and published it in the Federal Register your chances of influencing the policy diminish. By this point, the agency has invested a great deal of time, resources and political capital in the rule and is fully committed to it. Interested parties may petition EPA to reconsider the rule. 5 U.S.C. § 553(e) (2006). But unless they can present the agency with a compelling reason to change or rescind the rule, they will have little success.

The only remaining alternative is to challenge the rule in court. Here, too, you will be fighting an uphill battle. When reviewing a final rule, courts tend to defer to the agency's expertise in its area of regulation. They will uphold a duly promulgated agency rule so long as it reflects a "reasonable interpretation" of the enabling statute, *Chevron, U.S.A., Inc. v. Natural Resources Defense Council*, 467 U.S. 837, 844 (1984), and the policy conclusions contained in the rule are the product of "reasoned analysis," *Motor Vehicle Manufacturers Ass'n v. State Farm Mutual*, 463 U.S. 29, 42 (1983).

Nonetheless, if you have participated well during the comment stage of the rulemaking process and have built an administrative record that supports your client's position, you may be able to succeed in a legal challenge to a final rule. Bringing such a case may also gain your client a seat at the bargaining table with EPA. The agency may not want to run the risk of losing the case and may be willing to modify a regulation in order to reach a settlement. Bear Field & Robb, *EPA Rule Makings*, *supra* note 11 at 19–20. Thus, there are some potential benefits to challenging an EPA regulation in court. But this should not

---

12. For additional instruction on how to draft effective comments, *see* Elizabeth D. Mullin, the Art of Commenting: How to Influence Environmental Decision-making with Effective Comments (Environmental Law Institute, 2000); Cornelius M. Kerwin, Rulemaking: How Government Agencies Write Law and Make Policy (Cong. Quarterly Press, 4th ed., 2010).

be the preferred or exclusive method by which you represent your client's interests. You will best serve your client by engaging EPA while it is still formulating its proposed rule and by submitting comments on the proposal once the agency issues it.

Problem 5.13: Challenging a Regulation

Environmental statutes often restrict the timing and venue of legal challenges to agency regulations. If your client fails to follow the proper procedures it can lose its opportunity to challenge the regulation. It is therefore important to keep these statutory restrictions in mind.

Assume that you represent the Heartland Power Company, a large producer and supplier of electricity in the Midwest. In 1969, Heartland commenced negotiations with Combustion Construction (CC) regarding the building of a new oil-fired boiler to generate steam for Heartland's Kansas City electric generating facility. In May 1970, Heartland wrote to CC stating its "intent to award the construction contract for the new boiler to you." Based on this letter, but before the parties signed a formal contract, CC began designing the boiler. Heartland and CC eventually signed a contract on September 1, 1971, by which time CC had already completed ten percent of the work on the project. It is common industry practice for an electrical utility to issue a letter signifying its intent to award a contract, and for a contractor to begin work based only on such a "letter of intent." CC broke ground on the project in early 1972 and completed construction in 1973.

The EPA has published a New Source Performance Standard (NSPS) for fossil fuel-fired steam generating units with an effective date of August 17, 1971. 40 CFR §60.40 et seq. (2009). Heartland's Kansas City boiler has never complied with the terms of this performance standard. In 1980, EPA commenced a civil action in Missouri District Court alleging that Heartland was in violation of the NSPS regulation and seeking $25,000 per day of violation.

You represent Heartland in this litigation. Recall from Chapter I that the NSPS program applies to all "affected facilities" that "commenced construction" after the effective date of the applicable standard. Recall further that NSPS regulations define "commenced construction" as meaning that the owner has "undertaken a continuous program of construction or ... has *entered into a contractual obligation* to undertake and complete ... a continuous program of construction." 40 CFR §60.2 (2009) (emphasis added). This definition was included in the initial NSPS regulations promulgated in 1971 (36 Fed. Reg. 24877).

The principal issue in the case is whether Heartland "commenced construction" of the Kansas City boiler after August 17, 1971 (the effective date of the NSPS for fossil fuel-fired steam generating units). Heartland believes that, in light of the industry practice, its May 1970 "letter of intent" to CC and the preliminary work that CC performed prior to August 17, 1971 should qualify as "commencement" of construction, even if no formal "contract" had been signed at that time. Heartland wants you to challenge the NSPS regulations' narrow focus on "contractual obligation[s]," and to argue that the definition of "commenced construction" at 40 CFR §60.2 should be broadened to include arrangements such as the "letter of intent" that it sent to CC.

Answer the following questions: (A) Can Heartland challenge the regulation in this way, at this time, and in this court? If not, when and where could it have done so? Explain with appropriate citation to the Clean Air Act. (B) Even if Heartland cannot challenge the regulation, is there another way to make the argument that it wants to make? (C) Why do you think that Congress limits the time frame within which interested parties can challenge the substance of an EPA regulation?

D. Introduction to the Environmental Justice Movement

In the materials that follow, you will be asked to apply some of your new knowledge about the policy aspects of environmental practice to an EPA guidance document on the topic of environmental justice. A short introduction to the environmental justice issue will begin to prepare you for this task.

Environmental justice focuses on the distributional effects of environmental policies, *i.e.,* how environmental pollution and health risks are distributed among the various segments of American society. Environmental justice advocates believe that "environmental laws, regulations and policies have not been applied fairly across all segments of the population," and that consequently "low-income communities and communities of color bear a disproportionate burden of the nation's pollution problem." Robert D. Bullard, *Unequal Protection: Environmental Justice and Communities of Color XV* (1994). They use political and legal advocacy to remedy this unequal distribution of environmental harms.

1. Facts about the Discriminatory Siting of Facilities

Environmental justice concerns have been raised on a number of fronts, ranging from disparate exposure to toxic air emissions, to unequal provision of environmental amenities such as parks or open space. This section will focus on the claim that environmental agencies discriminate by issuing permits that disproportionately allow polluting facilities to be built in minority communities. A 1982 protest against the placement of a polychlorinated biphenyl (PCB) landfill in Warren County, North Carolina, a predominantly African-American area, played a key role in the bringing this issue to light.[13] The non-violent demonstrations, and the over 500 arrests that followed, convinced the U.S. General Accounting Office (GAO) that it should investigate the siting of hazardous waste facilities in the Southeast. In 1983, GAO published a report in which it concluded that, of the four major offsite hazardous waste facilities that existed in the region, three were located in predominantly African-American communities even though the region was only one-fifth African-American. U.S. Gen. Accounting Office, GAO/RCED 83-168, *Siting of Hazardous Waste Landfills and their Correlation with Racial and Economic Status of Surrounding Communities 1* (1983). The United Church of Christ Commission for Racial Justice (CRJ) subsequently undertook a national study of the siting of commercial hazardous waste facilities. The researchers identified the zip codes in which such facilities were located. They then compared the demographics of these areas with those of the zip code regions that did not contain such facilities. The 1987 CRJ report concluded that commercial hazardous waste facilities tend disproportionately to be located in minority areas and that race—not income level—was the most significant variable in explaining this pattern. United Church of Christ Commission for Racial Justice, *Toxic Wastes and Race in the United States* (1987). The report further found that three out of every five Blacks and Hispanics, and approximately half of all Asian/Pacific Islanders and Native Americans, lived in communities with uncontrolled toxic waste sites. *Id.* The GAO and CRJ reports and other, more recent, studies are widely cited for the proposition that polluting facilities are disproportionately sited in minority communities. At least one study has reached the opposite conclusion. *See* Douglas Anderton, et al., *Environmental Equity: The Demographics of Dumping*, 31 Demography 229 (May

---

13. On the history of the environmental justice movement, *see generally* Eileen Gauna, *Federal Environmental Citizen Provisions: Obstacles and Incentives on the Road to Environmental Justice*, 22 Ecology Law Quarterly 1 (1995), which provides a concise account.

1994) (finding no statistically significant difference in the race or poverty level of those living in census tracts with commercial hazardous waste sites as compared to those living in census tracts without such facilities).[14]

Some have argued that the results of the GAO and CRJ studies are better explained by market dynamics than by discriminatory permitting decisions of regulatory authorities. *See* Vicki Been, *Locally Undesirable Land Uses in Minority Neighborhoods: Disproportionate Siting or Market Dynamics?*, 103 Yale L.J. 1383 (1994). According to this view, the placement of a polluting facility in a neighborhood will likely result in a lowering of property values in that community. This may lead minorities, who tend to have fewer financial resources, to move into the area and wealthier, White residents to move out. *Id.* This argument has implications for the best way to remedy current disparities. If market dynamics are largely to blame, then a decision to place future facilities in majority White areas may not prevent the phenomenon from repeating itself. *Id* at 1392. Other solutions that focus on the dynamics of the residential housing market might be called for. *Id.* Empirical studies have thus far provided little support for the market dynamics theory. A 1997 examination of 544 commercial hazardous waste facilities looked at population demographics before, and after, each facility was built. It concluded that the construction of these facilities had little effect on the racial, ethnic, or socio-economic characteristics of the surrounding neighborhood. *See* Vicki Been and Francis Gupta, *Coming to the Nuisance or Going to the Barrios? A Longitudinal Analysis of Environmental Justice Claims*, 24 Ecology Law Quarterly 1 (1997). Two other studies have reached a similar conclusion. *See* John Michael Oakes, et al., *A Longitudinal Analysis of Environmental Equity in Communities with Hazardous Waste Facilities*, 25 Soc. Sci. Res. 125 (1996); Manuel Pastor, et al., *Which Came First: Toxic Facilities, Minority Move-in, and Environmental Justice*, 23 J. Urban Affairs 1 (2001). However, one study found that the percentage of poor and minority individuals in several St. Louis, Missouri neighborhoods increased after commercial waste facilities were sited there. Thomas Lambert & Christopher Boerner, *Environmental Inequity: Economic Causes, Economic Solutions*, 14 Yale J. on Reg. 195 (1997).

---

14. One commentator has pointed out that many hazardous waste landfills were built before the passage of the Resource Conservation and Recovery Act (RCRA) of 1976, and hence before the RCRA permitting process was put into place. *See* Michael B. Gerrard, *Fear and Loathing in the Siting of Hazardous and Radioactive Waste Facilities: A Comprehensive Approach to a Misperceived Crisis*, 68 Tulane L. Rev. 1047, 1099–1100 (1994).

Controversies over empirical evidence aside,[15] there is a strong logic to the environmental justice thesis. The Not In My Backyard (NIMBY) phenomenon is well-documented. Wealthy and politically-powerful communities use their clout to keep out undesirable land uses such as hazardous waste facilities or pollution-creating manufacturing facilities. Since minority communities tend to be poorer and politically weaker, it stands to reason that they would lose out in the NIMBY battle and receive a disproportionate share of the facilities that nobody wants. *See* Richard J. Lazarus, *Pursuing "Environmental Justice," The Distributional Effects of Environmental Protection*, 87 Northwestern L.J. 787, 806–11 (1993); *but see* Michael B. Gerrard, *The Victims of NIMBY*, 21 Fordham Urb. L.J. 495, 521 (1994) (arguing that the NIMBY phenomenon has not increased the siting of new landfills and incinerators in minority communities, although it has perpetuated the existence of old disposal units in those communities).

2. Federal Actions to Promote Environmental Justice

The federal government has been sufficiently convinced of the environmental justice claim that it has taken several high-profile steps to address the issue. In 1992, EPA established an Office of Environmental Justice (OEJ) to oversee the integration of environmental justice into the agencies' policies, programs and activities. In 1993, it created the National Environmental Justice Advisory Council (NEJAC), a group of grassroots activists, environmentalists, business representatives and state government officials that advises EPA on how to integrate environmental justice into federal environmental programs and related areas. In 1994, President Clinton issued Executive Order 12,898, 59 Fed. Reg. 7629 (1994), which requires each federal agency to "make achieving environmental justice a part of its mission" and establishes an Interagency Working Group on Environmental Justice (IWG) chaired by EPA Administrator. In 1995 EPA, responding to the Executive Order, adopted an Environmental Justice Strategy to "ensure the integration of environmental justice into the agency's programs, policies and activities."[16] In 1996, it adopted an Environmental Justice Implementation Plan.[17] In 2005, EPA Administra-

---

15. For an excellent overview of the possible causes of, and empirical evidence for, environmental injustice see Clifford Rechtschaffen & Eileen Gauna, Environmental Justice: Law, Policy & Regulation 27–85 (2002).

16. U.S. Environmental Protection Agency, *The Environmental Protection Agency's Environmental Justice Strategy* 1 (April 3, 1995).

17. U.S. EPA, *Environmental Justice Implementation Plan* (1996).

tor Stephen L. Johnson issued a memorandum reaffirming EPA's commitment to environmental justice. In 2008, he issued another memorandum calling on the Agency to strengthen its work in this area and directing EPA's national program managers and Regions to conduct environmental justice reviews.[18]

The EPA has provided grants to support organizations seeking to resolve environmental justice concerns and issues.[19] Moreover, in 2008, EPA instituted the Environmental Justice Achievement Awards, which are given to eligible academic institutions and community organizations to recognize their successes in addressing environmental justice issues. Notwithstanding these positive steps, the cumulative pollution burdens that environmental justice communities experience has proven to be a persistent problem that is not easily remedied.

3. Environmental Justice Litigation

Recent years have also seen a surge in environmental justice legal claims. These complaints have primarily challenged environmental permitting decisions (*e.g.*, the permitting of a hazardous waste landfill in the complainant's community), and have alleged either a violation of the Equal Protection Clause of the Fourteenth Amendment, or a violation of Title VI of the Civil Rights Act of 1964.

The equal protection claims typically assert that the state has racially discriminated against minority plaintiffs by issuing a permit for a polluting facility (or a series of polluting facilities) in their community and has thereby denied them the equal protection of the law. *See, e.g., Bean v. Southwestern Waste Management Corp.*, 482 F. Supp. 673 (S.D. Tex. 1979), *aff'd without op.*, 782 F.2d 1038 (5th Cir. 1986). To succeed in such a claim, plaintiffs must

---

18. Administrator Stephen L. Johnson, *EPA's Commitment to Environmental Justice* (Nov. 4, 2005); Administrator Stephen L. Johnson, *Strengthening EPA's Environmental Justice Program* (June 9, 2008).

19. The Agency's Environmental Justice Collaborative Problem-Solving Cooperative Agreement Program provides eligible community organizations with federal financial assistance to pursue a collaborative, problem-solving approach to addressing local environmental justice issues using EPA's "Environmental Justice Collaborative Problem-Solving Model." EPA's Environmental Justice Small Grants Program provides eligible recipients with financial assistance to foster collaborative partnerships in communities facing environmental justice issues and to enable them to provide education, training and outreach. Since its inception in 1994, the Program has awarded more than $20 million in funding to 1,130 community-based organizations. The Agency's State Environmental Justice Cooperative Agreements Program promotes environmental justice in state government activities.

demonstrate that the defendant acted with racially discriminatory intent. *See Washington v. Davis*, 426 U.S. 229, 238–48 (1976); *Arlington Heights v. Metropolitan Hous. Dev. Corp.*, 429 U.S. 252, 264–66 (1977). Plaintiffs have found it very difficult to find the "smoking gun" that will allow them to meet this standard in the environmental justice context. *See Bean v. Southwestern Waste Management Corp., supra* (dismissed for failure to show discriminatory intent); *East Bibb Twigs Neighborhood Ass'n v. Macon-Bibb County Planning and Zoning Comm'n*, 706 F. Supp. 880 (M.D. Ga.), *aff'd*, 888 F.2d 1573 (11th Cir.), *amended*, 896 F.2d 1264 (11th Cir. 1989) (same); *R.I.S.E. v. Kay*, 768 F. Supp. 1144 (E.D. Va. 1991), *aff'd*, 977 F.2d 573 (4th Cir. 1992) (same).

Since equal protection claims have rarely succeeded, environmental justice plaintiffs have come to rely more heavily on Title VI of the Civil Rights Act of 1964. Title VI provides that programs or activities funded by the federal government cannot discriminate on the basis of race, color or national origin. Section 601 of the Act reads: "No person in the United States shall, on the ground of race, color or national origin, be excluded from participation in, be denied the benefits of, or be subjected to discrimination under any program or activity receiving Federal financial assistance." 42 U.S.C. 2000d (2006). Section 602 of the Act authorizes federal agencies to issue regulations that implement the prohibition contained in §601 and to terminate financial assistance to recipients of federal funding that fail to comply with such regulations. 42 USC 2000d-1 (2006). The EPA has promulgated a set of regulations implementing Title VI. *See* 40 CFR §7.10 *et seq.* (2009). These rules spell out EPA's approach to implementing Title VI and set up a process, administered by EPA's Office of Civil Rights, for filing and handling administrative complaints alleging Title VI violations.

Historically, claims brought under Title VI have alleged racial discrimination in the provision of federally-financed services such as hospitals. Recently, however, environmental justice plaintiffs have sought to use Title VI to challenge the permitting of polluting facilities in minority communities. Plaintiffs in these actions have argued that the state environmental agencies that issue the permits for these facilities are "recipients" of federal funding and that, under Title VI, they cannot discriminate on the basis of race in their permitting decisions. Plaintiffs have attempted to show that the state agencies have discriminated against minorities in their permitting decisions, and that they have thereby violated Title VI. Under Title VI, once plaintiffs establish a *prima facie* case of discrimination the burden shifts to the recipient-defendant to demonstrate "a legitimate nondiscriminatory reason" for its action. *NAACP v. Medical Center, Inc.*, 657 F.2d 1322, 1333 (3rd Cir. 1981). If the defendant can make this showing, then the burden shifts back to the plaintiff to show that there are reasonable alternatives to defendant's actions and that the defendant's justification is, accordingly, a pretext for discrimination. *Id.* at 1333–37.

The courts have interpreted §601 of the Civil Rights Act of 1964 to require a showing of intentional discrimination. *See, e.g., Alexander v. Sandoval*, 532 U.S. 275, 280–81 (2001). Plaintiffs filing suit directly under §601 accordingly face many of the same evidentiary hurdles as those who have sought to challenge discriminatory permitting practices under the Equal Protection Clause. The situation is quite different for §602. Supreme Court precedents appear to allow agencies to adopt a discriminatory *effects* test in their implementing regulations. *See Guardians Ass'n v. Civil Serv. Comm'n of City of New York*, 463 U.S. 582, 584 & n. 2, 591–94 (1983); *Alexander v. Choate*, 469 U.S. 287, 293–94 (1985); *but cf. Alexander v. Sandoval*, 532 U.S. 275, 281–82 (2001) (questioning this conclusion but not reaching the issue). The EPA has adopted such a test. 40 CFR §7.35 (2009). Thus, under EPA's regulations, minority claimants challenging the issuance of a permit under Title VI need only show that a state agency's permitting decisions resulted in a racially discriminatory *effect* (also referred to as a "disparate impact"). They do not have to show a discriminatory *intent.* This may make such claims more winnable.

Environmental justice plaintiffs have used two different methods to bring their §602 disparate impact claims. Some have filed suit in court under §602 asserting that a state environmental agency has violated EPA's Title VI disparate impact regulations by engaging in discriminatory permitting practices. *See e.g. South Camden Citizens in Action v. N.J. Dep't of Envtl. Protection*, 145 F.Supp.2d 446 (D.N.J. 2001). Such actions have sought injunctive relief prohibiting the state from granting the permit at issue or from taking other discriminatory action. *Id.* Alternatively, environmental justice complainants have filed administrative complaints with EPA's Office of Civil Rights (OCR) alleging that a recipient's permitting practices violate the agency's disparate impact Title VI regulations. The OCR investigates these complaints and, if it finds a violation, can move to terminate the recipient's federal funding.

In 2001, the Supreme Court closed the door on private actions under Title VI seeking to enforce agency §602 discriminatory effects regulations. In the case of *Alexander v. Sandoval* the Court held that Congress, in passing Title VI, did not create a private right of action to enforce agency Title VI regulations promulgated under §602. *Alexander v. Sandoval*, 532 U.S. 275, 293 (2001). This holding has essentially precluded environmental justice plaintiffs from bringing claims directly in court based on EPA's Title VI disparate impact regulations. *See generally*, Clifford Rechtschaffen & Eileen Gauna, Environmental Justice: Law, Policy & Regulation 369–381 (2002); Michael D. Mattheisen, *The Effect of Alexander v. Sandoval on Federal Environmental Civil Rights (Environ-*

mental Justice) Policy, 13 Geo. Mason U. Civ. Rights L.J. 35 (2003). Some environmental justice plaintiffs responded to *Sandoval* by recasting their claims as actions brought under 42 U.S.C. § 1983. Section 1983 provides a remedy for deprivation, under color of state law, of rights secured by the federal "Constitution or laws." 42 U.S.C. § 1983 (2006). However, in 2001, the Third Circuit held that § 1983, much like Title VI itself, does not create a private right of action to enforce agency Title VI disparate impact regulations. *South Camden Citizens in Action v. N.J. Dep't of Envtl. Protection,* 274 F.3d 771 (3rd Cir. 2001); *see generally* Brad C. Mank, *South Camden Citizens in Action v. New Jersey Department of Environmental Protection: Will Section 1983 Save Title VI Disparate Impact Suits?,* 32 ENVT'L L. REP. 10454 (2002) (discussing this case). At least one lower court has held that plaintiffs may use § 1983 as the basis of a private right of action to enforce certain HUD regulations under Title VIII, the Fair Housing Act of 1968. *Langlois v. Abington Housing Authority,* 234 F. Supp.2d 33 (D. Mass. 2002). This court further suggested in dicta that parties might also use § 1983 to enforce Title VI disparate impact regulations. There is likely to be more litigation on this question. *See generally* 1A-31 BROWNFIELDS LAW AND PRACTICE § 31.06 (M. Gerrard, ed., 2009).

Litigants who do not possess a private right of action may still pursue another form of legal recourse: EPA's administrative complaint process. The EPA's Title VI regulations allow parties to file a Title VI complaint at any EPA office. 40 CFR § 7.120(b) (2009). Complaints are referred to EPA's Office of Civil Rights which evaluates whether they are sufficient on the pleadings and, if they are, accepts them for further processing. *Id.* at § 7.120(d)(1). OCR then investigates the allegations of discrimination. If it finds a violation of Title VI, and if the recipient resists taking voluntary measures to correct it, EPA can either withdraw federal funding from the recipient-defendant, or turn the case over to the Department of Justice for further litigation. *Id.* at § 7.130(a).

In 1998, EPA issued a guidance document entitled "Interim Guidance for Investigating Title VI Administrative Complaints Challenging Permits" (the "Interim Title VI Guidance") (reprinted below) in which it sought to explain its process for handling Title VI administrative complaints challenging State permitting decisions. U.S. EPA, *Interim Guidance on Investigating Title VI Administrative Complaints Challenging Permits* (Feb. 1998). EPA offered the public a limited opportunity to comment on the document. However, it stated that it would not subject the document to full notice-and-comment rulemaking procedures, nor would it respond to the comments that it did receive, since the document was merely "guidance."

The following problems and exercises will ask you to play the role of a lawyer whose client has an interest in the Interim Guidance. In Exercise 4.1, you will draft written comments on the document. Your comments will address the substance of the Guidance. They will also speak to the procedural question of whether the document should have been promulgated pursuant to notice-and-comment rulemaking procedures, rather than simply issued as a guidance document. In Exercise 4.2, you will assume that EPA has changed its mind and has decided to promulgate the policy through notice-and-comment rulemaking. It has reissued the document as a proposed rule. Given the high degree of controversy surrounding the policy, EPA has decided to hold a public hearing on the proposal. You will represent your client at this hearing. Before beginning the exercises, you should complete problems 4.14 to 4.19, which will introduce you further to EPA's Interim Title VI Guidance. [Note: On June 27, 2000, EPA issued two draft guidance documents that replace and supercede the Interim Guidance. *See* 65 Fed. Reg. 39650 (June 27, 2000). Thus, the Interim Guidance published in this book *no longer reflects current agency policy*. It nonetheless remains an excellent vehicle for learning about EPA's handling of Title VI environmental justice complaints, and for practicing the drafting of comments. It is used here for those pedagogical purposes. Students interested in the more recent Draft Guidances should see the Federal Register notice cited above and EPA's Web site, http://www.epa.gov/ocr/pol guid.htm, where the Draft Guidance documents are available.]

* * *

Interim Guidance for Investigating Title VI Administrative Complaints Challenging Permits

INTRODUCTION

This interim guidance is intended to provide a framework for the processing by EPA's Office of Civil Rights (OCR) of complaints filed under Title VI of the Civil Rights Act of 1964, as amended (Title VI),[1] alleging discriminatory effects resulting from the issuance of pollution control permits by state and local governmental agencies that receive EPA funding.

In the past, the Title VI complaints filed with EPA typically alleged discrimination in access to public water and sewerage systems or in employment practices. This interim guidance is intended to update the Agency's procedural and policy framework to accommodate the increasing number of Title VI complaints that allege discrimination in the environmental permitting context.

---

1. 42 U.S.C. §§2000d to 2000d-7.

As reflected in this guidance, Title VI environmental permitting cases may have implications for a diversity of interests, including those of the recipient, the affected community, and the permit applicant or permittee. EPA believes that robust stakeholder input is an invaluable tool for fully addressing Title VI issues during the permitting process and informally resolving Title VI complaints when they arise.

BACKGROUND

No person in the United States shall, on the ground of race, color, or national origin, be excluded from participation in, be denied the benefits of, or be subjected to discrimination under any program or activity receiving Federal financial assistance—Title VI.

On February 11, 1994, President Clinton issued Executive Order 12,898, "Federal Actions To Address Environmental Justice in Minority Populations and Low-Income Populations." The Presidential memorandum accompanying that Order directs Federal agencies to ensure compliance with the nondiscrimination requirements of Title VI for all Federally-funded programs and activities that affect human health or the environment. While Title VI is inapplicable to EPA actions, including EPA's issuance of permits, Section 2-2 of Executive Order 12,898 is designed to ensure that Federal actions substantially affecting human health or the environment do not have discriminatory effects based on race, color, or national origin. Accordingly, EPA is committed to a policy of nondiscrimination in its own permitting programs.

Title VI itself prohibits intentional discrimination. The Supreme Court has ruled, however, that Title VI authorizes Federal agencies, including EPA, to adopt implementing regulations that prohibit discriminatory *effects*. Frequently, discrimination results from policies and practices that are neutral on their face, but have the effect of discriminating.[2] Facially-neutral policies or practices that result in discriminatory *effects* violate EPA's Title VI regulations unless it is shown that they are justified and that there is no less discriminatory alternative.

EPA awards grants on an annual basis to many state and local agencies that administer continuing environmental programs under EPA's statutes. As a condition of receiving funding under EPA's continuing environmental program grants, recipient agencies must comply with EPA's Title VI regulations, which are incorporated by reference into the grants. EPA's Title VI regulations

---

2. Department of Justice, Attorney General's Memorandum for Heads of Departments and Agencies that Provide Federal Financial Assistance, The Use of the Disparate Impact Standard in Administrative Regulations Under Title VI of the Civil Rights Act of 1964, (July 14, 1994).

define a "[r]ecipient" as "any state or its political subdivision, any instrumentality of a state or its political subdivision, any public or private agency, institution, organization, or other entity, or any person to which Federal financial assistance is extended directly or through another recipient...."[3] Title VI creates for recipients a nondiscrimination obligation that is contractual in nature in exchange for accepting Federal funding. Acceptance of EPA funding creates an obligation on the recipient to comply with the regulations for as long as any EPA funding is extended.[4]

Under amendments made to Title VI by the Civil Rights Restoration Act of 1987,[5] a "program" or "activity" means all of the operations of a department, agency, special purpose district, or other instrumentality of a state or of a local government, any part of which is extended Federal financial assistance.[6] Therefore, unless expressly exempted from Title VI by Federal statute, all programs and activities of a department or agency that receives EPA funds are subject to Title VI, including those programs and activities that are not EPA-funded. For example, the issuance of permits by EPA recipients under solid waste programs administered pursuant to Subtitle D of the Resource Conservation and Recovery Act (which historically have not been grant-funded by EPA), or the actions they take under programs that do not derive their authority from EPA statutes (e.g., state environmental assessment requirements), are part of a program or activity covered by EPA's Title VI regulations if the recipient receives any funding from EPA.

In the event that EPA finds discrimination in a recipient's permitting program, and the recipient is not able to come into compliance voluntarily, EPA is required by its Title VI regulations to initiate procedures to deny, annul, suspend, or terminate EPA funding.[7] EPA also may use any other means authorized by law to obtain compliance, including referring the matter to the Department of Justice (DOJ) for litigation.[8] In appropriate cases, DOJ may file suit seeking injunctive relief....

---

3. 40 C.F.R. §7.25 (1996). Title VI applies to Indian Tribes as EPA recipients only when the statutory provision authorizing the Federal financial assistance is not exclusively for the benefit of Tribes. Otherwise, Tribes are exempt from Title VI.

4. 40 C.F.R. §7.80(a)(2)(iii)(1996).

5. Pub. L. No. 100-259, 102 Stat. 28 (1988); S. Rep. No. 64 at 2, 11–16, 100th Cong., reprinted in 1988 U.S. Code Cong. & Admin. News at 3–4, 13–18.

6. 42 U.S.C. §2000d-4a.

7. 40 C.F.R. §§7.115(e), 7.130(b)(1996); Id. at 7.110(c).

8. 42 U.S.C. §2000d-1; 40 C.F.R. §7.130(a).

Overview of Framework for Processing Complaints

While this guidance is directed at the processing of discriminatory effects allegations, as a general proposition, Title VI complaints alleging either discriminatory intent and/or discriminatory effect in the context of environmental permitting will be processed by OCR under EPA's Title VI regulations at 40 C.F.R. Part 7. The steps that the Agency will follow in complaint processing are described below. EPA's Title VI regulations encourage the informal resolution of all complaints with the participation of all affected stakeholders (see step 8 below).

1. Acceptance of the Complaint

Upon receiving a Title VI complaint, OCR will determine whether the complaint states a valid claim. If it does, the complaint will be accepted for processing within twenty (20) calendar days of acknowledgment of its receipt, and the complainant and the EPA recipient will be so notified. If OCR does not accept the complaint, it will be rejected or, if appropriate, referred to another Federal agency. 40 C.F.R. §7.120(d)(1).

2. Investigation/Disparate Impact Assessment

Once a complaint is accepted for processing, OCR will conduct a factual investigation to determine whether the permit(s) at issue will create a disparate impact, or add to an existing disparate impact, on a racial or ethnic population. If, based on its investigation, OCR concludes that there is no disparate impact, the complaint will be dismissed. If OCR makes an initial finding of a disparate impact, it will notify the recipient and the complainant and seek a response from the recipient within a specified time period. Under appropriate circumstances, OCR may seek comment from the recipient, permittee, and/or complainant(s) on preliminary data analyses before making an initial finding concerning disparate impacts.

3. Rebuttal/Mitigation

The notice of initial finding of a disparate impact will provide the recipient the opportunity to rebut OCR's finding, propose a plan for mitigating the disparate impact, or to "justify" the disparate impact (see step 4 below regarding justification). If the recipient successfully rebuts OCR's finding, or, if the recipient elects to submit a plan for mitigating the disparate impact, and, based on its review, EPA agrees that the disparate impact will be mitigated sufficiently pursuant to the plan, the parties will be so notified. Assuming that assurances are provided regarding implementation of such a mitigation plan, no further action on the complaint will be required.

4. JUSTIFICATION

If the recipient can neither rebut the initial finding of disparate impact nor develop an acceptable mitigation plan, then the recipient may seek to demonstrate that it has a substantial, legitimate interest that justifies the decision to proceed with the permit notwithstanding the disparate impact. Even where a substantial, legitimate justification is proffered, OCR will need to consider whether it can be shown that there is an alternative that would satisfy the stated interest while eliminating or mitigating the disparate impact.

5. PRELIMINARY FINDING OF NONCOMPLIANCE

If the recipient fails to rebut OCR's initial finding of a disparate impact and can neither mitigate nor justify the disparate impact at issue, OCR will, within 180 calendar days from the start of the complaint investigation, send the recipient a written notice of preliminary finding of noncompliance, with a copy to the grant award official (Award Official) and the Assistant Attorney General for Civil Rights. OCR's notice may include recommendations for the recipient to achieve voluntary compliance and, where appropriate, the recipient's right to engage in voluntary compliance negotiations. 40 C.F.R. §7.115(c).

6. FORMAL DETERMINATION OF NONCOMPLIANCE

If, within fifty (50) calendar days of receipt of the notice of preliminary finding, the recipient does not agree to OCR's recommendations or fails to submit a written response demonstrating that OCR's preliminary finding is incorrect or that voluntary compliance can be achieved through other steps, OCR will issue a formal written determination of noncompliance, with a copy to the Award Official and the Assistant Attorney General for Civil Rights. 40 C.F.R. §7.115(d).

7. VOLUNTARY COMPLIANCE

The recipient will have ten (10) calendar days from receipt of the formal determination of noncompliance within which to come into voluntary compliance. 40 C.F.R. §7.115(e). If the recipient fails to meet this deadline, OCR will start procedures to deny, annul, suspend, or terminate EPA assistance in accordance with 40 C.F.R. §7.130(b) and consider other appropriate action, including referring the matter to DOJ for litigation.

8. INFORMAL RESOLUTION

EPA's Title VI regulations call for OCR to pursue informal resolution of administrative complaints wherever practicable. 40 C.F.R. §7.120(d)(2). Therefore, OCR will discuss, at any point during the process outlined above, offers by recipients to reach informal resolution, and will, to the extent appropriate, endeavor to facilitate the informal resolution process and involvement of affected stakeholders. Ordinarily, in the interest of conserving EPA investigative resources for truly intractable matters, it will make sense to encourage dialogue at the beginning of the investigation of complaints accepted for processing. Accordingly, in notifying a recipient of acceptance of a complaint for investigation, OCR will encourage the recipient to engage the complainant(s) in informal resolution in an effort to negotiate a settlement.

REJECTING OR ACCEPTING COMPLAINTS FOR INVESTIGATION

It is the general policy of OCR to investigate all administrative complaints that have apparent merit and are complete or properly pleaded. Examples of complaints with no apparent merit might include those which are so insubstantial or incoherent that they cannot be considered to be grounded in fact.

A complete or properly pleaded complaint is:[9]

1. in writing, signed, and provides an avenue for contacting the signatory (e.g., phone number, address);
2. describes the alleged discriminatory act(s) that violates EPA's Title VI regulations (i.e., an act of intentional discrimination or one that has the effect of discriminating on the basis of race, color, or national origin);
3. filed within 180 calendar days of the alleged discriminatory act(s);[10] and
4. identifies the EPA recipient that took the alleged discriminatory act(s).

EPA's Title VI regulations contemplate that OCR will make a determination to accept, reject, or refer (to the appropriate Federal agency) a complaint within twenty (20) calendar days of acknowledgment of its receipt. 40 C.F.R. §7.120(d)(1). Whenever possible, within the twenty-day period, OCR will establish whether the person or entity that took the alleged discriminatory act is in fact an EPA recipient as defined by 40 C.F.R. §7.25. If the complaint does not specifically mention that the alleged discriminatory actor is an EPA financial assistance recipient, OCR may presume so for the purpose of deciding whether or not to accept the complaint for further processing.

---

9. The EPA's Title VI regulations require that the complaint be in writing, describe the alleged discriminatory acts that violate the regulations, and be filed within 180 calendar days of the alleged discriminatory act(s). 40 C.F.R. §7.120(b)(1),(2). The criteria listed above satisfy these regulatory requirements.

10. Also, see discussion below on Timeliness of Complaints.

Timeliness of Complaints

Under EPA's Title VI regulations a complaint must be filed within 180 calendar days of the alleged discriminatory act. 40 C.F.R. § 7.120(b)(2). EPA interprets this regulation to mean that complaints alleging discriminatory effects resulting from issuance of a permit must be filed with EPA within 180 calendar days of issuance of the final permit. However, OCR may waive the 180-day time limit for good cause. 40 C.F.R. § 7.120(b)(2).

OCR will determine on a case-by-case basis whether to waive the time limit for good cause. EPA believes that, in order to encourage complainants to exhaust administrative remedies available under the recipient's permit appeal process, thereby fostering early resolution of Title VI issues, it is appropriate to consider in making a good cause determination a complainant's pursuit of its Title VI concerns through the recipient's administrative appeal process. Under such circumstances and after considering other factors relevant to the particular case, OCR may waive the time limit if the complaint is filed within a reasonable time period (e.g., 60 calendar days) after the conclusion of the administrative appeal process.

In addition, it is OCR's policy not to reject automatically complaints challenging permits where such complaints are filed prior to final permit issuance by the recipient. Rather, OCR should provide the recipient with the information contained in the complaint for consideration in the permit issuance process. OCR also may notify the complainant that the complaint is premature, but that OCR is keeping the complaint on file in an inactive status pending issuance of a final permit by the recipient. Should the recipient issue a final permit, OCR could initiate an investigation if OCR or the complainant believe that issuance of the final permit may be discriminatory.

Permit Modifications

EPA believes that permit modifications that reduce adverse impacts and improve the environmental operation of the facility should be encouraged. Similarly, the Agency does not want to discourage merely administrative modifications, such as a facility name change, or otherwise beneficial modifications that are neutral in terms of their impact on human health or the environment. Because such modifications do not cause or add to adverse impacts, Title VI discriminatory effects claims based on them are likely to be dismissed.

Permit modifications that result in a net increase of pollution impacts, however, may provide a basis for an adverse disparate impact finding, and, accordingly, OCR will not reject or dismiss complaints associated with permit modifications without an examination of the circumstances to determine the nature of the modification.

In the permit modification context (as opposed to permit renewals), the matter under consideration by the recipient is the modified operation. Accordingly, the complaint must allege, and, to establish a disparate impact OCR must find, adverse impacts specifically associated with the modification.

INVESTIGATIONS OF ALLEGEDLY DISCRIMINATORY PERMIT RENEWALS

Generally, permit renewals should be treated and analyzed as if they were new facility permits, since permit renewal is, by definition, an occasion to review the overall operations of a permitted facility and make any necessary changes. Generally, permit renewals are not issued without public notice and an opportunity for the public to challenge the propriety of granting a renewal under the relevant environmental laws and regulations.

IMPACTS AND THE DISPARATE IMPACT ANALYSIS

Evaluations of disparate impact allegations should be based upon the facts and totality of the circumstances that each case presents. Rather than use a single technique for analyzing and evaluating disparate impact allegations, OCR will use several techniques within a broad framework. Any method of evaluation chosen within that framework must be a reasonably reliable indicator of disparity.

In terms of the types of impacts that are actionable under Title VI in the permitting context, OCR will, until further notice, consider impacts cognizable under the recipient's permitting program in determining whether a disparate impact within the meaning of Title VI has occurred. Thus, OCR will accept for processing only those Title VI complaints that include at least an allegation of a disparate impact concerning the types of impacts that are relevant under the recipient's permitting program.[11]

---

11. Even where a recipient's authority to regulate is unclear concerning cumulative burden or discriminatory permitting pattern scenarios (see step 3 below), OCR will nonetheless consider impacts measured in these terms because Title VI is a Federal cross-cutting statute that imposes independent, nondiscrimination requirements on recipients of Federal funds. As such, Title VI, separate from and in addition to the strictures of state and local law, both authorizes and requires recipients to manage their programs in a way that avoids discriminatory cumulative burdens and distributional patterns. Thus, while Title VI does not alter the substantive requirements of a recipient's permitting program, it obligates recipients to implement those requirements in a nondiscriminatory manner as a condition of receiving Federal funds.

The general framework for determining whether a disparate impact exists has five basic steps.

STEP 1: IDENTIFYING THE AFFECTED POPULATION

The first step is to identify the population affected by the permit that triggered the complaint. The affected population is that which suffers the adverse impacts of the permitted activity. The impacts investigated must result from the permit(s) at issue.

The adverse impacts from permitted facilities are rarely distributed in a predictable and uniform manner. However, proximity to a facility will often be a reasonable indicator of where impacts are concentrated. Accordingly, where more precise information is not available, OCR will generally use proximity to a facility to identify adversely affected populations. The proximity analysis should reflect the environmental medium and impact of concern in the case.

STEP 2: DETERMINING THE DEMOGRAPHICS OF THE AFFECTED POPULATION

The second step is to determine the racial and/or ethnic composition of the affected population for the permitted facility at issue in the complaint. To do so, OCR uses demographic mapping technology, such as Geographic Information Systems (GIS). In conducting a typical analysis to determine the affected population, OCR generates data estimating the race and/or ethnicity and density of populations within a certain proximity from a facility or within the distribution pattern for a release/impact based on scientific models. OCR then identifies and characterizes the affected population for the facility at issue. If the affected population for the permit at issue is of the alleged racial or ethnic group(s) named in the complaint, then the demographic analysis is repeated for each facility in the chosen universe(s) of facilities discussed below.

STEP 3: DETERMINING THE UNIVERSE(S) OF FACILITIES AND TOTAL AFFECTED POPULATION(S)

The third step is to identify which other permitted facilities, if any, are to be included in the analysis and to determine the racial or ethnic composition of the populations affected by those permits. There may be more than one appropriate universe of facilities. OCR will determine the appropriate universe of facilities based upon the allegations and facts of a particular case. However, facilities not under the recipient's jurisdiction should not be included in the universe of facilities examined.

If in its investigation OCR finds that the universe of facilities selected by the complainant is not supported by the facts, OCR will explain what it has found and provide the complainant the opportunity to support the use of its proposed universe. If the complainant cannot adequately support the proposed universe, then OCR should investigate a universe of facilities based upon the facts available and OCR's reasonable interpretation of the theory of the case presented. Once the appropriate universe(s) of facilities is determined, the affected population for each facility in the universe should be added together to form the Total Affected Population.

Ordinarily, OCR will entertain cases only in which the permitted facility at issue is one of several facilities, which together present a cumulative burden or which reflect a pattern of disparate impact.[12] EPA recognizes the potential for disparate outcomes in this area because most permits control pollution rather than prevent it altogether. Consequently, permits that satisfy the base public health and environmental protections contemplated under EPA's programs nonetheless bear the potential for discriminatory effects where residual pollution and other cognizable impacts are distributed disproportionately to communities with particular racial or ethnic characteristics. Based on its experience to date, the Agency believes that this is most likely to be true either where an individual permit contributes to or compounds a preexisting burden being shouldered by a neighboring community, such that the community's cumulative burden is disproportionate when compared with other communities; or where an individual permit is part of a broader pattern pursuant to which it has become more likely that certain types of operations, with their accompanying burdens, will be permitted in a community with particular racial or ethnic characteristics.

STEP 4: CONDUCTING A DISPARATE IMPACT ANALYSIS

The fourth step is to conduct a disparate impact analysis that, at a minimum, includes comparing the racial or ethnic characteristics within the affected population. It will also likely include comparing the racial characteristics of the affected population to the non-affected population. This approach can show whether persons protected under Title VI are being impacted at a disparate rate. EPA generally would expect the rates of impact for the affected population and comparison populations to be relatively comparable under properly implemented programs. Since there is no one formula or analysis to be applied, OCR may identify on a case-by-case basis other comparisons to determine disparate impact.

---

12. In some rare instances, the EPA may need to determine whether the impacts of a single permit, standing alone, may be considered adequate to support a disparate impact claim. While such a case has not yet been presented to the EPA, it might, for example, involve a permitted activity that is unique (i.e., "one of a kind") under a recipient's program.

STEP 5: DETERMINING THE SIGNIFICANCE OF THE DISPARITY

The final phase of the analysis is to use arithmetic or statistical analyses to determine whether the disparity is significant under Title VI. OCR will use trained statisticians to evaluate disparity calculations done by investigators. After calculations are informed by expert opinion, OCR may make a prima facie disparate impact finding, subject to the recipient's opportunity to rebut.

MITIGATION

EPA expects mitigation to be an important focus in the Title VI process, given the typical interest of recipients in avoiding more draconian outcomes and the difficulty that many recipients will encounter in justifying an "unmitigated," but nonetheless disparate, impact. In some circumstances, it may be possible for the recipient to mitigate public health and environmental considerations sufficiently to address the disparate impact. The sufficiency of such mitigation should be evaluated in consultation with experts in the EPA program at issue. OCR may also consult with complainants. Where it is not possible or practicable to mitigate sufficiently the public health or environmental impacts of a challenged permit, EPA will consider "supplemental mitigation projects" (SMPs), which, when taken together with other mitigation efforts, may be viewed by EPA as sufficient to address the disparate impact. An SMP can, for example, respond to concerns associated with the permitting of the facility raised by the complainant that cannot otherwise be redressed under Title VI (i.e., because they are outside those considerations ordinarily entertained by the permitting authority).

JUSTIFICATION

If a preliminary finding of noncompliance has not been successfully rebutted and the disparate impact cannot successfully be mitigated, the recipient will have the opportunity to "justify" the decision to issue the permit notwithstanding the disparate impact, based on the substantial, legitimate interests of the recipient. While determining what constitutes a sufficient justification will necessarily turn on the facts of the case at hand, OCR would expect that, given the considerations described above, merely demonstrating that the permit complies with applicable environmental regulations will not ordinarily be considered a substantial, legitimate justification. Rather, there must be some articulable value to the recipient in the permitted activity. Because the interests of a state or local environmental agency are necessarily influenced and informed by the broader interest of the government of which it is a part, OCR will entertain justifications based on broader governmental interests (i.e., interests not limited by the jurisdiction of the recipient agency). While the sufficiency of the justification will necessarily depend on the facts of the case at hand, the types of factors that may bear consideration in assessing sufficiency can include, but are not limited to, the seriousness of the disparate impact, whether the permit at issue is a renewal (with demonstrated benefits) or for a new facility (with more speculative benefits), and whether any of the articulated benefits associated with a permit can be expected to benefit the particular community that is the subject of the Title VI complaint.

Importantly, a justification offered will not be considered acceptable if it is shown that a less discriminatory alternative exists. If a less discriminatory alternative is practicable, then the recipient must implement it to avoid a finding of noncompliance with the regulations. Less discriminatory alternatives should be equally effective in meeting the needs addressed by the challenged practice. Here, again, mitigation measures should be considered as less discriminatory alternatives, including additional permit conditions that would lessen or eliminate the demonstrated adverse disparate impacts.

The statements in this document are intended solely as guidance. This document is not intended, nor can it be relied upon, to create any rights enforceable by any party in litigation with the United States. EPA may decide to follow the guidance provided in this document, or to act at variance with the guidance, based on its analysis of the specific facts presented. This guidance may be revised without public notice to reflect changes in EPA's approach to implementing the Small Business Regulatory Enforcement Fairness Act or the Regulatory Flexibility Act, or to clarify and update text.

* * *

Those who wish to obtain more information about environmental justice issues can consult the following list of sources:

Environmental Justice—generally: Unequal Protection: Environmental Justice and Communities of Color (Robert D. Bullard ed., 1994); Bunyon Bryant, Environmental Justice: Issues, Policies and Solutions (1995); Eileen Gauna, *Federal Environmental Citizen Provisions: Obstacles and Incentives on the Road to Environmental Justice,* 22 Ecology L. Q. 1, 1–40 (1995); Christopher Foreman, The Promise and Peril of Environmental Justice (1998); Luke Cole & Sheila Foster, From the Ground Up: Environmental Racism and the Rise of the Environmental Justice Movement (2001); Clifford Rechtschaffen & Eileen Gauna, Environmental Justice: Law, Policy and Regulation (2002).

Environmental Justice—empirical claims: U.S. Gen. Accounting Office, GAO/RCED 83-168, *Siting of Hazardous Waste Landfills and their Correlation with Racial and Economic Status of Surrounding Communities* (1983); United Church of Christ Commission for Racial Justice, *Toxic Wastes and Race in the United States* (1987); Robert Bullard, Dumping in Dixie: Race, Class and Environmental Quality (1990); Paul Mohai & Bunyan Bryant, *Environmental Racism: Reviewing the Evidence*, in Race and the Incidence of Environmental Hazards: A Time for Discourse (Bunyan Bryant & Paul Mohai, eds., 1992); Vicki Been, *Locally Undesirable Land Uses in Minority Neighborhoods: Disproportionate Siting or Market Dynamics?*, 103 Yale L.J. 1383 (1994); Andrew Szasz & Michael Meuser, *Environmental Inequalities: Literature Review and Proposals for New Directions in Research and Theory*, 45 Current Sociology 99 (July 1997); Vicki Been & Francis Gupta, *Coming to the Nuisance or Going to the Barrios? A Longitudinal Analysis of Environmental Justice Claims*, 24 Ecology L. Q. 1 (1997).

Environmental Justice—legal claims: Rachel D. Godsil, Note, *Remedying Environmental Racism*, 90 Mich. L. Rev. 394 (1991); Richard J. Lazarus, *Pursuing "Environmental Justice": The Distributional Effects of Environmental Protection*, 87 Nw. U. L. Rev. 787 (1993); James H. Colopy, Comment, *The Road Less Travelled: Pursuing Environmental Justice Through Title VI of the Civil Rights Act of 1964*, 13 Stan. Envtl. L.J. 125 (1994); The Law of Environmental Justice: Theories and Procedures to Address Disproportionate Risks (Michael B. Gerrard, ed., 1999); Alice Kaswan, *Environmental Laws: Grist for the Equal Protection Mill*, 70 U. Colo. L. Rev. 387 (1999); Bradford Mank, *Reforming State Brownfield Programs to Comply with Title VI*, 24 Harv. Envtl. L. Rev. 115 (2000); Eileen Gauna, *EPA at Thirty: Fairness in Environmental Protection*, 31 Envtl. L. Rep. 10528 (2001); Bradford Mank, *Using Section 1983 to Enforce Title VI's Section 602 Regulations*, 49 U. Kansas L. Rev. 321 (2001).

After having read the Interim Title VI Guidance, complete the following problems.

Problem 5.14: Parties to Complaint

Who are the formal parties in an environmental justice administrative complaint? Who else is likely to be have an interest in the proceeding?

Problem 5.15: OCR Procedures

Pursuant to the document, what are the procedural steps that the Office of Civil Rights (OCR) takes in processing an environmental justice administrative challenge to a state or local permitting decision?

Problem 5.16: Timing of Complaint

How long after the issuance of a permit does a party have to submit a Title VI administrative complaint? At what point will a complaint be deemed "untimely"?

Problem 5.17: Investigation of Complaint

What are the steps that OCR goes through in investigating whether a given permitting decision creates a disparate impact?

Problem 5.18: Mitigation

How does OCR evaluate "mitigation" under the Guidance?

Problem 5.19: Justification

How does OCR evaluate "justification" under the Guidance?

Exercise 5.1: Drafting Comments on EPA's Interim Title VI Guidance

In this Exercise, you will represent a client with an interest in EPA's Interim Title VI Guidance. You are to assume that your client has asked you to comment on the Guidance on its behalf. Your assignment is to draft the comments.

You will represent one of the following four clients (your professor will determine which one): (1) The New Jersey Department of Environmental Protection (NJ DEP), *a state environmental agency that, among other things, issues permits under the Clean Air Act, Clean Water Act and Resource Conservation and Recovery Act (RCRA) and receives federal funding under each of these programs; (2)* The Environmental Justice Legal Defense Fund (EJLDF), *a group of attorneys based in New Orleans, Louisiana that represents poor and minority communities in environmental justice actions; (3)* The Chemical Manufacturers Association (CMA), *a trade association representing companies that manufacture bulk chemicals, including businesses that operate large plants in Louisiana; (4)* The Flint Area Economic Development Authority (FAEDA), *a city government office whose mission is to bring business development back to Flint, Michigan, a city that has a large African-American population and that has one of the highest unemployment rates in the country.*

Your professor will provide you with a confidential memorandum from your client that outlines its principal interests with respect to the Guidance. Your goal is to represent these interests as effectively as you can in your client's written comments on the Interim Guidance. Your comments should be divided into two major sections: (1) Procedural issues: *does the law require EPA to proceed by notice-and-comment rulemaking in developing this policy, or is EPA's decision to use a guidance format legally sustainable? (You may have to do some legal research in order to develop your argument on this question.) (2)* Substantive issues: *explain how the Guidance impacts your client's interests and develop arguments as to why EPA should revise the document (or maintain it in its current form) in light of these interests.*

Exercise 5.2: Representing Your Client at a Public Hearing

In this Exercise you are to assume that EPA has changed its mind and has decided to promulgate its Title VI strategy through full notice-and-comment rulemaking. The Interim Guidance will now serve as the text of the proposed rule. The agency has published it in the Federal Register (with some minor revisions to make clear that it is now a proposed rule rather than a guidance document). In addition to taking written comment on the proposal, EPA has decided to hold a public hearing at which it will hear oral presentations from interested parties. The hearing is the subject of this Exercise. At the hearing, you will represent the same client on whose behalf you drafted comments in Exercise 4.1. You will orally present to an agency staff member (played by your professor, or by another student) your client's views on the substantive issues related to the proposed rule. The EPA official may ask you questions during the course of the presentation. After each interested party has had a chance to make its presentation, the parties will have an opportunity to rebut each others' stated views.

Appendix

In the Matter of
GEC Precision Corporation

UNITED STATES ENVIRONMENTAL PROTECTION AGENCY

REGION VII
726 MINNESOTA AVENUE
KANSAS CITY, KANSAS 66101

BEFORE THE ADMINISTRATOR

IN THE MATTER OF	)	EPCRA Docket No. VII-94-T-381-E
	)	
GEC Precision Corporation	)	COMPLAINT AND NOTICE OF
Wellington, Kansas	)	OPPORTUNITY FOR HEARDING
	)	
Respondent	)	

COMPLAINT

Jurisdiction

1. This is an administrative action for the assessment of civil penalties instituted pursuant to Section 325 of the Emergency Planning and Community Right-to-Know Act of 1986 (hereinafter "EPCRA"), 42 U.S.C. § 11045.

2. This Complaint serves as notice that the United States Environmental Protection Agency (hereinafter "EPA") has reason to believe that Respondent has violated EPCRA, 42 U.S.C. § 11001 et. seq. and the regulations promulgated thereunder and codified at 40 C.F.R. Part 372, governing the submission of toxic chemical release inventories by owners and operators of covered facilities.

Parties

3. The Complainant, by delegation from the Administrator of the EPA, and the Regional Administrator, EPA, Region VII, is the Director, Air and Toxicx Division, EPA, Region VII.

4. The Respondent is GEC Precision Corporation, an aircraft parts and equipment company, incorporated and registered to do business in the State of Kansas, located at 1515 Highway 81 North, Wellington, Kansas 67152.

Statutory and Regulatory Requirements

5. Section 313 of EPCRA and 40 C.F.R. §§ 372.22 and 372.30 require the owner or operator of a facility that: (a) has 10 or more full time employees; (b) has a Standard Industrial Classification (SIC) code of 20 through 39; (c) that manufactured, processed or otherwise used a toxic chemical listed under Section 313(c) of EPCRA and 40 C.F.R. §-372.65, in excess of the threshold quantity established under Section 313(f) of EPCRA and 40 C.F.R. § 372.25 during the calendar year, to

complete and submit a toxic chemical release inventory form
(hereinafter "Form R") to the Administrator of EPA and to the
State in which the subject facility is located by July 1 for
the preceding calendar year for each toxic chemical know by
the owner or operator to be manufactured, processed, or otherwise
used in quantities exceeding the established threshold quantity
during that preceding calendar year.

6. As set forth at Section 313(f) of EPCRA and 40 C.F.R.
§ 372.25, the reporting threshold amount for calendar year
1987 for chemicals manufactured or processed at a facility
is 75,000 pounds, 50,000 pounds for calendar year 1988, and
25,000 pounds for calendar years subsequent, to and including
1989. The reporting threshold for a toxic chemical otherwise
used at a facility is 10,000 pounds for calendar years subsequent
to and including 1987.

VIOLATIONS

The Complainant hereby states and alleges that Respondent
has violated EPCRA and regulations thereunder as follows:

Count I

7. On or about May 17, 1994, an authorized EPA representative
conducted an inspection pursuant to EPCRA § 313 at Respondent's
facility located at 1515 Highway 81 North, Wellington, Kansas
67152.

8. Respondent has 10 or more full-time employees, as defined as
40 C.F.R. § 372.3, at said facility.

9. Respondent's facility is in SIC Codes 20 through 39.

10. Respondent is a person as defined at Section 329(7) of EPCRA
and is the owner or operator of a facility as defined at Section
329(4) of EPCRA.

11. The May 17, 1994, inspection of Respondent's facility
revealed that in calendar year 1992, Respondent otherwise used
1,1,1 Trichloroethane in excess of 10,000 pounds.

12. 1,1,1 Trochloroethane is a toxic chemical listed under
Section 313(c) of EPCRA and 40 C.F.R. § 372.65.

13. Respondent failed to submit a Form R for 1,1,1
Trochloroethane to the Administrator of EPA and to the State of
Kansas by July 1, 1993.

GEC Precision Corporation
EPCRA Docket No.VII-94-T-381-E
Page 3 of 8

14. Respondent's failure to submit a Form R for 1,1,1
Trichloroethane by July 1, 1993, is a violation of EPCRA ~ 313,
42 U.S.C. § 11023, and of the requirements of 40 C.F.R. Part 372.

15. Pursuant to Section 325 of EPCRA, 42 U.S.C. § 11045, and
based upon the facts stated in paragraphs 7 through 14 above, it
is proposed that a civil penalty of $17,000 be assessed against
Respondent.

Count II

16. The facts stated in paragraphs 7 through 10, are herein
restated and incorporated.

17. The May 17, 1994, inspection of Respondent's facility revealed
that in calendar year 1992, Respondent otherwise used methyl ethyl
ketone (MEK) in excess of 10,000 pounds.

18. Methyl ethyl ketone (MEK) is a toxic chemical listed under
Section 313(c) of EPCRA and 40 C.F.R. § 372.65.

19. Respondent failed to submit a Form R for methyl ethyl ketone
(MER) to the Administrator of EPA and to the State of Kansas by
July 1, 1993.

20. Respondent's failure to submit a Form R for methyl ethyl
ketone (MEK) by July 1, 1993, is a violation of EPCRA § 313, 42
U.S.C. § 11023, and of the requirements of 40 C.F.R. Part 372.

21. Pursuant to Section 325 of EPCRA, 42 U.S.C. § 11045, and
based upon the facts stated in paragraphs 16 through 20 above, it
is proposed that a civil penalty of $17,000 be assessed against
Respondent.

Count III

22. The facts stated in paragraphs 7 through 10, are herein
restated and incorporated.

23. The May 17, 1994, inspection of Respondent's facility
revealed that in calendar year 1991, Respondent otherwise used
methyl ethyl ketone (MEK) in excess of 10,000 pounds.

24. Methyl ethyl ketone (MEK) is a toxic chemical listed under
Section 313(c) of EPCRA and 40 C.F.R. § 372.65.

25. Respondent failed to submit a Form R for methyl ethyl ketone
(MEK) to the Administrator of EPA and to the State of Kansas by
July 1, 1992.

GEC Precision Corporation
EPCRA Docket No.VII-94-T-381-E
Page 4 of 8

26. Respondent's failure to submit a Form R for methyl ethyl ketone (MEK) by July 1, 1992, is a violation of EPCRA § 313, 42 U.S.C. § 11023, and of the requirements of 40 C.F.R. Part 372.

27. Pursuant to Section 325 of EPCRA, 42 U.S.C. § 11045, and based upon the facts stated in paragraphs 22 through 26 above, it is proposed that a civil penalty of $17,000 be assessed against Respondent.

Count IV

28. The facts stated in paragraphs 7 through 10, are herein restated and incorporated.

29. The May 17, 1994, inspection of Respondent's facility revealed that in calendar year 1990, Respondent otherwise used methyl ethyl ketone (HEK) in excess of 10,000 pounds.

30. Methyl ethyl ketone (MEK) is a toxic chemical listed under Section 313(c) of EPCRA and 40 C.F.R. § 372.65.

31. Respondent failed to submit a Form R for methyl ethyl ketone (MEK) to the Administrator of EPA and to the State of Kansas by July 1, 1991.

32. Respondent's failure to submit a Form R for methyl ethyl ketone (MEK) by July 1, 1991, is a violation of EPCRA § 313, 42 U.S.C. § 11023, and of the requirements of 40 C.F.R. Part 372.

33. Pursuant to Section 325 of EPCRA, 42 U.S.C. § 11045, and based upon the facts stated in paragraphs 28 through 32 above, it is proposed that a civil penalty of $17,000 be assessed against Respondent.

Relief

34. Section 325(c) of EPCRA, authorizes a civil penalty of up to $25,000 per day for each violation of the Act. The penalties proposed in paragraphs 15, 21, 27, and 33 above are based upon the
facts stated in this Complaint, and on the nature, circumstances, extent, and gravity of the above-cited violations, as well as the Respondent's history of prior violations and degree of culpability, in accordance with EPCRA and the Enforcement Response Policy for Section 313 of EPCRA.

35. A Summary of the Proposed Penalties is contained in the enclosed Penalty Calculation Summary attached hereto and incorporated herein by reference.

GEC Precision Corporation
EPCRA Docket No.VII-94-T-381-E
Page 5 of 8

36. Payment of the total penalty — $68,000 — may be made by
certified or cashier's check payable to the Treasurer, United
States of America, and remitted to:

> Mellon Bank
> EPA — Region VII
> Regional Hearing Clerk
> P.O. Box 360748M
> Pittsburgh, Pennsylvania 15251

Note that payment of the proposed penalty alone does not satisfy
Respondent's legal obligation to file a complete and accurate
Form R as required by Section 313 of EPCRA and 40 C.F.R.
Part 372. Failure or refusal to file Form R may subject Respondent
to additional civil penalties of up to $25.000 per day of
violation.

NOTICE OF OPPORTUNITY TO REQUEST A HEARING

Answer and Request for Hearing

37. In accordance with 5 U.S.C. Section 554, Respondent has the
right to request a hearing to contest any material fact contained
in this Complaint above or to contest the appropriateness of the
proposed penalty set forth herein. Such a hearing will be held
and conducted in accordance with the Consolidated Rules of
Practice Governing the Administrative Assessment of Civil
Penalties and the Revocation or Suspension of Permits, 40 C.F.R.
Part 22, one copy of which is enclosed herein.

38. To avoid being found in default, which constitutes an
admission of all facts alleged in this Complaint and a waiver
of the right to hearing, Respondent must file a written answer
and request for hearing within twenty (20) days of service of
this Complaint and Notice of Opportunity for Hearing. Said
answer shall clearly and directly admit, deny, or explain each
of the factual allegations contained in this Complaint with
respect to which Respondent has any knowledge, or shall clearly
state that Respondent has no knowledge as to particular factual
allegations in this Complaint. The answer shall also state
(a) the circumstances or arguments which are alleged to
constitute the grounds of defense; (b) the facts that Respondent
intends to place at issue; and (c) whether a hearing is
requested.

39. The denial of any material fact or the raising of any
affirmative defense shall be construed as a request for hearing.
Failure to deny any of the factual allegations in the Complaint

GEC Precision Corporation
EPCRA Docket No.VII-94-T-381-E
Page 6 of 8

constitutes an admission of the undenied allegations. Said
answer shall be filed with the following:

> Regional Hearing Clerk
> United States Environmental Protection Agency
> Region VII
> 726 Minnesota Avenue
> Kansas City, Kansas 66101

40. If Respondent fails to file a written answer and request
for a hearing within twenty(20) days of service of this
Complaint and Notice of Opportunity for Hearing, such failure
will constitute a binding admission of all allegations made in
this Complaint and a waiver of Respondent's right to a hearing
under EPCRA. A Default Order may thereafter be issued by the
Regional Administrator and the civil penalties proposed herein
shall become due and payable without further procedings.

Informal Settlement Conference

41. Whether or not Respondent requests a hearing, an informal
conference may be requested in order to discuss the facts of this
case, the proposed penalty, and the possibility of a settlement.
To request a settlement conference, please contact:

> Anne E. Rauch
> Attorney
> United States Environmental Protection Agency
> Region VII
> 726 Minnesota Avenue
> Kansas City, Kansas 66101
> Telephone 913/551-7010

42. Please note that a request for an informal settlement
conference does not extend the twenty (20) day period during
which a written answer and request for a hearing must be
submitted.

43. EPA encourages all parties against whom a civil penalty
is proposed to pursue the possibilities of settlement as a result
of informal conference. Any settlement which may be reached as a
result of such a conference shall be embodied in a written
Consent Agreement and Consent Order issued by the Regional
Judicial Officer, EPA Region VII. The issuance of such a Consent
Agreement and Consent Order shall constitute a waiver of
Respondent's right to request a hearing on any matter stipulated
therein.

GEC Precision Corporation
EPCRA Docket No.VII-94-T-381-E
Page 7 of 8

44. If Respondent has neither achieved a settlement by informal
conference nor filed an answer within the twenty (20) day time
period allowed by this Notice, the penalties proposed above may
be assessed by the entry of a Default Order.

Date 9/2/94   /s/ William A. Spratlin
                                    William A. Spratlin, Director
                                    Air and Toxics Division

/s/ Anne E. Rauch
Anne E. Rauch
Attorney
Office of Regional Counsel.

Enclosures: Penalty Calculation Summary
             Consolidated Rules of Practice Governing the
             Administrative Assessment of Civil Penalties and
             the Revocation or Suspension of Permits, 40 C.F.R.
             Part 22
             Enforcement Response Policy for Section 313 of EPCRA

GEC Precision Corporation
EPCRA Docket No.VII-94-T-381-E
Page 8 of 8

CERTIFICATE OF SERVICE

I certify that on the date noted below I hand delivered
the original and one try and correct copy of this Complaint
and Notice of Opportunity for Hearing to the Regional Hearing
Clerk, United States Environmental Agency,
726 Minnesota Avenue, Kansas City, Kansas 66101

I further certify that on the date noted below I sent
by certified mail, return receipt requested, a true and correct
copy of the signed original Complaint and Notice of Opportunity
for Hearing; a copy of the Penalty Calculation Summary; a copy of
the Consolidated Rules of Practice Governing the Administrative
Assessment of Civil Penalties and the Revocation or Suspension of
Permits, 40 C.F.R. Part 22; and a copy of the August 19, 1992,
Enforcement Response Policy for Section 313 fo EPCRA to the
following registered agent for GEC Precision Corporation:

The Corporation Company
515 South Kansas Avenue
Topeka, Kansas 66603

Sept. 21, 1994   /s/ Bonnie Andrews
     Date   Bonnie Andrews

PENALTY CALCULATION FOR
GEC Precision Corporation
Wellington, Kansas
EPCRA Docket No. VII-94-T-381-E

COUNT I

VIOLATION: Failure to report toxic chemical release
                 inventory emissions for 1,1,1 Trichloroethane
                 in a timely manner during reporting year
                 1992.

EXTENT: LEVEL B — Description: Less than 10 times
                 reporting threshold; greater than $10 million
                 annual sales; greater than 50 employees

CIRCUMSTANCE: LEVEL 1 — Description: Failure to submit
                 1992 Form R report for 1,1,1 Trichloroethane
                 by July 1, 1993

GRAVITY BASED
PENALTY: $17,000 + Adjustments: None

PROPOSED
PENALTY: $17,000

COUNT II

VIOLATION: Failure to report toxic chemical release
                 inventory emissions for methyl ethyl ketone
                 (MEK) in a timely manner during reporting
                 year 1992

EXTENT: LEVEL B — Description: Less than 10 times
                 reporting threshold; greater than $10 million
                 annual sales; greater than 50 employees

CIRCUMSTANCE: LEVEL 1 — Description: Failure to submit
                 1992 Form R report for methyl ethyl ketone
                 (MEK) by July 1, 1993

GRAVITY BASED
PENALTY: $17,000+Adjustments: None

PROPOSED
PENALTY: $17,000

COUNT III

VIOLATION: Failure to report toxic chemical release
                          inventory emissions for methyl ethyl ketone
                          (MEK) in a timely manner during reporting
                          year 1991.

EXTENT: LEVEL B — Description: Less than 10 times
                          reporting threshold; greater than Slo million
                          annual sales; greater than 50 employees

CIRCUMSTANCE: LEVEL 1 — Description: Failure to submit
                          1991 Form R report for methyl ethyl ketone
                          (MEX) by July 1, 1992

GRAVITY BASED
PENALTY: $17,000 + Adjustments: None

PROPOSED
PENALTY: $17,000

COUNT IV

VIOLATION: Failure to report toxic chemical release
                          inventory emissions for methyl ethyl ketone
                          (MEK) in a timely manner during reporting
                          year 1990.

EXTENT: LEVEL B — Description: Less than 10 times
                          reporting threshold; greater than $10 million
                          annual sales; greater than 50 employees

CIRCUMSTANCE: LEVEL 1 — Description: Failure to submit
                          1990 Form R report for methyl ethyl ketone
                          (MEK) by July 1, 1991

GRAVITY BASED
PENALTY: $17,000 + Adjustments: None

PROPOSED
PENALTY: $17,000

TOTAL PROPOSED PENALTY: $68,000

UNITED STATES ENVIRONMENTAL PROTECTION AGENCY

REGION VII
726 MINNESOTA AVENUE
KANSAS CITY, KANSAS 66101

MAY 24, 1995

MEMORANDUM

SUBJECT: Penalty Calculation for GEC Precision Corporation
            Wellington, Kansas, EPCRA Docket No. VII-94-T-381-E

FROM: Mark A. Smith
            Environmental Scientist
            Toxic Substances Control Section

TO: Anne Rauch
            Office of Regional Counsel

     The following information supports the appropriateness of
the U.S. Environmental Protection Agency, Region VII's assessment
of civil penalties in regard to the subject administrative
action. The proposed penalties were calculated pursuant to the
August 10, 1992, Enforcement Response Policy for Section 313 of
the Emergency Planning and Community Right-To-Know Act (EPCRA).

     The purpose of the above-mentioned Enforcement Response
Policy (ERP) is to assure that enforcement actions for violations
of EPCRA Section 313 are arrived at in a fair, uniform, and
consistent manner. Furthermore, the ERP aims to provide
appropriate enforcement responses for violations committed, as
well as, providing deterrent from the violation of Section 313.

     The ERP states that the determination of the gravity-based
penalty is made according to two factors, which are the
circumstances and the extent of the violation. These two factors
are incorporated into a matrix which allows the determination of
an appropriate base penalty amount. After the base penalty has
been determined, upward or downward adjustments may be made to
the
base penalty in consideration of the following factors: voluntary
disclosure; history of prior violations; delisted chemicals;
attitude; other such matters as justice may require; supplemental
environmental projects; and, ability to pay. According to the ERP,
the first three of the above adjustment factors may be made prior
to issuing the civil complaint. The total proposed penalty is
determined by calculating the penalty for each violation on a per
chemical, per facility basis, and then applying any appropriate
penalty adjustment factors.

2

Facility Information

GEC Precision Corporation is listed in the Dun & Bradstreet
Database (D&B) with a Standard Industrial Classification (SIC)
code of 3728 — principally involved in the manufacture of
aircraft parts and equipment. GEC Precision Corporation
otherwise used chemicals listed under EPCRA Section 313 above
thresholds required for reporting during calendar years 1990,
1991, and 1992. According to D&B, annual sales at GEC Precision
were greater than $10 Million, and GEC Precision employed more
than 50 employees.

Summary of Alleged Violations

GEC Precision Corporation failed to report the otherwise use
of methyl ethyl ketone (MEK), a listed chemical under EPCRA
Section 313, for calendar years 1990, 1991, and 1992. GEC
Precision Corporation also failed to report the otherwise use of
1, 1,1 Trichloroethane (TCA), a listed chemical under EPCRA
Section 313, for calendar year 1992.

Penalty Calculations

Circumstance Level: According to the ERP, the circumstance
of the violation is determined by the seriousness of the
violation as it relates to the availability and accuracy of the
information to the community, to states, and to the government.
The ERP states that failure to report in a timely manner
(Category I — failure to submit report one year or more after the
July 1 due date) the otherwise use of a listed EPCRA Section 313
chemical is a "Level 1" circumstance.

Extent Level: The extent factor for a violation is based on
the quantity of EPCRA Section 313 chemical otherwise used by the
facility in violation, and the size of the total corporate entity
in violation. The size of the total corporate entity is defined
by the amount of sales or number of employees of all sites taken
together owned or controlled by the domestic or foreign parent
company. According to the ERP, a facility with total corporate
entity sales of $10 million or more and 50 employees or more,
which uses a Section 313 chemical less than 10 times the
threshold level is a "Level B" extent.

Summary of Proposed Penalties

COUNT I

VIOLATION: Failure to report toxic chemical release
                    inventory emissions for 1,1,1 Trichloroethane
                    in a timely manner during reporting year
                    1992.

3

EXTENT: LEVEL B — Description: Less than 10 times
                   reporting threshold; $10 million or more
                   annual sales; 50 employees or more

CIRCUMSTANCE: LEVEL 1 — Description: Failure to submit
                   1992 Form R report for 1,1,1 Trichloroethane
                   by July 1, 1993

GRAVITY BASED
PENALTY: $17,000+Adjustments: None

PROPOSED
PENALTY: $17,000

COUNT II

VIOLATION: Failure to report toxic chemical release
                   inventory emissions for methyl ethyl ketone
                   (MER) in-a timely manner during reporting
                   year 1992

EXTENT: LEVEL B — Description: Less than 10 times
                   reporting threshold; $10 million or more
                   annual sales; 50 employees or more

CIRCUMSTANCE: LEVEL 1 — Description: Failure to submit
                   1992 Form R report for MEK by July 1, 1993

GRAVITY BASED
PENALTY: $17,000+Adjustments: None

PROPOSED
PENALTY: $17,000

COUNT III

VIOLATION: Failure to report toxic chemical release
                   inventory emissions for methyl ethyl ketone
                   (MEK) in a timely manner during reporting
                   year 1991.

EXTENT: LEVEL B — Description: Less than 10 times
                   reporting threshold; $10 million or more
                   annual sales; 50 employees or more

CIRCUMSTANCE: LEVEL 1 — Description: Failure to submit
                   1991 Form R report for MEK by July 1, 1992

4

GRAVITY BASED PENALTY:	$17,000 + Adjustments: None

PROPOSED PENALTY:	$17,000

COUNT IV

VIOLATION: Failure to report toxic chemical release
                  inventory emissions for methyl ethyl ketone
                  (MEK) in a timely manner during reporting
                  year 1990.

EXTENT: LEVEL B — Description: Less than 10 times
                  reporting threshold; $10 million or more
                  annual sales; 50 employees or more

CIRCUMSTANCE: LEVEL 1 — Description: Failure to submit
                  1990 Form R report for MEK by July 1, 1991

GRAVITY BASED PENALTY:	$17,000 + Adjustments: None

PROPOSED PENALTY:	$17,000

TOTAL PROPOSED PENALTY: $68,000

INDEX